STUDIES IN CHRISTIAN HISTORY AND THOUGHT

Aspects of Reforming

Theology and Practice in Sixteenth Century Europe

STUDIES IN CHRISTIAN HISTORY AND THOUGHT

Aspects of Reforming

Theology and Practice in Sixteenth Century Europe

Edited by Michael Parsons

Foreword by David W. Hall

Copyright © Paternoster 2013

First published 2013 by Paternoster

Paternoster is an imprint of Authentic Media
52 Presley Way, Crownhill, Milton Keynes, Bucks, MK8 0ES

www.authenticmedia.co.uk
Authentic Media is a division of Koorong UK, a company limited by guarantee

09 08 07 06 05 04 03   8 7 6 5 4 3 2 1

The right of Michael Parsons to be identified as the Editor of this Work
has been asserted by him in accordance with the Copyright, Designs
and Patents Act 1988.

All rights reserved. No part of this publication may be reproduced, stored in a retrieval system, or transmitted, in any form or by any means, electronic, mechanical, photocopying, recording or otherwise, without the prior permission of the publisher or a license permitting restricted copying. In the UK such licenses are issued by the Copyright Licensing Agency, 90 Tottenham Court Road, London W1P 9HE.

British Library Cataloguing in Publication Data A catalogue record for this book is available from the British Library

ISBN 978–1–84227–806–2

Typeset by Michael Parsons
Printed and bound in Great Britain for Paternoster
by Lightning Source, Milton Keynes

Neville Atkinson and Billy Strachan

'The one who plants and the one who waters have one purpose, and they will each be rewarded according to their own labour,' 1 Corinthians 3.8

STUDIES IN CHRISTIAN HISTORY AND THOUGHT

Series Preface

This series complements the specialist series of Studies in Evangelical History and Thought and Studies in Baptist History and Thought for which Paternoster is becoming increasingly well known by offering works that cover the wider field of Christian history and thought. It encompasses accounts of Christian witness at various periods, studies of individual Christians and movements, and works which concern the relations of church and society through history, and the history of Christian thought.

The series includes monographs, revised dissertations and theses, and collections of papers by individuals and groups. As well as 'free standing' volumes, works on particular running themes are being commissioned; authors will be engaged for these from around the world and from a variety of Christian traditions.

A high academic standard combined with lively writing will commend the volumes in this series both to scholars and to a wider readership

Series Editors

Alan P.F. Sell	Visiting Professor at Acadia University Divinity College, Nova Scotia
D.W. Bebbington	University of Stirling, Stirling, Scotland
Clyde Binfield	Professor Associate in History, University of Sheffield, UK
Gerald Bray	Anglican Professor of Divinity, Beeson Divinity School, Samford University, Birmingham, Alabama, USA
Grayson Carter	Associate Professor of Church History, Fuller Theological Seminary SW, Phoenix, Arizona, USA
Dennis Ngien	Professor of Theology, Tyndale University College and Seminary, Founder of the Centre for Mentorship and Theological Reflection, Toronto, Canada

CONTENTS

Preface ix

Foreword by David Hall xi
Notes on Contributors xv

1. Martin Luther

Chapter 1 Luther, the priesthood of believers, and the theological interpretation of scripture
Uche Anizor 1

Chapter 2 No alternatives to Jesus: Martin Luther's definition of idolatry as evident in his *house postils*
Cameron MacKenzie 16

Chapter 3 Some implications of Martin Luther's *solus Christus* in his theological validation of the Jews
Berthold Schwarz 33

Chapter 4 Luther as a practical theologian: his input into the 1526 visitation
Brett James Muhlhan 52

Chapter 5 Luther's insights into grief: his pastoral letters
Michael Parsons 68

2. John Calvin

Chapter 6 John Calvin on revelation and the use of feminine imagery for God
Karin Spiecker Stetina 83

Chapter 7 Calvin's final verdict on the Augsburg Confession.
Peter A. Lillback 96

Chapter 8 Calvin's School of Christ for preachers
Peter Adam 118

Chapter 9 'A new embassy': John Calvin's gospel
Martin Foord 138

3. Exegesis and theology

Chapter 10	The Christoscopic interpretation of John Oecolampadius on the child named in Isaiah 7–11 *Jeff Fisher*	150
Chapter 11	Theological interpretation in the reformers: a case study of the 'Son of Man' texts in Matthew *Jason Lee*	165
Chapter 12	Socinus and the Racovian Catechism on justification *J.V. Fesko*	182
Chapter 13	'Let us not . . . call God to account.' John Calvin's reading of some difficult deaths *Michael Parsons*	202
Chapter 14	The Trinitarian shape of Calvin's theology and exegesis of scripture *Guenther ('Gene') Haas*	217
Chapter 15	Reformed worldviews and the exegesis of the Apocalypse *Rodney Petersen*	242

Bibliography	260
Indexes	286
Author index	286
Scripture index	290
General index	293

PREFACE

The Bible really came alive in the reformation period, or, rather, people came alive to the Bible in those years—theologians and pastors as well as 'ordinary' men and women. It was absolutely central to the reforming process from the reformation's inception to the conclusion of the century and beyond. Whether it was through fresh translation, expository preaching, rigorous commenting, or informed reading, the Bible—Old and New Testaments—became pivotal to the work in hand. The reformers saw it as the Word of God by which the Holy Spirit, who inspired the Scriptures, would call people to Christ, and both inform and form men and women of faith. Martin Luther spoke of it as follows, 'The true treasure of the church is the holy gospel and the grace of God' and spoke of preachers 'who extract the living Word from the Old Scripture' (*WA* 1.236, *WA* 10^1.626). John Calvin, similarly, speaks of true pupils of Scripture and looks for the emergence of true knowledge and obedience from a study of its pages (*Inst.* 1.6.2).

During the reformation the Word was liberated to do its divinely-given task of conforming men and women to the image of Jesus Christ by the power of the Holy Spirit. Conscientious exegesis was, therefore, a significant exercise, as was prudent study, preaching, teaching and attentive listening, followed by careful obedience. This volume of essays seeks to demonstrate a variety of areas in which the reformers sought understanding from the pages of Scripture. It reveals men who looked first to God for understanding; and men who, then, felt obliged to teach and to preach for the good of their particular communities of faith. The third section, exegesis and theology, focuses on their careful and strategic reading of the text of Scripture with the purpose of gaining insight into God's purposes and ways. Throughout, there is clearly displayed the practical intent and application of the reformers' theology and exegesis.

Whilst others have been written specifically for this volume, many of these essays started life at the Evangelical Theological Society's annual conference in San Francisco, 2011—a conference I was privileged to attend. Chapter 5, 'Luther's insights into grief: his pastoral letters,' was given as a paper at the ETS conference at Milwaukee, 2012. The papers have been reworked, enhanced and enlarged to fit better into an academic book such as the present one. They demonstrate attention to detail, a profound understanding of the subject matter and a commitment to the study of the reformation period. I am grateful to the contributors who took the effort to produce such excellent work and who made the task of editing very straightforward indeed. I am grateful, too, to David Hall for taking the time and trouble to read the whole manuscript and for writing the Foreword. His work on the reformation—in editing and writing, in leading the ETS reformation group—is very much appreciated.

Particular thanks go as always to my wife, Becky, and our children, Chris and Katy, for their love, encouragement and support. They know the significance of the sixteenth century and its importance to me. But they also keep my feet firmly planted in the twenty-first century and my prayers in today's struggles.

I trust that this short volume might add to our growing understanding of the reformers—their exertions and their progress. My prayer, though, is that the Lord might reveal himself and might liberate his Word amongst us today as he did in that turbulent, but exciting period of the reformation.

Michael Parsons
Didcot, Oxfordshire, 2013

FOREWORD

For both the uninitiated and for the illuminati, appreciation of a fine symphony or opera is enhanced by the program notes that accompany the production. As a courtesy to the audience, the expert performers provide sufficient background for greater appreciation for the non-expert audience. Such is this volume: it is a guide to a concert.

Like the discography (or liner notes for a CD), these essays orient an audience far removed from the sixteenth century to the thoughts and morés of a day that—in an age of lightning-paced social media—would likely be lost if moderns were not informed. We can thank our adroit editor for his selection, and his selectivity, that has yielded a fine and helpful volume.

The scholarly essays included have several things in common. First, they are written by practitioners, who have studied well the period. Second, they are written by students of the period who have invested the time and effort to understand a virtually foreign age—that hermeneutical task is not slight. Third, these essays take seriously the historical period without falling into the seduction of thinking of these as hollow halcyon years. Finally, these essays are broad enough in scope as to provide an adequate cross-sectional glimpse into the vibrant age of the reformation.

The mixture of sources and perspectives is tantalizing; it makes the reader pine for more—surely an accomplishment of its own in a day of cyber textual gluttony.

The chapters on Luther are like monographs in miniature. Uche Anizor's exploration of Luther's use and understanding of Scripture is a fine beginning point for any student of liturgy, history, or theology. Similarly, Luther's treatment of idolatry and how that impacts preaching makes Dr. Luther come alive—as if he needed a more colorful palette—yet, Cameron MacKenzie provides that. Berthold Schwarz's treatment of Luther's view of the Jews—a topic that will never recede subsequent to the errors of the Third Reich's ideological kidnapping of the church—is explained as flowing from Luther's intense desire to defend Jesus of Nazareth as the exclusive basis of salvation. While it is easy to criticize Luther's abuses—and he had many, as did Calvin and other reformers—it is also important to seek to understand how his thought led to those abuses. That is precisely how this volume helps us: it not only seeks to explain but to provide background for those 16th century explanations.

A fine example of the above assertion may be seen in Brett Muhlhan's enlightening essay on Luther as a practical theologian. Using the foil of the Visitation-Catechizing plan of the first generation of the reformation, Muhlhan poses the question whether or not Luther would fit into the "New Perspective" insistence on dialogical theology with a praxis orientation. Not only is that juxtaposition addressed but this essay also provides a primer on practical theology—worthy of use in any course containing that phrase. Such value is this aspect of reformation that one should hardly proceed without perusing this fine chapter.

Moreover, the exhibitions that show aspects of Luther's contribution also reveal a poignant human side as Michael Parsons takes the reader on a very informed tour through an immensely practical and perennial topic: dealing with grief. Luther is a detergent for much of the sappy experientialism of our day, which lends so very little help in dealing with real grief. From the Word to idolatry to Christian exclusivity as a religious tenet, and to Luther's practical theology and pastoral care for the grieving, the opening section of this anthology provides a satisfying orientation to key aspects of the reformation concert.

After a brief intermission, as the volume proceeds to consider the other major reformer, light is shed on Calvin's variegated contributions to the reformation. On the heels of the Luther connection, Peter Lillback's essay on Calvin's (and Melanchthon's) adherence to the Augsburg Confession provides the basis for an explanation into what is meant by each reformer on the meaning of confessional subscription. Lillback nuances Calvin's position and reveals a glimpse into the reformer's ecumenical penchant as well as to his sincere confessionalism.

Karin Stetina helps modern readers to see how Calvin made a distinction between metaphoric language and titles of identity. On one hand, Calvin wished to follow Scripture wherever it led; on the other, he did not identify God with a gender. Stetina emphasizes that Calvin's epistemology allows for imagery and that God is free to make use of the created, comparing himself to that which he has made. Knowing the freedom of God leads to the personal liberation that charged the reformation.

While Stetina and Lillback help explore deep aspects of Calvin's reformation, Peter Adam introduces us to how Calvin mentored a generation of preachers. Lest Calvin be thought of as a sterile theoretician, he pioneered educational reforms for clergy and laity alike. This aspect of reformation is motivated by a love for truth and love for our neighbor. Adam also sees Calvin's expository preaching as integral to that educational reform. So important was ministerial education that Calvin provided for the educational institution to tradition the faith.

Some of the most helpful chapters in this volume are those that compare some aspect of a major reformer with other contemporaries. Martin Foord contrasts Calvin's broad and narrow sense of the term 'gospel' from commentaries and the *Institutes* both with medieval precursors and also with Martin Luther. These comparative studies bring a fullness to these aspects of the reformation. Similarly, John Fesko's 'Socinus and the Racovian Catechism on Justification' details how this proto-Unitarian contemporary of Beza both deviated from the orthodox view of justification while also viewing himself as emanating from the same repudiation of Medievalism shared by the reformers.

Clarity is brought to this subject when Socinius' work is compared with other Protestant Trinitarians.

Fesko's contribution is a fitting companion to Guenther Haas' study of how Calvin not only was Trinitarian in concept but moreover he appealed to the economic Trinity often to explicate other theological notions. Calvin's exegesis of Scripture frequently appeals to this Triunity in order to make sense of Scripture. Haas even spies a 'Trinitarian shape of Calvin's exegesis of Scripture' that simultaneously prevents distortion of interpretation as well as undergirds the harmony of Scripture.

As the score reaches its lively finalé, we are introduced to several new theologians and new studies in the final section of this fine anthology.

Jeff Fisher's exploration into an oft-neglected source, Oecolampadius and his commentaries, indicates the breadth of the Reformed tradition. In fact, even though there is occasional methodological difference between Oecolampadius and Calvin, their exegesis was energized by the reformation's return *ad fontes*.

Mike Parsons' article on how Calvin dealt with some of the most ticklish exegetical issues yields a broader portrait of both the humanity and the realism that characterizes Calvin, except to those who wish only to vilify him. Indeed, as Parsons shows, one of the aspects of the reformation was in dealing with unavoidable issues presented by the text, rather than hiding behind a canon law skirt. One leaves with greater appreciation of the reformers after seeing how they chose not to dodge difficult exegetical issues.

Jason Lee's examination of the reformer's exegesis reminds us not to ignore the past. He is surely wise to advise modern exegetes to enhance their own interpretive skills by consulting the previous interpretations of these reformers. The subsequent assertion of this essay, that hermeneutical excellence will only flourish as modern exegetes 'relearn the habits and practices that constituted a flourishing pattern of theological interpretation in the past,' is a gem from this essay.

The final chapter by Rodney Peterson explores how facile it is to have one's exegesis impacted by a worldview; it is especially tempting to over-realize the *eschaton* and identify good and evil with persons or institutions that the exegete loves or fears.

These fine essays, composed by an international, interdenominational, and interdisciplinary faculty, seek to move the conversation of our guild forward. The best trajectory is both perennially dis-satisfied with the state of our knowledge and also seeks to submit our scholarship to a test of time, i.e., will this iteration of scholarship merely entertain—tantamount to being reduced to a court jester of a high order—or will it enrich our knowledge base and help the church that it professes to serve?

Theological scholarship that is always seeking such unassuming utility, if it seeks the latter, will be humble enough to admit that we are not as brilliant as often wished, nor are we infallible in our perspectives that determine which values are important to research. The editor has chosen well in pursuit of that latter goal.

The reader is in for a treat in the coming pages. Enjoy the music, guided by these apt conductors.

David W. Hall
December, 2012

CONTRIBUTORS
(IN ALPHABETICAL ORDER)

Peter Adam served, until recently, as the Principal of Ridley Theological College, Melbourne.

Uche Anizor is Assistant Professor of Theology at Talbot School of Theology, Biola University, USA.

John V. Fesko is Academic Dean and Associate Professor of Systematic and Historical Theology at Westminster Seminary, Escondido, California, USA.

Jeff Fisher is an ordained minister in the Christian Reformed Church in North America and a Ph.D. candidate at Trinity Evangelical Divinity School in Deerfield, Illinois, USA.

Martin Foord is Lecturer in Theology and Reformation Church History at Trinity Theological College, Perth, Australia.

Guenther Haas is Professor of Religion & Theology, Redeemer University College, Ancaster, Ontario, Canada.

David W. Hall is Senior Pastor at Midway Presbyterian Church, Powder Springs, GA, USA.

Jason Lee is Associate Professor of Historical Theology, Southwestern Baptist Theological Seminary, Fort Worth, USA.

Peter A. Lillback is President and Professor of Historical Theology at Westminster Theological Seminary, Philadelphia.

Cameron MacKenzie is Forrest E. and Francis H. Ellis Professor of Historical Theology, Concordia Theological Seminary, Fort Wayne, Indiana, USA.

Carl Mosser is Associate Professor of Biblical Studies at Eastern University in St. Davids, Pennsylvania, USA.

Brett James Muhlhan is Lecturer in Theology and Church History at the Perth Bible College, Western Australia.

Michael Parsons is the Commissioning Editor for Paternoster, and an Associate Research Fellow at Spurgeon's College, London, UK.

Rodney Petersen is Executive Director of the Boston Theological Institute (BTI), co-director of the Religion and Conflict Transformation program at Boston University School of Theology.

Berthold Schwarz is Professor of Systematic Theology at the Giessen School of Theology, Giessen, Germany.

Karin Spiecker Stetina is a part-time Lecturer in Theology at Wheaton College and an Associate Editor for *Luther Digest*.

ABBREVIATIONS

ATR	Anglican Theological Review
AUSS	Andrews University Seminary Studies
BT	Bible Translator
CH	Church History
ChH	Christian History
CNTC	*Calvin's New Testament Commentaries*, 12 vols (ed. David W. Torrance and Thomas F. Torrance. (Grand Rapids: Eerdmans, 1960).
CO	*Ioannis Calvini Opera Quae Supersunt Omnia.*, 59 vols., *Corpus Reformatorum* (ed. Guilielmus Baum, August Eduard Cunitz, and Eduard Reuss: Bad Feilnbach, Germany: Schmidt Periodicals, 1990).
CR	Corpus Reformatorum (Halle: C. A. Schwetschke, 1834-1900; reprint, New York: Johnston Reprint, 1964).
CTJ	Calvin Theological Journal
CTS	*Calvin's Commentaries* from the Calvin Translation Society, 1843-55.
DB	*Deutsche Bibel*, that part of the Weimar edition devoted to Luther's German Bible.
EQ	Evangelical Quarterly
ETR	Études Théologiques et Religieuses
1536 *Inst.*	*Institutes of the Christian Religion, 1536* (ed. and trans., Ford Lewis Battles; H.H. Meeter Center for Calvin Studies; Grand Rapids: Eerdmans, 1986).
1541 *Inst.*	*Institutes of the Christian Religion: 1541 French Edition*, (trans. Elsie Anne McKee: Grand Rapids: Eerdmans, 2009).
1559 *Inst.*	*Institutes of the Christian Religion, 1559* (ed. John T. McNeill, trans. Ford Lewis Battles: Philadelphia: Westminster Press, 1960).
Int	*Interpretation*
JRH	Journal of Religious History
JSNT	Journal for the Study of the New Testament
JRR	Journal from the Radical Reformation
JCE	Journal of Christian Education
JISCA	Journal of the International Society of Christian Apologetics
JTI	Journal of Theological Interpretation
JTS	Journal of Theological Studies
KI	Kirche und Israel
LQ	Lutheran Quarterly
LW	Jaroslav Pelikan and Helmut T. Lehmann (eds), *Luther's Works* (55 vols; St. Louis: Concordia, and Philadelphia: Fortress Press, 1955-86).

PSB	*The Princeton Seminary Bulletin*
RRR	*Reformation and Renaissance Review*
RRJ	*Reformation and Revival Journal*
SJT	*Scottish Journal of Theology*
SCJ	*Sixteenth Century Journal*
T & T	*Calvin's Tracts and Treatises*. Selected Works of John Calvin. Volume 2 (trans. Henry Beveridge: Edinburgh: Calvin Translation Society, 1858).
WA	*D. Martin Luthers Werke, kritische Gesamtausgabe* (Weimar: Hermann Böhlaus Nachfolger, 1883-).
WJT	*Westminster Journal of Theology*

1. *Martin Luther*

CHAPTER 1

Martin Luther, the priesthood of believers and the theological interpretation of scripture

Uche Anizor

Martin Luther protested the loss of a biblical vision for the royal priesthood of all believers, which, he believed, resulted in a tragic decline in the use, proper interpretation, and general attention to the Word of God in its many forms. According to the reformer, royal priesthood is an invitation to mutual ministry of the Word; and this ministry takes the form of a variety of theologically-oriented reading practices, that is, ways of engaging Scripture that bring out and are consonant with its divine character. The aim of this brief essay is to examine one way that Luther offers a concrete, though underdeveloped, attempt to integrate the themes of royal priesthood and the theological interpretation of Scripture. In employing the somewhat anachronistic phrase 'the theological interpretation of Scripture' with reference to Luther, I speak primarily of Scripture reading practices encouraged by Luther that (1) are concerned chiefly with soteriological, ecclesiological, and missiological—thus, theological—issues, and (2) desire to present Scripture as the *viva vox Dei*, the living voice of God. What Luther hoped, and what is here suggested, is that regaining a vision for the royal priesthood of all believers might open up possibilities for the Word's broader activity in and transformation of the church's life. I begin by looking, briefly, at Luther's understanding of the 'Word of God', then, examine what he means when he declares the priesthood of all believers as essential for a proper 'reading' of this Word.

The multifaceted Word of God

To understand best how Luther relates the Word of God to the priesthood of believers, it is essential to grasp what he means by the 'Word of God'. It will be evident in the following that this term has many dimensions, which will make its connection to Christian priesthood all the more rich.

It is understandable to assume that when Luther speaks of the Word of God he has only Scripture in mind, as the primacy of Scripture was a central commitment of his reform. However, this would be a false assumption. In Luther, the Word of God consists in three broad forms: oral, sacramental, and written.

He writes in the *Smalcald Articles* (1537) that the gospel is given, first, 'through the spoken word, by which the forgiveness of sins is preached to the whole world (which is the proper function of the Gospel); second, through baptism; third, through the holy Sacrament of the Altar; fourth, through the power of keys and also through the mutual conversation and consolation of brothers and sisters.[1] Through these various forms of his Word, God graciously presents himself to human beings. More than just pointing to God and his disposition toward sinners, these forms of his Word, actually, convey and perform his saving will. Writing on Luther's view, Robert Kolb observes, 'God designed his Word in these forms as instruments of his re-creating power which accomplish what they announce. More than performative speech, they are creative speech, parallel to God's speaking in Genesis 1.'[2] Luther presents God as 'a *person* who engaged his people in conversation through his Word in its several forms,' and through it 'exercises *his* power to claim and restore sinners'.[3] Let us examine each of these forms in order.

God encounters his people, primarily, in his Word. For Luther this Word is, predominantly, a spoken word, uttered in the proclamation of the gospel and in the absolution of sins. The oral proclamation of the Word, first, places emphasis on the living confrontation and conversation between the Creator and humanity. Luther writes,

> The word 'Gospel' signifies nothing else than a sermon or report concerning the grace and mercy of God merited and acquired through the Lord Jesus Christ with His death. Actually, the Gospel is not what one finds in books and what is written in letters of the alphabet; it is rather an oral sermon and a living Word, a voice that resounds throughout the world and is proclaimed publicly, so that one hears it everywhere.[4]

Since God is a speaking God, one most powerfully encounters him through the medium of the human voice. This truth is summed up well in the eighth of the *Marburg Articles* (1529) which states that 'the Holy Spirit, ordinarily, gives

---

[1] *Smalcald Articles* 3, 5 in Robert Kolb and Timothy J. Wengert (eds), *The Book of Concord* (Minneapolis: Fortress, 2000), 319. We will return to these specific forms of the Word and expand this list in what follows.

[2] Robert Kolb, *Martin Luther: Confessor of the Faith* (Oxford: OUP, 2009), 132. Lohse argues that Luther's view is rooted in Augustine's distinction between the sign and reality. For Augustine, words were only a reference to a reality behind them, which could not be communicated or expressed. Words were merely signs. Luther retained those distinctions but went beyond Augustine by tying word and reality, or outer and inner word, more closely together. For him, the human word becomes the 'bearer of the divine Spirit' and, actually, conveys the reality in some real way. Bernhard Lohse, *Martin Luther's Theology: Its Historical and Systematic Development* (edited and translated by Roy A. Harrisville; Minneapolis: Fortress, 1999), 191, points out the parallels with Luther's view on the Lord's Supper.

[3] Kolb, *Martin Luther*, 131, emphasis added.

[4] *Sermons on the First Epistle of St. Peter* (1522), *LW* 30.3.

such faith or his gift to no one without preaching or the oral word or the gospel of Christ preceding, but that through and by means of such oral word he effects and creates faith where and in whom it pleases him'.[5] The Word of God, as the proclamation of the gospel, brings Christ to us and us to Christ through a human voice.

Second, the pronouncement of forgiveness in the sacrament of penance is a word of God's comfort to troubled sinners. In his treatise, *The Sacrament of Penance* (1519), Luther argues that the Word of God, and not the priest, accomplishes what is important in the sacrament of penance, namely, absolution from the guilt of sin.[6] He does not deny the role of the priest in extending God's forgiveness, but he emphasizes that God's Word, itself, conveyed forgiveness to those who trusted in it. The words of the priest 'show, tell, and proclaim to you that you are free and that your sins are forgiven by God according to and by virtue of the above-quoted words of Christ to St. Peter [Matt. 16.19]'.[7] That is, the word of Christ's promise, that whatever is loosed on earth will be loosed in heaven, is articulated and rearticulated through the word of the priest's absolution. To disbelieve it is to make God out to be a liar. However, if with 'unshakeable faith' we 'give place to the word of God spoken through the priest' we may receive the forgiveness of our sins and have a joyful conscience.[8] It is this oral Word that, in the hearing of the one who has faith, conveys what it promises.

The sacraments—baptism and the Lord's Supper—are, also, forms of God's Word to his people. Concerning the first, Luther, typically, presents speech as an image of the mode of God's activity in baptism. He asserts that 'baptism is nothing other than God's Word in the water, commanded by God's institution'.[9] Baptism proclaims and actualizes the promises of God for forgiveness,

---

[5] *The Marburg Colloquy and The Marburg Articles* (1529), *LW* 38.87. In *The Sacrament of the Body and Blood of Christ—Against the Fanatics* (1526), he, moreover, writes, 'I preach the gospel of Christ, and with my bodily voice I bring Christ into your heart, so that you may form him within yourself. If now you truly believe, so that your heart lays hold of the word and holds fast within it that voice, tell me, what have you in your heart? You must answer that you have the true Christ . . . [T]he one Christ enters so many hearts through the voice, and that each person who hears the sermon and accepts it takes the whole Christ into his heart' (*LW* 36.340). See, also, *The Adoration of the Sacrament* (1523), *LW* 36.278, and *A Brief Instruction on What to Look For and Expect in the Gospels* (1521), *LW* 35.121.

[6] 'It follows further that the forgiveness of guilt is not within the province of any human office or authority, be it pope, bishop, priest, or any other. Rather it depends exclusively upon the word of Christ and your own faith' (*LW* 35.12). Cf. Kolb, *Martin Luther*, 134.

[7] *LW* 35.11.

[8] *LW* 35.14-16. It is noteworthy that when Luther later excluded penance from the list of sacraments, he still urged Christians to partake of the absolution pronounced by pastors, both publicly and privately (Kolb, *Martin Luther*, 134).

[9] *Smalcald Articles* 3, 5:1, in *The Book of Concord*, 319.

cleansing, and new life: 'In Baptism . . . it is said to us: "I am the Lord your God, do not be troubled! I will care for you! Cast your care on Me! You have a God who has promised that He will care for you."'[10] It is precisely its attachment to God's Word of promise that renders baptism itself a word, and particularly a word of any value.[11] The emphasis in baptism is on divine action and initiative, not on the response of the recipient.[12] The God who graciously makes the promise provides a visible word through which he effects what he has pledged. Similar things may be said of the Eucharist. Following Paul's account (1 Cor. 11.24-26) Luther holds that the sacred meal proclaims Christ. As the signs of bread and water are combined with the words of institution, they preach and praise Christ, glorify his sufferings, and speak of his grace, 'to the end that our faith, provided with and confirmed by divine words and signs, may thereby become strong against all sin, suffering, death, and hell, and everything that is against us'.[13] Contrary to Rome's view, the sacrament was not a sacrifice but a testament of the forgiveness of sins and God's gracious disposition toward his own, and like baptism, bestows what it proclaims, particularly as faith receives the promises that are intertwined with the signs.[14] Yet, the importance of faith is somewhat mitigated by the reality of Christ's presence in the Supper, which is made certain by Christ's creative words of institution, and this apart from faith. Thus, there is a kind of objectivity to the work done in the sacramental word of the Lord's Supper. In fact, in at least this way, the sacrament is meant to arouse or strengthen faith.[15] For Luther, as Kolb points out, 'all talk of Christ's presence in the sacrament must serve to assure the faithful that God works through the sacrament to give them eternal life, for "the forgiveness of sins, consolation of souls, and strengthening of faith"'.[16] Luther's vehement

---

[10] *Lectures on Genesis 37* (1544), *LW* 6.364. Cf. *Lectures on Genesis 17* (1539), *LW* 3.124.

[11] Trigg, helpfully, draws attention to the multivalence of 'word' in relation to the sacrament. The term may refer to the ministry of the word that accompanies baptism or the divine word of promise, which is joined to the sacrament. The former is merely a human word intended to remind those who are weak in faith, while the latter is already given in Scripture and, therefore, continues to be given—Jonathan D. Trigg, *Baptism in the Theology of Martin Luther* (Leiden: Brill, 1994), 35.

[12] In his earlier work on baptism, Luther emphasized the necessity of faith for the efficacy of baptism (see, e.g., *The Holy and Blessed Sacrament of Baptism* [1519], *LW* 35.33-36). However, in his later works he stressed the objectivity of baptism, sometimes over against the claims of the Anabaptists (see, e.g., *Concerning Rebaptism* [1528], *LW* 40.249).

[13] *Treatise on the New Testament* (1520), *LW* 35.105-106.

[14] *LW* 35.84-87. On Luther's stress on the necessity of faith to receive the benefits of the sacrament, see *LW* 35.88-89 and *LW* 36.349-50.

[15] The *Marburg Articles* state, 'That the use of the sacrament, like the word, has been given and ordained by God Almighty in order that weak consciences may thereby be excited to faith by the Holy Spirit' (*LW* 38.88).

[16] Kolb, *Martin Luther*, 147.

opposition to the views of Zwingli and other Swiss theologians was intended to secure this assurance for God's people. Bread and wine are visible words that guarantee Christ's presence and promises, especially to those who believe.

That Luther holds Scripture to be the Word of God is beyond dispute.[17] What emerges from the above discussion, however, is the question of the interplay between Scripture and the oral and sacramental forms of the Word of God. Luther sometimes speaks of Scripture as merely the preservation of the prior proclaimed Word, leading some, like Lohse, to conclude, too strongly, that 'Luther emphasized the priority of the oral proclamation *over* the written deposit.'[18] Rather, by highlighting the oral proclamation of the gospel Luther was making a basic distinction between the Old and New Testament eras and their respective scriptural writings. He averred that, although both testaments were written down, the New Testament should properly be 'contained in the living voice which resounds and is heard everywhere'. It is, therefore, not necessary that it be written. While the Old Testament is available only in writing and merely points to the Christ who was to come, the gospel or New Testament 'is a living sermon on the Christ who *has* come'.[19] The gospel is an announcement of good news, and that news is the reality of Jesus Christ who has come to save humankind. Althaus, more accurately, captures Luther's heart. While affirming that for Luther the Word is 'first and last the spoken word', he, also, notes that this living, oral Word is limited because its content is the apostolic Word. The apostles, alone, are the infallible teachers of the Christian message, whose writings are the authoritative accounts of their own preaching.[20] Therefore, all true Christian proclamation can only transmit and explain this apostolic Word.[21] Written Scripture provides the sure message, oral proclamation brings it into conversation with human persons, and each reinforces the other. Absolution functions in a more straightforward manner. The pronouncement of forgiveness is merely a repetition or re-verbalization of Christ's promise of clemency. Because the Lord pledges that what is forgiven on earth is truly forgiven, the

---

[17] See, e.g., *Preface to the Wittenberg Edition of Luther's German Writings* (1539), *LW* 34.284; *The Gospel for the Festival of the Epiphany, Matthew 2* (1522), *LW* 52.211; *The Small Catechism* (1529), Small Catechism Baptism 1–8, in *The Book of Concord*, 359. Lohse, *Martin Luther's Theology*, 188, rightly, points out that Luther's view of the relationship between God and Scripture is complex. He outlines three ways that Luther speaks of Scripture: as God's Word, containing God's Word, and as a mere creature. At the very least, what this alerts us to is the flexibility of Luther's statements about Scripture. However, this flexibility does not mute Luther's constant refrain that the Scriptures are the final authority in all matters.

[18] Lohse, *Martin Luther's Theology*, 189, emphasis added. Also, see *LW* 52.205-207, where Luther makes the point that the apostles first preached before they wrote and that their writings were for the preservation of what they had preached.

[19] *LW* 30.19, emphasis added.

[20] *LW* 52.206.

[21] Paul Althaus, *The Theology of Martin Luther* (translated by Robert C. Schultz; Philadelphia: Fortress, 1970), 72.

priest who absolves simply gives breath and voice to the written Word and makes it a living word of comfort to the hearer amidst his circumstances.

Luther makes explicit the connection between Scripture and baptism in his *Small Catechism*, where he defines the latter as 'water used according to God's command and connected with God's Word'. What is God's Word? It is Matthew 28.19, which commands Christ's followers to baptize in the triune name. The second question in this section of the catechism asks what gifts or benefits are bestowed by baptism. The answer: 'It effects forgiveness of sins, delivers from death and the devil, and grants eternal salvation to all who believe, as the Word and promise of God declare.' What is this Word and promise? Again, it is Scripture, specifically Mark 16.16, which declares that all who believe and are baptized will be saved.[22] Thus, baptism is commanded and defined by the written Word, and, furthermore, confers what it promises on the basis of God's promise in this same Word. The Lord's Supper, also, derives its power from the scriptural Word alone. Against anti-sacramentalists, like Karlstadt, Luther avers that even if the bread and wine were only symbolic, the sacrament would still grant the forgiveness of sins on account of Christ's words of institution. 'Everything,' he says, 'depends on the Word.'[23] The sacraments as visible, tangible words are rooted in the prior Word that established them and continues to undergird their work in the lives of believers.[24]

We may, therefore, sum up the interplay between Scripture and the other forms of the Word of God, and, therefore, Luther's view, as follows: oral and sacramental proclamation are forms of the Word of God when they correspond to the written Word that instituted and makes promises through them. Now that we have some grasp of Luther's use of 'the Word of God' we are better able to understand how he connects this to the Christian's priesthood.

The mutual ministry of the Word

One important way Luther establishes the priesthood of every Christian is to take what his opponents, and medieval Christianity, generally, believed are the functions of a priest and demonstrate that all Christians are permitted to perform those same functions. In *Concerning the Ministry* he identifies seven such priestly functions: (1) to teach and preach the Word of God, (2) to baptize, (3) to administer the Lord's Supper, (4) to bind and loose sins, (5) to pray for oth-

---

[22] *Small Catechism* Baptism 1–8, in *The Book of Concord*, 359. This is, also, Luther's argument against the Anabaptists. He argues that, if they believed God's word (Mk. 16.16) about the efficacy of baptism, they would not rebaptize anyone (see *LW* 40.249).

[23] *Against the Heavenly Prophets in the Matter of Images and Sacraments* (1525), *LW* 40.214.

[24] See Trigg's entire discussion on the relation of water and word in Luther's baptismal theology—Trigg, *Baptism*, 61-109, especially, 70.

ers, (6) to sacrifice, and (7) to judge all doctrine and spirits.[25] It should be no surprise that he views the first duty as the highest and the one upon which the others depend, for 'we teach with the Word, we consecrate with the Word, we bind and absolve sins by the Word, we baptize with the Word, we sacrifice with the Word, we judge all things by the Word'.[26] These seven priestly duties are nothing other than expressions of the various forms of the Word of God outlined above. Everything a priest does is, in essence, a ministry of the Word, and this ministry defines priesthood.[27] The remarkable move Luther makes is to extend this manifold priestly ministry of the Word to all Christians—men and women, alike. He argues that if all Christians are given access to the same Word of God, and if all, as priests, are given a ministry, namely, to proclaim the excellencies of God (1 Pet. 2.9), then, no priestly duty should be denied any believer since they are all derivative of the ministry of teaching and preaching the Word. Every 'splendid' and 'royal' duty is to be exercised by every Christian.[28] In *Concerning the Ministry* and elsewhere he expands on what it means, and what it does not mean, for every believer to perform these priestly functions.

First, preaching, teaching, and proclaiming the Word is within the province of every believer. 'Even though not everybody has the public office,' Luther writes, 'every Christian has the right and the duty to teach, instruct, admonish, comfort, and rebuke his neighbor with the Word of God at every opportunity and whenever necessary.'[29] Two things should be observed: (1) he distinguishes between the *office* and *function* of preaching, and, therefore, (2) grants every believer a non-official ministry of the Word. He is clear throughout his writings that the public ministry of the Word is for those called by a congregation to exercise this office on the congregation's behalf. No one may take it upon himself, but must be elected by the church.[30] Another way to understand

---

[25] *LW* 40.21.
[26] *LW* 40.21.
[27] 'The duty of a priest is to preach, and if he does not preach he is as much a priest as a picture of a man is a man' (*The Babylonian Captivity of the Church* [1520], *LW* 36.115). 'The priesthood is properly nothing but the ministry of the Word. . . . Whoever, therefore, does not know or preach the gospel is not only no priest or bishop, but he is a kind of pest to the church, who under the false title of priest or bishop, or dressed in sheep's clothing, actually does violence to the gospel and plays the wolf in the church' (*LW* 36.116). 'To declare the praises of Christ is the priesthood and kingdom of the Christians' (*Lecture on Isaiah 43* [1527-1530], *LW* 17.98).
[28] *LW* 40.21.
[29] *Commentary on Psalm 110*, *LW* 13.333. Cf., *Lecture on Zechariah 17* (1527), *LW* 20.346.
[30] 'Although we are all equally priests, we cannot all publicly minister and teach' (*The Freedom of the Christian* [1520], *LW* 31.356). Writing against radical reformers who used the doctrine of the priesthood of all believers to justify their usurpation of the office of pastor, he urges, 'It is true that all Christians are priests, but not all are pastors. For to be a pastor one must be not only a Christian and a priest but must have an

Luther's view is to note the way he distinguishes between 'public' and 'private' spheres. For him, these terms do not designate corporate vs. personal spheres, but, rather, official vs. non-official. Thus, the priesthood of all believers obliges every Christian to declare God's Word in the private sphere, that is, to mediate the Word of God to a fellow believer in personal conversation.[31] A parent who acquaints her child with the gospel, a brother who teaches another the Lord's Prayer, or a peasant who admonishes an ignorant friend concerning the Ten Commandments—these are truly priests.[32] When any Christian speaks to another a word of correction, instruction, or consolation, the priesthood of all believers, vis-à-vis the ministry of the Word of God, is properly exercised.

Second, the administration of baptism is permitted to all the baptized. According to church law only priests were permitted to baptize. However, Luther's opponents allowed even ordinary women to baptize in emergency situations. According to their logic, he argues, every Christian is then made a priest since every Christian is allowed to baptize. And baptism, being the proclamation of the life-giving Word of God, is the greatest official ministry in the church. Therefore, every believer is given the great honor of visibly and verbally preaching Christ in the church.[33]

The third function of the universal priesthood is the consecration and administration of the Lord's Supper. Luther argues that the words of institution (Lk. 22.19; 1 Cor. 11.24) were originally spoken to all those present at the Last Supper and to those who in the future would come to the table. It follows, therefore, that what was given there was given to all. Furthermore, in 1 Corinthians 11.23 ('For I received from the Lord what I also delivered to you . . .') Paul addresses all the Corinthians, making each of them consecrators.[34] Finally, Luther concludes that if the two greatest ministries—preaching the Word and baptism—are given to all Christians, it is no great thing that all should be able to

---

office and a field of work committed to him. This call and command make pastors and preachers' (*Sermons on Ps 82* [1530], *LW* 13.65). Cf. *LW* 39.157; *That a Christian Assembly or Congregation Has the Right and Power to Judge All Teaching and to Call, Appoint, and Dismiss Teachers, Established and Proven by Scripture* (1523), *LW* 39.310-11. Some even took the priesthood of believers so far as to exclude the need for training for the ministry. Luther rejects this notion (see *To the Councilmen of All Cities in Germany That They Establish and Maintain Christian Schools* [1524], *LW* 45.343). Luther did make necessity an exception to this hard and fast rule. If there were no official ministers, then, anyone, including a woman, might preach to the congregation. The most important thing was the proclamation of the Word (*LW* 39.310; cf., *Explanations of the Ninety-five Theses* [1518], *LW* 36.152).

[31] Brian A. Gerrish, 'Priesthood and Ministry in the Theology of Luther,' *CH* 34 (1965), 416-17. Cf., *LW* 40.34.

[32] See *The Estate of Marriage* (1522), *LW* 45.46; *LW* 13.333.

[33] *LW* 40.23.

[34] *LW* 40.24.

administer the Eucharist.[35] If God gives the greater, how much more would he grant the lesser?

Fourth, Luther holds that the power of the keys belongs to all Christians on the basis of Matthew 18.15-20, which is spoken not only to the apostles but all believers.[36] Binding and loosing are nothing else than the proclamation and application of the gospel. 'For what is it to loose,' he asks, 'if not to announce the forgiveness of sins before God? What is it to bind, except to withdraw the gospel and to declare the retention of sins?'[37] The word Christ spoke to Peter ('Whatever you loose . . . shall be loosed') is the power behind every absolution; 'indeed every absolution depends upon it'.[38] Thus, since the ministry of this and every form of the Word belongs to all, the power to forgive and withhold forgiveness is the prerogative of all.

Fifth, prayer is the common right of all believers. Luther does not make equally clear connections between prayer, the Word of God, and universal priesthood. He, simply, argues that since the Lord's Prayer is given to all Christians, all may take part in the priestly duty of making intercession for others.[39] Prayer is, simply, every believer's response to the command, promise, and provision of God.

The sixth function, sacrifice, is a spiritual activity carried out by all believers. The only sacrifice in the New Testament is a spiritual sacrifice, that is, our bodies, which includes our praise and thanksgiving (Rom. 12.1; 1 Pet. 2.5). Luther relates the Word of God to this sacrifice in two ways. First, the sacrifice is perfected by the Word, which means that it must be offered according to Scripture and as a result of the gospel.[40] Second, he interprets the Old Testament priestly sacrifice as the offering of Christians through the ministry of the Word. That is, the 'office of slaughter and sacrifice signifies nothing else than the preaching of the gospel, by which the old man is slain and offered to God, burned and consumed by the fire of love in the Holy Spirit'.[41] Sacrifice is putting to death the sinful nature by constant use of the Word of God, and this is something all Christians are permitted, indeed commanded, to do.

---

[35] *LW* 40.25.
[36] Here, Luther embarks on an argument against the false distinction between power and use. His opponents held that it might be true that all believers have the power of the keys, but they asserted that the use was not common to all. Luther objects that Scripture does not make such a distinction and, if it were to be upheld, it would have to apply to Peter as well (Matt. 16.19) (*LW* 40.26-27).
[37] The papist priests, on the other hand, bound and loosed on the basis of their own laws. In this way they undermined the gospel and closed the door of heaven to the church (*LW* 40.28).
[38] *LW* 35.13.
[39] *LW* 40.30.
[40] *LW* 40.29.
[41] *Preface to the Old Testament* (1545), *LW* 35.248.

Finally, the right to judge doctrine belongs to the whole church, as is firmly established in Scripture by passages that deal with testing false teachers (John 10.5, 27; Matt. 7.15; 16.6; 24.4-5; 1 Thess. 5.21) and those which affirm that each believer has the Spirit of truth (John 14.26; 1 Cor. 2.15; 2 Cor. 4.13; 1 John 2.27).[42] The judging of doctrine is a corollary of the teaching ministry.[43] Both activities require knowledge of God's Word and are concerned with its proclamation. In this vein, both seek to edify—the latter by the positive presentation of the gospel, the former by the refutation of destructive teaching. If every Christian as a priest can preach the Word, the same may judge doctrine.[44] 'It is the duty of a Christian,' Luther exclaims, 'to espouse the cause of the faith, to understand and defend it, and to denounce every error.'[45] This is part of what it means for believers to live out their priesthood.

The relationship of the priesthood of all believers to the Word of God is a rich and multifaceted one. Far from being an affirmation of an individual's right to read the Bible and form private judgments, it combines the many different expressions of God's Word with an emphasis on ministry to others. Althaus captures the reformer's view well:

> Luther never understands the priesthood of all believers merely in the 'Protestant' sense of the Christian's freedom to stand in a direct relationship to God without a human mediator. Rather he constantly emphasizes the Christian's evangelical authority to come before God on behalf of the brethren and also of the world. The universal priesthood expresses not religious individualism but its exact opposite, the reality of the congregation as a community.[46]

All Christians have access to God's Word in order that they might minister it in its many forms to one another. Luther's linking of the priesthood of believers with the Word of God brings out the New Testament emphasis on the community—the 'one another' aspects of the Christian's calling. As a priest, the baptized person lives for their Christian brother and sister. But, the primary way they help the other is by holding to and proclaiming the manifold Word of God.

Luther's contribution: toward a theology of priestly readers

In what ways does Luther enrich our understanding of the priesthood of all believers, the Word of God, and their interconnectedness? The answer to this question brings to the fore the contribution Luther makes to contemporary reflection on the theological nature of 'reading' the Word and, thus, the central concerns of this essay. I would suggest at least four contributions.

---

[42] *LW* 40.32-33; *LW* 39.306-308; *To the Christian Nobility of the German Nation Concerning the Reform of the Christian Estate* (1520), *LW* 44.135.
[43] *LW* 40.32-33.
[44] *LW* 44.135.
[45] *LW* 44.136.
[46] Althaus, *Theology of Martin Luther*, 314.

First, he is uniquely aware that when the priesthood of all believers is denied or neglected, attention to the Word of God is somehow diminished. Though the manifold Word of God might still be proclaimed by the ordained priesthood, its full effects, including its power to reform the church, are weakened because laypeople are not enjoined to handle the Word as priests to one another. What Luther posits is that when the priesthood of believers is, rightly understood and appreciated it results in freeing the Word of God to function more fully in the life of the church. Thus, in one sense, Luther democratizes access to and ministry of the Word, but not to the exclusion of ordained ministers or to encourage individualism in Scripture reading practices. Rather, he delivers the Word of God to every believer so that each is made responsible for the encouragement, comfort, and discipline of others, and all this for the benefit of the whole church.[47] Stephen Fowl and L. Gregory Jones, in *Reading in Communion*, share Luther's instinct, arguing for the need of a more expansive notion of the church in order to combat potentially sectarian and, thus, unfaithful readings of Scripture. They contend that the 'we' who read and hear Scripture must take into account the voices of supposed outsiders, as these may serve to correct our sometimes arrogant and destructive readings.[48] Although one need not follow Fowl and Jones at every turn, they point to the importance of openness in the reading of Scripture, particularly openness to silenced and neglected voices within the church of Jesus Christ. The priesthood of *all believers* emphasizes that even the un- and under-educated must have a voice. Furthermore, but related, on an inter-ecclesial level, non-Western voices must be heard, appreciated, and appropriated.[49] If all believers are royal priests, then all are responsible to minister the Word. This democratization of priestly privilege does not ignore concerns about the unformed and individualistic Western Bible reader.[50] Rather, this expansion of the 'we' is a wise measure to keep in check potentially parochial and political readings of Scripture. Again, there is a faint echo of Luther's concerns here. When the church ceases hearing the voices of 'outsiders', it becomes turned in on itself, falling prey to bias-confirming interpretations

---

[47] Cyril Eastwood, *The Priesthood of All Believers: An Examination of the Doctrine from the Reformation to the Present Day* (Minneapolis: Augsburg, 1962), 3-4, remarks that Luther, rightly, places the task of ministry *in* the church and not *above* it. He adds that the ministry of the gospel, which is the primary ministry of the church, does not occur 'outside the congregation but within it, and in this way the Gospel is mediated through the congregation'.

[48] Stephen E. Fowl and L. Gregory Jones, *Reading in Communion: Scripture and Ethics in Christian Life* (Grand Rapids: Eerdmans, 1991), 113-34.

[49] For a helpful introduction to the issues surrounding the intersection of globalization and theological hermeneutics, see Daniel J. Treier, *Introducing Theological Interpretation of Scripture: Recovering a Christian Practice* (Grand Rapids: Baker Academic, 2008), 157-86.

[50] See, for example, Stanley Hauerwas, *Unleashing the Scripture: Freeing the Bible from Captivity to America* (Nashville: Abingdon, 1993), 15-18.

and, in many respects, losing its way. Thus, Luther's appeal to the priesthood of all believers may be seen as an affirmation of the centrality of the Word of God in the church's life. When one emphasis declines, the other is soon to follow.

Second, Luther's emphasis on the relative importance of oral forms of the Word draws attention to the living character of this Word. He gives prominence to preaching and proclamation because he sees the Word of God as a summons, a call to faith from almighty God. The gospel is presented, most appropriately, with a living voice; its proper form is oral; it is to be vocalized and heard. The practice of confession and absolution surfaces similar concerns. When forgiveness is pronounced verbally, the hearer is assured of God's promise of mercy as if God spoke the Word himself. What this points to is that believers are to be mouthpieces for the Word of God; they are mediators of an address the living God seeks to make to his people. Their words, when congruent with the written Word, become God's Word of invitation, promise, and discipline. Thus, what Luther, unwittingly, underlines is the need for more reflection on the place of orality in the theological reading of Scripture. How might the insights of some experts, regarding oral cultures and orality, aid a properly theological interpretation of the Scriptures? For example, one writer observes that 'knowing' in oral cultures, in contrast to literate cultures, 'means achieving close, empathetic, communal identifications with the known'.[51] Another author contrasts literate and oral practices and states the differences in terms of participation vs. non-participation in the stories told:

> Where memory collapses time spans, writing tends to fix events temporally and heighten the sense of their distinctiveness as well as their 'pastness', or separation from the present and the individual person. The sense of participation in the events narrated becomes more difficult. . . . In other words, literacy changes the relationship between a society and its traditions, as well as that between individuals and their past, because it fixes traditions and that past in a way that distances both from the present.[52]

Oral practices, thus, foster a sense of self-involvement or participation in the events narrated. Of course, vocalizing stories does not guarantee participatory hearing, but it can mitigate some of the distancing effects of silent reading. These observations are all the more important for Christians, who must recognize the history of Adam, Israel, and Jesus Christ as their own history. A distancing from these stories can be a distancing from the life-altering realities these stories communicate.

Moreover, these insights provide some justification for the pre-eminence of the sermon as possibly the most common and effective means of theological

---

[51] Walter J. Ong, *Orality and Literacy: The Technologizing of the Word* (New York: Routledge, 2005), 45-46.

[52] William A. Graham, *Beyond the Written Word: Oral Aspects of Scripture in the History of Religion* (Cambridge: CUP, 1987), 16.

interpretation. In fact, the recurrent plea for concrete examples of theological interpretation in action has been, in some sense, answered by the inclusion of sermons in texts like Hays and Davis' *The Art of Reading Scripture*, or the publication of volumes of sermons by contemporary theologians.[53] Moreover, Stephen Webb's recent study on Christian acoustemology is a sustained argument that the sermon is the most appropriate medium for understanding the Bible.[54] Certainly, the theological reading of Scripture—as the complex interplay between God the Word, readers, concrete situations, and the Bible—lends itself to the more fluid and dynamic environment embodied by the event of Christian proclamation. Indeed, the place of the sermon in the overall apparatus of learning and appropriating Scripture is a question contemporary advocates of the theological interpretation of scripture might seek to answer.

Third, Luther points us to the important place of the sacraments as visible *and* vocal words in the presentation of the gospel to God's people. When the elements of the Lord's Supper, for example, are combined with the scriptural words of institution, the signs themselves preach Christ. As such, the sacraments *are* the faithful performance of Scripture because they proclaim the very heart of the biblical message—Christ crucified and resurrected for us and our salvation. Kevin Vanhoozer hints at this relationship between faithful reading and the sacraments:

> The sacraments, like the proclaimed word, are 'real presentations' of the gospel of Jesus Christ. . . . The sacraments facilitate *a theo-dramatic participation in the eschatological action* through faith's attestation of the work of Son and Spirit. Through baptism and the Lord's Supper, Christ *presents* himself to believing communicants via a *real presentation* of the climactic events of redemptive history. By performing the biblical words and the sacramental actions, we are *really* drawn into the ongoing theo-dramatic action by the Spirit.[55]

If the sacraments truly present the scripturally mediated gospel, then they are theological Scripture reading practices in the truest sense. The sacraments are the embodiment of the oral Word, which itself is the vocalization of the scriptural Word. Thus, through the sacraments we are directed away from the centrality of silent reading toward the importance of oral reading practices, while affirming (even elevating) tangible and symbolic elements as effective means of proclaiming and hearing the Word of God. Faithful reading in the light of

---

[53] See the six sermons by Davis and Hays in *Art of Reading Scripture*, 277-325. See, also, for example, Colin E. Gunton, *Theology Through Preaching: The Gospel and the Christian Life* (London: T. & T. Clark, 2001); Gunton, *The Theologian As Preacher: Further Sermons from Colin Gunton* (London: T. & T. Clark, 2004).

[54] Stephen H. Webb, *The Divine Voice* (Grand Rapids: Brazos, 2005), especially, 24-29.

[55] Kevin J. Vanhoozer, *The Drama of Doctrine: A Canonical-Linguistic Approach to Christian Theology* (Louisville: Westminster John Knox, 2005), 412, original emphasis.

Luther's contribution, then, is an oral and physical act, or better, an oral-physical act, where fidelity to the Word of God is increased, not diminished, by the employment of visible, symbolic words.

Finally, Luther underscores the missionary component of the church's reading practices.[56] It is common in missiological discussions to see the church as a missionary church. If, now, mission is the essence of the church, then all of the church's practices must conform to that essence. Thus, the reading of Scripture, as a central practice, must reflect the missionary nature of the church. In that light, reading Scripture must be seen as a centrifugal act directed toward those separated from the community of Christ. Few advocates of the theological interpretation of Scripture have connected theological interpretation (or reading) specifically with mission in their treatments. In his study, J. Todd Billings argues, notably, that the church's reading of Scripture is missional when it lives up to its identity as those who belong to Jesus Christ. He writes, 'Scripture is the means by which the living Christ instructs, builds up, and continually converts the church to be a people of his mission and his way by the Spirit's enabling power.'[57] He adds, 'There is no activity more missional than Christ-centered, Spirit-empowered worship, which speaks, hears, smells, and tastes the great drama of the gospel.'[58] As we encourage one another through the use of Scripture to be shaped in a Christ-like direction, and, actually, do reflect the way of Jesus, we *are* witnesses. Vanhoozer moves in a similar direction when he describes the missionary role of the church, writing, 'Preaching and teaching should be "evangelistic," then, in the sense of enabling people to indwell the gospel (=evangel) as the primary framework for all that they say and do.'[59] The church's reading is missionary, inasmuch as it forms a community that indwells the gospel. This more community-focused aspect of mission, certainly, echoes aspects of Luther's treatment, not to mention God's calling of Israel as a royal priesthood and holy nation (Exod. 19.5-6). As the people of God reflect their difference and distinctiveness to the nations, God is revered as the holy One. Similarly, as God, through Scripture, shapes the church, the outside world will

---

[56] André Gounelle, 'Le sacerdoce universel,' *ÉTR* 63 (1988), 434, in fact, concludes that the doctrine of the priesthood of all believers is an affirmation of the mission of the community to the world.

[57] J. Todd Billings, *The Word of God for the People of God: An Entryway to the Theological Interpretation of Scripture* (Grand Rapids: Eerdmans, 2010), 222-23.

[58] Billings, *The Word of God*, 223. Similar points are being made by many in current missional church conversations. Darrell L. Guder, *The Continuing Conversion of the Church* (Grand Rapids: Eerdmans, 2000), 151-55, for example, writes: 'The evangelizing congregation is continuously being evangelized. . . . Evangelization as the heart of ministry means that the gospel-centered community encounters and celebrates Christ. This is the purpose and witness of public worship. . . . Our worship is therefore the first demonstration before the world of our sentness, as we respond to God's grace in the good news of Jesus Christ.'

[59] Vanhoozer, *Drama of Doctrine*, 74, emphasis added.

become cognizant of the work of the triune God in our midst. However, while focusing on this aspect of the missionary reading of Scripture, we cannot neglect the more active aspect, the proclamatory component: 'But you are a chosen race, a royal priesthood, a holy nation, God's own people, *in order that you may proclaim* the mighty acts of him who called you out of darkness into his marvelous light' (1 Pet. 2.9, emphasis added). According to Luther, preaching, absolution, baptism and the Eucharist function to vocalize and symbolize God's words of promise and hope to those *outside* the church as well; the proper use of the Word of God—its proper 'reading'—must have unbelieving others in mind. In a real way, right reading seeks to bring the written Word to life in order that others might truly *hear* God and respond to him as the living Judge and Savior of their souls. It might be said that evangelistic or missionary preaching is the consummation or completion of the entire reading act, indeed as the achievement of one of Scripture's chief aims. As Luther remarked repeatedly, the New Testament gospel comes to full flower when it is proclaimed in the world. If, in one sense, 'interpretation is practice', then the church's verbal declaration of the good news is the performed meaning of the missionary scriptural Word.[60] Faithful reading *is* proclamation, publication, declaration.

Conclusion

In Luther's vision of priesthood, to be a Christian is to be a priest, and this carries with it various rights and responsibilities. As God's priests in God's house, all believers are called to declare the Word of God in its many forms for the edification of one another and the salvation of the world. Only in this way will the royal priesthood of all believers come into its own and the Word of God be given full and free rein in the Church. What Luther provides is a concrete application of the biblical motif of royal priesthood to the reading of Scripture, one that accounts for both the dignity and calling of the epithet. The being and action of readers are a unity when viewed through the lens of royal priesthood.

---

[60] See David Scott, 'Speaking to Form: Trinitarian-Performative Scripture Reading,' *ATR* 77 (1995), 145-46.

CHAPTER 2

No alternatives to Jesus: Luther's understanding of idolatry as evident in his *house postils*

Cameron A. MacKenzie

Although the Eucharist and Christology are the two most prominent topics cited when pointing to differences between Martin Luther and the Reformed, another issue that arose in Luther's controversies with fellow Evangelicals was that of sacred images. While reformers like Andreas Karlstadt said, 'Pull them down,' Luther responded, 'Not so fast.' Subsequently, Lutherans and other Protestants continued to develop along different lines with the former being quite tolerant of much of what the latter denounced as idolatry.[1] But that does not mean that the German reformer was 'soft' on 'false gods'. Quite the contrary. In fact, Luther's understanding of idolatry went far beyond statues, and in his discussion of the First Commandment in his *Large Catechism* he explained that a person's 'god' is whatever he trusts most—whether he calls it 'god' or not.[2] In the con-

---

[1] Even before the Evangelicals began to divide over the presence of Christ's body in the sacrament, they were disagreeing over sacred images. Carlos Eire has pointed this out in summary fashion in his article on 'Iconoclasm' in Hans J. Hillerbrand (ed.), *Oxford Encyclopedia of the Reformation* (New York: OUP, 1996) and at greater length in his book, *War Against the Idols: The Reformation of Worship from Erasmus to Calvin* (Cambridge: CUP, 1986), 54-73. Irena Dingel has demonstrated the difference over images between Lutheran and Reformed in the 16th century in her '"Dass wir Gott in keiner Weise verbilden": Die Bilderfrage zwischen Calvinismus und Luthertum' in Andreas Wagner, Volker Hörner, Günter Geisthardt (eds), *Gott im Wort—Gott im Bild: Bilderlosigkeit als Bedingung des Monotheismus?* (n.p.: Neukirchener Verlag, 2005), 97-111. According to Dingel, the elimination of pictures and images was a signal that a church was switching from Lutheran to Reformed—along with introducing the breaking of the bread in the communion rite, eliminating the exorcism in the baptismal rite, and promoting a new kind of church music.

[2] *Large Catechism* 1.1-15 First published in 1529, Luther's two catechisms—large and small—are a part of the Lutheran Confessions, *Die Bekenntnisschriften der evangelisch-lutherischen Kirche, herausgegeben im Gedenkjahr der Augsburgischen Konfession 1930* (Göttingen: Vandenhoeck & Ruprecht, 1959). In this essay, citations of the English version are from Theodore G. Tappert (ed.), *The Book of Concord: The Confessions of the Evangelical Lutheran Church* (Philadelphia: Fortress, 1959).

temporary world, Luther's definition is immediately relevant in a way that railing against sacred images is not.

But how did Luther, himself, apply this definition? In his sermons, what 'idols' did he identify as especially threatening to the people among whom he ministered? Did he even mention sacred images? Using a set of sermons that Luther originally delivered to his own household, this essay explores Luther's preaching for what it can tell us about competition to Jesus Christ for first place in the lives of those who were among the first hearers of the Protestant gospel. Luther's sermons reveal his theology in action.[3]

Luther on idols

First, however, we need to consider Luther's position regarding idolatry outside of the sermons in order to determine what it is that we should look for in the sermons. For those familiar with the Old Testament, the term 'idol' immediately calls to mind the continuous struggle of the prophets against pagan images that the children of Israel were tempted to worship and often did. From Moses and the golden calf (Exod. 32) to the three men in the fiery furnace (Dan. 3), the first part of the Christian Bible regularly contrasts faithfulness to the true God with the worship of false gods in the form of images. In the era of the reformation, therefore, it did not take a lot of imagination for Protestants who rejected medieval worship in preference to what they considered a more biblically based piety to identify the sacred images of their Catholic neighbors with idolatry.

Indeed, even before the reformation, Erasmus had sharply criticized the cult of the saints and an excessive reliance on images and relics.[4] Huldrych Zwingli went even further and taught that the invisible God forbids people to make visible representations of him and demanded the removal of all sacred images from

---

[3] For Luther's preaching, see Fred W. Meuser, *Luther the Preacher* (Minneapolis: Augsburg, 1983) and, by the same author, 'Luther as Preacher of the Word of God' in Donald K. McKim (ed.), *The Cambridge Companion to Martin Luther* (Cambridge: CUP, 2003), 136-48; Gerhard Heintze, *Luthers Predigt von Gesetz und Evangelium* (München: Chr. Kaiser Verlag, 1958); Ulrich Asendorf, *Die Theologie Martin Luthers nach seinen Predigten* (Göttingen: Vandenhoeck & Ruprecht, 1988); Eberhart Winkler, 'Luther als Seelsorger und Prediger' in Helmar Junghans (ed.), *Leben und Werk Martin Luthers von 1526 bis 1546* (Göttingen: Vandenhoeck und Ruprecht, 1983), 1.225-39, 2.792-97; Robert Kolb, *Luther and the Stories of God: Biblical Narratives as a Foundation for Christian Living* (Grand Rapids: Baker Academic, 2012).

[4] Eire, *War*, 36-45. For examples of Erasmus's criticism, see 'The Handbook of the Militant Christian' in John P. Dolan (ed.) *The Essential Erasmus* (New York: New American Library of World Literature, 1964), 60-61, and 'The Praise of Folly' in Dolan, 129-30, 135-36.

the churches.⁵ Later, John Calvin also maintained that God forbids displaying any reverence toward images like bowing, kneeling, or uncovering one's head.⁶ In general, therefore, Reformed Protestants characterized the Second Commandment of the Decalogue as an absolute prohibition against sacred images.⁷

In developing such arguments, however, both reformers were following the lead of still another one, Luther's one time colleague at the University of Wittenberg, Andreas Karlstadt.⁸ During Luther's absence from Wittenberg after the Diet of Worms (1521), Karlstadt had begun calling for practical changes in the life of the church in the university and town, including the removal of sacred images. In December 1521 and February 1522, Karlstadt's campaign resulted in iconoclastic riots. In March 1522, Luther returned home.⁹

This then became the occasion for Luther publicly to address the question of sacred images, and he did so—along with other issues – in the Invocavit Sermons, a series of eight homilies preached on successive days almost immediately upon his return.[10] Luther rejected not only Karlstadt's approval of violence in the removal of images but also his colleague's total rejection of such images in the first place. On the one hand, Luther's remarks hardly constituted a ringing endorsement of images, 'It is true that they are unnecessary, and we are free to have them or not, although it would be much better if we did not have them at all. I am not partial to them.'[11] On the other hand, Luther placed them in the category of things indifferent, 'we are free to have them or not.' But to insist on something that God has left open was to violate one of Luther's most cherished principles, Christian liberty: 'They wished to make a "must" out of that which is free. This God cannot tolerate.'[12]

---

[5] Eire, *War*, 73-86. See, also, Zwingli's *Commentary on True and False Religion* (edited by Samuel Macauley Jackson and Clarence Nevin Heller; Durham, NC: The Labyrinth Press, 1981), 330-37.

[6] Eire, *War*, 212-20. For Calvin's own discussion of idolatry and images, see *Inst.* 1.11 and 2.8.17-18.

[7] See, for example, the 'Second Commandment' in Joel R. Beeke and Sinclair B. Ferguson (eds), *Reformed Confessions Harmonized* (Grand Rapids: Baker Books, 1999), 140-44.

[8] In the early years of the reformation, Andreas Bodenstein von Karlstadt (1481-1541) was Luther's close associate at Wittenberg and cooperated in the cause of reform. The two men broke, however, in connection with the reforms promoted in Wittenberg while Luther was at the Wartburg. Karlstadt subsequently left Wittenberg, was exiled from Saxony, found refuge in Zurich, before finally residing at Basel as a professor in the university there. See OER, s.v. 'Bodenstein von Karlstadt, Andreas'.

[9] OER, s.v. 'Iconoclasm'; Eire, *War*, 55-65.

[10] For the historical context of these sermons, see Neil R. Leroux, *Luther's Rhetoric: Strategies and Style from the Invocavit Sermons* (St. Louis: Concordia Academic, 2002), 41-53.

[11] *LW* 51.81 (*WA* 10³.26.4-7).

[12] *LW* 51.82 (*WA* 10³.26.11-12). For 'Christian liberty' in Luther, see Gerhard Ebeling, *Luther: An Introduction to His Thought* (London: William Collins, 1970), 212-14;

Of course, whether or not Christians were truly free in the matter of such images was precisely the question, so Luther went on to explore the biblical evidence. Regarding the prohibition in the Decalogue, Luther argued that it is unclear whether the text of Exodus 20 meant to forbid all images absolutely, 'You shall not make for yourself a carved image' (v. 4, ESV), or only as objects of worship, 'You shall not bow down to them or serve them' (v. 5). But given at least a couple of examples in which God himself employed images, the 'birds [*vögel*]' placed on the mercy seat of the ark of the covenant (Exod. 37.7) and Moses's bronze serpent to heal the people (Nu. 21.9), Luther concluded that 'we may have images and make images, but we must not worship them.'[13]

Luther was not naïve about the possible misuse of such images. After all, Hezekiah finally destroyed the bronze serpent when people began to worship it (2 Kings 18.4); but Luther thought that the best approach was to preach against idols just like St. Paul at Athens (Acts 17). Luther's advice was this, 'It should have been preached that images were nothing and that no service is done to God by erecting them; then they would have fallen of themselves.' For Luther, the real problem lay not with the statues but with the people who worshipped them, 'Outward things [can] do no harm to faith, if only the heart does not cleave to them or put its trust in them. This is what we must preach and teach, and let the Word alone do the work.'[14]

Following this first confrontation over the question of images, Luther never changed his opinion that God did not prohibit images per se; and in fact, he even argued for using them positively in the Christian life as teaching devices. In a later work directed against Karlstadt, *Against the Heavenly Prophets* (1525), Luther still advocated preaching against idolatrous images but also insisted that 'images for memorial and witness, such as crucifixes and images of saints, are to be tolerated'. Luther explicitly defended the use of pictures in German Bibles and advocated using them in churches:

> Now there are a great many pictures in those books, both of God, the angels, men and animals, especially in the Revelation of John and in Moses and Joshua. . . . Pictures contained in these books we would paint on walls for the sake of remembrance and better understanding. . . . It is to be sure better to paint pictures on walls of how God created the world, how Noah built the ark, and whatever other good stories there may be, than to paint shameless worldly things.[15]

Gustaf Wingren, *The Christian's Calling: Luther on Vocation* (Edinburgh: Oliver and Boyd, 1957), 93-107.

[13] *LW* 51:82 (*WA* 10³.28.3-4).

[14] *LW* 51.83 (*WA* 10³.29.13-30.2).

[15] *LW* 40.91, 99 (*WA* 18.74.15-18; 18.82.23-83.3). According to Kurt Hendel, 'The Material as a Vehicle of the Divine,' *Currents in Theology and Mission* 28 (2001), 333, the first complete Luther Bible (1534) contained illuminated initials and 124 colored woodcuts.

Not surprisingly, therefore, Lutheran churches continued to be highly decorated. Territories that became Lutheran did not remove the images; and, under the leadership of Luther's friend, Lucas Cranach, Lutherans developed a genre of didactic paintings with which to decorate their churches and to edify the faithful.[16]

But what about idolatry? In his controversy with Karlstadt, Luther not only rejected an identification of idols with images, he also thought deeply about what constituted idolatry in the first place. It was not a matter of the thing but of the heart. In *Against the Heavenly Prophets*, he urged Christians to destroy images 'with the Word of God. . . . This means to instruct and enlighten the conscience that it is idolatry to worship them, or to trust in them, since one is to trust alone in Christ'.[17] For Luther that was the key. Idolatry was a matter of misplaced trust. Christ alone is the object of faith.

Therefore, a few years later, when Luther prepared the *Large Catechism* (1529) for pastors to use in instructing their parishioners in the basics of the Christian religion,[18] he offered several examples of such misplaced trust as instances of idolatry that had nothing to do with images. For instance,

> Many a person thinks he has God and everything he needs when he has money and property; in them he trusts and of them he boasts and so stubbornly and securely that he cares for no one. Surely such a man also has a god—mammon by name, that is, money and possessions—on which he fixes his whole heart.

Mammon, Luther added, 'is the most common idol on earth' and afflicted even those who had none of it. Such a person 'doubts and despairs as if he never heard of God. Very few . . . do not fret and complain, if they do not have mammon.'[19] In addition, however—besides money—Luther specified learning, wisdom, power, prestige, family, and honor. Anyone who 'trusts in them, he also has a god, but not the one, true God'.[20] A real idol did not have to be a statue.

Of course, Luther also mentioned the cruder forms of idolatry, like that of the pagans who looked to Jupiter, Mercury, and other false deities for well-being and pleasures, or Christians who called on the saints when danger threatened or needs were felt. Some even made pacts with the devil. But the worst of

---

[16] See Carl C. Christensen, *Art and the Reformation in Germany* (Athens, OH: Ohio University Press, 1979), 42-65, 110-80; John Tonkin, 'Word and Image: Luther and the Arts', *Colloquium* 17(1985), 45-54; Christopher Weimer, 'Luther and Cranach on Justification in Word and Image,' *LQ* 18 (2004), 387-405; and Steven Ozment, *The Serpent and the Lamb: Cranach, Luther, and the Making of the Reformation* (New Haven: Yale University Press, 2011).

[17] *LW* 40.91 (*WA* 18.74.6-9).

[18] For background to both catechisms, see Martin Brecht, *Martin Luther* (Philadlphia: Fortress, 1990), 2.273-80.

[19] *Large Catechism* 1.5-9.

[20] *Large Catechism* 1.10.

all, according to Luther, was the idolatry of works righteousness, practiced by those who sought 'help, comfort, and salvation in [their] own works and presume[d] to wrest heaven from God'. Where God offered gifts, they demanded rewards for works 'just as if God were in our service. . . . [W]hat is this but making God into an idol . . . and setting up ourselves as God?'[21] The ultimate idolatry! To turn oneself into God! But in every case of idolatry, one was looking to something other than God as his source of good and his refuge from trouble. Misplaced trust rather than images constituted the essence of this sin:

> Idolatry does not consist merely of erecting an image and praying to it. It is primarily in the heart, which pursues other things and seeks help and consolation from creatures, saints, or devils. It neither cares for God nor expects good things from him sufficiently to trust that he wants to help, nor does it believe that whatever good it receives comes from God.[22]

But if these were Luther's instructions to pastors in the *Large Catechism* about how to teach the people about idolatry, the question remains, how did Luther himself do it when he preached? Did Luther follow his own advice? The answer is 'Yes'—as will become clear in our examination of the issue of idolatry in the house postils.

Luther and the house postils

But why these sermons in particular, the so-called 'house postils'?[23] Not merely because Luther originally aimed them at the servants and young people of his own household—reason enough for our purposes. But, also, because they represent an effort by one of Luther's closest disciples to make the reformer's preaching to ordinary people available to others —ordinary people and their pastors! The process by which Luther's theological insights became Lutheranism is a complicated one. But not least in significance is the role played by the mediators of Luther's thought—people like Veit Dietrich, the editor of the first printed version of the house postils. Dietrich developed a close relationship with Luther, first as a student and, then, as a colleague when he lived in Wit-

---

[21] *Large Catechism* 1.22-23.
[22] *Large Catechism* 1.21.
[23] According to John M. Frymire, *The Primacy of the Postils: Catholics, Protestants, and the Dissemination of Ideas in Early Modern Germany* (Leiden: Brill, 2010), 12, the term 'postil' refers to a homiletical genre developed in the late Middle Ages to assist preachers by offering outlines, exegesis, or even model sermons for the standard Bible lessons—'gospels' and 'epistles'—read annually in church on the Sundays and festival days of the church year. Luther and his disciples made extensive use of this genre in order to promote Evangelical preaching. Their Catholic opponents did the same. For Luther's postils in general, see John W. Doberstein, 'Introduction' to *LW* 51: *Sermons I*, xiv-xv, and Gerhard Ebeling, *Evangelische Evangelienauslegung: Eine Untersuchung zu Luthers Hermeneutik* (Darmstadt: Wissenschaftliche Buchgesellschaft, 1962), 30-37.

tenberg (1522-1535), in fact, with Luther himself at the Black Cloister. Dietrich accompanied Luther to the Marburg Colloquy (October, 1529), the occasion of Luther's face-to-face confrontation with Zwingli, and then stayed with Luther at Coburg during the Diet of Augsburg (April to October, 1530). For many years he served Luther as a kind of secretary and organized his correspondence, took dictation for future publications, transcribed the 'table talk', and recorded Luther's sermons and lectures. Albert Freitag has described Veit Dietrich—along with Georg Rörer—as the 'most significant' of those who constructed the 'Luther tradition'.[24]

One piece of that tradition has been Luther's house postils. These were sermons on the traditional Bible readings for Sunday services and festivals. For health reasons, Luther limited his public preaching from 1531 to 1535, but he continued to proclaim the Word to the members of his own household—which could be quite a group since it included relatives, friends, boarders, and servants, as well as Luther's wife and children.[25] In so doing, Luther claimed that he was acting as a 'house father' in order to instruct his servants (*gesinde*) in how to lead a Christian life.[26] Once delivered, Luther thought no more about the sermons. But Veit Dietrich had been taking notes on them, and about ten years later, in 1544, Dietrich published them for the first time. During the next year or so, they were reprinted seven times as well as in low German and Latin editions. John Frymire has published a chronological listing of 94 printed editions of the *House Postils* from 1544 to 1609, including 11 low German; 10 Latin; 1 Polish; and 1 Slovak edition. An alternative edition to Dietrich's work—based on Georg Rörer's notes, but prepared by Andreas Poach[27]—appeared in 1559, but by that time Dietrich's edition had been printed 35 times, not including the 8 low German and 4 Latin versions that were based on it. The Rörer/Poach version appears only 7 more times in Frymire's entire list.[28] In the formative years of Lutheranism, therefore, the house postils, especially Die-

---

[24] Albert Freitag, 'Veit Dietrichs Anteil an der Lutherüberlieferung' in Karl Drescher (ed.), *Lutherstudien zur 4. Jahrhundertfeier der Reformation veröffentlicht von den Mitarbeitern der Weimarer Lutherausgabe* (Weimar: Hermann Böhlaus Nachfolger, 1917), 171. For Dietrich's biography, see Bernhard Klaus, *Veit Dietrich: Leben und Werk* (Nürnberg: Verein für bayerische Kirchengeschichte, 1958); OER, s.v. 'Dietrich, Veit'.

[25] Brecht, *Luther*, 2.204.

[26] *WA* 52.1.4-6.

[27] Poach's version appeared more than a decade after Luther's death. In so doing, he charged Dietrich with numerous inaccuracies, and modern editors likewise have agreed that Dietrich did not publish an exact copy of Luther's original preaching. For background to both versions, see the introduction by Georg Buchwald in *WA* 52.vii-xii. The Weimar edition also provides data on the relationship between Dietrich's edition and Rörer's still extant manuscripts. See, also, Emanuel Hirsch's introductory comments to each version in *Luthers Werke in Auswahl*, vol. 7: *Predigten* (Berlin: Walter de Gruyter, 1962) 7.69, 84.

[28] Frymire, 546-48.

trich's version, were available as models of Evangelical preaching and teaching; and Emil Hirsch has described them as the postils from which entire generations of Lutheran clergy learned about Luther's doctrine and preaching.[29]

Modern scholarship is agreed that Dietrich did not publish a stenographic version of what Luther originally said in the house postils.[30] In reconstituting Luther's sermons from his own transcriptions, Dietrich often combined multiple homilies on a text into just one sermon and on a few occasions when Luther originals were lacking he used the preaching of others, including himself, to fill in the gaps. Therefore, as is often the case with certain kinds of Luther's works—lectures, sermons, and table talk—we are dealing with a highly edited version of the reformer, but that does not necessarily mean an inauthentic version, especially if Luther himself validated what was published as he did with Dietrich's version of the house postils. Nobody could have reasonably expected a word for word recounting of what Luther originally said, but they could expect what Dietrich in fact gave them—sermons on the texts of the church year that went back to Luther's own preaching—preaching transcribed at the time and later reconstructed and developed for pastoral purposes by Luther's close associate, Veit Dietrich.

For the very first edition, Luther prepared an introduction, in which he acknowledged, 'I have preached these sermons from time to time in my house for my household' after the example of the patriarchs and according to the command of Christ to the apostles that they preach first of all in houses, to which, Luther suggested, neighbors might also come.[31] Though not feeling up to mounting the pulpit in the city church, Luther still felt responsible for leading his servants and children through the appointed gospel lessons for each Sunday and the main festivals of the church year.[32] Also, according to Luther's introduction, he did not originally intend their publication. In fact, he didn't even realize that they were being taken down when he preached them. However, Veit Dietrich was recording them—at least, that is the claim that Dietrich set forth in his dedication to the city fathers of Nuremberg that accompanied their

---

[29] Hirsch, 69.
[30] Ebeling, 35-36; Hirsch, 69; Klaus, 351-53.
[31] *WA* 52.1.3-4. There is an English translation of Dietrich's version of the house postils by Matthias Loy (and others), *Sermons on the Gospels for the Sundays and Principal Festivals of the Church Year by Dr. Martin Luther* (Rock Island, IL: Augustana Book Concern, 1871) as well as a more recent one of Poach's version, Eugene F.A. Klug (ed.), *Sermons of Martin Luther: The House Postils* (Grand Rapids: Baker, 1996). Loy's version is helpful but not always accurate, so the translation in this essay is my own.
[32] The title for one of the first editions is, 'Hausspostil D. Martin Luther, uber die Sontags, und der fürnembsten Fest Evangelia, durch das gantze Jar.' *WA* 52.xxx. In the table prepared for the Weimar edition, the editors have indicated only 8 sermons (out of 94) based on something other than a text from one of the four Gospels. See *WA* 52.xii-xxvi.

publication in 1544, 'I alone recorded them . . . and have kept them until the present.'[33]

Luther called them 'crumbs' and 'fragments';[34] but Dietrich saw them as a 'treasure' especially on account of their simplicity and brevity, perfect, he thought, for ordinary folk:

> These sermons were presented in a fine, short, and simple fashion and are especially useful for young and simple people. In such circumstances, one must not employ great artistry but should present the doctrine briefly and simply and by means of words to impress them that they can grasp and notice something of the teaching.[35]

Dietrich, also, thought they were especially appropriate for 'unlearned' clergy who often pastored poor peasant parishes. If such pastors lacked the training and skills to construct their own sermons, their churches should be content if only the pastors would read materials like the house postils that presented pure doctrine in an orderly, simple, and understandable way.[36] Dietrich was also concerned that heads of households who could not get to church on a Sunday would have appropriate materials to hear or read at home for the hallowing of the Sabbath with God's Word.[37] Finally, Dietrich offered the postils to those who still lived under bishops and clergy who had not yet embraced the reformation. By means of Luther's house sermons, people who had had no expectation of hearing true doctrine in their churches might at least read it at home.[38]

A principal concern of Dietrich was 'pure doctrine'.[39] These sermons provided just that and, of course, had the advantage of coming from Luther himself. Dietrich praised him as the one through whom 'God has brought the Scriptures and knowledge of God to light, has abolished the terrible abuses that the papacy introduced into the Church, and has established both pure doctrine and right worship in the Church.'[40] Dietrich was convinced that exposure to these sermons would produce much 'fruit', viz., strengthen faith, improve lives, and so result in praising and thanking God.[41]

In short, Dietrich recommended the house postils as a simple but comprehensive presentation of the truths of the Christian religion, useful for the per-

---

[33] *WA* 52.5.38-39.
[34] 'brosamen' and 'brocken'. *WA* 52.2.5.
[35] *WA* 52.5.40-6.4.
[36] *WA* 52.6.18.
[37] *WA* 52.6.20-26.
[38] *WA* 52.7.34-8.13.
[39] *WA* 52.6.17.
[40] *WA* 52.5.21-25. For Luther's reputation among the Lutherans as God's special agent for reformation of the church, see Robert Kolb, *Martin Luther as Prophet, Teacher, and Hero: Images of the Reformer, 1520-1620* (Grand Rapids: Baker, 1999).
[41] *WA* 52.6.17-19, 8.22-24.

Luther, the house postils and idolatry

So how do the house postils handle the theme of idolatry? As in the *Large Catechism*, Luther understands it broadly as encompassing all alternatives to faith in Jesus. Thus, idolatry becomes a principal topic in these sermons because justification by faith in Jesus Christ is the main theme. This understanding of the gospel—the forgiveness of sins on account of Jesus and appropriated only by faith—is the center of Luther's theology, generally,[42] and these sermons that the reformer intended for the children and servants of his own household are no exception. From the first sermon to the last, Luther preaches the gospel. In the first of the series, a homily on Jesus' entry into Jerusalem on Palm Sunday (Matt. 21.1-9), Luther describes Jesus as the 'Righteous One and Savior, who shall bring with himself righteousness and salvation, attack sin and death, be an enemy of sin and of death' so that 'those who believe in him and accept him as their king . . . , their sins will be forgiven and death will not harm them but they will have eternal life.'[43]

For the last Sunday of the church year, the text is Matthew 5.1-12, the Beatitudes. Luther understands this text as a description of Christians, their lives and attitudes; nevertheless, he still finds opportunity to present Jesus as Savior. The first Beatitude, for example, speaks of the 'poor in spirit', i.e., according to Luther, the person who 'on account of his sins has no peace either day or night'. But God wants 'to comfort such a person with his grace, that he may not despair on account of such fears; but rather that through his holy gospel, the Lord Christ may shine into his heart with the result that he will have consolation and joy and inherit the kingdom of heaven.'[44] Similarly, when interpreting those who are 'pure in heart' a few verses later, Luther understands such people not as pure in themselves but as sincerely devoted to the gospel:

> Therefore, we should hold on diligently to the Word and permit it alone to dwell in and enlighten our hearts, so that we will see God rightly and be certain that he is a kind and gracious God and even though no one is innocent before him, nevertheless he will forgive our sins and save us forever for the sake of Christ.[45]

As one might readily expect, Luther has no trouble finding justification by faith in texts like John 3.16-21 (for the Monday after Pentecost):

---

[42] See my essay, 'The Evangelical Character of Martin Luther's Faith' in Kenneth J. Stewart and Michael Haykin (eds), *The Advent of Evangelicalism: Exploring Historical Continuities* (Nashville: B&H Academic, 2008), 171-98.
[43] *WA* 52.11.35-12.2.
[44] *WA* 52.554.8, 24-27.
[45] *WA* 52.560.26.

> For just as God has given such a treasure [the gift of the Son of God] through love and mercy, we therefore obtain such a treasure and can only obtain it through faith. To enter a cloister, or to do this or that cannot earn it, for our works have nothing to do with such a great treasure. The only thing that is appropriate is for a person through faith to hold out his hands; and just as God through love becomes the giver, so we through faith in Christ become the receiver.[46]

But Luther can also find his version of the gospel in much more legalistic texts like those in which Jesus told his disciples how to live, e.g., Luke 6.36-42 (for the fourth Sunday after Trinity) or Matthew 5.20-26 (for the sixth Sunday after Trinity). The former text instructs disciples in the virtue of mercy and the dangers of hypocrisy, but Luther in the very first paragraph of his homily reminds his hearers that good works are a consequence of justification, 'For if we have become believers and now have the name and are called Christians, who have been saved by the Lord Christ from sin, from death and all evil, then we also should lead a new life and do what God desires from us.'[47]

The latter text is from that portion of the Sermon on the Mount in which the Lord sharpens the demands of the commandment, 'Thou shalt not kill.' In this case, Luther not only begins his sermon as previously with a reminder that his hearers are already the recipients of God's undeserved mercy so they should act like Christians, he also interprets the Lord's demand for a righteousness that 'exceeds' that of the scribes and Pharisees at the beginning of the text (v. 20) as something that *cannot* be accomplished, a law therefore that demonstrates the futility of relying on one's own righteousness and the need for relying on Christ.[48] Luther then proceeds to a clear statement of justification, 'Whoever knows that such sins [i.e., a heart full of evil lusts and sins] have been forgiven, that person is righteous, not for his own sake because he is a sinner; but on account of grace, such sins have been forgiven through faith in Christ.'[49]

Luther's preaching is textual. He always considers the actual words of the Scripture text placed before him, but it is also evangelical for he also always finds the opportunity to proclaim the good news of forgiveness of sins in Jesus Christ, received by faith alone. But in presenting his version of the gospel, Luther also describes alternatives to the good news to which his hearers might be tempted—everything from monasticism to money. Whether Luther uses the term or not (and frequently he does), alternatives to Jesus are the essence of what Luther understands by idolatry.

---

[46] *WA* 52.331.34-332.2.
[47] *WA* 52.383.26-29.
[48] This so-called 'theological' function of the Law to reveal sin in contrast to its 'civic' use in regulating temporal society is another great theme in Luther's theology. See Bernhard Lohse, *Martin Luther's Theology: Its Historical and Systematic Development* (Minneapolis: Fortress, 1999), 270-73.
[49] *WA* 52.406.22-24.

Luther says this explicitly in his Third Sermon for Christmas, devoted to the praise of the angels (Lk. 2.13-14), 'The dear angels meant to say: Before this Child was born, things were far different. There was nothing going on in this world except blasphemy [*Gotteslesterung*] and idolatry [*abgötterey*]; for everything that is outside of and without Christ, no matter how glorious and great it may be, is nothing but blasphemy.' But blasphemy and idolatry are more than just ignorance about who the true God is. For knowing Christ means knowing, first and foremost, that God is merciful to sinners.

> But if God is supposed to be God, that is, held and honored by the people as God, it must be done through this Child. For in this way only can people learn and know for certain that God is a gracious, merciful, and kind God, since he has not spared his only-begotten Son but has sent him to become a human being for our sakes.[50]

With this gospel as his premise, Luther proceeds to indict the world before the birth of Christ, including God's chosen people, as so 'full of idolatry' that they worshipped—'one here, one there, in as many places as there were hills or even beautiful trees in the land'—with all kinds of works, sacrifices, fastings, and sufferings. But this served no one 'except the devil and his plans, for they gave to him the honor that belonged to God'.[51]

But idolatry is not just a thing of the past. Luther finds it in contemporary society as well, 'the world is full of idolatry'; but he does not single out false gods and their images like those of the pagans.[52] Instead, he points to the fact that 'people worship money, possessions, and similar things. . . . For there go kings, princes, merchants, and farmers after this rough log [*klotz*], this shameful mammon, this miserable helper, to which they ascribe everything.'[53] But earthly wealth is just one of the things that people use as substitutes for God. Luther, also, talks about pride, going all the way back to the Garden of Eden, 'The human race is afflicted with desire for praise. The devil in paradise persuaded Adam and Eve that they wanted to be like God, and this still adheres to us. Therefore, if God gives skill, money, property, or power, if he presents to a wife or a maid a beautiful belt or dress, everyone expects it to be praised.'[54] Now, however, the Christmas angels point us to the source of all blessings that we might worship God aright:

---

[50] *WA* 52.53.13-21.
[51] *WA* 52.53.30-36.
[52] Of course, in other places he does. For example, in connection with the Song of Simeon (Lk. 2.25-32) Luther mentions the situation of the Gentiles, 'idolatry, blasphemy, and all kinds of degeneration and sins' (*WA* 52:162.29-30). In an Easter Sermon (Matt. 28), Luther explains that apart from Christ the little spark of knowledge that people have by nature about God is soon lost and they fall into 'error and idolatry' (*WA* 256.38-257.1).
[53] *WA* 52.54.2-5.
[54] *WA* 52.54.25-29.

ASPECTS OF REFORMING

For all who accept the angels' song will say: My righteousness, my holiness, my wisdom, skill, money, and power are all nothing. The child Jesus is everything. Therefore, God receives his honor that he alone is our strength, confidence, joy, our money and wealth and that we with our whole hearts put our trust, consolation, confidence, and joy in him alone.[55]

True worship is to acknowledge God alone as the giver of all good things, especially the gospel, 'that we are free from the devil, free from and unencumbered by our sins'.[56] But it is idolatry to look anywhere else.

Throughout the house postils, Luther warns against alternatives to Jesus.[57] Sometimes he uses the term 'idolatry' (*Abgötterei*), sometimes not, but the point in every case is to describe something that detracts from the true God and the true way of salvation. As indicated above, such alternatives can include real blessings from God which people then abuse by placing their trust in them. Such things have good and appropriate uses, but are routinely perverted into objects of trust.

There are other 'idols,' however, that are not so much perversions as they are wrong from the start. From this perspective, Luther regularly cites the papacy and its misguided religious activities.[58] These works are never good. 'Papists,' Luther complains, 'hear the gospel but don't accept it. . . . They are not satisfied with this Savior but go after other "saviors" and rely upon them.'[59] Accordingly, Luther often indicts medieval (papal) religious practices as forms of idolatry, ways of salvation other than faith in Jesus.[60] On one occasion, Luther uses the humility and preaching of John the Baptist (John 1.19-28, Fourth Sunday in Advent) to indict the papal system. Luther begins his homily with

---

[55] *WA* 52.54.31-35.
[56] *WA* 52.55.8-9.
[57] Another excellent example is Luther's second sermon for New Year's Day (*WA* 52.82-88) which Luther devotes to the name 'Jesus' that signifies him as the world's only Savior. Similarly, Luther's sermon on the Parable of the Sower (Sexagesima Sunday, Lk. 8.4-15) gives him the opportunity to discuss alternatives to the true faith in connection with the different kinds of soil. The Temptation of Jesus (First Sunday in Lent, Matt. 4.1-11) also provides Luther with an occasion to discuss a wide variety of alternatives to Jesus (*WA* 52.171-77). His sermon for Laetare Sunday on the Feeding of the Five Thousand (John 6.1-15) presents the challenges of providing for material well-being while still trusting solely in God and his Word (*WA* 52:192-198).
[58] Luther came to the conclusion that the pope was the Antichrist quite early in the reformation largely on account of his hostility to Luther's doctrine of justification and his oppression of people's consciences through a theology of works. For Luther and the papacy, see Scott H. Hendrix, *Luther and the Papacy: Stages in a Reformation Conflict* (Philadelphia: Fortress, 1981).
[59] *WA* 52.48.38-40.
[60] Luther frequently uses the word 'idolatry [*Abgötterei*]' for such practices. Here are some examples: *WA* 52.69.1-11, 70.1-3, 125.9-25, 159.9-10, 177.3-7, 191.10-11, 196.1-3, 212.13-15, 219.29-37, 221.1-5, 233.7-12, 257.38-259.5, 532.37, 533.39-41, 534.29-32.

yet another affirmation of Christ, the world's only Savior, 'through whom alone all patriarchs, prophets, and apostles have been saved from the beginning of the world'. But, immediately, Luther adds that too many reject Christ, preferring their own 'way to go to heaven', e.g., entering a cloister, becoming a monk, fasting, or sleeping on the ground.[61]

In this sermon, John the Baptist, himself, is Luther's great example of the inability of works to save. Addressing himself especially to the clergy, 'pope, bishops, priests, monks, and all the world,' Luther challenges them, 'be as pious and holy as you want, you will not be as holy as John.' Then Luther indicts them, 'But they do not want to let the holiness of Christ be their treasure the way John did. He throws all his own righteousness away and does not value it as much as an old rag with which one wipes a dirty shoe.'[62] Instead of following John in rejecting all forms of works righteousness, the church leaders of Luther's day have invented a wide variety of 'meritorious' works. Among those to which the papists direct people instead of Christ, Luther enumerates: 'entering a cloister, saying mass, conducting masses for the dead, vigils, paying for worship, going on pilgrimages, and buying indulgences'.[63] Works like these cannot save.

Instead, Luther maintains, 'becoming a monk or a priest, entering a cloister, and whatever works that can be mentioned similar to these, belong to the devil and in hell'. With such works people expect to merit salvation, but in reality they are 'denying Christ and mocking him'. Through their 'cloister life' they may aim at heaven but they will find it a heaven 'where the flames and fire burst out the windows'.[64]

In addition to John the Baptist in this sermon, Luther mentions 'Paul, Peter, and other saints' who likewise could not save themselves with their own works and righteousness. They, too, had to rely on Christ.[65] The saints and their cult are still another part of the papal system that Luther preaches against in his house postils, but this is one area of medieval religion that Luther tries to rescue by presenting the saints as examples of true sanctity, i.e., faith in Christ and the works that follow.[66] So, here in this sermon on John 1.19-28, in which John the

---

[61] *WA* 52.30.27-28, 31-33.
[62] *WA* 52.33.22-24, 30-32.
[63] *WA* 52.33.7-9.
[64] *WA* 52.35.19-21, 24, 34-35. In his sermon on the temptation of Jesus (Invocavit Sunday, Matt. 4.1-11; *WA* 52.175.36-176.19), Luther identifies monasticism with idolatry. In explaining the third temptation, Luther notes the devil's efforts to lead people into idolatry [*Abgötterey*] through externals that people admire and honor though against God's Word, such as abstaining from marriage and raising children, wearing distinctive clothes, fasting, making pilgrimages, and entering a cloister to separate from the world.
[65] *WA* 52.35.27-30.
[66] In 1530, the Lutherans had made this same point in the *Augsburg Confession* (21.1): 'It is also taught among us that saints should be kept in remembrance so that our faith

Baptist humbles himself in comparison to Christ, Luther, also, cites Paul (Phil. 3.7-8) who described all his works as 'dirt and filth [*dreck und kot*]'. This, says Luther, 'is speaking horribly clear about our holy living'.[67] So, Luther draws the conclusion from the example of Paul that even if in the eyes of the world, our life is exemplary, when it comes to eternal life, we must hold entirely and exclusively to Christ and his holiness.

If Luther were at all inclined to admonish his hearers regarding the dangers of sacred images, it would be in connection with the saints whose statues and relics were popular objects of veneration in the medieval world. But Luther does not. Instead—as with other forms of 'idolatry' in the house postils—he speaks against trusting the saints instead of Christ. One can find references to this effect throughout the house postils, but an early discussion of this kind of idolatry occurs in connection with Luther's Christmas preaching. In commenting on the angel's announcement to the shepherds of the miraculous birth in Bethlehem, Luther emphasizes the Christ-child's uniqueness as the Savior. That being the case, Luther concludes, then no one else is the Savior, 'not his mother Mary, St Peter, or St Paul. Neither are Augustine, Francis, and Dominic with their "rules".' And yet, Luther continues, 'up till now in the papacy people have been directed to the intercession of the saints, to monasticism, and other things. But how does this fit with the preaching of the angel?'[68] Of course, from Luther's perspective, it doesn't fit at all.[69]

But if the saints are not heaven's helpers, they are earthly examples. As we have already seen, Luther employed this idea when describing the humility of John the Baptist and of St. Paul, but he does it elsewhere as well. A revealing instance of this is his pair of sermons for 'The Festival of the Purification of Mary or Candlemas [*Liechtmessen*]'.[70] In the first of these, Mary is presented simply as an example of obedience—not an intercessor and certainly not the

---

may be strengthened when we see what grace they received and how they were sustained by faith. Moreover, their good works are to be an example for us.'

[67] *WA* 52.34.33-34.

[68] *WA* 52.50.39-51.4. A few lines further, Luther mentions, specifically, the perversity of appealing to the Virgin Mary when the gospel and even Christmas songs identify Christ as the Savior (*WA* 52.51.36). Elsewhere, Luther is horrified by the practice of pronouncing absolution in the name of Mary, the apostles, or other saints (*WA* 52.265.26-36).

[69] Luther frequently rejects the intercession of the saints. Here are some examples: *WA* 52.86.22, 89.24-33, 170.8-13, 212.13-15, 219.34-35, 233.10-11, 535.26-30.

[70] This is one of three Marian festivals for which Dietrich provided Luther sermons. The others are the Annunciation and the Visitation. All three, of course, have a biblical basis and the last was offered as a replacement for the Assumption [*Hymmelfart*] of Mary which Luther describes as 'full of idolatry and without foundation in Scripture' (*WA* 52.681.6-70).

queen of heaven.[71] Along with her Son, Mary submits herself to the law of Moses. Luther uses their behavior as a rebuke to our own, 'Such examples . . . should be preached in order that we might be ashamed of the fact that we . . . do not do what we are supposed when he [the Child Jesus] has done for our sakes what Moses commands although rightfully he was not required to do it.'[72] At this point, Mary drops out of the sermon and Luther proceeds to discuss at length the significance of first born sons to which the mosaic law in the text applied.

In the second sermon, Luther focuses on Simeon and his song (Lk. 2.25-32) and presents him as an example of faith, 'All of his hope was based on the conviction that God would soon keep his promise and send the Lord Christ.' Luther, also, believes that the Holy Spirit worked such confidence in Simeon 'undoubtedly' from reading the Word of God (Genesis 49 and the prophecies of Daniel) and concluding that the coming of Christ was imminent.[73] Finally, Luther interprets Simeon's words as a confession of the gospel, 'This child is a savior from sin, death, and hell. . . . The fact that Simeon calls this child only by the name "savior" must mean . . . that there can be no other savior. . . . Whoever holds to another savior must be deceived and remain in sin and death.'[74]

This is Luther's regular way of treating the saints in the house postils. They exemplify the Christian life and the mercy of God in Christ. Luther's church calendar retained several (biblical) saints days, so Dietrich included 21 additional homilies in order to complete the year—from St. Andrew's Day to St. Michael's.[75] Luther routinely calls these saints examples [*Exempel*] in his sermons. Thus, Andrew is an example of 'firmly holding to God's Word'; Thomas first for his unbelief but then for his 'glorious confession of Christ'; James as a warning against false security since 'sin and weakness' strike even the best Christians; and Matthew for how Christ wants to be gracious to 'all troubled sinners'.[76] Mary Magdalene teaches the nature of true repentance and how one

---

[71] Luther sharply rejects appeals to Mary and depending on her intercession and indicts the pope for wanting to make 'the mother equal to the Son in everything' (*WA* 52.681.27-31).
[72] *WA* 52.150.10-14.
[73] *WA* 52.154.26-155.6.
[74] *WA* 52.158.20-27.
[75] According to Buchwald, 'Einleitung,' xi, Dietrich included homilies for St. Bartholomew and for the Ascension of our Lord since these were in the Nuremberg calendar though not in Wittenberg's. He may have based them on Luther materials but they did not originate in Luther's house preaching. They have not been printed in volume 52 of the Weimar Edition.
[76] *WA* 52.565.4, 572.7-8, 674.2-3, 706.35-707.1.

can receive the forgiveness of sins;[77] and Stephen shows the faithful how to find consolation and hope in the midst of persecution.[78]

Without dwelling on medieval abuses,[79] Luther used his preaching to redefine the role of the saints in the church. They were definitely not intercessors. Instead, they were real people—like his hearers—who personified what it meant to be a Christian, i.e., someone who recognized their sin, believed in Christ alone for their salvation, and then served God in this life, surrounded by trials and temptations, until at last delivered safely into heaven.

Conclusion

As in all of his preaching, Luther's main concern was to proclaim justification by faith in its various ramifications. But at the center of justification was always the person and work of Jesus. Therefore, Luther was always on his guard against anything that threatened to obscure or replace Christ as the world's only Savior—whether the abuses of medieval religion or the perennial temptation offered by temporal wealth. Trusting in *anything* other than Jesus was idolatry. There simply was no alternative to him.

---

[77] *WA* 52.664.21-22
[78] *WA* 588.1-4.
[79] They surface only occasionally. One interesting example is Luther's description and denunciation of putting one's trust in candles consecrated in connection with the Purification of Mary (*WA* 52.164.6-32). Another interesting passage is one in which Luther discusses the 'lying wonders' performed by agents of the devil, who pretends to be afraid of candles, salt, and water in order to lead people into idolatry and superstition (*WA* 52.191.3-20). In another place, he indicts confraternities for—among other things—distributing the 'good works' of dead saints (*WA* 52.258.1-2). Similarly, the pope through indulgences (*WA* 52.263.23-24).

CHAPTER 3

Some implications of Martin Luther's *solus Christus* in his theological validation of the Jews

Berthold Schwarz

To talk or to teach about Luther's *solus Christus* in his theological validation of the Jews could be a dangerous undertaking, dangerous at least because of two major reasons. First, 'Because Luther was terribly wrong in his reasoning against Jews, he can't be right in other parts of theology. He should not be received as an authority of the church anymore.' I do not share this opinion. But it *is* taught in several ways. And—this is also a major problem in dealing with the topic—if someone does not share this judgment against Luther, they find themselves immediately labeled as an anti-Semite, too.

Second, another danger could be that Luther's reasoning against the Jews is wrongly understood. Indeed there exist several interpretations. The popularized, non-academic extremes are either: 'Luther is all in all the believer's enemy because of his cruel words against Jews' (ie. total condemnation); or, 'Luther has said some wrong things against Jews, but he is still our hero of faith. Therefore his words against Jews are of minor importance' (ie. somehow a glorification).

I do not accept Luther's anti-Jewish writings.[1] He was deeply wrong in saying what he said. I have sadness and anger towards Luther's later anti-Jewish writings and his treatment of Jews therein.[2] Neither can I accept Luther's teaching on Jews as if it was just a minor lapse (it was not!), nor can I condemn him as a *persona non grata*, as if he should be erased out of Christian theology. Both extremes are taught today among Christians, Jews, scholars and in messianic-Jewish circles. But both extremes should be avoided. Having said this I

---

[1] And neither do many representative Lutherans. '[W]e who bear his name and heritage must with pain acknowledge . . . Luther's anti-Judaic diatribes and violent recommendations of his later writings against the Jews.' See *Documents from the Evangelical Lutheran Church in America* (1994) and *The Evangelical Lutheran Church in Canada* (1995). Cf. Kenneth A. Strand, 'Current Issues and Trends in Luther Studies,' *AUSS* 22.1 (1984), 144-46.

[2] Cf. Beatrice Acklin-Zimmermann, *Die Gesetzesinterpretation in den Römerbriefkommentaren von Peter Abaelard und Martin Luther. Eine Untersuchung auf dem Hintergrund der Antijudaismusdiskussion* (Frankfurt a.M. 2004), 255.

will now present some aspects of Luther's teaching on the Christ with its implications for the Jewish people.

Luther on Christ Jesus

To talk or to teach about the meaning of 'Jesus Christ' in the theology of Martin Luther we talk about 'all and everything'. Luther holds this to be the center of the gospel. And, of course, the Bible, itself, is certainly not unclear when it speaks about what the reformation later called *solus Christus*—see, for example, Matthew 1.21, John 14.6, Acts 4.12, 1 Timothy 2.5. Such examples could easily be multiplied from the text of the New Testament. It teaches that Jesus Christ alone, Jesus Christ and no other, saves sinners. Therefore, according to Martin Luther, the Bible is about Jesus Christ. The reformer said that Jesus Christ is the 'center and circumference of the Bible,' meaning that its fundamental content is Jesus Christ—who he is and what he did for us in his death and resurrection. To miss him as the center and key to Scripture is to remain in darkness and ignorance.

This is the judgment and punishment which God permits to come upon those who do not see this light, that is, do not accept and believe God's Word concerning Christ. They would stay in darkness, and they would understand no article of Christian teaching: what sin is, what human ability is, how one gets rid of sin and becomes righteous, what law or gospel is, what faith is, what good works are, what the Christian estates are. And since they do not know Christ, they cannot really know and see a Christian, but must condemn and persecute the true church and Christians, who teach the Word of Christ.[3]

Of course, the reformers knew that we do not see the centrality of Christ in the Scriptures on the basis of our immediate, intuitive, and inherent rational abilities. The Scriptures tell us that one of the many aspects of the Fall was that our intellects were darkened in respect to any knowledge of our Creator and his will toward us. Any theological or saving 'knowing' we have concerning Christ will only be the result of the Father's gracious initiative. He must open our eyes to understand the Scriptures. If God does not act in that way in us, we will remain trapped in darkness concerning the gospel.

One aspect of this darkness is our blindness concerning Christ as the sum and substance of Scripture. We may, if we are well trained in the art of reading a book, grasp the centrality of Christ in the Bible in what the reformers called 'an outward way'. But we will never, on our own, grasp Christ in a truly saving or theological way. The Holy Spirit must use the gospel in the text to open our eyes to Christ and his work on our behalf. Having said this, let us consider what

---

[3] Ewald Plass (ed.), *What Luther Says* (St. Louis: Concordia, 1959), 145-48.

Luther's understanding of *solus Christus* means in his theological validation of the Jews

Luther on the Jewish people

Luther on Jews—peripheral to his life's work

Popularly speaking, Luther's ministry as a reformer begins in 1517 with the posting of the 95 theses at the door of Wittenberg's Schlosskirche. For around 20 years, Luther said little about the Jews, and what he did say was all-in-all relatively positive (when judged by the standards of popular culture of his time). Luther's 'anti-Jewish' writings span his last 8 years (1538-1546). Luther's attitude towards the Jews is somewhat peripheral to his overall life's work. As the largest collections of his writings show, comparatively, very few of those pages are dedicated to his opinions on the Jews.[4] But there is no getting around it, in his later years, Luther said some awful things about the Jewish people. Where Luther was gravely mistaken, Protestants must admit his faults.

Luther's treatment of the Jews—not based on biological reasons

It can be shown that Luther's writings began favorably toward the Jews, but as the years progressed, he developed a deep hostility that was nurtured in medieval stereotype and bias, as well as his apocalyptic expectations.

It should be kept in mind that Luther's later anti-Jewish tracts were written from a position different than current anti-Semitism. Luther was born into a society that was anti-Jewish, but it was not the current anti-Judaic type of society that bases racism on biological factors. Luther had no objections to integrate converted Jews into Christian society. He had nothing against Jews as Jews. He had something against their religion because he believed it denied and blasphemed Christ.[5] Heiko Oberman points out,

> Luther was anti-Jewish in his repeated warnings against the Jews as bearers of an anti-Christian religion which had established itself both within and outside Christianity. But Luther was not an anti-Semite or racist of any kind because—to apply the test appropriate to his time—for him a baptized Jew is fully Christian. Conversely, he said that among us Christians in Germany there are horrifyingly many

---

[4] See Lewis W. Spitz, *The Protestant Reformation* (New York: 1985), 357. George S. Robbert, 'Martin Luther's Later Years' *ChH* 39. 12.3 34, points out that 'Luther wrote some 60,000 pages, much of it later in life.' The material Luther wrote in regards to the Jews probably spans some hundred pages. Of that amount, only a small percentage of it involves hostile rhetoric.

[5] Luther says, '[I]n itself there is nothing wrong with living like a Jew, for it is a matter of indifference whether you eat pork or any other meat. But to live like a Jew in the sense that you abstain from certain foods for the sake of conscience is a denial of Christ and the destruction of the Gospel,' *LW* 26.118.

who in their hearts deny Christ. Those are the true Jews! Not race but belief in the law, in good works, makes Jews.[6]

I agree with Oberman. Luther cannot rightly be labeled an anti-Semite.[7] Rather than being motivated by biological factors, Luther's criticisms were motivated by theological concerns.[8]

In his commentary on Galatians 3.28, Luther explains that we are all equal. No particular people has any right to claim special privilege before God:

> There is neither magistrate nor subject, neither professor nor listener, neither teacher nor pupil, neither lady nor servant. For in Christ Jesus all social stations, even those that were divinely ordained, are nothing. Male, female, slave, free, Jew, Gentile, king, subject – these are, of course, good creatures of God. But in Christ, that is, in the matter of salvation, they amount to nothing, for all their wisdom, righteousness, devotion, and authority."[9]

Luther's most well known anti-Jewish writing was *On The Jews and Their Lies*, it is often quoted and cited as the clearest example of Luther's anti-Semitism. Interestingly though, this very document proves that Luther was not against the Jews as *people*, nor did he seek for their extermination.[10] In that treatise, Luther launches into a long section against any notion that the Jews are better than anyone else. He puts forth an *alleged* popular anti-Jewish argument that they thanked God that they were not born gentiles or women. In arguing against this

---

[6] Heiko A. Oberman, *The Impact of the Reformation* (Michigan: 1994), 76. See, also, Oberman: *The Roots of Anti-Semitism* (Philadelphia: 1984), 102; Strand, 'Current Issues,' 141-42.

[7] Eric Gritsch, 'Was Luther Anti-Semitic?' *ChH* 39. 12.3, 39, echoes Oberman's point, 'Luther was not an anti-Semite in the racist sense. His arguments against the Jews were theological, not biological.' Also, Gritsch: *Martin—God's Court Jester: Luther in Retrospect* (Philadelphia: 1983), 145.

[8] See Carter Lindberg, 'Tainted Greatness: Luther's Attitudes Toward Judaism and their Historical Reception' in Nancy A Harrowitz (ed.), *Tainted Greatness: Antisemitism and Cultural Heroes* (Philadelphia: 1994), 20-21.

[9] *LW* 26.353.

[10] It should be noted that while Luther recommended expulsion of the Jews, he did not recommend their annihilation. Cf. Bertold Klappert, 'Erwählung und Rechtfertigung' in Heinz Kremers (ed.), *Die Juden und Martin Luther—Martin Luther und die Juden: Geschichte, Wirkungsgeschichte, Herausforderung* (Neukirchen-Vluyn: 1987), 368-410, esp. 377. Cf., also, Carter Lindberg, 'Tainted Greatness,' 30n.1. Even Luther's treatise *On The Jews and Their Lies* was not geared toward annihilating the Jews. 'This was not an appeal to the mob to rise up in a surge of riotous patriotism and attack the Jews in cruel revenge, for Luther had unequivocally prefaced his reeducation program with this statement: "We must not avenge ourselves." His demands were directed at the temporal rulers, the princes and nobility,' says Heiko A. Oberman: *Luther: Man Between God and the Devil* (New York: 1989), 294.

'nonsense,' Luther mocks those who think any one particular people is better than another.

Luther was born into a society of animosity towards the Jews

Martin Luther was born into a society of (largely accepted) animosity toward the Jews. Since the early church the Jews were stigmatized as those who killed Christ, and deserved to experience God's wrath as his rejected people. They had become—as a sad development over the centuries—the scapegoats of society, blamed for countless evils befalling the medieval age. The populace had gone as far to create fictional crimes to charge to their account. They were said to partake in ritual murders: slaughtering Christian children for blood to use during Passover.[11]

In the earliest days of Luther's academic career, Luther held four theological opinions on the Jews, which were to remain unchanged. Gordon Rupp presents these as follows:

1. God's wrath has fallen on his disobedient people and only God can take it away.
2. Humanly speaking, the Jews are unconvertible and they cannot be saved by human action.
3. Because they reproach God and blaspheme against Christ their faith is an actively anti-Christian religion.
4. And this one makes the difference: All these things are true not only of the Jews, but of all human beings who set themselves against God, so that unbelieving Jews and unbelieving gentiles are comprehended within one solidarity of guilt.[12]

Luther's changing views towards the Jews

Many Luther scholars say that Luther's views of the Jews underwent an extreme change in his lifetime. They claim that Luther at first showed friendly interest and compassion to the Jews, only to turn against them later on. Luther's earliest known dealing with the Jews occurred in 1510. A converted Jew named Pfefferkorn accused his former people (the Jews) of all kinds of cruelties and blasphemies. He then arranged to have Jewish books burned. Johannes Reuchlin, the foremost Hebrew scholar of Germany, opposed Pfefferkorn's actions. Luther sided with Reuchlin. Some take this to be an indication of Luther's early pro-Jewish views. But Luther's actions, of course, were not strictly pro-Jewish, but were more in support of true scholarship, especially where it would aid biblical study. But some of the Jews of the day failed to understand Luther correctly. A Jewish historian correctly notes, 'They were overjoyed that at last

---

[11] Mark U. Edwards, Jr., *Luther's Last Battles* (Ithaca: 1983), 118-19.
[12] Gordon Rupp, *Martin Luther and the Jews* (London: 1972), 9.

a famous Christian teacher spoke of them as human beings. A few enthusiasts among the Jews of Germany went so far in their misunderstanding of Luther that they actually congratulated him on the steps he was taking to come closer to Judaism.'[13] Luther apparently was not troubled by this development at this time. He was optimistic that the Jews would be converted once the abuses of the Roman Catholic Church were removed.

In 1516, one finds Luther moving towards a warmer attitude towards the Jews—explicit in his work in the 1520s:

> [M]any people are proud with marvelous stupidity when they call the Jews dogs, evildoers, or whatever they like, while they too, and equally, do not realize who or what they are in the sight of God. Boldly they heap blasphemous insults upon them, when they ought to have compassion on them and fear the same punishments for themselves. Moreover, as if certain concerning themselves and the others, they rashly pronounce themselves blessed and the others cursed. Such today are the theologians of Cologne, who are so stupid in their zeal, that in their articles, or rather their inarticulate and inept writings, they say that the Jews are accursed. Why? Because they have forgotten what is said in the following chapter: 'Bless and do not curse' (Rom. 12.14), and in another place: 'When reviled, we bless; when slandered, we try to conciliate' (1 Cor. 4.12–13). They wish to convert the Jews by force and curses, but God will resist them.[14]

With Luther's proclamation of the gospel in the early 1520s, against the prevailing culture of his day, Luther re-evaluated the plight of the Jews. For a time, he rose above cultural conformity and extended the gospel message to the Jewish people. Perhaps it was due to the persecution he received from the Roman Catholic Church. In his exposition of the *Magnificat* (1521) Luther said, 'We ought, therefore, not to treat the Jews in so unkindly a spirit, for there are future Christians among them, and they are turning every day.'[15]

It is sometimes suggested that Luther was overwhelmingly positive towards Judaism early in his career (previous to 1517) and did not suffer from all of the cultural stereotypes of his day. However, the editors of *Luther's Works* make it clear that this is not so:

> Luther's earliest lectures—those on the Psalms, delivered in 1513-1515—already contained in essence the whole burden of his later charges against the Jews. The Jews, Luther asserts in these lectures, suffer continually under God's wrath; they are paying the penalty for their rejection of Christ. They spend all their efforts in self-justification, but God will not hear their prayers. Neither kindness nor severity will improve them. They become constantly more stubborn and more vain.

---

[13] Solomon Grayzel, *A History of the Jews* (New York: 1968), 374.
[14] *LW* 25.428.
[15] *LW* 21.354.

> Moreover, they are active enemies of Christ; they blaspheme and defame him, spreading their evil influence even into Christian hearts.[16]

Against the spirit of his day, Luther, nevertheless, did not singularly blame the Jews for the death of Christ. Eric Gritsch points out, 'Luther did not, however, hold Jews responsible for the death of Christ. As he wrote in a hymn, "We dare not blame . . . the band of Jews; ours is the shame." And he felt that at least a few Jews might be won for Christ.'[17] It was the sins of all people that brought about Christ's death.[18]

In the early days of the reformation Luther placed the origin of the blame for Jewish unbelief on the Catholic Church. In 1523 his pen produced a favorable tract, *That Christ was born a Jew*. He told the Jews that he could understand why they didn't want to join the Catholic Church. He writes, 'The papists have so demeaned themselves that a good Christian would rather be a Jew than one of them, and a Jew would rather be a sow than a Christian.'[19] Not only was Luther understanding toward them, he also optimistically thought that they would then become true Christians according to his own understanding of the gospel.[20] He wrote,

> Let [the Jews] first be suckled with milk, and begin by recognizing this man Jesus as the true Messiah; after that they may drink wine, and learn also that he is true God. For they have been led astray so long and so far that one must deal gently with them, as people who have been all too strongly indoctrinated to believe that God cannot be man.[21]

Against the spirit of medieval culture, Luther took bold steps of tolerance towards the Jews. He said,

> I would request and advise that one deal gently with them and instruct them from Scripture; then some of them may come along. Instead of this we are trying only to drive them by force, slandering them, accusing them of having Christian blood if they don't stink, and I know not what other foolishness. So long as we thus treat them like dogs, how can we expect to work any good among them? Again, when we forbid them to labor and do business and have any human fellowship with us, thereby forcing them into usury, how is that supposed to do them any good? If we really want to help them, we must be guided in our dealings with them . . . by the law of Christian love. We must receive them cordially, and permit them to trade

---

[16] See *LW* 47.127-28.
[17] Eric Gritsch, 'Was Luther Anti-Semetic?' *ChH* 39. 12.3, 38.
[18] See, also, Oberman: *Luther*, 296; cf. Johannes Wallmann, Kirche und Israel im Mittelalter und in der Reformationszeit, *KI* 34 (1989), 69-90.
[19] Roland Bainton, *Here I Stand* (New York: 1950), 297.
[20] *LW* 45.200; cf. *WA* 56.436,7-23 (Rom. 11.22) or *WA* 6.140,16-20 (Rom. 15.13f).
[21] *LW* 45.229.

and work with us, that they may have occasion and opportunity to associate with us, hear our Christian teaching, and witness our Christian life. If some of them should prove stiff-necked, what of it? After all, we ourselves are not all good Christians either.[22]

Luther's hope for Jewish conversion seems to have reached its zenith of frustration in 1536. Sometime previous to this year, Luther met with three learned Jews who disagreed with his interpretation of messianic passages from the Old Testament based on rabbinic tradition. The argument centered around the Christological interpretation of Jeremiah 23.6. The Rabbis refused to see Christ in the passage.[23] That these learned Jews refused this, as well as the Christological nature of the Old Testament, must have evoked deep frustration. Coupled with the failure of Jewish conversion since his writings from 1523, Luther vowed never to enter into dialogue with the Jews again.

The Jews completely ignored his theological exhortations and proclamation of the gospel. Heiko Oberman describes Luther's mindset toward them:

> For Luther the Jews were doing anything but improving. What was worse, encouraged by their misreading of his own words, they had become more daring, defaming and cursing Jesus of Nazareth and regarding Christians as their "worst enemies," so much so that "if you could, you would [now] rob [all Christians] of what they are and what they have". However, the decision not to speak for the Jews in Saxony hinged on the analysis that they were appealing to religious tolerance while irreligiously rejecting their own God . . . the Father of Jesus Christ.[24]

Luther's writings and discussions did not produce the results that he was expecting. Luther's views of the Jews began to change. A Jewish historian said this about Luther, 'He thought he could win the Jews with a few kind words. When this did not happen, he was bitterly disappointed. . . . A movement, hopeful in its beginning for the Jews, ended in utter disillusionment.'[25] These frustrating experiences, however, build only a small factor in Luther's change.

At this point in Luther's development, he had been reading anti-Jewish works of Lyra, Paul of Burgeos, Victor of Carben, and Antonius Margaritha.[26]

---

[22] *LW* 45.229; cf. H. Boockmann: Kirche und Frömmigkeit vor der Reformation in G. Bott (ed.), *Martin Luther und die Reformation in Deutschland. Ausstellung zum 500. Geburtstag Martin Luthers. Veranstaltet vom Germanischen Nationalmuseum Nürnberg in Zusammenarbeit mit dem Verein für Reformationsgeschichte* (Frankfurt a.M.: 1983), 41-72.

[23] See *LW* 47.191.

[24] Oberman, *Luther*, 293-94.

[25] Grayzel, *A History*, 374.

[26] Gordon Rupp, *Martin Luther*, 14-15, explains: 'The effect on Luther of one of these writings was catastrophic. Antonius Margaritha was of a famous Jewish family and he claimed to describe faithfully the life and worship of the Jews, and especially their

These writings greatly influenced Luther.[27] By 1538, he came to believe the popular stories about the Jews' attempts to convert Christians. In Moravia Lutherans were—so was the rumor—beginning to keep the Sabbath day and enforce the rite of circumcision. Luther was upset that people were preaching law instead of gospel freedom. He was informed that the Jews had convinced some Christians that they should be circumcised, that the messiah had not yet come, that the Jewish law was externally valid, and that it should be observed by gentiles.

So Luther wrote the tract, *Against the Sabbatarians* (1538). Luther begins this writing (an 'open letter') stating exactly what topics he will cover:

> You informed me that the Jews are making inroads at various places throughout the country with their venom and their doctrine, and that they have already induced some Christians to let themselves be circumcised and to believe that the Messiah or Christ has not yet appeared, that the law of the Jews must prevail forever, that it must also be adopted by all the Gentiles, etc. Then you inquired of me how these allegations are to be refuted with Holy Scripture. . . . I will convey my advice and opinion briefly in this matter.[28]

This, however, did not stop this activity. Zealous rabbis began enticing Christians away from their faith. They even began to write Jewish apologetic pam-

---

anti-Christian prayers and practices, in a work, *The Whole Jewish Faith*, published in Augsburg in 1530. But at the Diet of Augsburg, Josel withstood Margaritha to his face, accused him of lies and exaggerations, to such good effect that Margaritha was arrested and finally banned from the city. Yet it was the third edition of this work which Luther had read aloud to his friends at supper-time and which he said had come as a revelation to him, confirming his fears that they practiced what amounted to public blasphemy.'

[27] In *On The Jews And Their Lies*, these sources played a key role: 'Luther offered a Christological interpretation of the Old Testament in opposition to the Jewish claims based on Scripture that the Messiah had not yet come. Here Luther relied on traditional methods of interpretation, especially those developed by Nicholas of Lyra (1270-1349) and by Paul of Burgos (1351-1435), a Spanish rabbi who had converted to Christianity and had become an archbishop. Both had used rabbinical methods in their Old Testament interpretations to show that Christ was the Messiah foretold in the Jewish Bible. Luther followed their example and cited four passages of the Old Testament as proof texts for the coming of the Messiah. Nevertheless, Luther enjoyed reading Margaritha's stories at table and cited them whenever he dealt with the Jewish question. One of these items was that Jews considered Jesus the product of adultery—the whore Mary had relations with a blacksmith—and therefore Luther called for stern measures against the people who so abused the toleration extended to them by Christians. Since Jews had slandered the holiest of holy in Christendom, Jesus, Mary, and the Trinity, they should be deprived of Christian mercy'—Gritsch, 'Was Luther Anti-semitic?', 139.

[28] *LW* 47.65.

phlets in reply to Luther. Luther's patience simply ran out. In the reformer's eyes, the Jews were a clear example of *hardened hearts*: they were no longer the church's responsibility, but rather needed to be given over to God's judgment.

Luther laid out a number of scriptural arguments to counter their claims. By and large, Luther treats the Jews in this writing as he would any group that opposed the gospel. He uses rhetoric, *argumentum ad absurdum*, and appeal to a clear exposition of the Scriptures. Luther ends this writing by admitting defeat in converting the Jews:

> If you are unable to convert the Jews, then consider that you are no better than all the prophets, who were always slain and persecuted by this base people who glory solely in the boast that they are Abraham's seed, though they surely know that there have always been many desperate, lost souls also among them, so that they might well recognize that it requires more to be a child of God than just to be the seed of Abraham. . . . Because God for fifteen hundred years has failed to do this with the Jews but lets them live on and on in exile without any word or prophecy to them regarding it, it is evident that he has forsaken them, that they can no longer be God's people, and that the true Lord, the Messiah, must have come fifteen hundred years ago.[29]

Mark Edwards comments, 'Luther was uncompromising in his insistence on the error of the Jews, but his language is still, for the most part, temperate and restrained.'[30] After this treatise, Luther decided, 'to write no more either about the Jews or against them'.[31] Had Luther kept to this decision, he would have avoided writing one of his most controversial treatises, *On The Jews And Their Lies*.

Finally (May 1542) Luther received from a Moravian friend, Count Schlink, a copy of a Jewish apologetic work along with the request that he reply to it. Luther's anger boiled over; restraint could not contain his anger, and the result was a lengthy tract, *Against the Jews and Their Lies*. This treatise may come as a shock to many. The language is very biting; his proposals almost seem inhumane. Luther very thoroughly and systematically condemned the religious errors of the Jewish people. He was no longer writing to convert them: 'It is not my purpose to quarrel with the Jews, nor to learn from them how they interpret the scriptures, I know all that very well already. Much less do I propose to convert the Jews, for that is impossible.'[32] So, the change in Luther's approach is obvious from the start. First, he lashes out against the false boasts of the

---

[29] *LW* 47.96.
[30] Edwards, *Luther's Last Battles*, 127.
[31] *LW* 47.133.
[32] *LW* 47.137.

Jewish people. The Jews took special pride in their ancestry; they were thankful that they were God's chosen people, the physical descendants of the patriarchs.

Following this section, Luther proceeds to an exegesis and explanation of key Old Testament prophecies. Using a book they too regarded as sacred, he cites several key Messianic prophecies. He proves to them from God's Word that *olam* need not mean 'forever,' that David's ruling house was not an earthly dynasty and that Christ perfectly fulfilled all the Messianic requirements. Luther says, 'When I debated with them, they gave me their glosses, as they usually do. But when I forced them back to the text, they soon fled from it, saying they were obliged to believe their rabbis. The more one tries to help them, the baser and more stubborn they become. Leave them to their own devices.'[33]

Nevertheless, he spends nearly one-half of this lengthy treatise explaining scriptural proofs for the Jews. Luther then lists a few reasons for his dislike of them. A medieval rabbi wrote *Der gantz Juedisch glaub*, which contained this interesting sidelight; 'Jesus is a whore's son, his mother Mary was a whore, who conceived him in adultery with a blacksmith.'[34] Another matter that Luther, along with almost all Europeans, could not tolerate was the Jewish practice of usury. He found this particularly detestable. Had Luther stopped here, his treatise probably would be of little interest to anyone. However, he went on to propose what he thought should be done about the situation.[35]

Luther moved from his earlier writings of attacking Jewish theology to attacking Jewish people.[36] Still, Luther was not against the Jews for being Jews – he had no objections to integrating converted Jews into Christian society: 'Now, in order to strengthen our faith, we want to deal with a few crass follies of the Jews in their belief arid their exegesis of the Scriptures, since they so maliciously revile our faith. If this should move any Jew to reform and repent, so much the better.'[37] Nevertheless, Luther no longer holds out any hope for Jewish conversion: 'Much less do I propose to convert the Jews, for that is impossible.'[38] Nor is there to be any debate over their scriptural interpretation: 'Therefore a Christian should be content and not argue with the Jews,'[39] and, 'it

---

[33] *LW* 47.191-92.

[34] *LW* 47.257.

[35] Bainton, *Here I Stand*, 297, 'One could wish that Luther had died before ever this tract was written.'

[36] Written pre-holocaust, the Roman Catholic historian Hartmann Grisar, *Luther* (St Louis: 1915), 4.306, comments, 'It is clear that [Luther] was within his rights when he scourged the anti-Christian blasphemy and seductive wiles of the Jews, however much he may have been wrong in allowing himself to be carried away by fanaticism so far as to demand their actual persecution.'

[37] *LW* 47.140.

[38] *LW* 47.137.

[39] *LW* 47.138. Luther qualifies, 'But if you have to or want to talk with them, do not say any more than this: "Listen, Jew, are you aware that Jerusalem and your sovereignty,

is useless to argue with them about how God is triune, how he became man, and how Mary is the mother of God. No human reason nor any human heart will ever grant these things, much less the embittered, venomous, blind heart of the Jews.'[40] Luther has completely given up writing in order to dialog with Jews, he now writes for the sole purpose of warning Christians against them. Luther repeats many of the arguments he put forth in his earlier writing, *Against the Sabbatarians*,[41] though it is obvious his tone and demeanor have changed.

Because of the Jewish blasphemy against Jesus Christ, Mary, the Trinity, and the whole of the Christian faith, Luther's understanding of the Jewish people reduces them to being murderers, blasphemers, liars and thieves. He has stereotyped an entire group of people to be the worst of criminals. With this prejudice, Luther launches into the section of the treatise for which *On The Jews and Their Lies* is most remembered. He says, 'We must exercise harsh mercy with fear and trembling, in the hope that we could save some from the flames and embers. We must not avenge ourselves. They are under God's wrath—a thousand times worse than we could wish it upon them.'[42] Luther considered his early treatise from 1523 *soft mercy*, an appeal to the Jews to

---

together with your temple and priesthood, have been destroyed for over 1,460 years?" For this year, which we Christians write as the year 1542 since the birth of Christ, is exactly 1,468 years, going on fifteen hundred years, since Vespasian and Titus destroyed Jerusalem and expelled the Jews from the city. Let the Jews bite on this nut and dispute this question as long as they wish.'

[40] *LW* 47.139.

[41] Luther again sees that the historical misery of the Jews is the result of their rejection of Christ and his Word: 'For such ruthless wrath of God is sufficient evidence that they assuredly have erred and gone astray. . . . For one dare not regard God as so cruel that he would punish his own people so long, so terribly, so unmercifully, and in addition keep silent, comforting them neither with words nor with deeds, and fixing no time limit and no end to it. . . . Therefore this work of wrath is proof that the Jews, surely rejected by God, are no longer his people, and neither is he any longer their God.' And, 'If there were but a spark of reason or understanding in them, they would surely say to themselves: "O Lord God, something has gone wrong with us. Our misery is too great, too long, too severe; God has forgotten us!" etc. To be sure, I am not a Jew, but I really do not like to contemplate God's awful wrath toward this people. It sends a shudder of fear through body and soul, for I ask, What will the eternal wrath of God in hell be like toward false Christians and all unbelievers? Well, let the Jews regard our Lord Jesus as they will. We behold the fulfillment of the words spoken by him in Luke 21: "But when you see Jerusalem surrounded by armies, then know that its desolation has come near . . . for these are days of vengeance. For great distress shall be upon the earth and wrath upon this people".'

[42] This sentence, left out of the English translation, is found in *WA* 53.522,34-37—Oberman, *Luther* 290.

convert. Now, Luther attempts to use *harsh mercy*, forcing the Jews to convert and to protect Christians from blasphemy.

Luther gives his infamous seven recommendations to the political authorities.[43] (1) burn their synagogues and schools, (2) raze and destroy their homes, (3) take away their books, (4) forbid their rabbis to teach, (5) allow no safe conduct for them on the highways, (6) prohibit usury, take their money from them, and (7) put an ax, hoe, or spindle into the hands of young, strong Jews to let them earn their bread. As if this were not enough, Luther was still bothered about the abusive blasphemy of the Jews. He writes, 'We are at fault in not avenging all this innocent blood of our Lord and of the Christians which they shed . . . we are at fault for not slaying them.'[44]

Yet, one should not concentrate only on these several pages of aggression and anger. In this same writing he calls on God to soften their hearts with this entreaty: 'O God, heavenly father, relent and let your wrath over them be sufficient and come to an end, for the sake of your dear Son.'[45] Finally, Luther closes with this prayer for their conversion, 'May Christ, our dear Lord, convert them mercifully and preserve us steadfastly in the knowledge of him, which is eternal life.'[46] This was no mere cover-up for his harsh statements: Luther wrote this way out of religious considerations.[47]

Gordon Rupp provides a remarkable citation from Luther's last sermon preached at Eisleben (February 15, 1546):

> Now I am going home, and perhaps I will never preach to you again, and I have blessed you and prayed you to stay always close to God's Word. . . . I see the Jews are still among you. Now we have to deal with them in a Christian manner and try to bring them to the Christian faith that they may receive the true Messiah who is their flesh and blood and of the seed of Abraham. . . . [T]hey must be invited to turn to the Messiah and be baptized in him. . . . If not then we must not suffer them to remain for they daily abuse and blaspheme Christ. I must not, you must not be a partaker of the sins of others. God knows I have enough to do with sins of my own, but if they will give up usury and receive Christ we will willingly

---

[43] *LW* 47.268.
[44] *LW* 47.267.
[45] *LW* 47.292.
[46] *LW* 47.306.
[47] Luther went on to publish two more anti-Jewish writings: *On The Ineffable Name and On Christ's Lineage* (1543) and *On The Last Words of David* (1543)—not in the English edition of Luther's Works. *On The Ineffable Name and On Christ's Lineage* is in the book, Gerhard Falk, *The Jew in Christian Theology: Martin Luther's Anti-Jewish Vom Schem Hamphoras, Previously Unpublished in English, and Other Milestones in Church Doctrine Concerning Judaism* (North Carolina: 1992). In these writings, Luther intended to show the superiority of Christian interpretation over rabbinical interpretation.

receive them as our brethren . . . but if they call Mary a whore and Jesus her bastard still we must exercise Christian love towards them that they may be converted and receive our Lord. . . . If they turn from their blasphemies we must gladly forgive them, but if not we must not suffer them to remain!'[48]

Heiko Oberman notes, '[I]n his final Admonition . . . the concept of tolerance that leaves room for conversion is certainly retained. But his imminent expectation of the Last Judgment lets him interpret and evaluate the "signs of the times" so as to keep this tolerance within very narrow bounds, as it is the very last chance to avert expulsion.'[49]

Luther's attitude towards the Jews within his eschatological framework

Luther's eschatological framework is essential to understanding his attitude towards the Jews. As early as 1522, Luther preached that his generation was living in the last days: 'I do not wish to force any one to believe as I do; neither will I permit anyone to deny me the right to believe that the last day is near at hand. These words and signs of Christ compel me to believe that such is the case. For the history of the centuries that have passed since the birth of Christ nowhere reveals conditions like those of the present.'[50] In 1542, Luther said, 'I hold that Judgment day is not far away. I say this because the drive of the gospel is now at its height.'[51] Thus, the entirety of his reformation career embraced an impending consummation of history.[52]

Toward the end of his life, this expectation increased. Luther spoke out strongly against those groups who went against the gospel: the Papacy, Turks,

---

[48] These words probably are not from Luther's last sermon, but rather from his *An Admonition Against The Jews* (1546), which was added to his last sermon. If these are Luther's last words about the Jews, they summarize what his later position was towards them with minimal rhetoric and abusive language (at least in this section). Luther admonishes his hearers to 'try to bring them to the Christian faith' and to treat them in a 'Christian manner,' which harkens back to his positive treatise of 1523. On the other hand, he is firm that if the Jews do not embrace Christianity 'then we must not suffer them to remain for they daily abuse and blaspheme Christ' and if they continue partaking in an anti-Christian religion, 'we must not suffer them to remain'. This is indeed the later Luther, intolerant of non-Christian religions that he considered in league with the devil. Cf. *WA* 51.195-96. The English edition includes Luther's last sermon of February 15, 1546, but it does not include this section—their translation covers *WA* 51.187-94, while Rupp's section is from 195-96. Rupp is probably citing Luther's *Admonition Against The Jews*.

[49] Oberman, *Luther*, 296.

[50] Martin Luther, *The Sermons of Martin Luther* (Grand Rapids: 1996), 1.62. Available online at http://www.orlutheran.com/html/mlselk21.html.

[51] Ewald M. Plass, *What Luther Says: An Anthology* (St. Louis: 1959), 2.696.

[52] See Edwards, *Luther's Last Battles*, 97. See, also, Paul Althaus: *The Theology of Martin Luther* (Philadelphia: 1966), 420-21.

radicals and the Jews. These groups were led by the devil, used for continued opposition of the gospel.[53] Early in his career, his treatise *That Jesus Christ Was born a Jew* kindly appealed to the Jews to embrace the gospel. Later, the impending Judgment Day compelled Luther to appeal to the authorities to protect Christendom against those groups that continually chose not to convert and opposed the gospel. Heiko Oberman explains,

> [Luther] spoke to the Christian authorities: the Last Judgment is fast approaching, so woe to those temporal rulers who have neglected their duty to protect Christendom! Now is the time for defense against the storm troopers of the Antichrist, whether they descend upon Christendom from the outside in the form of the Turks, subvert the preaching of the Gospel and order in the empire from inside the Church like the pope and clerics beholden to him, or, like the Jews, undermine the public welfare from the inside. Luther had discovered this concatenation of Jews, pope, and Turks as the unholy coalition of the enemies of God long before he began leveling his massive assaults on the Jews. Now that the terrors of the Last Days had been unleashed, the Church and temporal authorities were forced into their own defensive battle, one without the promise of victory but with the prospects of survival.[54]

Luther's harsh language

Some think that Luther's harsh language against the Jews was unique, but it is to be mentioned that his language against the Papacy was much stronger, and his words against the Turks and false brethren were almost as strong. The polemics of the older Luther against the Turks and Protestant opponents are only slightly more restrained. Against each of these opponents—Catholics, Turks, other Protestants and Jews—he occasionally passed on libelous tales and gave credence to improbable charges. In all these respects Luther treated the Jews no differently than he treated his other opponents.[55]

---

[53] 'As he grew older, Luther became increasingly convinced that Satan had rallied many forces against him and the gospel's cause. Papists, Turks, other Protestants . . . and Jews were to him Satan's agents attacking the gospel he had rediscovered'—E. Gritsch, 'The Unrefined Reformer,' *Christian History* 39. 12.3, 36.

[54] Oberman, *Luther*, 294. Oberman, *Impact of the Reformation*, 56, 'Luther as the reformer cannot be understood unless he is seen located between God and the devil, who have been involved in a struggle—not in a *metaphysical* but *a real* battle—ever since the beginning of the world—a battle which now "in these last days" is reaching a horrible climax. As the assiduous reader of Augustine and Bernard, Luther knew that after the first phase of persecutions in the Roman empire and the second phase of attacks by heretics assailing the church from without, in the third phase the enemy would come from within, when the antichrist would successfully disguise himself as the *vicarious Christi*.'

[55] Edwards, *Luther's Last Battles*, 140; cf. Grisar: *Luther*, 4.287-88.

Oberman traces Luther's harsh language as far back as a sermon preached in 1515, thus showing the *young* Luther used the same type of speech as the *old* Luther. Oberman provides insight in pointing out, 'In the total historical context, . . . Luther's scatology-permeated language has to be taken seriously as an expression of the painful battle fought body and soul against the Adversary, who threatens both flesh and spirit.'[56] Luther's rough language was, therefore, a weapon to use against the devil. '[A]ll true Christians stand in a large anti-defamation league and are called upon to combat the God-awful, filthy adversary, using his own weapons and his own strategy: "Get lost Satan."'[57] Since Luther felt Satan was the mastermind behind works-centered religions (like Judaism), Luther attacks those religions using Satan's own weapons against him.[58]

For Luther, his use of scatological language exposes the devil, who has hidden himself in the papacy, behind the Turks, and in the theology of Judaism. Since it is the Last Days, Satan must be resisted with all one's might, with as much energy and all the vehemence possible. By exposing Satan in these systems, Satan becomes enraged and fights harder against God. By fighting harder, the Last Day approaches quicker.[59]

Luther also felt he was following the example of Christ. Luther asks rhetorically if the Lord used abusive language against his enemies: 'Was he abusive when he called the Jews an adulterous and perverse generation, an offspring of vipers, hypocrites, and children of the Devil? . . . The truth, which one is conscious of possessing, cannot be patient against its obstinate and intractable enemies.'[60] In similar fashion, Luther responded to his opponent Latomus,

> I have never insisted that anyone consider me modest or holy, but only that everyone recognize what the gospel is. If they do this, I give anyone freedom to attack my life to his heart's content. My boast is that I have injured no one's life or repu-

---

[56] Oberman, *Luther*, 108-109. Paul Althaus, *Theology of Martin Luther*, 162-63, summarizes Luther's view of Satan: 'It is the devil who stands behind all enemies of the word, behind the misinterpretation of Scripture, behind all false doctrine and sects, and behind philosophy. He cannot bear the pure word and the true doctrine and attempts to falsify them: particularly to falsify their decisive content, justification through faith alone.'

[57] Oberman, *The Impact*, 61.

[58] Grisar, *Luther*, 4.286, provides examples: 'The "devil" also is drawn into the fray the better to enable Luther to vent his ire against the Jews. At the end of the passage just quoted he says: "For the devil has entered into the Jews and holds them captive so that perforce they do his will, as St. Paul says, mocking, defaming, abusing and cursing God and everything that is His. . . . The devil plays with them to their eternal damnation."

[59] Cf. Oberman, *The Impact*, 63.

[60] Martin Luther, cited in Gritsch, 'The Unrefined Reformer,' 36.

tation, but only sharply reproached, as godless and sacrilegious, those assertions, inventions, and doctrines which are against the Word of God. I do not apologize for this, for I have good precedents. John the Baptist [Luke 3.7] and Christ after him [Matt. 23.33] called the Pharisees the 'offspring of vipers'. So excessive and outrageous was this abuse of such learned, holy, powerful, and honored men that they said in reply that He had a demon [Jn. 7.20]. . . . Elsewhere Christ calls them 'blind' [Matt. 23.16], 'crooked,' 'liars,' 'sons of the devil' [John 8.44, 55]. Good God, even Paul lacked evangelical modesty when he anathematized the teachers of the Galatians [Gal. 1.8] who were, I suppose, great men. Others he calls 'dogs' [Phil. 3.2], 'empty talkers' [Tit. 1.10], 'deceivers' [Col. 2.4, 8]. Further, he accused to his face the magician Elymas with being a 'son of the devil, full of all deceit and villainy' [Acts 13.10].[61]

'Luther was a product of his times. The writers of his day were unrestrained by modern standards. It is important to note that Luther did not reserve this harsh language for the Jews alone. Luther called princes, "the greatest fools and worst knaves on earth," monks, "tame dogs that lie on pillows and whistle with their hind ends". He also said of his own people: "I know that we Germans are brutes and stupid swine." . . . This rough, graphic language was the style of the day: Luther was by no means the worst: Luther delighted less in muck than many of the literary men of his age.'[62] The vulgarity of Luther in his tracts against Jews, then, is of no special significance.

The historical setting and the anti-Jewishness of Luther's time

Luther was not the first to speak unkindly about the Jews. The Romans disliked them, Christians slaughtered thousands of them during the Crusades. In 1290 England expelled them, thirty years later France did likewise. In 1492 they were murdered and expelled from Spain. Bainton says, 'If similar tracts did not appear in England, France, and Spain in Luther's day, it was because the Jews had already been completely expelled from these countries.'[63]

Johann Eck, also, wrote some virulent anti-Jewish tracts.[64] 'The absolute champion of anti-Jewish polemic in the early modern period was Luther's Catholic opponent Johannes Eck, whose 1541 *Refutation of a Jew Book* was "a summa of the anti-Jewish literature of the Middle Ages, leaving out no accusation of genocide, blasphemy, or treason".'[65] The Catholic Church of Luther's

---

[61] *LW* 32.141.
[62] Montgomery, *In Defense of Martin Luther* (Milwaukee: NPH, 1970), 144.
[63] Bainton, *Here I Stand*, 297.
[64] Most of Johann Eck's writings were in Latin, but some feel that since his anti-Jewish writings were written in German, they were intended for a popular audience; cf. Edwards, *Luther's Last Battles*, 120.
[65] Lindberg, 'Tainted Greatness,' 17.

time doesn't have a spotless record of defending the Jews and other groups against intolerance and hatred. 'In 1553 all copies of the Talmud found in Rome were burned in public. Pope Paul IV (1555-1559) ordered measures to be taken against the Jews, and twenty-four men and one woman were burned at the stake. On July 12, 1555, he issued a bull that renewed all the oppressive medieval legislation against the Jews, excluding them from professions, limiting their financial and commercial activities, forbidding them to own real estate, and humiliating them by obliging them to wear yellow hats.'[66]

Reflections: Christ and the Jews

Martin Luther was a sinful human being, and his writings against his opponents, especially against the Jews, show this. However, to reason that Luther's work is somehow nullified because of his anti-Jewish writings is perhaps an argument for an impossible standard. As I would stand against Peter's denial, Solomon's idolatry, David's adultery and conspiracy to murder, so I would stand against Luther's anti-Jewish writings. That a holy God chooses to use sinful men to accomplish his will is an example of his mysterious divine providence.

Simply because Luther was wrong on his attitude toward the Jews does not necessarily mean he was wrong on the need for church reform, the proclamation of the gospel of justification by faith alone (*sola fide*), the uniqueness of Christ for salvation (*solus Christus, sola gratia*), or the hermeneutical principle of *sola scriptura*. Luther was a man of many faults. Nevertheless, believers in Jesus Christ are challenged in several ways by Luther's position towards the Jews.

> (1) In Luther's view the bad example of the papacy with its self-righteousness was a hindrance for Jews to become believers in Christ. Being, instead, a good example of God's love and compassion, an example of true words and godly deeds, Jews could become more and more open to listen to the gospel-truth of Jesus, as their Messiah and Savior, their Lord and God (Jn. 20.28).
>
> (2) Compassion, endurance, kindness are necessary while sharing the gospel with Jews.

---

[66] Spitz: *The Protestant Reformation*, 357. Owen Chadwick likewise documents this: 'He forced every Jew to wear a yellow hat and live in a ghetto with only one exit . . . He caused to be published the first Index of prohibited books. . . . Sixtus of Siena was sent to Cremona, where there was a great Hebrew school (for the destruction of the Talmud was ordered), and reported that he had burnt a store of 12,000 volumes. . . . Under an Inquisition with extended powers, and a pope ready to suspect everyone, there was almost a reign of terror in the city.'—Owen Chadwick, *The Reformation* (New York: 1964), 271.

(3) The uniqueness of Christ and the salvation in him has to be deeply understood by everybody who ministers among Jews. Luther's emphasis on these central issues should to be discussed and reflected. Luther had stressed the one way of salvation in the crucified and resurrected Christ. Is there any second or even a third way of salvation 'without faith in Christ' (as a matter of *revelatio generalis*), e.g., for Jews, because of their relationship to Jahweh from biblical times on? Luther rejected this view, stressing, as he did, the center of reformation theology—justification by faith in Christ.

Luther is a warning example to anybody who is active in evangelizing Jews. He started somehow well in 1510, 1514 and 1523, and ended tragically in 1537 and in the 1540s. Today's missionaries among Jewish people should be aware that there could be frustration ahead in their ministry, because the conversion of Jews needs patience and endurance. Quick conversions are usually not to be expected.

Luther's theology is still a challenge. His teaching was clearly not inerrant, nor his writing inspired. He was terribly wrong in his cruel teaching on the Jews. But even as a sinner his emphasis on the uniqueness of Christ, on salvation, on justification by faith in Christ without works or merit should be discussed in fulfilling the task of evangelizing the world which is without hope without Christ.

CHAPTER 4

Luther as a practical theologian: his input into the 1527 Visitation[1]

Brett James Muhlhan

In their *Primer on Practical Theology* Heyns and Pieterse make what could be an interesting assertion for the Luther student.

> The reformer Martin Luther concurred with Duns Scotus by rejecting the distinction between 'theoretical' and 'practical' and declaring all true theology to be practical. Although he did not recognize practical theology as an independent discipline, this did not mean that the subject did not feature.[2]

The inference that Luther rejected the 'distinction between "theoretical" and "practical" theology' and that practical theology 'featured' in his labors as theologian and pastor have been well enforced.[3] Michael Parsons has convincingly shown Luther's practical/pastoral concerns to be of central significance to his theological work.[4] Yet, the way in which Heyns and Pieterse are appealing to Luther here as a practical theologian is of a distinct type; a type that distances itself from the general understanding of practical theology—for instance, that developed in Wengert's work sub-titled *Essays on Martin Luther's Practical Theology*.[5] Therefore, the question this raises is whether the definitions offered by Heyns and Pieterse correlate with the general understanding of Luther as a 'practical theologian'. Can Pieterse and Heyns' inclusion of Luther into their practical theological heritage be sustained? An *a priori* working hypothesis of what follows will contend for an answer of both yes and no.

Can Martin Luther be seen as a practical theologian in accordance with the current 'new perspective' definition of the discipline? The answer will largely

---

[1] This paper was originally presented at the 12th International Luther Congress in Helsinki, 2012.
[2] L.M. Heyns and H.J.C. Pieterse, *A Primer in Practical Theology* (Pretoria, SA: Gnosis, 1990), 85.
[3] See T.J. Wengert, *The Pastoral Luther: Essays on Martin Luther's Practical Theology* (Grand Rapids: Eerdmans, 2009).
[4] See, for example, M. Parsons, *Martin Luther's Interpretation of the Royal Psalms. The Spiritual Kingdom in a Pastoral Context* (New York: Edwin Mellen, 2009), 14.
[5] Wengert, *The Pastoral Luther*.

depend on an ability to arrive at consolidating a definition that is accepted by the parties within the new perspective on practical theology. With this in mind, the study will then investigate a significant historical situation (*praxis*) in which Luther was involved in bringing to bear a specific theological theory (*theoria*)—the 1527 Saxon Visitation. An analysis of Luther's role in shaping the Visitation, the Visitation Articles and the resultant catechisms reveal both a correspondence and a dissonance with the new perspective on practical theology's methodology. These two aspects will then be reviewed in light of both the theoretical underpinning that Luther provided the Visitation (his doctrine of freedom) and the way in which this theory shaped, and was shaped by the Wittenbergers' investigation of the praxis. One of the primary justifications for pursuing this course of investigation is that Luther, himself, seems to suggest that he is somewhat of a precursor to the new perspective's understanding of practical theology as Heyns and Pieterse contend. Luther says, 'True theology is practical, and its foundation is Christ, whose death is appropriated to us through faith.'[6]

The new perspective on practical theology

The 1974 publication of Klostermann and Zerfass' collection of essays, *Praktische Theologie heute*, marked a distinct literary beginning for a new perspective on practical theology.[7] This new perspective defined itself as a discrete academic discipline in its own right and in doing so distanced itself from a number of similar paradigms. It is here that the question of Luther as practical theologian becomes more complex than is often assumed. Pieterse makes a statement that seems to incorporate a number of perspectives on practical theology with the following: 'Practical Theology studies the *practice* of the communication of the gospel, the mediating of the Word of God to people in order to help them to accept Jesus Christ as their savior, to mature faith and to become disciples of the Lord.'[8] He says this, though, within a literary context that makes very concrete distinctions. The most obvious of these distinctions is the way in which the new perspective on practical theology defines itself over against the pastoral/clerical model and the ecclesiastical model. It seems obvious that Luther would support any method that encourages the 'communication of the gospel'. Yet, Luther's support for the new perspective on practical theology may have waned once he learned that his cherished shepherd/pastor-flock (*Seelsorge*) framework for church was being undermined.

---

[6] *LW* 54.22.
[7] See D.A. van Oudtshoorn, 'Video as effektiewe Bedieningsmiddel in die Plaaslike Gemeente' (unpublished dissertation: University of South Africa, 1988), 221. See, also, Pieterse, *Contextual Theology for Ministry* (Perth Bible College: Visiting Scholar Lectures, 2011) 8.
[8] H. Pieterse, *Contextual Theology for Ministry* (Perth: Snowgoose Media, 2010), 1.

ASPECTS OF REFORMING

While it seems that the pastoral model existed from the earliest of Christian times, Pieterse recognizes that, as a distinct university discipline, this model can only be traced as far back as 1774, when the theologian, Rautenstrauch, headed up a new faculty at the University of Vienna, Austria. For the first time, at least in an explicit academic sense, the practice of the pastor was examined through the means of theological and scientific inquiry. Pieterse says, 'From the outset this new university discipline was seen as the method, skills, and tactics learnt by the pastor to exercise his practical ministry expertly and competently.'[9] However, though the pastoral model seems to concur largely with the Wittenberg method, the new perspective on practical theology is quite critical of it. Pieterse represents this well in the following,

> From hindsight today, we must evaluate this approach critically. This approach created the so-called shepherd-flock congregations where the pastor knows everything and the church members are inactive minors (sheep in the metaphor shepherd-flock) that just have to listen and follow the pastor.[10]

While there is enough anecdotal and academic evidence to support this claim, it seems there is similarly enough evidence to suggest that the shepherd-flock model has been sufficient for genuine Christian community.[11] One could ask whether the misconstrual of a biblical image for church by some abrogates its effectiveness for all. It is plain here that the new perspective on practical theology wants to go beyond the traditional pastoral model even if it means undermining it to some degree.

Another way in which the new perspective on practical theology defines itself negatively is in the distancing of itself from the ecclesiological model. The way in which the ecclesiological model differs from the pastoral, is that it expands its focus to include both pastor and congregation in its investigation. This broader perspective is attributed to the practical theologian, Anton Graf (1814-1867). According to Pieterse, Graf 'saw Practical Theology as the science of the maintenance, building and fulfilment of the Church. The fundamental principles of his thinking are both ecclesiastic and scientific.'[12] One of the benefits of this broadening of perspective is that it takes seriously into consideration each member of the congregation, their gifts and the way in which each member contributes through their actions. Added to this is that the ecclesiological model developed a means of studying the way in which a congregation's actions affected each member and in what manner this interrelated context is influenced by their particular cultural matrix. In Pieterse's words, '[I]t asked for a

---

[9] Pieterse, *Contextual Theology*, 2.
[10] Pieterse, *Contextual Theology*, 3. Pieterse goes as far as saying that the pastoral model was partly responsible for the situation in Nazi Germany and for the apathy of the church during the South African apartheid.
[11] See Wengert, *The Pastoral Luther*.
[12] Pieterse, *Contextual Theology*, 4.

communication of the gospel that fits into the problems, questions and terminology of the people.'[13] According to this definition, then, Luther's driving convictions about the need for the German people of his time to be given the opportunity to hear and read the gospel in their own language serves as an example of resonance with the ecclesiological model.

Yet, practical theology, as a new perspective, is keen to move beyond both pastoral and ecclesiological models, in an attempt to engage pastor, congregation and the world in which they live and relate. Browning quotes Farley in this regard, 'Farley's emphasis upon centering practical theology on a phenomenology of "ecclesial presence" is designed to shift away from exclusive concentration upon the internal life of the church and accentuate more the life of the church in the world.'[14] Farley speaks for himself, 'Ecclesiology in the narrower sense and themes of the church, its ministries, and tasks of ministry should have their thematization within this larger theme of the world-transforming character of ecclesiality.'[15]

In a section below, this study will examine this methodology more closely; for now, it demonstrates one of the key distinctions that the new perspective on practical theology makes concerning other paradigms. The new perspective is keen to examine all aspects of the gospel's communicative process in an effort to improve this communication, and by implication, to bring to bear the transformative power of the gospel to pastor, church and the world in which they live and relate.[16]

One of the primary concerns for the new perspective on practical theology is that the theory of the church remains in a constant creative tension with its praxis and the unique contexts in which these two exist. In this way, the pastor and the church are held accountable for the base and operational theories that influence its impact on any given praxis. Added to an emphasis on accountability is the notion that the maintenance of a dynamic tension between theory and praxis will lend itself to genuine transformative action. Pattinson and Woodward elaborate on this: 'Practical theology is often deeply committed to the notion of understanding leading to and from action, or praxis. This means that it aspires to be transformative in both theory and practice.'[17] This infers, then, that rather than a pastor or such bringing to bear a concrete theory on a congre-

---

[13] Pieterse, *Contextual Theology*, 4.
[14] D.S. Browning (ed.), *Practical Theology* (San Francisco: Harper & Row, 1983), 10.
[15] E. Farley, 'Theology and practice outside the clerical paradigm' in Browning, *Practical Theology*, 39.
[16] D.A. Smith, *The Preaching Community* (unpublished dissertation: University of Pretoria, 2007), 5, concurs: 'Practical theology is the study concerning the improvement of human-divine interactive communicative actions involved in the service of the gospel.'
[17] S. Pattinson and J. Woodward, 'An Introduction to Pastoral and Practical Theology' in James Woodward and Stephen Pattison (eds), *The Blackwell Reader in Pastoral and Practical Theology* (New Jersey: Blackwell, 2000), 11.

gation in a monological and authoritative posture, an engagement with the praxis (both congregation and its cultural context) may in fact re-shape the original theory in an effort to improve the communicative event. It attempts to introduce—by way of theological, philosophical and scientific means—a sense of humility into a dialogical framework that seeks to understand the theoretical presuppositions of all aspects of the praxis. The question this raises in regard to whether Luther can be appealed to as a practical theologian along these lines will be examined below when we ask about his theory for action and the unique praxis events he was involved with during the Visitation. To assist this process it is necessary to draw some principal conclusions about the new perspective on practical theology so as to act as a framework for guidance.

First, practical theology is the practical application of theology to everyday life.[18] Richard Osmer explains that the four key questions and tasks in practical theology which will assist our analysis of the Visitation are: (1) What is going on? (the descriptive-empirical task); (2) Why is this going on? (the interpretative task); (3) What ought to be going on? (the normative task) and (4) How might we respond? (the pragmatic task).[19] Another helpful principle is a definition of practical theology offered by Heyns and Pieterse that seems to track well with Luther's pastoral heart, 'Practical theology is that part of theology that concerns itself with this event—the encounter between God and humanity—and particularly with the role of human beings in this encounter.'[20]

To propose that Luther was deeply concerned about the encounter between God and humanity would be an understatement in light of his passion and life's work. However, what emphasis he placed on the 'role of human beings' in this encounter will need to be unpacked in light of the Visitation as a series of praxis situations and, of course, the interaction of the theological theories of both Luther and Melanchthon.

To summarize thus far, it seems clear that the new perspective on practical theology, while holding some common ground with the older perspectives, intends making several concrete distinctions about its methodology. This methodology drives an effort to both define itself as a discipline in its own right and to engage the church and its context with a transformative gospel. In defining itself, the new perspective questions two of the more traditional approaches to pastoral/practical ministry. The pastoral model (clerical) and the ecclesiological model (congregational) are incorporated, with varying degrees of criticism, into

---

[18] Heitink's definition is much broader, 'Practical theology consists of several related sub-fields: applied theology (such as missions, evangelism, pastoral psychology or the psychology of religion), church growth, administration, homiletics, spiritual formation, pastoral theology, spiritual direction, spiritual theology, political theology, theology of justice and peace and similar areas' (G. Heitink, *Practical Theology: history, theory, action domains: manual for practical theology* (Grand Rapids: Eerdmans, 1999), 6.

[19] R.R. Osmer, *Practical Theology: Introduction* (Grand Rapids: Eerdmans, 2008), 4.

[20] Heyns and Pieterse, *A Primer*, 6.

a much broader framework that makes the cultural and worldly context a legitimate dialogue partner. The central aspect of this framework is the intentional holding together of the theory-praxis tension, which is expected to generate a continuous dialogue between both pastoral and ecclesiastical theory with the concrete communicative contexts with which they live and interact. Heyns offers his own helpful summary:

> From its particular vantage point [practical theology] studies the object of all theology, namely people's faith and their religious statements about God. The focus is particularly on those religious actions designed to mediate God's coming to humankind—in other words, actions that enable people to hear the gospel properly and to understand, accept and actualize it in their lives.[21]

The question that presents itself from here on, then, is in what sense does Luther's role in the Visitation correspond with these distinct principles and more specifically—while keeping a keen eye on avoiding anachronism—did Luther in some way exercise an implicit understanding of the theory-praxis tension?

The 1527 Visitation

In a letter to Nicholas Hausmann, dated 13 July 1527, Luther declared 'the visitation has begun'.[22] Two months later, in a letter to Spalatin, he would indicate that he had reviewed and approved the Visitation Instructions drafted by Melanchthon.[23] The Saxon Visitation, according to Luther's 1528 Preface to these Instructions, clearly outlines a theory/praxis tension with regard to the collateral impact the evangelical movement had effected with the removal of the Roman system (interpretive task). Luther says,

> Now that the gospel through the unspeakable grace and mercy of God has again come to us or in fact has appeared for the first time, and we have come to see how grievously the Christian church has been confused, scattered, and torn, we would like to have seen the true Episcopal office and practice of visitation re-established because of the pressing need.[24]

Luther's belief/theory in the genuine place of the episcopal office and its role in building up the health of the Christian community was set in definite tension with the reality of the praxis. Once the dust had settled after the travesty of the Peasant's War, the Wittenberg community—especially Luther—by means of a

---

[21] Heyns and Pieterse, *A Primer*, 10.
[22] P. Smith, *Luther's Correspondence and other Contemporary Letters* (Philadelphia: Lutheran Publication Society, 1918), 408.
[23] Smith, *Luther's Correspondence*, 410.
[24] *LW* 40.271 (*WA* 26.197).

number of complaints and several minor visitations came to realize the extent of the devastation left by the Romanists and their particular theories of practice.

According to Luther, the divinely-ordained offices of Archbishop, Bishop and Pastor, and the responsibilities they implied, had been thoroughly abrogated by the Romanists (interpretive-empirical task). Luther sums up the situation thus,

> In brief this is what befell so worthy an office and nothing remained of it except the burdening and banning of people because of money, debts, and temporal goods and the making of a divine order out of the bellowing of antiphons and versicles in churches. No attention is paid to how one teaches, believes, loves, how one lives a Christian life, how to care for the poor, how one comforts the weak, or punishes the unruly, and whatever else belongs to such an office. They are altogether officious and gluttonous fellows who destroy what belongs to the people and do worse than nothing for them. This office has fared like all holy and ancient Christian doctrine and order—it has become the farce and contempt of the devil and Antichrist with awful and terrible destruction of souls.[25]

Instead of finding a 'divinely wholesome' work from an ordained office (normative task), in his later Preface to his Small Catechism Luther reflects on the stark reality of a theory gone wrong.

> The deplorable, wretched deprivation that I recently encountered while I was a visitor [22 Oct 1528–9 Jan 1529] has constrained and compelled me to prepare this catechism, or Christian instruction. Dear God what misery I beheld! The ordinary person, especially in the villages, knows absolutely nothing about the Christian faith, and unfortunately, many pastors (*Pfarrherr*) are completely unskilled and incompetent teachers.[26]

The theory/praxis tension for Luther in this situation is not simply the neglect of the office by the Romanists (interpretive task), but that his own doctrine of freedom (normative task), the return of the gospel, was being mastered by the ordinary people into the fine art of 'misusing all their freedom'.[27]

This prompted Luther to revise his pastoral theory, or more specifically, to nuance it to accommodate a grave situation (pragmatic task).[28] Where Luther had held the spiritual government of Christ and the temporal government of the prince in a distinct, but not separate, tension, he now, with a fair degree of anx-

---

[25] *LW* 40.270 (*WA* 26.196).
[26] R. Kolb and T.J. Wengert, *The Book of Concord: The Confessions of the Evangelical Lutheran Church* (Minneapolis: Fortress, 2000), 347.
[27] Kolb and Wengert, *The Book of Concord*, 348.
[28] At a later stage, it will be necessary to make clear the difference between confessional theory and doctrinal theory. Luther was free to nuance doctrinal theory but was not prepared to move from the confessional convictions he found in the Scriptures. This point draws attention to a possible weakness with the new perspective on practical theology as below.

iety, called on the prince (Elector John) to take up a spiritual challenge. The broad theoretical framework that allowed Luther to do this was his tried and tested doctrine of freedom. Luther called on John to conduct a visitation, not because he was a Christian and not because he was the temporal authority, but because he was a Christian authority. To some degree, Luther saw this as the only option, given the desperate nature of things with the church at the time. Grimm adds,

> It was a dangerous step [Elector John and the Visitation] and the entering wedge of a new caesaropapacy—the rule of statecraft over priesthood. But it seemed to be the only available help under the circumstances, and certainly served a very useful purpose. Luther had full confidence in the God-fearing Elector, that he would not abuse the authority thus temporarily conferred on him.[29]

In this way, Luther demonstrates an ability to move—as per practical theological methodology—from theory to praxis and back to theory which indicates, in some way, an ability to work with the theory/praxis tension. In an added sense, Luther, also, demonstrates an implicit sense of practical theological methodology in his ability to move beyond the sphere of the church and into his worldly/temporal context. Estes supports this and brings the important Melanchthon into the discussion, 'Luther and Melanchthon both started with the assumption that Christian princes had an appropriate role to play in the achievement of the religious reforms that the bishops had signally failed to provide.'[30]

The failure of Romanist theory and its woeful effect on Saxon ecclesiastical praxis, prompted the Wittenbergers—particularly, Luther and Melanchthon—to understand their own praxis of Christian community in light of their theoretical criteria. Even after the struggle of the 1524-1525 Peasants' War, Luther was still compelled to nuance his theoretical anxieties about involving the territorial prince in the hope that it would only be a temporary necessity.[31]

In summary, it seems that Luther's involvement in the recognition, instigation and theoretical underpinning of the 1527 Saxon Visitation, resembles the theory-praxis-theory schema of the new perspective on practical theology, as outlined by Osmer above. This will be critically analyzed further in a following section; for now, it is worth noting a degree of correspondence in the methods used by the Wittenbergers and the new perspective's methodology.

To examine this statement more closely, a process is needed for understanding how Luther's doctrine of freedom, as a theory for transformation, underpinned the development of Melanchthon's *Instructions for the Visitors of Par-*

---

[29] H.J. Grimm, *The Reformation Era: 1500-1650* (New York: Macmillan, 1973), 547.
[30] J.M. Estes, 'The Role of the Godly Magistrate in the Church: Melanchthon as Luther's interpreter and collaborator,' *CH* 67.3 (1998), 463–83.
[31] Estes, 'The Role of the Godly Magistrate,' 481, adds, 'There is ample evidence that Luther was still anxious lest the magisterial authority in the church that he had now so positively endorsed be abused and that he continued to dream of a church with a greater degree of administrative independence than circumstances would allow.'

ish Pastors in Electoral Saxony.[32] Following proponents of the new perspective's assertion that they are concerned primarily with the 'improvement of divine-human' communicative events, it seems reasonable to suggest that this is exactly what drove the core convictions of Luther and his colleagues. What follows, then, is an overview and analysis of the way in which Luther's doctrine of freedom manifests itself in Melanchthon's theoretical, preparatory response to the crisis of visitation.

Luther's doctrine of freedom as theory for transforming praxis

A close reading of the *Visitation Articles* reveals a striking consistency between what Melanchthon wrote here and what Luther had defined as a Christian way of freedom in his 1520 *De Libertate Christiana*. While there are many instances in which Luther brings his theory of freedom to bear on a specific praxis throughout 1520-1527 (especially the 1522 Wittenberg iconoclastic crisis and the 1524-1525 Peasants' War) it seems most felicitous to see Luther's doctrine of freedom in action during the Visitation. As stated so far, there seems to be a level of correspondence between how the new perspective on practical theology defines itself and the way in which the Wittenberg community, led by Luther, manifests a theory-praxis-theory framework for transformation. What follows will be an overview of how Luther's doctrine of freedom (*Freiheitsbegriff*) in its fivefold structure, underpins the Visitation Articles. Rather than seeing a major disjunction between Luther and Melanchthon here, this approach takes Luther at his word when he suggests that he is in full agreement with the way in which Melanchthon had written up the instructions. In a letter to Spalatin, dated 19 August 1527, Luther states clearly that 'the visitation acts are fine'.[33] Therefore, Luther has no problem with the articles, in the sense that they are in general agreement with his doctrine of freedom. However, our analysis may reveal several nuances being weighted in other directions due to the impact the praxis of the visitation had on the Wittenberg theory of Christian freedom.

The law is the first of two indicative principles in Luther's doctrine of freedom. In the *Freedom Tractate*, he states it thus:

> Here we must point out that the entire Scripture of God is divided into two parts: commandments and promises. Although the commandments teach things that are good, the things taught are not done as soon as they are taught, for the commandments show us what we ought to do but do not give us the power to do it. They are intended to teach man [sic] to know himself, that through them he may recognize his inability to do good and may despair of his own ability.[34]

The Visitation Articles capitalize on this aspect of the law/gospel distinction in an effort to overcome the abuse of Luther's doctrine of freedom by antinomian-

---

[32] *LW* 40.269–320 (*WA* 26.195–240).
[33] Smith, *Luther's Correspondence*, 410.
[34] *LW* 31.348.

ism.[35] What has changed for the theory is that repentance and penance are now magnified as a causal link between law and gospel. The Articles read as follows.

> These two are the first elements of Christian life: Repentance or contrition and grief, and faith through which we receive the forgiveness of sins and are righteous before God. Both should grow and increase in us. The third element of Christian life is the doing of good works.[36]

The law drives repentance, contrition and grief while faith receives the promise of the forgiveness of sins (gospel). From here, and only in this order—as per the *Freedom Tractate*—can Melanchthon then speak/write of good works. So the imperative that looms large throughout the Visitation Articles, in response to antinomianism, is based firmly on Luther's law/gospel distinction.

The second element of the Christian life according to the Visitation Articles, the gospel, is the core component in Luther's doctrine of freedom. However, where Luther makes the gospel the key/explicit/central pillar of his doctrine of freedom in the *Tractate*, it seems to exist at an implicit level throughout the Articles. In the *Freedom Tractate* Luther develops the priority of the gospel under a threefold framework (the threefold power of faith).[37] Yet, in the Articles, it exists, implicitly, as forgiveness of sins or, more broadly, the concept of promise.[38] It seems reasonable, then, to conclude that, given the priority of praxis, Melanchthon's use of Luther's doctrine of freedom presupposes Luther's priority for the gospel (justification by faith) but is compelled by the praxis to shift the emphasis onto the imperatives contained in Luther's doctrine of freedom.

While all three imperatives are contained within the Visitation Articles, the priority is given to the official-social aspect of Luther's doctrine of freedom. This priority is in line with Luther's understanding of the eschatological tension, which he summarizes under his twofold thesis on Christian freedom. As per the way in which the doctrine of freedom functioned throughout the confrontation with the radicals during 1522-1525, the emphasis slowly shifted, because of the shifting nature of the praxis, to move from the personal imperative, through the personal-social imperative and, finally, to place an emphasis on the official-social imperative.[39]

Because of Luther's realistic perception of the now/not-yet eschatological tension, he could affirm the place of commandment in the Christian life, his

---

[35] Luther alluded to the threat/possibility of antinomianism in the appendix (*Anhang*) of his Latin version of the Freedom Tractate (*LW* 31.371–77).
[36] *LW* 40.277 (*WA* 26.203–204). See, also, *LW* 40.293–97 (*WA* 26.217–22).
[37] See *LW* 31.344–58.
[38] See *LW* 40.274, 275, 278 (*WA* 26.202, 205).
[39] For a detailed analysis of Luther's doctrine of freedom, including its fivefold structure, see B. Muhlhan, *Being Shaped by Freedom* (Eugene Oregon: Pickwick, 2012).

personal imperative. After developing the fundamental structures of law and gospel, Luther can, then, say,

> Here we shall answer all those who, offended by the word 'faith' and by all that has been said, now ask, 'If faith does all things and is alone sufficient unto righteousness, why then are good works commanded? We will take our ease and do no works and be content with faith.' I answer: not so, you wicked men, not so. That would indeed be proper if we were wholly inner and perfectly spiritual men. But such we shall be only at the last day, the day of the resurrection of the dead. As long as we live in the flesh we only begin to make some progress in that which shall be perfected in the future life.[40]

The Visitation Articles track with this thought wherever it highlights the need for prayer and other good works.[41] This principle, the third in Luther's fivefold schema on freedom, is a direct attack on the possibility of antinomianism. Yet, it seems at the time of the Visitation, that the situation called for a stronger approach, which seems to suggest, as per the Wittenberg iconoclastic crisis of 1522, that the personal imperative for good works—that they flow from justification by faith—had been abrogated in some sense.

Another aspect that appears to highlight that the given praxis encountered during the Visitation had an effect of Luther's doctrine of freedom, as a theory for transformation, is that the personal-social imperative (Luther's fourth principle of freedom) is, also, given a subordinate place. Luther develops the personal-social imperative, the servant love of the neighbor as a major aspect of genuine Christian freedom. In fact, Luther would go as far as saying in the *Freedom Tractate*, that if one did not do good work for the neighbor, then one's faith status as a Christian was suspect, just as the fruit of a tree says something specific about the tree itself.[42] The Articles correspond to this 'fourth principle' in the following,

> So they especially who bear the name of Christian should do this in love which willingly bears all burdens, and gives beyond what is due, which pays, even when burdened unjustly, and seeks no revenge through its own powers, as Christ teaches in Matt. 5[.39].[43]

This principle, though explicit in the *Freedom Tractate*, and of central concern for Luther in rectifying the iconoclastic crisis, exists in the Visitation Articles but is overshadowed by an overwhelming emphasis on Luther's fifth principle of freedom, his official-social imperative.

---

[40] *LW* 31.358.

[41] *LW* 40.277.

[42] 'We conclude, therefore, that a Christian lives not in himself, but in Christ and in his neighbor. Otherwise he is not a Christian. He lives in Christ through faith, in his neighbor through love. By faith he is caught up beyond himself into God. By love he descends beneath himself into his neighbor' (*LW* 31.371).

[43] *LW* 31.286.

Luther's official-social imperative concludes the fivefold framework of his doctrine of freedom. Research has shown that while Luther added the official-social imperative into his doctrine of freedom as early as 1520, it was most certainly then subordinated to the personal and person-social imperatives that are formed under the government of Christ. On the way in which a Christian relates under the temporal government, Luther says in the *Freedom Tractate,*

> Of the same nature are the precepts which Paul gives in Rom. 13[.1-7], namely, that Christians should be subject to the governing authorities and be ready to do every good work, not that they shall in this way be justified, since they already are righteous through faith, but that in the liberty of the Spirit they shall by so doing serve others and the authorities themselves and obey their will freely and out of love.[44]

This element of Luther's doctrine of freedom would undergo major revision and expansion during the 1522-1525 radical crises. This expansion set the tone for the theological theory that underpinned much of the Visitation Articles. As per the Peasant's War, Luther understood the situation of the Visitation to be so grave and of such dire consequence that the only way forward was the direct intervention of the temporal ruler. It is, also, possible to add that Luther may not have had too much choice in the Elector's involvement due to the fact that it was his territory and his subjects under Visitation.[45]

Luther's official-social imperative runs as a thread throughout both his preface and Melanchthon's articles. Luther says,

> We have respectfully appealed to the illustrious and noble prince and lord, John, Duke of Saxony, First Marshall and Elector of the Roman Empire, Landgrave of Thuringia, Margrave of Meissen, our most gracious lord and prince, constituted of God as our certain temporal sovereign, that out of Christian love (since he is not obligated to do so as a temporal sovereign) and by God's will for the benefit of the gospel and the welfare of the wretched Christians in his territory, His Electoral grace might call and ordain to this office several competent persons.[46]

Luther, here, resonates with Paul's insistence in Romans 13 that the temporal authority has its basis in God's constitution. What is important to remember, here, is that Luther sees that the devastation of the church left by the Romanists—via the thorough abrogation of the office of Bishop and priest—can only be remedied by the intervention of the authority in the re-institution of the ministerial office. That Luther and Melanchthon have a high regard for the purpose

---

[44] *LW* 31.369.
[45] See Grimm, *The Reformation Era*, 127.
[46] *LW* 40.271 (*WA* 26.197). See, also, *LW* 40.273 (*WA* 26.200). Much has been written on this aspect of the Visitation as a precursor to the Church-State. See B. Lohse, *Martin Luther: An Introduction to his Life and Work* (Philadelphia: Fortress, 1986), 82. Our intention here is not to pursue this but to demonstrate the nature of Luther's official-social imperative as a theory that underpinned the Visitation.

of this office is obvious in the Visitation Articles and the preface that accompanies them. Melanchthon has a seven page exposition of the official-social imperative.[47] At the heart of this exposition Melanchthon writes,

> Also that we obey the government. In Romans 13 Paul enumerates three points concerning government. First, the payment of taxes, namely that each shall give the authorities such money and labor as is required of him [Rom. 13.6f]. Second, respect, that is, that we have sincere respect for government. Even if government cannot in every instance punish our violations, still we should know that God will punish, for he has established and maintains government. Also we can be assured that all the rebellious will be punished, as Paul says in Rom. 13[.27]: 'Therefore he who resists the authorities resists what God has appointed, and those who resist will incur judgment.'[48]

Therefore, it seems reasonable to say that Luther and Melanchthon emphasize the official-social imperative as a necessary—though it was hoped as a short-term—solution to the crisis of faithlessness they discovered during the Visitation.

In summary, it is possible to conclude this section with an understanding that Luther's doctrine of freedom and the way it was shaped in the Visitation Articles (with Luther's approval) tracked with the theory-praxis-theory progression described by the new perspective on practical theology. In saying this, it may be more beneficial to add that the new perspective on practical theology seems to have systematized what happens intuitively in the church when the gospel is brought to bear on a specific historical occurrence. This nuance may help in the concern to avoid anachronism.

Luther as practical theologian

In concluding this study, we now ask the question explicitly. Can Luther's input into the 1527 Visitation be expanded into the new perspective on practical theology? Can Pieterse and Heyns' inclusion of Luther into their practical theological heritage be sustained? It seems that our study indicates a tentative answer for both a negative and a positive conclusion. In elucidating both answers, we will draw together a number of threads that define both a correspondence between Luther and the new perspective on practical theology and a dissonance between them, in order to arrive at a firm statement.

There seems to be a verifiable level of correspondence between Luther's theological methodological input into the Visitation and the new perspective on practical theology's methodology when one considers the three main theological paradigms under review.

---

[47] *LW* 40.280–87 (*WA* 26.206–11).
[48] *LW* 40.281 (*WA* 26.207).

In light of the way the new perspective positively appraises/incorporates the pastoral model, we can, confidently, say that there is a high degree of correspondence between Luther and the new perspective. According to Heyns and Pieterse, '[P]ractical theology is that which concerns itself with "the encounter between God an humanity".'[49] To say that this is Luther's concern, especially in light of the Saxon Visitation, would be a dramatic understatement. What gives this point more weight is that Luther, and his Wittenberg colleagues, were most concerned about the pastoral office and sought to apply a theological theory that re-instituted and strengthened pastoral ministry. Luther's preface to the Visitation Articles is shot through with this high regard for the pastoral (episcopal) office.

In view of the way in which the new perspective appraises/incorporates the ecclesiastical model, we can, confidently, say that there is a high degree of correspondence between Luther and the new perspective. Pieterse says that the ecclesiastical model 'asks for a communication of the gospel that fits into the problems, questions and terminology of the people'.[50] In light of this study, it seems reasonable to say that this definition is, exactly, what Luther intended/expected of the Visitation. There is considerable attestation to the fact that the Visitation engaged the interaction of congregations (the impact of individuals on the whole), that took into account the particular cultural matrix in which these congregations existed. It seems that the negative cultural matrix (the abrogation of the Episcopal office and the misconstrual of Luther's doctrine of freedom) generated a theory-praxis tension that needed further theoretical attention.

This leads us to conclude that what is basically intrinsic to a practical theological model—the theory-praxis-theory tension—is verifiable in the methodology of Luther and his colleagues throughout the 1527 Visitation. What seems to underpin this understanding is the way in which Luther's doctrine of freedom was nuanced to place major emphasis on repentance and the official-social imperative without compromising his doctrine of justification by faith. Rather than seeing a disjunction between Luther and Melanchthon in the Articles, we see Luther (in response to a particular praxis) give affirmation to the nuancing of his theological theory. This is, also, quite verifiable in the way in which the Wittenbergers called upon the temporal authority to enact its divine calling. The over-emphasis of the official-social imperative during the visitation is consistent with a theory-praxis-theory tension in that Luther's earlier doctrine of freedom (1520-1522) is, predominantly, characterized by justification by faith and the personal-social imperative. This seems to suggest that the new perspective's theory-praxis-theory tension is, at least, implicit in Luther's input into the 1527 Visitation.

---

[49] Heyns and Pieterse, *A Primer*, 6.
[50] Pieterse, *Contextual Theology*, 4.

However, there appears to be quite a degree of dissonance between Luther's methodology and that of the new perspective in a number of instances. First, the critical appraisal offered by the new perspective in regard to the shepherd/flock, pastoral model, seems as though it would have been quite an affront to Luther and his colleagues.[51] In fact, one of the key transformative conclusions of Luther's phenomenology, at the time, is that the pastoral office needed to be re-invigorated in such a way that took the highest of priorities. The involvement of the temporal authority was to be supposed as an interval solution while the pastoral/episcopal office was re-instituted.

Another key area of dissonance between Luther and the new perspective on practical theology—one which certainly calls into question a fair degree of actual correspondence—is the way in which practical theology opens itself to the philosophical constructs of the world. One wonders how Luther would respond to the following quotation by the new perspective on practical theology.

> [I] emphasize even more the need for practical theology to enter a revised correlational dialogue with the other religions and secular 'faiths' that make up our pluralistic society. They [I] want the practical theologian to enter an open and honest conversation with the secular educator, the secular mental health worker, the Marxist revolutionary, the local Jewish mayor, the feminist member of the municipal council, and the fundamentalist senator with his huge popular following.[52]

There seems to be a tension in practical theology in regard to what part of the Christian confession is open to critical dialogue and what is not. It seems that in the theory-praxis-theory tension, there is room for the most precious of Christian truths to be challenged. It is possible that the Wittenberg conception of the 'pure gospel' would find it hard to exist within the openness of the new perspective's methodology.

Conclusion

Can Luther be seen as a theological/practical forbear to the new perspective on practical theology? This can only be affirmed if we see practical theology reading back into history and systematizing what they find there. If so, then Luther can be included as one in the many throughout church history who have responded to unique praxis events with their theoretical methodology. In Luther's case, this theoretical framework was his doctrine of freedom.

There appears, then, a certain degree of correspondence between Luther's input into the 1527 Visitation in regard to the theory-praxis-theory paradigm offered up by the new perspective on practical theology. It seems clear that in response to the praxis of visitation, Luther was happy for his doctrine of freedom to be nuanced in order to engage with the specific needs that the context

---

[51] See Wengert, *The Pastoral Luther*, 23.
[52] Browning, *Practical Theology*, 11.

required. This is seen, explicitly, in the subordinating of his personal-social imperative by his official-social imperative throughout his preface to the Visitation Articles and the Articles themselves.

The affirmation of correspondence between Luther and the new perspective on practical theology needs to be balanced with a certain degree of dissonance. As this study suggests, there are a number of criteria set forth by the new perspective, which would simply clash with Luther's theological methodology. In addition to the new perspective's critical analysis of the pastor/shepherd model is the fact that Luther would probably have been reluctant to adopt the new perspective's over-confident appraisal of worldly philosophical methodologies.[53]

However, it could be possible that Luther would engage a 'secular educator,' but there is no way in which this study could suggest that Luther would have been willing to put his gospel on the table for critical dismemberment. This seems to suggest that Luther can only be invited onto the new perspective on practical theology's heritage list with a certain amount of caution. What is worth noting, in conclusion, is that what the new perspective has defined as their own unique discipline seems to be implicit in the reforming methodology of the Wittenberg community. This is especially apparent in the transformative dynamic that Luther's doctrine of freedom had during the Visitation.

---

[53] It would be hard to imagine Luther in an 'open and honest conversation' with a 'Marxist revolutionary', for example. There may be something to learn from a Marxist theory about sociology, but Luther would probably have struggled with this idea if the Marxist thought that the social problem was attributed to faith in Christ. See Browning, *Practical Theology*, 11.

CHAPTER 5

Luther's insights into grief: his pastoral letters[1]

Michael Parsons

In his remarkable work on Luther as a comforter, Neil Leroux, understandably, stresses that 'the "rhetorical situation" of consoling a bereaved person, particularly through a single letter, is a complicated and delicate matter'.[2] Subsequently, he suggests several persistent themes in the reformer's pastoral letters: (1) God, who knows better than we do, has taken the loved one; (2) God created us as feeling, loving creatures, who will naturally grieve over loss; (3) God, Christ and the Word are the best consolers; (4) a faithful death is better than a miserable life; and (5) there is a need for moderation in grief.[3] The following short essay, then, develops and qualifies these themes, and others. What does Luther say of grief, how does he respond to bereavement, and what consolation does he offer? In order to explicate Luther's insights, first, we turn to a number of specific pastoral letters in some detail. And, second, before a short reflection on this, we consider some of the reformer's repeated themes in his pastoral approach to those who suffer loss.

Luther's letters to the grieving

To Bartholomew von Staremberg, 1524

Late in 1524 Luther wrote to Bartholomew von Staremberg, whose wife Magdalene had just died.[4] Von Staremberg had served for a while as regent for the Emperor, Maximilian I, and seems to have tended towards a sympathetic understanding of evangelical doctrines. The reformer seems not to have known

---

[1] This chapter began as a paper given at the Evangelical Theological Society's annual conference in Milwaukee, 2012.
[2] Neil Leroux, *Martin Luther as Comforter. Writings on Death* (Leiden: Brill, 2007), 183-84.
[3] Leroux, *Martin Luther*, 188.
[4] To Bartholomew von Staremberg, September 1, 1524: *Luther: Letters of Spiritual Counsel* (translated by Theodore Tappert: Vancouver: Regent College, 2003—hereafter, *Letters*), 53-55 (*WA* 18.1-7).

von Staremberg personally as he begins the letter explaining that a mutual friend, Vincent Wernsdorfer, had urged him to write 'moved by Christian concern and loyalty'. Luther demonstrates some reticence, asking if the recipient might receive the letter 'kindly', and 'in good part'. He admits to second-hand knowledge of the situation, but that he had been assured that von Staremberg's wife had been remarkable for her 'love and fidelity'. However, Luther has heard that von Staremberg 'has been trying hard to help her soul with services and good works, particularly with Masses and vigils' and it is this issue in particular that he wishes to address.[5]

After the initial address and introductory material Luther makes two careful, but direct, requests. First, he suggests that von Staremberg 'should cheerfully give God what is his'; that he should try to accept the situation, as awful and excruciating as it is.[6]

> Let me remind you of what Job says: 'The Lord gave, and the Lord hath taken away; as it seemed good to the Lord, so hath he done.' You should sing the same song to a dear and faithful God who gave you a dear and faithful wife and has now taken her away. She was his before he gave her; she was his after he had given her; and she is still his ... now that he has taken her away. Although it hurts us when he takes his own from us, his good will should be a greater comfort to us than all his gifts, for God is immeasurably better than all his gifts. ... Although we cannot perceive God's will as well as we can perceive a wife, we can apprehend his will by faith. Accordingly you should cheerfully give God what is his and accept this just exchange ... whereby instead of a dear, tender wife you have a dear, tender will of God—and, what is more, God himself. How blessed and rich we would be if we could engage in such an exchange with God! We could do so, in fact, if we knew how to, for God confronts us with the opportunity daily, but we cannot ask him.[7]

It is worth making four brief observations at this early juncture. First, we notice that the reformer begins with an appropriate quotation from Scripture—Job 1.21. This characteristically grounds his advice in the truth of God, allowing him to rest on that authority as he encourages someone to face the continuing pain of loss and bereavement. This is almost invariably Luther's way of pastoral support: to lay a biblical foundation upon which he intends to build his advice.[8] Second, having shifted attention to the Word of God, he centres God, himself, within this terrible situation. Though von Staremberg acutely feels the loss, Luther reminds him that God is still at the centre of his world—in life *and* in death, in gain *and* in loss, in joy *and* in sorrow. So, though Luther acknowledges the hurt, he encourages the recipient to see that everything in

---

[5] *Letters*, 53.
[6] *Letters*, 54.
[7] *Letters*, 53-54.
[8] Dennis Ngien, *Luther as a Spiritual Adviser* (Milton Keynes: Paternoster, 2007), 133.

life, including his wife, is a gift from a loving God. However, God gives and he takes—he has that right—but he himself remains to comfort in sorrow and in loss. Third, Luther characteristically introduces the subject of faith. Those newly bereaved see a loving God in the situation only by the exercise of faith: 'Although we cannot perceive God's will as well as we can perceive a wife, we can apprehend his will by faith.' Behind this lies the typically reformational thought that reality is perceived by faith, not by sight. As human beings it is easier to be certain of the being and existence of our spouse whom we see, hear and touch every day, than to be certain of the being and existence of God whom we do not. It is absolutely necessary that we apprehend reality in a different way. Faith (*fiducia*) alone apprehends and maintains the certainty of a *loving* God, even in situations of pain. Fourth, Luther suggests that we might be better at this in the more acute problems that we face if we practised sacrificing ourselves daily to God's will at other, more routine times.

Luther's first request, then, is that the recipient accepts the situation of loss. His second request is that the recipient should 'discontinue the Masses and vigils and daily prayers for her soul'.[9] The second is clearly a consequence of the first being accomplished—if he accedes to the situation then he will find no need for the religious rituals with which, in his fear, he seems so obsessed. Luther is not against prayer! But he assures him that it is enough to pray just once or twice for her, being certain that God answers prayer. Again, he underlines this by quoting from the Word, 'If you ask anything in my name I will do it' (John 14.12-14). To pray too often about the same issue, says Luther, shows we don't really believe that God answers prayer. Von Staremberg must move on to setting his sights differently. More forcefully, Luther condemns Masses and vigils themselves as 'unchristian practices which greatly anger [*ertzürnen*] God'. 'Such vigils,' he says, 'are a mockery [*spot*] of God . . . a useless mummery [*Gemürmel*]'.[10]

This short early letter is both forceful and compassionate. The reformer seeks to move von Staremberg from the position in which bereavement has placed him, to realise *in the situation* that God continues with him in love and gentleness, to recognise that he needs to let go of the deceased, to release her into the Lord's loving and eternal care, and to move on, however painfully, himself.

To Ambrose Berndt, 1532

Ambrose Berndt had been a student at Wittenberg, matriculating in 1528. It is not impossible, therefore, that Berndt had been one of the fortunate students to sit around Luther's dining table, listening to his conversations around life and faith, theology and society. Unfortunately, Berndt's first wife had died in

---

[9] *Letters*, 54.
[10] *Letters*, 54. See Austra Reinis, *Reforming the Art of Dying* (Aldershot: Ashgate, 2007), 4.

childbirth and their newly born son had died with her. Into this unimaginable situation Luther writes words of comfort to the grieving husband.[11] One remarkable characteristic of this letter is the degree to which Luther acknowledges the grief of the bereaved: 'I am not so inhuman,' he says, 'that I cannot appreciate how deeply the death of Margaret distresses you.' He understands that this distress is grounded in 'the great and godly affection which binds a husband to his wife' and that it 'is so strong that it cannot easily be shaken off'. His conclusion is that 'No hurt as painful as this can befall a man in his domestic life.'[12] The reformer assures Berndt that this sorrow is *not* displeasing to God; 'since it is an expression of what God has assuredly implanted in you . . . Nor would I account you a man, to say nothing of a good husband, if you could at once throw off your grief.'[13] So, grief and distress are natural for a husband at the death of his wife; partly, because they have grown close in affection for each other, and, partly, because God creates in them mutual love.[14] The reformer recognises that the loss is very great indeed—almost insurmountable. However, Luther encourages the young man to hold his grief in check in order to insure that it does not become contrary to the will of God. It is necessary, he says, 'to put a limit to one's sorrow and grief'.

Luther reminds Berndt that Margaret had been faithful to her calling and her duties throughout her life, and even at the point of death. She had died in childbirth, 'that is, in the performance of her God-given duty'. It would be simplistic to read this as a misogynist evaluation of her death. Luther is really concerned here, not so much with duty *per se*, as with authentic faith and commitment on the wife's part: '[S]he did this,' he continues, 'with a resolute spirit and a firm faith in Christ. Knowing that she was facing death, she confessed him again and again, called upon Christ alone, and, offering herself wholly to God, was resigned to his will.'[15] Berndt is to remember this wonderful example of faith, to be comforted that his wife was a true believer in Christ, even in the painful realisation of death.

Furthermore, the reformer suggests to his friend that 'If you compare physical with spiritual gifts, you will certainly come to the conclusion that spiritual gifts are greater than physical ones.'[16] Again, this implies that division between that which we so tenaciously cling to as reality and that which is spiritual. Our preoccupation with the physical, as somehow ultimate, damages our ability to see the Lord's spiritual gifts in our lives—and, indeed, to see our lives as spiritual gifts. A few last encouragements further this idea: 'Occupy yourself with these thoughts unceasingly and control your grief as much as you

---

[11] To Ambrose Berndt, 1532: *Letters*, 62-63 (*WA Br* 6.279-81).
[12] *Letters*, 62. See Michael Parsons, *Reformation Marriage* (Eugene: Wipf & Stock, 2011), 172-73, 203-206.
[13] *Letters*, 62.
[14] See Parsons, *Reformation Marriage*, 142-45.
[15] To Ambrose Berndt, 1532: *Letters*, 63 (*WA Br* 6.281).
[16] *Letters*, 63.

can. Comfort yourself with the Word of God, the pre-eminent consolation.' Luther commends that he '[P]ray that our common Father may allow you and all of us to die in faith in Jesus Christ.'[17]

To John Reineck, 1536

Luther knew John Reineck, from Mansfeld—they had been friends from their school-days. He had just lost his wife when the reformer wrote to him a heartfelt letter, part of which follows.

> How should we conduct ourselves in such a situation? God has so ordered and limited [*geordnet und gemäsziget*] our life here that we may learn and exercise the knowledge of his very good will so that we may test and discover whether we love and esteem his will more than ourselves and everything that he had given us to have and love on earth. And although the inscrutable goodness of the divine will is hidden (as is God himself) from the old Adam as something so great and profound that man finds no pleasure in it, but only grief and lamentation [*Trauren und Klagen*], we nevertheless have his holy and sure Word which reveals to us this hidden will of his and gladdens the heart of the believer.[18]

The rhetorical question appears to highlight the questioning agony of those who lose loved ones to death. We notice, though, that the question is not, 'What should we believe in such a situation?' but, 'What should we *do*?' Luther wants Reineck to maintain his faith. There is that implicit acknowledgement that those suffering acute loss are tempted to change how they behave. There is an acknowledgement that we feel that God is against us in such a situation: he speaks of 'the inscrutable goodness of the divine will [being] hidden (as is God himself)'. Naturally, there is no pleasure in it, 'only grief and lamentation'. A little later he says that 'the old Adam is reluctant and unwilling to act like Job'—and Luther evidently has in mind Job's patience.

But, again, in this short letter we find that Luther's encouragement to the bereaved Reineck is to set his mind and heart on that which he has retained rather than on that which he has lost. He encourages him to rest in the 'holy and sure Word' of God, hoping that this will gladden his heart, that he might 'find more pleasure in God's grace and Fatherly will' than he will have pain from his loss. Luther knows, from experience, that it is often in the Word that we find God's fatherly grace—not in the circumstances of darkness and suffering.

To Conrad Cordatus, 1530

Conrad Cordatus was one of the pastors in the city of Zwickau. Luther was distressed to learn of his son's death, for only three months previously to this letter the reformer had written to congratulate him on the birth of this very

---

[17] *Letters*, 63.
[18] To John Reineck, April 18, 1536: *Letters*, 69-70 (*WA Br* 7.399-400).

child.[19] In the first paragraph, the reformer comes straight to the point, immediately turning the recipient's attention to Jesus Christ, whilst acknowledging the pain of his loss: 'May Christ comfort you in this sorrow and affliction (*humilitate et affliction*) of yours. Who else can soothe such a grief?' The rhetorical question implies the lack of any other possible balm. Noticeably, in attempting to acknowledge Cordatus' pain, the reformer refers to the death of his own daughter, Elizabeth, two years earlier, at the age of only seven months: 'I can easily believe what you write, for I too have had experience of such a calamity, which comes to a father's heart sharper than a two-edged sword, piercing even to the marrow, etc.'

Luther encourages the grieving father, '[I]t is not to be marvelled at if he, who is more truly and properly a father than you were, preferred for his own glory that your son—nay, rather, *his* son—should be with him rather than with you, for he is safer there than here.' It is questionable whether speaking in this way to a newly bereaved father is wise, of course, but the final words remind us that the times in which they lived were precarious. However, Luther himself recognises that this way of approach so early on in the grieving process may be questionable, for he says, 'But all this is vain, a story that falls on deaf ears, when your grief is so new. I therefore yield to your sorrow.' Before he concludes, the reformer implies that grief can be a snare and can bring men (and women, presumably) into sin: 'Greater and better men than we are have given way to grief and are not blamed for it.'[20] Luther believes that 'these agonies' may prove the power of the Word and of faith; he encourages Cordatus to suffer 'in glorious and trusting innocence—that is, with a good conscience'.[21]

Finally, he writes, acknowledging the recipient's wife for the first time, 'Greet the companion of your sorrow, and rejoice the while in the living Christ more than you grieve over your son who is dead—nay, who is alive but has been taken from you.'[22] And, in a touching personal conclusion, he says, 'My Katie and our whole household send you greeting.'[23]

To Benedict Pauli, June, 1533

Tappert tells us that the following were words spoken to Benedict Pauli at the death of Pauli's only son who apparently fell to his untimely death from the house-top. The words were recorded by Veit Dietrich.[24] Luther begins by assuring Pauli that the Scriptures do not prohibit grieving over deceased

---

[19] To Conrad Cordatus, April 2, 1530: *Letters*, 59-61 (*WA Br* 5.273-274).
[20] *Letters*, 60.
[21] *Letters*, 60.
[22] *Letters*, 60-61.
[23] *Letters*, 61.
[24] 'So, not a letter in the strict sense, but oral remarks. . . . [T]hese remarks take on many characteristics of a funeral sermon, except that there is no Scripture text'—Leroux, *Martin Luther*, 194.

children. On the contrary, there are many examples of godly patriarchs and kings who mourned (that is, 'mournfully wailed [*gravissime luxerunt*])' the death of their sons. Nevertheless, the reformer warns that there ought to be moderation in grieving. Pauli ought to leave room for consolation. And again, in this instance, Luther suggests that the consolation is that the Lord gave and now has taken away his son. In this circumstance Pauli is to imitate Job (Job 2.10). He reminds Pauli that we receive far more good things than bad from the Lord, but that at the present time, naturally enough, his 'eyes are fixed only on the evil'.[25]

The reformer concedes that the evil that has befallen Pauli is very grave. However, he insists that it is not unique to him. Many of his friends had experienced bereavement, as did many biblical characters, too. Luther briefly lists one or two examples. Abraham 'had more and greater grief'. He asks, dramatically, 'How do you think he felt when he grasped the sword to kill his son?'[26] Jacob 'suffered infinite grief'. And, David, 'What father was ever more grieved?' At one level, then, Luther is simply reminding his friend of the common lot of humanity which is to suffer bereavement, pain and loss. Yet the reformer goes further, concluding this argument with the following comment, 'If you reflect on these and similar examples, you will understand that your misfortune is not at all to be compared with even a part of the misfortune and grief of those men, and by this comparison your own grief will be greatly relieved and lightened.'[27] However difficult it may have been to accept this encouragement, it reveals Luther's perceptive pastoral understanding. He knows, from bitter experience as well as from pastoral insight, that in Pauli's situation you feel that this is worse than any other being has had to endure. Existentially, it seems as though the world's hurt has become focused on the individual. Luther wishes to counter that by suggesting the commonality of suffering in this life.

Luther suggests that death is not altogether a dreadful event; what we term 'horrible death' is not for those in Christ. Luther expands upon this. He realises that generally in dying there is that increase (*zuspitzung*) of fear; but for those who are in Christ dying is made easier (*eine Entlastung des Sterbens*), not because of their own virtue but purely on the basis of divine grace. In pastoral acknowledgement of the profound existential difficulty of maintaining trust in a gracious God in such a time of painful loss Luther says the following.

> Certainly it is the good will of God that your son should die, although human nature cries out against this and imagines that God is angry. It is a characteristic of our human nature to think that what we wish is best and what God does is

---

[25] *Letters*, 67-68.
[26] *Letters*, 68. See *Comm. Gen.* 22, *LW* 4.91-186 (*WA* 43.200-270).
[27] *Letters*, 68.

unsatisfactory to us. . . . It is enough for us that we have a gracious God. Why he permits this or that evil to befall us should not trouble us at all.[28]

The reformer acknowledges the agony of the experience of loss, '*human nature cries out against this and imagines that God is angry*'—in acute grief we have that awful existential, introverted, despairing sense of not only being alone but of being singled out for punishment. Luther understands that from his own periods of grief and anxiety. He, also, recognises the black and bottomless hole that seems to surround the inevitable question, Why does God allow this? He seeks to steer the sensitive bereaved away, implicitly calling for a strenuous faith that clings to a gracious God *despite* the appearances of present, painful experience.

Luther's approach to those who grieve

Having examined a few notable examples of Luther's letters to those who grieve we are in a position to elaborate upon our understanding of the reformer's general approach to the question of grief in the experience of evangelical believers. This will, also, give us a chance to widen the scope of letters examined.

Recognition of the trial

Luther recognises what grieving and hurting people are going through—he acknowledges their painful trial. He does not fight shy of commenting directly on this. Rhetorically, his purpose is clearly to gain a hearing for his later comfort and advice; but, pastorally, he wishes recipients to realise that he knows something of what they are experiencing; he empathises with them in their hurt. As we have seen, to von Staremberg, for instance, he admits the depth of hurt that bereavement inevitably brings; with Ambrose Berndt he empathises over the pain he suffers; to Conrad Cordatus he acknowledges, from his own experience, the agony of losing a child.

This is a favourite strategy. This explicit and, at times, very personal acknowledgement is a constant refrain in the majority of Luther's letters of comfort. For example, when John Zink died the reformer writes to the bereaved and sorrow-stricken father that 'It is only natural that your son's death and the report of it should distress and grieve you and your dear wife.'[29] And, sometimes, the reformer employs exaggerated language to make his point more graphic, for he knows that the situation warrants striking, over-stated language to reflect the tumultuous feelings involved. Generally, on the death of spouses, for example, he says, 'Our God is the greatest breaker of marriages' ('*Unser*

---

[28] *Letters*, 69.
[29] To Thomas Zink, April 22, 1532: *Letters*, 64-65 (*WA Br* 6.300-302). See letter to John Reineck, *Letters*, 69.

here Gott ist der gröste Ehebrecher.')[30] On the death of a wife he remarks to the husband, 'This is more than suffering and dying; it is being buried and descending into hell.'[31] And, beneath it all, he often assures the sufferers that he experiences something of their pain: 'I can well imagine how painful this parting is for you,' he writes to Wolf Heinze, 'and I assure you that I am deeply grieved for your sake . . . your loss moves me deeply.'[32]

Martin Luther, then, is a pastor who, knowing the uncertainty of life, has experienced that uncertainty in the lives of others through pastoral empathy and in his own life in the experience of vexation, loss, pain, and death. This gives him the boldness to acknowledge the trials of others explicitly and allows him to talk into their lives at the sharp end of their grief and agony. One never gains the sense of empty rhetoric or platitudes, with Luther; he feels their hurt for he has felt his own.

God's inscrutable kindness

Not only does Luther want to assure grieving people that he knows what they are going through, he also assures them that God himself knows what they are going through, that he is intimately involved in the midst of their suffering and that ultimately he is *for* them, not *against* them in their pain. This crucial, reformational understanding of a personal and involved God is central to Luther's pastoral agenda, of course, and very difficult to accomplish at that moment of loss and hurt. He needs to assure those who suffer that God is still on their side as he has always been, as it were, despite the very human (and fallen) propensity to accuse God in times of despair. It was vital that the reformer insist that God was positively, intimately and lovingly involved. His grace is greater than his judgement. He alone can heal the wounds that he has inflicted.

This becomes something of a refrain in the reformer's letters. For example, on the death of her husband, King Lewis, Luther turns the attention of Queen Mary of Hungary to the divine fatherhood, exhorting her to 'learn to trust alone in the true Father who is in heaven'.[33] The reformer suggests to the Elector of Saxony that God will take the place of his deceased brother, Frederick. In this way, he says, the Lord will give strength and comfort from his goodness, he gives courage 'to bear misfortune and in the end gives ways and means to escape it'.[34] We notice that Luther's intention here is not merely to suggest the

---

[30] Table Talk, July 1539: *Letters*, 73 (*WA Tr* 4, n°4709).
[31] To Lawrence Zoch, November 3, 1532: *Letters*, 66 (*WA Br* 6.302).
[32] To Wolf Heinze, September 11, 1543: *Letters*, 77 (*WA Br* 10.394-95).
[33] To Queen Mary of Hungary, November 1, 1526: *Letters*, 57-58; Table Talk, 1532: *Letters*, 63 (*WA Tr* 2 n°1361).
[34] To Elector John of Saxony, May 15, 1525: *Letters*, 55-56 (*WA Br* 3.496-97). See his letter to George Spalatin, July 10, 1527: *Letters*, 29 (*WA Br* 4.221-22); Table Talk, March 1536: *Letters*, 43-44 (*WA Tr* 3, n°3612c); letter to Thomas Zink, April 22, 1532: *Letters*, 64-65 (*WA Br* 6.300-302).

presence and reality of a heavenly Father, but also to suggest that he will be present in grace to end this pain, to allow peace and some sort of comfort—that is the nature of fatherly love, after all.

Christ is identified with suffering believers

Luther seeks to show that the Father's love is secured and exercised through Jesus Christ and he does this in a diversity of ways. Luther writes to Lawrence Zoch, for instance, who has recently lost his wife, and in a surprising way, perhaps, he discerns in the young man's experience of grief a type of Christ's.[35]

> Remember that Christ had this experience, and even worse. But God, who seemed to be assailing him, did not forsake him, but raised him up in honor. . . . But it is a far greater comfort that Christ has made you a type of himself and that you are suffering as he suffered—that is, punished and confounded not only at the devil's hands, but also as if by God himself, who is and wishes to be your comfort. Therefore, although your flesh murmurs and cries out, as Christ also cried out in his weakness, your spirit ought to be ready and willing and ought to cry with groanings that cannot be uttered, 'Abba, dear Father; that I know very well.'[36]

Note the explicit way in which Luther equates the experiences of Christ and the believer in suffering (though he is quick to point out that Christ's suffering was far worse).[37] And, note, too, the direct manner in which Christ is said to have 'made [Zoch] a type of himself'. This, fundamentally, is encouragement to look to the future rather than being steeped in the present, to the end of the dreadful experience, to see beyond that which feels like forsakenness (or, like punishment), and to see that there will be a kind of resurrection from acute suffering that will eventually occur by God's grace. As Christ is 'the model for all our suffering' so is his resurrection and ensuing honour a model for our being raised to peace and comfort.

Christ has overcome death

Jesus Christ is central to Luther's pastoral emphases as much as he is to his theology and biblical exegesis. At one point in his encouragement to prince Joachim of Anhalt he makes the profound, but simple, short statement that Jesus 'became incarnate to comfort'.[38] In other correspondence he shows what he means by this crucial phrase. In a letter to his mother, for instance, he almost preaches the idea in the following words.

> You know the real basis and foundation of your salvation, on which you must rest your confidence in this and all troubles, namely Jesus Christ. . . . He says, 'Be of good cheer; I have overcome the world.' If he has overcome the world, surely he

---

[35] To Lawrence Zoch, November 3, 1532: *Letters*, 65-67 (*WA Br* 6.382, 383).
[36] *Letters*, 66-67.
[37] See letter to Queen Mary of Hungary, November 1, 1526: *Letters*, 58 (*WA* 19.553).
[38] To Prince Joachim of Anhalt, December 25, 1535: *Letters*, 98 (*WA Br* 7.335).

has overcome the prince of this world with all his power. And what is his power but death? . . . But now that death and sin are overcome, we may joyfully and cheerfully listen to the sweet words, 'Be of good cheer; I have overcome the world.' . . . He is the Conqueror, the true Hero, who in these words, 'Be of good cheer,' gives me the benefit of his victory. I shall cling to him. To these words and comfort I shall hold fast.[39]

The repeated refrain, 'Be of good cheer,' speaks to one who is suffering, anchored as it is in the gospel statement that Jesus Christ has overcome the world, Satan and death. And he has done this for his people—'[He] gives me the benefit of his victory'—Jesus 'became incarnate to comfort'. This thought spoke powerfully to his father, John Luther, on his death-bed. Martin seeks to encourage him in this difficult time.

Let your heart be strong and at ease in your trouble, for we have yonder a true mediator with God, Jesus Christ, who has overcome death and sin for us and now sits in heaven with all his angels, looking down on us and awaiting us. . . . He has such great power over sin and death that they cannot harm us, and he is so heartily true and kind that he cannot and will not forsake us, at least if we ask his help without doubting.[40]

Christ is not only strong and powerful, but 'so heartily true and kind that *he cannot and will not* forsake us' (emphasis added). The encouragement to pray for the Lord's help is implicit in the reformer's words. Ultimately, Luther desires that those who are suffering grasp the point that they are objects of infinite and unconditional love—the love of God in Christ.

Grief is to be moderately expressed

Luther knew grief first hand. The death of his father, for example, caused him to despair. He grieves not only because his father gave him life and the many natural gifts he had, but also because he misses 'his kindness and . . . his pleasant conversation'. He writes to his friend, Philip Melanchthon, that 'This death has cast me into deep mourning' and speaks of 'so deep a wound in my heart that I have scarcely ever held death in such low esteem'.[41] And the death of his beloved daughter, Magdalene, at the age of fourteen, caused him deep grief that would last for many years.[42] Indeed, he alludes to this grief three

---

[39] To Mrs John Luther, May 20, 1531: *Letters*, 33-36 (34) (*WA Br* 6.103-104).
[40] To John Luther, February 15, 1530: *Letters*, 29-32 (31) (*WA Br* 5.238-41). See Robert Kolb, *Martin Luther. Confessor of the Faith* (Oxford: OUP, 2009), 169-70.
[41] To Melanchthon, June, 1530: *Letters*, 30 (*WA Br* 5.351).
[42] Susan Karant-Nunn, *The Reformation of Feeling. Shaping the Religious Emotions in Early Modern Germany* (Oxford: OUP, 2010), 195-96, reminds us that when Magdalene died Katherine wept openly. 'Luther wrestled with his pain, even urging the neighbors who accompanied her body to the grave not to express undue sympathy toward him.'

years later in a letter of comfort to Andrew Osiander on the loss of his second wife and a daughter at almost the same time, saying, 'I know from the death of my own dearest child how great must be your grief. It may appear strange, but I am still mourning the death of my dear Magdalene.' He adds, 'and I am not able to forget her,' by which he clearly means that he is unable to move from that locus of acute grief.[43] Significantly, Luther gives the impression of one who closely empathises with those who grieve, so he is able to grieve not only for his own loss but for the loss of others with a new-found depth to his own experience.[44]

So, from his own experience of grief the reformer knows that grief has to be expressed: 'It is quite inconceivable that you should not be mourning,' he says to a couple who have just lost their son after a long illness.[45] To Catherine Metzler, who had recently lost her son, he writes, 'It is natural and right that you should grieve.' He adds this reason, 'For God has not created us to be without feeling or to be like stones or sticks, but it is his will that we should mourn and bewail our dead. Otherwise it would appear that we had no love.'[46] Inasmuch as love for our family members is a God-given, created aspect to our make-up as human beings, pain and grief is a natural consequence to their loss.

However much grief and its expression are natural and the consequences of divinely-given affection, the reformer is insistent that it be expressed in moderation. Why? The answer lies succinctly in a brief comment, written to a father whose adult son had just died: 'I do not blame you for [grieving], for all of us, and I in particular, are stricken with sorrow,' he says. Then he adds this interesting and insightful instruction, 'Grieve in a way, therefore, as to console yourselves.'[47] Grief is natural and right, it is even in its way consoling, but it must not be excessive, for Luther is worried that excessive grief will lead the believer further and further away from coming to a place of acceptance—however difficult that may be—and, therefore, of consolation and genuine comfort.

In writing to the parents of John Knudsen Luther quotes Ecclesiasticus 22.11, 'Weep for the dead, for light hath failed him; but do not mourn much, for he hath found rest.' He adds that they (the parents), when they have 'mourned and wept moderately, should be comforted again'.[48] His longing for those who mourn is that they might find a point of peace, not that they should

---

[43] To Andrew Osiander, June 3, 1545: *Letters*, 80-81 (80), (*WA Br* 11.113-14).
[44] To Justus Jonas, December 26, 1542: *Letters*, 75-76 (75) (*WA Br* 10.226-28). See Luther's letter to Thomas Zink, April 22, 1532: *Letters*, 64-65 (*WA Br* 6.300-302).
[45] To Mr and Mrs Matthias Knudsen, October 21, 1531: *Letters*, 61-62 (61) (*WA Br* 6.212-13).
[46] To Catherine Metzler, July 3, 1539: *Letters*, 72-73 (*WA Br* 8.484-85). See letter to Wolf Heinze, September 11, 1543: *Letters*, 77 (*WA Br* 10.394-95); letter to Casper Heydenreich, April 24, 1545: *Letters*, 79-80 (*WA Br* 75-76).
[47] To Thomas Zink, April 22, 1532: *Letters*, 65 (*WA Br* 6.302).
[48] To Mr and Mrs Matthias Knudsen, October 21, 1531: *Letters*, 61 (*WA Br* 6.212).

bewail the situation excessively in a prolonged manner. This is his pastoral purpose, to lead people beyond the current situation—as harsh and awful as it presently is—and to enable them to move forward for themselves. To the grieving Andrew Osiander Luther makes the following fascinating remark:

> [Y]ou must yield up your dear Isaac as a burnt offering and for a sweet-smelling savor to God—not your daughter or your wife [who had just passed away], for these live and are blessed in the Lord, but the natural and strong affection which asserts itself too powerfully in us.[49]

The allusion to Abraham's near offering of his son, Isaac (Gen 22), is significant as the reformer often employs that passage to demonstrate the painfulness of death and loss.[50] But we notice, too, that here Luther says that it is the emotion of grief that is to be sacrificed or given up because it is too powerful in us; it is too assertive and destructive. Grief must give way to comfort; those who mourn 'should be comforted again'—and, ultimately, this is a matter of faith.

The importance of faith

Generally speaking, Luther knows that painful parting and grief are able to push us in one of two very different directions. This is clear from a comment he makes to his students sitting around the dinner table: 'God both loves and hates our afflictions. He loves them when they provoke us to prayer. He hates them when we are driven to despair by them.'[51] Sufferers must not be driven to despair by their circumstances, for despair indicates a loss of confidence and trust in God as gracious Father. To the Elector John of Saxony Luther writes that God desires that our faith be real and determinative, not merely superficial—so that our faith 'may have its true dwelling place in the depth of our hearts'.[52] It is this strong, rooted faith that is our victory.[53] Seeking to comfort John von Taubenheim, on the death of his wife, Luther makes this point.

> In the struggle with your grief let the peace of God, which passes all understanding keep the victory, even if the flesh gags and grumbles. . . . [Y]ou yourself know that the peace of God is not a matter of the five senses or of the understanding but goes beyond these and is a matter of faith.[54]

His allusion to Philippians 4.7 indicates that peace in this circumstance can derive only from the Lord who gives that peace, and that it comes through the

---

[49] To Andrew Osiander, June 3, 1545: *Letters*, 81 (*WA Br* 11.114).
[50] See *Comm. Gen.* 22, *LW* 4.91-186 (*WA* 43.200-270).
[51] See Table Talk, December 1531: *Letters*, 87.
[52] To Elector John of Saxony, May 15, 1525: *Letters*, 56 (*WA Br* 3.497).
[53] To John Ruehel, June 9, 1534: *Letters*, 38 (*WA Br* 7.82).
[54] To John von Taubenheim, January 10, 1539: *Letters*, 70-72 (*WA Br* 8.352-54).

believer's faith. The flesh fails people in distress—it complains about the situation, apprehending only through what it senses or through its own weak and insufficient understanding. It appears that Luther isn't naïve enough to think that we can reach a conclusive understanding of the dreadful situation of loss. Rather, he wants those suffering to reach a point of peace through the grace of God—peace that is victory, peace that 'passes all understanding'. Then 'after mourning for a season, we shall enter into joy unspeakable'.[55] This is the hope that the reformer puts before those who presently suffer, that they might finally know the joy of entering heaven where their loved ones await them. In the meantime, though, they are encouraged to moderate their grief, to be thankful that those for whom they grieve are safe and at peace in Christ,[56] to comfort themselves 'with the knowledge of eternal salvation'.[57] Finally, as Luther suggests to Catherine Metzler,

> Our grief should be moderate, for our dear Father is testing us here to see whether we can fear and love him in our sorrows as well as in joy and whether we can give back to him what he has given us.[58]

This is clearly more than an appeal to duty. The question for Luther is whether our faith is authentic and whether through faith, we can discern and trust God in traumatic and sorrowful days in the way that we can in joyful ones.

Reflections

The first matter that might usefully be addressed is the involvement that Luther allows God in the situation. He insists that God is central to the circumstance of grief—actively involved because he takes the deceased, Father to the one who has passed away and to the one who is left, the one who ultimately shows mercy and grace. Luther stresses the centrality of Christ—comfort will come from God through Christ—Luther asks Cordatus, for instance, 'Who else can soothe your grief?' Pastorally, this is a difficult road to take. The juxtaposition of pain and trust is a difficult balance in the traumatic event of bereavement. Luther realizes this problem. So why does he insist on this theme? Luther is convinced that everything that happens is somehow in the control of God.

This poses obvious problems for theodicy, but Luther speaks *from* theological understanding *towards* a situation, *from* doctrine *to* practice, not the other way around. The divine centrality in times of crisis and hurt is important, pastorally. He never refuses to separate sorrow from providence for he knows that if someone suffering makes that severance they face the danger of unbelief, of ingratitude, of angering the Lord and of falling away. The emphasis on God-

---

[55] To Justus Jonas, December 26, 1542: *Letters*, 76 (*WA Br* 10.228).
[56] To Mr and Mrs Matthias Knudsen, October 21, 1531: *Letters*, 61 (*WA Br* 6.212). See Karant-Nunn, *The Reformation of Feeling*, 195.
[57] To George Hoesel, December 13, 1544: *Letters*, 79 (*WA Br* 10.699).
[58] To Catherine Metzler, July 3, 1539: *Letters*, 73 (*WA Br* 8.485).

in-the-situation, also, allows the reformer a more concretely realistic view of grief.

The second matter that we might comment on, then, is the matter of grief, itself. Luther does not shy away from expressing his own grief. He speaks passionately concerning the deaths of his two children, Elizabeth and Magdalene, and of some of his friends. In this way, Luther encourages the expression of grief from others—certainly, that is the implication of his letters. Luther sees grief as natural, as a consequence of the divinely-given familial situation. Fellowship, closeness, the *alter Christus* situation in which families live by faith, are the background to the agony of grief being felt and expressed. Indeed, for Luther, familial affections are heightened in believers.[59] However, and this is important, Luther insists that grief be expressed carefully, or moderately. This has a theological basis for it clearly derives from his understanding of providence and God's intimate control of everything. But it also derives from a pastoral appreciation of the psychology of those grieving. Luther wants grief to be checked because of the natural propensity of fallen and sinful human beings in extremity to go against the will of God. But we saw, also, that Luther looks beyond that to the time of comfort and he longs for those who suffer to reach that point, exhorting them to 'leave room for consolation'.

The third matter is that of faith. Luther underlines the significance of faith in situations of suffering. Genuine faith, in the midst of the terrible situation, is able to discern reality from non-reality; the spiritual from the merely physical; the eternal from the temporal. It does not deny the situation; but it sees it through a different lens. Faith focuses on God and takes hold of Christ. Luther encourages sufferers to realise Christ's identification with them. He looks to the resurrection, at which time those who have been taken will be recovered because Jesus Christ has overcome death once and for all. In the meantime, faith trusts God the Father and is encouraged to look at what has been retained, not so much on what (or who) has been lost. Faith enables the struggling Christian to be further transformed into the image of Christ.

So Luther, the writer of pastoral letters, encourages their recipients to maintain their faith and their Christian practice. He certainly does not deny grief and lament.[60] On the contrary, he seems to encourage it as part of the personal psychological process through which these believers are going.

---

[59] See Luther on Genesis 22.8 (*WA* 43.215-16).
[60] Contra R.A. Hughes, *Lament, Death and Destiny* (New York: Peter Lang, 2004), 101-117, for example.

2. John Calvin

CHAPTER 6

John Calvin on revelation and the use of feminine imagery for God

Karin Spiecker Stetina

'O Jerusalem, Jerusalem, the city that kills the prophets and stones those who are sent to it! How often would I have gathered your children together as a hen gathers her brood under her wings, and you were not willing!'[1]

'What's in a name? That which we call a rose by any other word would smell as sweet.'[2] The question that Juliet raises in Shakespeare's *Romeo and Juliet* seems even more relevant today than it did when it was first posed. In the famous monologue, Juliet is willing to give up her name and her family identity to be with the man she loves. Juliet assumes that names and identities are separate. Are names so easily changed without altering the thing signified by the name? Would a rose really smell as sweet if we called it a skunk cabbage?

This question is particularly significant when we ask it in reference to God. The church has struggled with God-language since its inception, alternating between tying God-language to Scripture or to culture. What is in a name for God? What is revelatory and what is metaphoric? What is timeless and what is adaptable?

This essay is not intended to be a feminist or revisionist proposal for establishing feminine language for God. Rather it is to be seen as part of an examination of the bigger question of how God is revealed and how we respond to that revelation. Previously I have addressed that question with an examination of Calvin's use of the biblical term 'Fatherhood'.[3] This study will seek to follow-up that discussion with a brief look at the nature of God-language and the biblical use of feminine imagery. In particular, I will examine what wisdom John Calvin has to offer our generation about how we are to talk to and about God and whether or not that should include the use of feminine-language. I will

---

[1] Matthew 23.37, ESV.
[2] William Shakespeare, *Romeo and Juliet*, Norton's Anthology (Chicago: Hampton, 2004), 2.2.1-2.
[3] See Karin Spiecker Stetina, 'Abba Father: Calvin's biblical image of the Fatherhood of God' in Michael Parsons (ed.), *Since we are Justified by Faith: Justification in the Theologies of the Protestant Reformation* (Milton Keynes: Paternoster, 2012), 72-85.

also discuss Calvin's understanding of the nature of revelation and biblical metaphors, his usage of feminine imagery for God, and what that means for theology today.

The nature of revelation: God's accommodating[4]

Historically, proponents of the Christian faith have insisted that God is known most fully by self-revelation. God is revealed to Moses as 'I AM WHO I AM,'[5] a designation that goes beyond human limitations. While Adam was given the right to name finite creatures, God alone, not Adam or Moses, nor any other human, has the right to name God.

The Church Fathers understood God's self-revelation in Scripture as God's accommodation to our human capacity and need. Without this assistance, we would be without true knowledge of God. John Calvin, in continuity with this tradition, insists that God cannot be comprehended unless 'he accommodates himself to our standard' and 'anyone who does not allow God to be silent or to speak as he alone decides is striving to impose order on God'.[6] The reformer referred to the apostolic writers as 'sure and genuine scribes' of the Holy Spirit.[7] When the Spirit enters our hearts, then we realize that the Scriptures are the very word of God.[8] When people fashion Scripture according to their own will, Calvin argues, they 'depart from the true God and forsake him . . . having nothing left except an accursed idol'.[9]

Calvin called Scripture the 'School of the Holy Spirit', where 'nothing is omitted that is both necessary and useful to know'.[10] It is the place where God reveals and gives us the opportunity to respond. Ford Lewis Battles points out the importance of Calvin's training as rhetorician in his understanding of the Word. Just as human rhetoric seeks to bridge the gap between the educated and the uneducated through the use of clear, persuasive communication, Calvin taught that the inspired Word uses divine rhetoric to bridge the gap between God and humanity.[11] The reformer did not, however, see the task of the theologian as the same as the rhetorician or philosopher. It is not merely a persuasive

---

[4] Ford Lewis Battles, 'God Was Accommodating Himself to Human Capacity' in *Readings in Calvin's Theology* (Grand Rapids: Baker, 1984), 21. Battles points out that Calvin never uses the noun *accommodatio*, but the verb *accommodare* or *attemperare* in the *Institutes*.
[5] Exodus 3.14, ESV.
[6] *Comm. Ezek.* 9:3,4.
[7] *Inst.* 1.8.9 and 1.8.13.
[8] *Inst.* 1.7.5 and 1.8.13.
[9] Without the Word, people are 'worshipping not God but a figment and a dream of their own heart'—*Inst.* 1.4.1-3.
[10] *Inst.* 3.21.3.
[11] Battles, 'God Was Accommodating Himself,' 22. Battles argues that the root of Calvin's rhetoric background is grounded in the rhetoricians of classical Greece and Rome. He used this training to serve his pastoral role of expounding the Scriptures.

or speculative exercise, but a calling 'to instruct in sound godliness, in the fear of his name, in true trust'.[12] Calvin sought to prepare students to do this by teaching them to properly read the divine Word.[13]

It is necessary, according to Calvin, 'to know how Holy Scripture uses words . . . we cannot at all understand the doctrine of God if we do not know the procedure it employs and its style and language'.[14] In the Word, God speaks to us in baby talk like a nurse does to an infant. 'Such forms of speaking do not so much express clearly what God is like as accommodate the knowledge of Him to our slight capacity. To do this He must descend far beneath His loftiness.'[15] God accommodates to our weakness, representing himself to us 'as He seems', 'not as He is,' in his transcendence.[16] In the divine Scriptures, the reformer argues, God often accomplishes this through figurative language.

Due to blindness and rebellion, Calvin reminds us, the human mind is incapable on its own to bridge the chasm between God and humanity. The spectacles of faith enable one to see what God has revealed, bringing clarity to the otherwise confused knowledge of the Divine.[17] God, the originator of Scripture, has given the testimony of the Holy Spirit so that we 'seek our conviction in a higher place than human reasons, judgments, or conjectures'.[18] Rooted in Calvin's epistemology is the concept of biblical infallibility and a new emphasis on the Word and the Spirit as the source for true knowledge of God.[19] These con-

---

[12] Battles, 'God Was Accommodating Himself,' 22. 'The theologian's task is not to divert the ears with chatter, but to strengthen consciences by teaching things true, sure, and profitable'—*Inst.* 1.14.4.

[13] 'Moreover, it has been my purpose in this labor to prepare and instruct candidates in sacred theology for the reading of the divine Word, in order that they may be able both to have easy access to it and to advance in it without stumbling'—*Inst.* Introduction, 4.

[14] *Serm. John* 1.1-4, 465, quoted in William Bouwsma, *John Calvin: A Sixteenth Century Portrait* (Oxford: OUP, 1988), 188-99.

[15] *Inst.* 1.13.1.

[16] 'God represents Himself to us not as He is in Himself, but as He seems to us, to accommodate to our weak capacity His description of Himself'—*Inst.* 1.17.12f.

[17] *Inst.* 1.4.1-3.

[18] *Inst.* 1.7.4. 'Let this point therefore stand: that those whom the Holy Spirit has inwardly taught truly rest upon Scripture, and that Scripture indeed is self-authenticated; hence, it is not right to subject it to proof and reasoning. And the certainty it deserves with us, it attains by the testimony of the Spirit'—*Inst.* 1.7.5.

[19] Calvin claimed that we are given direct intuitive knowledge of God through Scriptures, where we experience God speaking to us personally. Calvin believed, however, that historic and philological scholarship is necessary in order to remove the opaqueness of scriptural language ('which is ancient and foreign and full of unfamiliar idioms, habits and toms') so the truth of God's Word may show through clearly (*Inst.* 1.6.1). He also discussed how the human condition stands in the way. Only through God's self-revelation and accommodation can humans have true knowledge of God—*Comm. Ps.* 78.60.

victions, coupled with Calvin's interpretative skills, shaped his use of God-language, in general, and his use of feminine imagery, in particular.

Biblical metaphors for God

Calvin, along with other humanists, had a new attentiveness to the nature and use of language.[20] While theologians had always made abundant use of figurative language, Calvin sought to raise people's consciousness of the proper biblical use of metaphors in theology. He believed that metaphorical language is one of the primary ways that God accommodates divine truth to human comprehension.[21]

Calvin held that the images revealed in the Word, even female images, are a revelation of God's character. In response to Isaiah 40.18 in which it is written, 'To whom then will you liken God? or what likeness will compare with him?'[22] Calvin explains that the only way to know God by human reason is to 'frame a likeness of him according to our own fancy'. Instead, he urges the reader to look to the Word, where his 'lively image is exhibited to us'. We should be satisfied with God's manner of communication, and not attempt our seeking God by human methods, which 'teach us vanity and falsehood,' not truth. Calvin writes,

> When the Lord sometimes compares himself to a lion, a bear, a man, or other objects, this has nothing to do with images, as the Papists imagine, but by metaphors either the kindness and mercy of God, or his wrath and displeasure, and other things of the same nature, are expressed; for God cannot reveal himself to us in any other way than by a comparison with things which we know.[23]

In the *Institutes*, Calvin warns the reader, however, to avoid believing that God is changeable 'merely because He accommodated diverse forms to different ages, as He knew would be expedient for each'.[24] God is immutable and the only reliable source for knowledge of the Divine.

---

[20] For further discussion of Calvin as a humanist rhetorician see William J. Bouwsma, 'Renaissance and Reformation: An Essay in the Affinities and Connection' in Heiko A. Oberman (ed.), *Luther and the Dawn of the Modern Era* (Leiden: Brill, 1975), 127-49.; Bouwsma, 'Calvin and the Renaissance Crisis of Knowing,' *CTJ* 17 (1982), 190-211; E. David Willis, 'Rhetoric and Responsibility in Calvin's Theology' in Alexander J. McKelway (ed.), *The Context of Contemporary Theology* (Atlanta: John Knox, 1974), 43-64.

[21] *Inst.* 1.13.1.

[22] Isaiah 40.18, ESV.

[23] *Comm. Isa.* 40.18.

[24] 'If a household instructs, rules, and guides, his children one way in infancy, another way in youth, and still another in young manhood, we shall not on this account call him fickle and say that he abandons his purpose. Why, then do we brand God with

One of the primary biblical self-portraits God uses to accommodate himself to our needs is that of Father, a term that is used in reference to the nation of Israel as well as in reference to all creation. Calvin describes God as 'not only a father but by far the best and kindest of all fathers' and he urges us to recognize that 'He willed that we call Him not only 'Father' but explicitly 'our Father'.[25] This image is essential, according to Calvin, for knowing God as both sovereign and personal, trustworthy and compassionate, just and merciful, and for realizing our kinship with the Trinity as adopted children of God.

God also offers many more self-portraits in Scripture. The Word portrays God as Teacher (Job 33.6), Physician (Jer. 17.5-8), Yahweh (Gen. 3.1-18), Creator (Isa. 45.5-12), Savior (Mark 10.35-45), Shepherd (Ps. 23), King (Ps. 24), Mother (Isa. 49.15), Comforter (Jer. 8.18), and Beloved (Eph. 1.6). What place should be given to these images, particularly the feminine ones?

Calvin's treatment of feminine imagery for God

While the theme of motherhood is scarce in church history, with the exception of Julian of Norwich, nevertheless the use of female imagery is evidenced in the Church Fathers, the 12th century devotional texts, the 14th century Medieval mystics, as well as some of the Scholastics. Two important Church Fathers who employed female imagery for God were Augustine and Clement of Alexandria. Augustine uses the analogy of a nursing Mother in order to explain the incarnation[26] and Clement describes Christ as both Father and Mother.[27] Both Augustine and Clement find the image of mother for God particularly useful in conveying God's love. Yet, neither used female God-language as a literal title given by God.

---

the mark of inconstancy when he has with apt and fitting marks distinguished a diversity of times?'—*Inst.* 2.11.13.

[25] *Inst.* 3.20.37.

[26] 'He who has promised food has nourished us on milk, having recourse to a mother's tenderness. For just as a mother, suckling her infant, transfers in her flesh the very same food which otherwise would be unsuitable to a babe (the little one actually receives what he (or she) would have received at table, but the food conveyed through the flesh is adapted to the child), so our Lord, in order to convert His wisdom into milk for our benefit, came to us clothed in flesh'—Augustine, *On the Psalms*, cited by Jennifer Heimmel, *'God is our mother': Julian of Norwich and the medieval image of Christian feminine divinity* (Salzburg, Austria: Institut fur Anglistik und Amerikanistik, Universitat Salzburg, 1982), 25.

[27] 'The Word is everything to the child, both father and mother, teacher and nurse. . . . The nutriment is the milk of the father . . . and the Word alone supplies us children with the milk of love, and only those who suck at this breast are truly happy. . . . For this reason seeking is called sucking; to those infants who seek the Word, the Father's loving breasts supply milk'—Clement of Alexandria, 'The Instructor' in Alexander Roberts and James Donaldson (eds), *The Ante-Nicene Fathers: Translation of the Writings of the Fathers down to AD 325* (Grand Rapids: Eerdmans, 1956), 1.6.

ASPECTS OF REFORMING

These examples suggest that Calvin came out of a tradition that was not adamantly opposed to feminine imagery and God-language. While the use of female imagery and God-language varied throughout the time prior to John Calvin a few general observations should be made. First, while female imagery and God-language was used throughout church history, it was never prominent. Second, when it was utilized, it was mainly in devotional works and not theological treatises. Third, the main purpose of female imagery, especially maternal imagery, was to declare God's love and nurturing care in redeeming and sustaining his children. In expressing this, God's love and nurturance is seen as extending beyond gender distinctions. This enabled writers to couple maternal imagery and masculine God-language together. Last, some of the writers extend feminine imagery and God-language beyond metaphorical usage to name and address God, yet they never attempt to have it function as a replacement for male God-language.

The traditional use of feminine imagery prior to John Calvin may have had an influence on his usage of it. Calvin diverged from tradition, however, in that he never sought to utilize female imagery for God unless Scripture called for it. Furthermore, based on his belief in *sola Scriptura*, Calvin opposed the dismissal of male God-language in favor of female, since male God-language, including the term 'Father,' is a fundamental part of God's self-revelation. Calvin did not, however, completely dismiss the use of feminine biblical images for God. In fact, Calvin's epistemology led him to employ these images freely when they accorded with Scripture. While Calvin did not employ any feminine language for God in *The Institutes of the Christian Religion*, he does not shy away from it in his biblical commentaries.

Calvin's biblical epistemology enables him to utilize many of the same female images for God that feminists[28] promote such as a woman in labor,[29] midwife,[30] nursing mother,[31] mother eagle,[32] and mother hen.[33] Yet, his use of them can be seen today as a critique of both feminists as well as some traditionalists. While he freely uses these maternal images primarily to express God's love and nurturing care and shows no apprehension that they would promote heretical views of God, he does so only when the Bible merits their use and never in place of masculine imagery. Furthermore, he makes a distinction between metaphoric language and titles of identity. While Calvin recognizes feminine imagery throughout Scripture and particularly in the Psalms, the Prophets

---

[28] Virginia Mollenkott, *The Divine Feminine: the Biblical Image of God as Female* (New York: Crossroad, 1983). In this book she explicates the feminine images listed for Calvin as well as others.
[29] *Comm. Isa.* 42.14.
[30] *Comm. Ps.* 22.9.
[31] *Comm. Isa.* 49.15.
[32] *Comm. Deut.* 32.11.
[33] *Comm. Ps.* 91.4 and *Harmony Matt, Mark, and Luke*, 3.68.

and some New Testament texts, this work will focus on a few key feminine images: mother bird, woman in labor, womb, and mother.

Mother bird

The images of God as bird and of God's sheltering wings have often been interpreted in feminine terms. This imagery is commonly found in Psalms 57, 91, 61 and 102, as well as Matthew 23. Calvin recognized the female imagery in these passages when his translation of Scripture called him to.

In Psalms 57 and 91, Calvin recognized the significance of the feminine imagery. In Psalm 91.4 it is written, 'He will cover you with his pinions, and under his wings you will find refuge; his faithfulness is a shield and buckler.'[34] In the tradition of Augustine, Calvin connects the protecting wings in Psalm 91 to Christ's description in Matthew of the sheltering wings of a mother hen. In linking the two images, Calvin explains the passage as a metaphor of the intimacy into which God invites believers.[35] Calvin writes that this passage 'beautifully expresses the singularly tender care with which God watches over our safety'. He points to the surprising nature of God's self-revelation.

> When we consider the majesty of God, there is nothing which would suggest a likeness such as is here drawn between him and the hen or other birds, who spread their wings over their young ones to cherish and protect them. But, in accommodation to our infirmity, he does not regard it as a burden to descent, as it were, from the heavenly glory which belongs to him in order to encourage us more alluringly to approach him under so humble a similitude as that of a hen. Since he condescends in such a gracious manner to our weakness, surely there is nothing to prevent us from coming to him with the greatest freedom.[36]

While Calvin freely connects the sheltering wings in Psalms 57 and 91 to the female imagery of a mother hen, he ignores the imagery in Psalms 61.3 and 102.6. These omissions, however, do not seem to be an intentional neglect of the feminine imagery, as some scholars have suggested.[37] They seem to be more a result of Calvin's skill as a text critic and Hebrew scholar rather than a patriarchal bias.[38]

---

[34] Psalm 91.4, ESV.
[35] He makes a similar connection in his interpretation of Psalm 57. See *Comm. Ps.* 57.1.
[36] *Comm. Ps.* 91.4.
[37] In Jane Dempsey Douglass' article, 'Calvin's Use of Metaphorical Language for God: God as Enemy and God as Mother,' *PSB* 8 (1987), 26, she suggests that Calvin is quick to dismiss female metaphors that denote some sort of power, such as midwife and mistress and emphasizes ones of humility.
[38] Calvin translates 'shelter' in Ps. 61.3 as 'refuge' and 'strength' and the bird in Ps. 102.6 as a melancholy bird rather than a sacrificial mother pelican. See Augustine's commentary on Psalm 61.3. Traditionally the bird in Ps. 102 was thought to be a mother pelican, which was believed to revive her chicks with her own blood. Augus-

Woman in labor

In his explication of the prophetic writings, Calvin recognizes the feminine image of a woman in labor. Isaiah 42.13-14 uses both the metaphor of a warrior and that of a woman in labor. In this passage Calvin sees the maternal image once again as God's accommodating to our capacity in order that we may know how eagerly God desires to preserve us. When God uses the metaphor of a laboring mother, God reveals 'love and tenderness of affection'. While this image may not seem appropriate for God, Calvin declares God must 'borrow comparisons from known objects, in order to enable us to understand those which are unknown to us'. While 'God loves very differently from human beings, that is, more fully and perfectly although he surpasses all human affections, yet nothing that is disorderly belongs to him.'[39] At first glance this statement seems to support the allegation that Calvin recognizes feminine imagery when it represents an image of weakness or self-humiliation.[40] While Calvin asserts the image of a laboring woman may be somewhat debasing, he does not imply this is due to God being compared to a woman. Rather, Calvin connects the degradation to the idea of God suffering.[41] In his explication of this passage, Calvin sees the female metaphor of a woman in labor as a positive expression of God's warm love and tender affection.

Womb

In Isaiah, Calvin also identifies the feminine imagery of the womb. The writer proclaims in Isaiah 46.3: 'Listen to me, O house of Jacob, all the remnant of the house of Israel, who have been borne by me from before your birth, carried from the womb.'[42] While Calvin could have understood this verse as a reference to God's parental care, he interpreted it in terms of maternal imagery. Since God spiritually begat his people, Calvin does not disapprove of the idea that they were brought forth from the womb of God.

The biblical scholar points out that this 'very expressive metaphor' which is a testimony of God's grace could be understood as simply a picture of how God nourished the Israelites, like a father or a nurse. But God reveals far more than this, as James 1.18 suggests. Calvin writes that God 'also "begat them" spiritually, I do not object to extending the words so far as to mean, that they were

---

tine connected this image with Christ's sacrifice proclaiming that he has both 'paternal authority and maternal feeling'—*Comm. Ps*, C.C. 40, 1430-32.

[39] *Comm. Isa.* 42.14.

[40] Dempsey Douglass, 'Calvin's Use of Metaphorical Language for God', 26.

[41] 'Because that comparison of a laboring woman might somewhat degrade the majesty and power of God, the Prophet determined to add here a different feeling. So far then as relates to love, he says that God resembles a mother; so far as relates to power, he says that he resembles a lion or a giant'—*Comm. Isa.* 42.14.

[42] Isaiah 46.3, ESV.

brought, as it were, out of the bowels of God into a new life and the hope of an eternal inheritance.'[43]

Contrary to those who oppose maternal imagery on the basis that it encourages heretical and pantheistic views of God,[44] Calvin sees maternal imagery, especially that of the womb, as a defense against idolatry, writing that in opposition to the Babylonian gods that had to be carried on carts, the God of Israel '"carries" his people, like a mother carries the child in her womb, and afterwards carries it in her bosom'. The prophet gives the Jews comfort by pointing out that God 'bore them and their burdens'. Unlike the dead weight of idols, Calvin points out that the Israelites have experienced God's power and benefits from their conception.[45] According to Calvin, the image of the womb is an indispensable revelation of God's power and love, both in Godself and in us.

In communicating this, Calvin posits that the love of God surpasses any metaphor. Therefore, we should not limit God to the image of Father. Instead, we should recognize God as he has manifested himself as both Father and through the metaphor of Mother. He writes,

> If it be objected, that God is everywhere called 'a Father,' (Jeremiah 31.9; Malachi 1.6) and that this title is more appropriate to him, I reply, that no figures of speech can describe God's extraordinary affection towards us. . . . By no metaphor, therefore, can his incomparable goodness be described. . . . In a word, the intention of the Prophet is to show . . . that God, who has manifested himself to be both their Father and their Mother, will always assist them; and likewise, that they have known his power by uninterrupted experience, so that they ought not to pay homage to idols.[46]

---

[43] *Comm. Isa.* 42.14. 'This is a very expressive metaphor, by which God compares himself to a mother who carries a child in her womb. He speaks of the past time, when he began to give them testimonies of his grace. Yet the words might be taken as meaning simply that God kindly nourished that people, like an infant taken from its mother's womb, and carried it in his bosom. . . . But as God not only begins to act as the father and nurse of his people from the time when they were born, but also "begat them" (James 1.18) spiritually, I do not object to extending the words so far as to mean, that they were brought, as it were, out of the bowels of God into a new life and the hope of an eternal inheritance.'

[44] Elizabeth Achtemeier argues in 'Exchanging God for "no gods": A Discussion of Female Language for God' in A. Kimel Jr. (ed.), *Speaking the Christian God* (Grand Rapids: Eerdmans, 1992), 9, that 'If God is portrayed in feminine language, the figures of carrying in the womb, of giving birth, and of suckling immediately come into play. . . . But if the creation has issued forth from the body of the deity, it shares in deity's substance; deity is in, through, and under all things, and therefore everything is divine if God is identified with his creation, we finally make ourselves gods and goddesses.'

[45] *Comm. Isa.* 46.3.

[46] *Comm. Isa.* 46.3.

While Calvin never suggests that the term 'Father' for God should be usurped by the term 'Mother', nonetheless, in his interpretation of this passage, he suggests the inadequacy limiting God to this designation. He sees the image of the womb and our begetting by God as God's self-revelation of love and power which calls us to recognize him as both Father and Mother, our source of life and sustenance.

Mother

Closely related to the image of the womb in the prophetic writings is the metaphor of God as Mother. Calvin discusses the importance of this image in his exposition of Isaiah 49.15, 66.12-13 and 31.5. In the first of these, the writer compares God's love to that of a mother. Calvin suggests that a mother's love is an even stronger metaphor than that of a father's love.[47]

Calvin proposes that the female image of a mother for God, particularly when it is connected with the womb, is a stronger expression of affection. In this passage, God gave us this metaphor alongside the father image to show us God's ardent love. Yet, it, too, should be recognized as inadequate if it is grounded in human experience. He asserts that God's affection is 'far stronger and warmer than the love of all mothers'. Calvin compares God's love to the self-indulgent love of human parents who are 'anxious about their children,' asking, 'What shall God do, who is goodness itself? Will it be possible for him to lay aside a father's love?' He responds with the biblical answer 'certainly not'. Even though a human mother at times may forsake her children, God will never forsake them. Though we may experience afflictions, Calvin reminds us that God watches over our salvation with perfect, unremitting, motherly love.[48] God is compared to both a father and mother in Scripture to accommodate the knowledge of God's love and power to us. God, however, transcends these images, defining a perfect, unconditional love.[49]

---

[47] 'In order to correct that distrust, . . . he shows how strong is his anxiety about his people, comparing himself to a mother, whose love toward her offspring is so strong and ardent, as to leave far behind it a father's love. Thus he did not satisfy himself with proposing the example of a father (which on other occasions he very frequently employs,) but in order to express his very strong affection, he chose to liken himself to a mother, and calls them not merely "children" but *the fruit of the womb*, towards which there is usually a warmer affection. What amazing affection does a mother feel toward her offspring, which she cherishes in her bosom, suckles on her breast, and watches over with tender care, so that she passes sleepless nights, wears herself out by continued anxiety, and forgets herself!'—*Comm. Isa.* 49.15.

[48] *Comm. Isa.* 49.15.

[49] Calvin returns to this metaphor in Isaiah 66. 'He continues his metaphor, and compares the children of God to infants, that are carried in the arms, and warmed in the bosom of their mothers, who even play with them. And in order that he may express more strongly his affection toward us, he compares himself to a mother, whose love, as we have formerly seen, exceeds every other by a wide interval. The Lord wishes to be to us in the room of a mother, that, instead of the annoyances, reproaches, dis-

Church as mother

While Calvin does not shy away from using female metaphors for God when Scripture calls him to, it is important to realize that he never uses these female images as God-given titles for God.[50] The concept of mother coupled with the image of God as our Father enables us to understand our position as children of God. The Father gathers his offspring in church 'not only that they may be nourished by her help and ministry as long as they are infants and children but also that they may be guided by her motherly care until they mature and at last reach the goal of faith'.[51] While Calvin includes biblical, maternal imagery in his conception of God, it is the church that is rightly attributed this title. Scripture reveals that God the Father gave us over to the motherly care of the church.

While Calvin advocates the title 'Mother' for the church, in examining his works it is readily apparent that he does not advocate the use of the title 'Mother' for God in worship or prayer. In fact, it may even be said that the reformer, in general, reads much less female imagery for God than some of his predecessors and those that come after him.[52] It has been suggested that his lack of attentiveness to this imagery is a result of the reformer's patriarchal tendencies.[53] Whenever Calvin finds a female image for God in the biblical text, however, he consistently accepts it as genuine and acknowledges it. He is careful, though, to recognize the limitations of metaphoric language about God and not to extend the feminine or masculine images beyond their biblical use.[54] While some people might find it offensive to liken God to a woman in labor or a brooding hen, Calvin sees these biblical metaphors as God-given accommodations. He does not, however, extend these allusions to titles, since God does not use these metaphors as self-given names in the Word, ultimately leaving God's name to God.

---

tresses, and anxieties, which we have endured, he may treat us gently, and, as it were, fondle us in his bosom'—*Comm. Isa.* 46.12.

[50] 'There is no other way to enter into life unless this mother conceive us in her womb, give us birth, nourish us at her breast, and lastly unless she keep us under her care and guidance until, putting off mortal flesh, we become like the angels (Matt. 22.30). Our weakness does not allow us to be dismissed from her school until we have been pupils all our lives. Furthermore, away from her bosom one cannot hope for any forgiveness of sins or any salvation'—*Inst.* 4.1.4.

[51] *Inst.* 4.1.5

[52] Dempsey Douglass, 'Calvin's Use of Metaphorical Language for God,' 26.

[53] Eleanor L. McLaughlin, 'Male and Female in Christian Tradition: Was there a Reformation in the sixteenth century?' in Ruth Tiffany Barnhouse and Urban T. Holmes, III (eds), *Male and Female: Christian Approaches to Sexuality* (NY: Seabury, 1976), 50.

[54] However, he never attempts to explain the Fatherhood of God in terms of metaphoric language. God does not gain his identity as our Father from human fathers. Instead, God's Fatherhood is grounded in God's relationship to Jesus Christ. Through our adoption, we are given the right to be called children of God.

ASPECTS OF REFORMING

Conclusion

So how should we respond to Juliet's question in reference to God? What is in a name? How much should God-language be adapted or changed to speak to the current culture? In order to answer this question the Church must examine its epistemology.

Calvin's epistemology is clear. God is the source of true knowledge of the Divine. Therefore, Calvin felt free to utilize both masculine and feminine imagery for God as long as it is rooted in Scripture. Calvin is not only conscious of female metaphors for God in the Bible, but believes that these metaphors are edifying to Christian people. While, at times, he does not recognize some of the images that had previously been explicated this seems more due to his interpretative skills than to a bias against this imagery. Calvin assumes that whatever manner God chooses to use to speak is absolutely proper and purposeful.

This approach helps us to see that the answer to the question 'What's in a name?' is very different when we ask it about God than when we ask it about creatures. Calvin points out that God alone has the authority to name God. While God uses metaphors, similes, images, and titles, God is Spirit and beyond figurative language. God's self-revelation gives us a glimpse of God's identity and God's relationship to creation, but God is far beyond the human limitations of knowing.

When the knowledge of God moves away from a theocentric approach, like Calvin's, and is grounded solely in human experience, inaccurate ideas can be deposited onto God. Though little flashes of God can be perceived naturally through reason and perception, they are quickly obscured by sin and rebellion. Natural knowledge of God, as Calvin described, is like a 'traveler passing through a field at night who in a momentary lightening flash sees far and wide, but the sight vanishes so swiftly that he is plunged again into the darkness of the night before he can take even a step—let alone be directed on his way by its help'.[55] As Calvin would insist, this can only be corrected by the light of God, which is most clearly expressed in Christ's revelation of his relationship with the Father.[56] As Jesus himself proclaims in John 8.12, Christ is 'the light of the

---

[55] *Inst.* 2.2.18.
[56] Donald Bloesch, *Is the Bible Sexist?* (Westchester, IL: Crossway, 1982), 78, reinforces this idea saying, 'The criterion for deciding what analogical language is most appropriate is the self-revelation of God in Jesus Christ given in the Bible. To begin from human nature and experience and then posit in God the perfection of the creature is to end in the impasse of natural theology. This is the path taken by both ideological patriarchalists and feminists; it has also been the course followed by German Christians and Christian Marxists, who have sought to read into the faith their own ideological commitments. The way of faith on the other hand, begins with the Word of God in Scripture and listens to God's own self-witness, which comes to us in the form of analogy to be sure but in an analogy determined by divine revelation and not by human wisdom.'

world. Whoever follows' him 'will not walk in darkness, but will have the light of life.'

At forefront of Calvin's mind is what should be at the forefront of our minds: God reveals not only so we can know God, but also so we can respond. Knowledge of God is not for puffing up the human mind, but rather for equipping people to glorify God. Our love of God and neighbor is directly related to our knowledge of God. If we know God only through our marred, natural perceptions, we know nothing of God's glory and love. If we know God through God's accommodating self-portrait, we can call out to our 'Abba Father' and find liberation.[57]

---

[57] For further discussion of this see Bernard Cooke, 'Non-Patriarchal Salvation,' *Horizons* 10 (1983), 30-31.

CHAPTER 7

Calvin's final verdict on the Augsburg Confession.

Peter A. Lillback

'I am carefully on the watch that Lutheranism gain no ground,
nor be introduced into France.'

The *Augsburg Confession* has served as an important Protestant ecumenical symbol since it was written in 1530 by Philip Melanchthon. As the first Lutheran creed, it summarizes the biblical teachings of Luther's reformation.[1] The Reformed tradition had previously produced various statements of faith, such as Zwingli's 67 Articles (1523), The Ten Theses of Bern (1528) and Bucer's Tetrapolitan Confession (1530), since he and others chose not to sign the *Augsburg Confession*. For the Protestant reformers who held to the principle of *sola Scriptura*, the Scriptures were the superior standard or the 'norming norm' (*norma normans*) while their confessions were the subordinate standards or the 'normed norms' (*norma normata*).[2] Given that such a commitment to *sola Scriptura* was absent in Roman Catholic theology, confessional subscription in the sixteenth century Roman Catholic context required, instead, an adherence to the teaching of the 'holy mother Church'.[3] Thus, the *Augsburg Confession*,

---

[1] See F. Bente, *Historical Introductions to the Book of Concord* (St. Louis: Concordia, 1965), 8-9; *The Book of Concord* (translated and edited by Theodore G. Tappert; Philadelphia: Fortress, 1978), 7-8, 14, 95-96, 316-17, 636; 'Subscription' in John McClintock and James Strong (eds), *Cyclopedia of Theological Literature* (New York: Harper, 1881), 10.3-4.

[2] Cf., Philip Schaff, *The Creeds of Christendom* (Grand Rapids: Baker, 1977), 1.7-8.

[3] Cf., Philip Schaff, *History of the Christian Church* (Grand Rapids: Eerdmans, 1979), 8.609; 2.207-10. In this post-Vatican II era, and with the apparent warming of relationships between American evangelicals and American Catholics, it is important to understand that Vatican II in no way lessened the Church's allegiance to the decrees of the Council of Trent. Cf., Austin Flannery (ed.), *Vatican Council II: The Conciliar Documents* (Northport: Costello, 1979), 11, 18, 104, 121, 137-38, 153, 157-61, 186, 206, 412, 435, 489, 724. Cf., especially, 18, which says, 'The dogmatic principles which were laid down by the Council of Trent remaining intact. . . .', and 121, which says, '. . . leaving intact the principles of the Council of Trent'.

with its dependence upon Scripture and its origin in Luther's reforms, held important ecumenical significance for the early years of Lutheran and Reformed Protestantism.[4] Its ecumenical implications have continued through the centuries, in part due to the *Augsburg's* teaching on the unity and nature of the church.[5] Thus, these ecclesiastical perspectives, coupled with its primal Protestant theology, have made the *Augustana* an important ecumenical document from its reformation context to the union and ecumenical efforts of European Protestantism. In the nineteenth century this can be seen in the German Evangelical Kirchentag,[6] in the twentieth with the Hochkirchliche Vereinigung Augsburgischen Bekenntnisses (*High Church Union of the Augsburg Confession*),[7] and in the twenty-first with The Protestant Church in the Netherlands (PCN).[8]

With this backdrop, consider, then, the following remark made by Arthur C. Cochrane, 'Recently Dr. James I. McCord, President of Princeton Theological Seminary, expressed to me his profound regret that The United Presbyterian Church in the USA did not include the *Augustana* in its Book of Confessions of 1967. And I now publicly express my embarrassment that I did not include it in my collection, *Reformed Confessions of the 16th Century* (Westminster,

---

[4] Cf. Schaff, *Creeds*, 1.529. J.V. Fesko writes, 'Evidence of the basic agreement between the Lutherans and Reformed appears in the *Harmonia Confessionum Fidei Orthodoxarum et Reformatarum* (1581) that was compiled by Theodore Beza. . . . The *Harmonia Confessionum* was approved by the pastors of Geneva, Zurich, Schaffhausen, Bern and Neustadt. Beyond the Swiss formal adoption, the *Harmonia Confessionum* was published in the name of the churches of France and Belgium. The overall goal of the *Harmonia Confessionum* was to demonstrate the unity of opinion among the Reformed churches spread across Europe and the British Isles. Moreover, the intention of the work was to demonstrate Reformed agreement with Lutheran theology.'

[5] See *Augsburg Confession* Article VII: Of the Church, Article VIII: What the Church Is. See http://www.elca.org/Who-We-Are/Our-Three-Expressions/Churchwide-Organization/Office-of-the-Presiding-Bishop/Ecumenical-and-Inter-Religious-Relations/Full-Communion-Partners.aspx.

[6] See the minutes of the proceedings of the German Evangelical Kirchentag's annual meeting in Berlin, in September, 1853, in *Evangelical Christendom*, volumes 7-8 by Evangelical Alliance.

[7] Hochkirchliche Vereinigung Augsburgischen Bekenntnisses (*High Church Union of the Augsburg Confession*) is a Lutheran High Church organization in Germany. It was founded in Berlin, October 1918, inspired by High Church theses Stimuli et Clavi, 1917, by Heinrich Hansen. Later, it has been greatly influenced by the Evangelical Catholic theology of Friedrich Heiler. See http://en.wikipedia.org/wiki/Hochkirchliche_Vereinigung_Augsburgischen_Bekenntnisses

[8] The Protestant Church in the Netherlands (PCN) (Formerly, Reformed Churches in the Netherlands and Uniting Protestant Churches in the Netherlands). See http://www.google.com/#sclient=psy-ab&hl=en&source=hp&q=The+Protestant+Church+in+the+Netherlands.

1966).'⁹ This is a remarkable admission. Public profound presidential regret and a written admission of scholarly embarrassment are relatively rare, particularly in the Reformed tradition. This suggests that the slight against the *Augsburg Confession* must have been construed as a major *faux pas*! To add insult to injury, Calvin, the great founding father of the Reformed tradition, subscribed to the *Augsburg Confession*. And, according to Richard Stauffer, Calvin even signed the *Augustana* in its original 1530 form—the unaltered version that has been adhered to by the staunchest Lutherans since it presents Luther's Eucharistic doctrine of consubstantiation.[10]

In 1540, Melanchthon softened the Lutheran teaching on the Lord's Supper, making it easier for Reformed believers to sign the Confession. This act created the distinction between the 1530 *Invariata* (unaltered) and the 1540 *Variata* (altered) versions of the *Augsburg Confession*. It, also, created a firestorm of debate that lasted for decades that was only brought to a conclusion through an imposed unity in 1580 by the Lutheran Formula of Concord.

So, in what manner did Calvin sign the *Augsburg Confession*? The view of Richard Stauffer, as we have just seen, declares that Calvin signed the *Invariata*. The view of Irene Dingel is that should this be true, Calvin signed it with an exception.[11] Unfortunately, the historic confessional documents that would help us determine Calvin's intentions when he subscribed to the *Augsburg* were lost in World War II. Moreover, this raises the question of whether Calvin's subscription was *because* he held that the *Augsburg* was the Word of God (a *quia* subscription) or *as far as* it was in agreement with the Word of God (a *quatenus* subscription).[12] The evidence that is available and that will be considered below leads to the conclusion that contrary to Calvin's ideal, his subscription to the *Augsburg Confession* was a *quatenus* subscription, not a *quia* subscription. Moreover, contrary to Arthur Cochrane's apology and President James

---

[9] Arthur C. Cochrane, 'Reading the *Augustana* from the Reformed Tradition' in *Currents in Theology and Mission* (St. Louis, Faculty of Concordia Seminary in Exile, 1980).

[10] Richard Stauffer, *The Quest for Church Unity: From John Calvin to Isaac d'Huuisseau* (Allison Park, PA: Pickwick, 1986), 9. See Willem Nijenhuis, *Calvinus Oecumenicus: Calvijn en de eenheid der kerk in het licht van zijn briefwisseling* (La Haye, 1958). Cf. *Ecclesia Reformata. Studies on the Reformation* (Leyden, 1972), 113. I am indebted to Professor Anthony Lane for directing me to Stauffer's work.

[11] This is based on a personal conversation with Dr. Irene Dingel, August 22-27, 2010.

[12] A confession of faith is a norm that is normed by Scripture. To what *extent*, then, can a confession be considered authoritative? Is it to be subscribed because (*quia*) it is Scripture or is it to be subscribed as far as (*quatenus*) it is Scripture? Cf. E.H. Klotsche, *Christian Symbolics or Exposition of the Distinctive Characteristics of the Catholic, Lutheran and Reformed Churches as well as the Modern Denominations and Sects Represented in this Country* (Burlington: Lutheran Literary Board, 1929), 15-16. Cf., James R. Payton, Jr., 'The Background and Significance of the Adopting Act of 1729' in *Pressing Toward the Mark* (Philadelphia: Committee for the Historian of the Orthodox Presbyterian Church, 1986), 136ff.

McCord's profound regret, it is clear that Calvin would *not* have included the *Augustana* in a French collection of sixteenth century Reformed confessions, at least not after 1561.

To establish these claims, we will consider Calvin's engagement with the *Augsburg Confession* from his initial subscription to his final verdict on the *Augustana*.[13] In particular, we will explore several letters written by Calvin from August 1561 to September 1563,[14] and, we will review a confession written by Calvin at that time to resist the entrance of Lutheranism into France.

Calvin's views of confessional subscription

So did Calvin advocate a *quia* (because it is Scripture) or a *quatenus* (as far as it is Scripture) subscription? An early example of Calvin's encounter with confessional subscription is with Peter Caroli in respect to the *Athanasian Creed*. In a letter to Megander (1537) Calvin writes,

> That he [Caroli] might, therefore, appear to have got the better of us in something or other, he accused the whole meeting of Arianism. I rose up immediately and brought forward the confession in our Catechism, which is repeated in our public letter to your college. Even this did not quiet him, but he declared that we would be suspected in that matter, until we subscribed to the creed of Athanasius. I replied, that it was not my practice *to approve any thing as the words of God, unless upon due consideration*.[15]

This passage is instructive since it shows that Calvin viewed subscription to a confession as ideally a *quia*-subscription, that is, 'as the words of God'.

Similarly, when differences broke out on the doctrine of the Trinity in the Italian congregation in Geneva (1558), Calvin developed a creed entitled, *Summary of the Confession of Faith of the Students of the Academy of Geneva*, that required a high subscription that was tantamount to a *quia* subscription.[16] Thus, in the wake of the anti-Trinitarian controversy Calvin essentially sought a *quia* subscription. But was Calvin able to subscribe to the *Augsburg Confession* in this way?

---

[13] This article builds on P.A. Lillback, 'Confessional Subscription Among 16th Century Reformers' in David Hall (ed.), *The Practice of Confessional Subscription* (University Press of America, 1995), 33-65.

[14] These were written to royal figures: The King of Navarre, August 1561; Admiral Coligny, September 24, 1561; Comte of Erbach, September 30, 1561; The Prince of Conde, May 10, 1563; September 17, 1563; as well as theological leaders: Theodore Beza, September 10, 1561; October 1, 1561; Heinrich Bullinger, November 5, 1561; July 2, 1563; September 9, 1563.

[15] John Calvin, *Selected Works* (Grand Rapids: Baker, 1983), 4.49, emphasis added.

[16] Of this incident, see Calvin's letter to the Marquis De Vico, *Selected Works*, 6.442-44 (443n.2). For the text of the Confession, see *The Register of the Company of Pastors of Geneva in the Time of Calvin* (edited and translated by Philip E. Hughes; Grand Rapids: Eerdmans, 1966), 345-46.

ASPECTS OF REFORMING

The *Augsburg Confession* in the various stages of Calvin's career

Calvin's sojourn in Strasbourg (1539-1541) under the Augsburg Confession (1530-1540)

Calvin's exile from Geneva brought him to Strasbourg (1539-1541). Strasbourg adhered to the original 1530 *Augustana*, before it had been changed by Melanchthon in 1540. Melanchthon's original Confession presented Luther's doctrine of the Lord's Supper as follows:

> Article X: Of the Lord's Supper.
>
> Of the Supper of the Lord they teach that the Body and Blood of Christ are truly present, and are distributed to those who eat the Supper of the Lord; and they reject those that teach otherwise.[17]

The altered *Augsburg Confession* states:

> Concerning the Lord's Supper, they teach that 'with' bread and wine are truly exhibited the body and blood of Christ to those that eat in the Lord's Supper.[18]

Melanchthon's changes to the *Augsburg Confession* especially impacted the Lutheran view of the Lord's Supper. As its author, he felt a certain freedom to 'improve' the Confession in light of changes in his understanding of theology. Consequently, in 1540 the *Variata* was born. The rationale for Melanchthon's changes was, in part, found in a decided move in a Reformed direction in his understanding of the Sacrament of the Lord's Supper.[19]

The timing of Calvin's stay in Strasbourg might corroborate Stauffer's assessment that he had signed the *Invariata*:

> During his stay in Strasbourg, the French Reformer had had the occasion to participate, side by side with Lutheran theologians, in the Colloquies of Haguenau, Worms, and Ratisbon, . . . to participate in these encounters, and to represent Strasbourg, he had to sign that charter of Lutheranism, the Augsburg Confession,

---

[17] The Latin version with German additions with an English translation are as follows: *De Cœna Domini docent, quod corpus et sanguis [wahrer Leib und Blut] Christi vere adsint [unter Gestalt des Brotes und Weines], et distribuantur vescentibus [da ausgetheilt und genommen wird] in Cœna Domini; et improbant secus docentes [Derhalben wird auch die Gegenlehr verworfen].*
Of the Supper of the Lord they teach that the [true] body and blood of Christ are truly present [under the form of bread and wine], and are [there] communicated to those that eat in the Lord's Supper [and receive]. And they disapprove of those that teach otherwise [wherefore also the opposite doctrine is rejected].

[18] See Schaff, *Creeds*, 3.13; Stauffer, *Quest*, 23n.37. Cf. *Die Bekenntnisschriften der evangelisch-luterischen Kirche* (Gottingen, 1959), 64-65.

[19] Bard Thompson, 'Historical Background of the Catechism' in *Essays on the Heidelberg Catechism* (Philadelphia: United Church, 1963), 12-13. See Calvin to Farel, March 1539, *Selected Works*, 4.129-30.

not, as it has often been claimed, in its 1540 version, the *Confessio Augustana Variata*, but in its primitive version, . . . the *Invariata* of 1530.[20]

While this sounds like a compelling argument, given the dates of Calvin's ministry in Strasbourg, the claim does not necessarily square with the facts. James William Richard and Philip Schaff present substantive evidence that the *Variata* was the version of the *Augsburg* that was used at the Colloquies of Haguenau, Worms, and Ratisbon.[21] Nevertheless, during these years, whether with the *Variata* or the *Invariata*, Calvin was impacted by both Luther and the Swiss reformers.[22]

From Strasbourg Calvin engaged various reformers wherein his views of Luther, the Zwinglians and their theology were revealed. He wrote on February 21, 1538, to Bullinger expressing his hope of reconciliation between Luther and the Reformed.[23] But in October of that year he wrote to Farel confessing that the efforts of Bucer and others to reconnect the Zurichers with the Lutherans was unsuccessful.[24] The failure to unite the Protestants, in Calvin's mind, was due to all sides, including Luther.[25] The casualty in the process was Bucer's reputation.[26] Nevertheless, in spite of it all, Calvin could celebrate that 'For the first time, we have administered the sacrament of the Supper in our little church [The French Church of Strasbourg] according to the custom of the place, which we purpose to repeat every month.'[27]

The following February, Calvin wrote to Farel, who had urged efforts for Protestant union. Calvin explained that strenuous, if unsuccessful, efforts had

---

[20] Stauffer, *Quest*, 9. See Nijenhuis, *Calvinus Oecumenicus*. Cf. *Ecclesia Reformata. Studies on the Reformation* (Leyden, 1972), 113.

[21] See James William Richard, books.google.comhttp://books.google.com/books/about/Philip_Melanchthon_the_Pro testant_precep.html?id=3fYEAAAAYAAJ&utm_source=gb-gplus-sharePhilip Melanchthon, the Protestant preceptor of Germany, 1497-1560. Philip Melanchthon, the Protestant Preceptor of Germany, 1497-1560 (NY: Putnam, 1898), 281-95. Cf. Schaff, *Creeds*, 1:241-42.

[22] Cf. Stauffer, *Quest*, 1, 6-7.

[23] While Calvin felt as though he was not receiving sufficient intelligence during this time, there seemed to be a growing hope of a union between Luther and the Reformed as some of the correspondence shows. See Calvin, *Selected Works*, 4:67, To Henry Bullinger, February 21, 1538; to Capito, December 6, 1537. Luther wrote, 'I write these things that you may know that our heart is upright and sincere in the hope of agreement; may the Lord himself complete the work. Amen.' In a letter to Bullinger, March 4, 1538, Luther expressed a remarkable respect to the memory of Zwingli and Oecolampadius: 'I can freely declare that, after having seen and heard Zwingli at Marbourg, I have considered and esteemed him as a most excellent man, as also Oecolampadius; so that their calamity has well-nigh disheartened me.'

[24] Cf. Calvin, *Selected Works*, 4.89n.2. Calvin to Farel, October 1538, 4.89.

[25] Calvin, *Selected Works*, 4.89-90.

[26] Calvin, *Selected Works*, 4.89-90. Cf. 4.108ns1-2.

[27] Calvin, *Selected Works*, 4.92, October, 1538.

already been attempted to that end. In the process, Calvin, also, articulated his high respect for Luther and Zwingli, while confiding a sense of the primacy of Luther.[28] Efforts to connect Zurich and Calvin's Strasbourg continued in spite of misunderstandings. After a lengthy silence, Calvin wrote to Bullinger in March, 1539, to strengthen the bonds of friendship and to address what Calvin believed was the Zurichers' unjust prejudice against Bucer and the Reformed ministers in Strasbourg.[29] In November Calvin wrote to Farel relating news that Luther had actually spoken well of Calvin and his writings even though Calvin had been critical of Luther.

> Crato, one of our engravers, lately returned from Wittenberg, who brought a letter from Luther to Bucer, in which there was written: 'Salute for me reverently Sturm and Calvin, whose books I have read with special delight.' Now, consider seriously what I have said there about the Eucharist; think of the ingenuousness of Luther: it will now be easy for you to see how unreasonable are those who so obstinately dissent from him. Philip, however, wrote thus: 'Luther and Pomeranus have desired Calvin to be greeted; Calvin has acquired great favour in their eyes.' Philip has informed me at the same time by the messenger, that certain persons, in order to irritate Luther, have shown him a passage in which he and his friends have been criticised by me; that thereupon he had examined the passage, and feeling that it was undoubtedly intended for him, had said at length: 'I hope that Calvin will one day think better of us; but in any event it is well that he should even now have a proof of our good feeling towards him.' If we are not affected by such moderation, we are certainly of stone.[30]

Thus we find that Calvin, while in Strasbourg, was not only supportive of the Lutherans, but he was aware of the value of the *Augsburg Confession* in his ministry there. Writing on July 28, 1540, to Monsieur Du Tailly, one of the Genevans who desired his return, he explained that the *Augsburg Confession* was a key tool in answering Catholic officials sent to Strasbourg by the King in the context of the Council of Haugenau.[31] So, in Strasbourg, whether he had subscribed to the *Variata* or the *Invariata*, Calvin was favorably inclined to seek union with the Lutherans and the Reformed as he ministered in the context of the *Augsburg Confession*.

Calvin's return to Geneva (1541); his assessment of Luther in the renewed controversy concerning the Eucharist (1544)

Upon his return to Geneva in 1541, Calvin pursued his reforms in earnest. However, he did not employ the *Augsburg Confession* as the standard for the Genevan Reformation. Nor did Calvin simply rely upon the recently adopted

---

[28] Calvin, *Selected Works*, 4.107-108, February 28, 1539.
[29] Calvin, *Selected Works*, 4.112-115, March 12, 1539.
[30] Calvin, *Selected Works*, 4.166-67, November 20, 1539.
[31] Calvin, *Selected Works*, 4.194-95.

Swiss Reformed confessions such as The First Confession of Basel (1534), The First Helvetic Confession (1536), The Lausanne Articles (1536), or the Geneva Confession (1536). Instead, he wrote an extensive catechism of his own, publishing the final version in 1545. His catechism was completed during the Eucharistic controversy that broke out again between Luther and the Reformed. In Calvin's 1557 debate with Westphal, the defender of Luther's Eucharistic doctrine, Calvin declared that over 200,000 subscribed to his Catechism![32]

While Calvin chose not to adopt the Lutheran *Augsburg Confession* in Geneva, his distinct catechetical standard did not mean that he had distanced himself from being identified with Luther. Calvin's continuing identification with Luther is seen in his comments on Isaiah 22.17, written in 1551, where he described Thomas More's persecution of the Reformed believers, 'Among other applauses the most conspicuous was, that he had been a very great persecutor of the Lutherans, that is, of the godly.' [The French has *'C'est a dire, des enfans de Dieu'*, i.e., 'That is, of the children of God.'] In the same year, Calvin related to Bullinger that adherents of 'Lutheran doctrines' in France were facing persecutions of all kinds. This persecution included a mandated oath in order to expose any Protestant sympathies, which was effected by the reading every Sabbath day of the 1542 *Sorbonne Articles*. Calvin writes,

> A penalty is imposed, besides, on all citizens who may, by their suffrages, have raised to the magistracy, any individual known to hold, or suspected of holding, *the Lutheran doctrines*. The Supreme Council is bound by law to compel any of their number, who may seem to have a leaning to our doctrines, to clear himself by oath. All are commanded, with more than usual earnestness, to adore the breaden god on bended knee. All parsons of parishes are commanded to read the Sorbonne articles every Sabbath for the benefit of the people, that a solemn abnegation of Christ may thus resound throughout the land.[33]

Calvin's assessment of Luther, however, became particularly evident in the renewed sacramental controversy. In spite of the peace established in 1538, the controversy over the Lord's Supper broke out again between the German and Swiss Churches in 1544. With renewed disdain for Zwingli, Luther's stinging invective condemned the doctrines of the Zurich reformer and his church, comparing them to the heresies of the radical reformers. Deeply troubled and feeling Luther's wrath, Melanchthon had written to Bucer on August 28, 1544,

> I have written to you about our Pericles, who has again begun to thunder most vehemently on the subject of the Lord's Supper, and has written a fierce attack, in which you and I are beaten black and blue. I am a quiet peaceable bird, nor would

---

[32] Calvin, *Selected Works*, 2.434.
[33] Calvin, *Selected Works*, 5.320, emphasis added.

be unwilling if I may depart out of this prison-house, if our disturber shall constrain me.[34]

Seeking to keep the peace, the clergy of Zurich, at first, remained silent. But Luther's sustained attacks compelled them to answer, doing so indirectly by publishing Zwingli's works with a preface that defended his teaching. In this context, Calvin wrote to Farel on October 10, 1544, praising the patience of the brethren in Zurich while admitting 'the rage of Luther,' 'Luther's unkindness' and 'the danger . . . from Luther,'[35] referring to Luther's recently published *Short Confession concerning the Supper* (*Kurzes Bekenntniss vom Abendmahl*).

Calvin strove to limit the conflict by writing to Bullinger on November 25, 1544, reminding him of Luther's extraordinary giftedness and the Reformed movement's indebtedness to him.[36] Under these difficult circumstances, Calvin went on to give high praise for Luther's work.[37] Calvin, however, did not ignore Luther's 'evil qualities' that 'beset him'. Moreover, he referred to Luther's 'violence' and 'fierce invective' that 'harassed' the Reformed, revealing Luther's 'serious faults' and 'vehemence of natural temperament'. Calvin wished Luther was 'more observant and careful in the acknowledgment of his own vices' instead of being so 'prone to be over-indulgent to himself'.[38]

Offended by Luther's attacks, the ministers of Zurich in 1545 published a defense of their doctrine, with a title that loosely translates as *The Confession of the Orthodox Ministers of the Swiss Church, A Modest Response to the Vain and Offensive Calumnies and Condemnations of Dr. Martin Luther*. 'Provoked by Luther's violence, this reply irritated the zealous Lutherans, afflicted Melanchthon, delighted the adversaries of the Reform by the unseemly divisions which had got the upper hand among them.'[39] In June, 1545, Calvin wrote to encourage Melanchthon who labored under Luther's 'overbearing tyranny'.[40]

Thus, Calvin maintained an abiding respect for Luther in spite of the sacramental conflict in 1544-1545, yet he did not diminish Luther's offenses in the struggle. Nor did Calvin base his reforms on the Lutheran *Augsburg Confession*. Instead, on November 28, 1545, he dedicated his perfected Catechism that was printed in Strasbourg to 'the faithful ministers of Christ who preach the pure doctrine of the gospel in East Friesland'.[41] His catechism presents a Reformed and not a Lutheran view of the Supper for the children of Geneva.[42]

---

[34] Calvin, *Selected Works*, 4.433.
[35] Calvin, *Selected Works*, 4.428-29.
[36] Calvin, *Selected Works*, 4.432-34.
[37] Calvin, *Selected Works*, 4.433.
[38] Calvin, *Selected Works*, 4.433.
[39] Calvin, *Selected Works*, 4.466n.2.
[40] Calvin, *Selected Works*, 4.466-68.
[41] Wulfert de Greef, *The Writings of John Calvin* (translated by Lyle Bierma; Westminster John Knox, 2008), 117.
[42] See, for example, http://camosun.ca/learn/programs/history/johnston/120_topic3.pdf.

The Commendation of the Augsburg Confession (1554-1558) in Calvin's Consensus with Zurich

Consensus Tigurinus or *Mutual Consent in regard to The Sacraments; Between the Ministers of the Church of Zurich and John Calvin, Minister of the Church of Geneva* was published in 1554. In Calvin's letter to the pastors of Zurich, printed with this treatise, he writes, 'I wish it however to be understood that nothing is here contained which our colleagues also, as many as serve Christ under the jurisdiction of the city of Geneva or in the Canton of Neufchatel, have not approved by their subscription. Farewell, most excellent men and brethren, whom I truly love in my heart.'[43] Although written by Calvin, all had subscribed the work that was being sent to the Zurichers. The Zurich pastors declared their approval in their response to Calvin, also published with the *Consensus*,

> [I]t has admirably fulfilled its office in having attested to all clearly, and without equivocation, that we, whom God has enabled to think and speak the same thing on the doctrines of religion, do not at all differ in the exposition of its ordinances. Farewell, dearest Brother.[44]

But the *Consensus* did not come without substantial dialogue, including dialogue about the appropriateness of mentioning the *Augsburg Confession*.[45] The Zurichers, non-subscribers to the *Augsburg Confession*, and frequently the brunt of Luther's invective for their differences about the sacrament, were uncomfortable with Calvin's mention of the Confession. Calvin's defense for including it is significant. First, it was the *Variata*. The *Variata* enabled Reformed theologians more easily to sign the *Augsburg Confession* in good conscience. Second, when the changes in the *Variata* were discovered by the Roman Catholics, it caused a stir. But, surprisingly, to Calvin, Luther did not object to it. Thus, the *Variata* had indirect approval from Luther beside the fact that it was from the pen of Melanchthon. Clearly in Calvin's mind, this Lutheran support for an article that sounded like the Reformed view of the Supper, was too good simply to ignore. Ultimately, Calvin prevailed with the Zurichers, and the *Consensus* said,

> [R]eaders will find in our Agreement everything contained in the Confession published at Ratisbon, and called the confession of Augsburg, provided only that it be not interpreted as having been composed under fear of torture, to gain favour with the Papists. The words are 'In the holy Supper, the body and blood of Christ are truly given with the bread and wine.' Far be it from us either to take away the re-

---

[43] Calvin, *Selected Works*, 2.201.
[44] Calvin, *Selected Works*, 2.204.
[45] Calvin, *Selected Works*, 6.91-92. Calvin's seeming slight upon Luther's character is actually rather mild compared to his assessment of Luther in his January 12, 1538, letter to Martin Bucer—7.384-85.

ality from the sacred symbol of the Supper, or to deprive pious souls of so great a benefit. We say that lest the bread and wine should deceive our senses, the true effect is conjoined with the external figure, so that believers receive the body and blood of Christ. Nay, as it was our design to leave pious readers in no doubt, we have attempted to explain more clearly and fully what that Confession only glanced at.[46]

Calvin's success in bringing about a union with the Zurichers and doing it under the aegis of the *Augsburg Confession* would not long go unnoticed by Lutherans. In fact, Calvin appeals to this fact in his *Last Admonition to Joachim Westphal*, one of Calvin's several treatises in his ongoing debate with Lutherans on the Lord's Supper, and his third against Westphal (1557).[47] By Calvin's appeal to Melanchthon's *Variata*, published at Ratisbon in 1540, he was able to resist the Lutheran consubstantiation doctrine and still subscribe to the *Augsburg Confession*, as interpreted by its author. Forty years later, with the publication of the *Book of Concord*, the repercussions of Melanchthon's changes were still being felt.

The 1555 Peace of Augsburg established a legal existence for both the Roman Catholic Church and the Lutheran Church. This agreement, under Charles V, officially sanctioned a divided Church in the German Kingdoms. The concept was '*cujus regio ejus religio*' ('whose kingdom, his religion'). The importance of this was that 'each prince was entitled to determine which religion would prevail in his realm; but no rights whatever were extended to any except Roman Catholics and adherents of the *Augsburg Confession*'.[48] This reality made Calvin's approach to the *Variata* attractive to Reformed Christians in the German lands, as it enabled them to have religious freedom. Nevertheless, writing to Bullinger, in 1557, Calvin speaks of a coerced subscription to the *Augsburg Confession* for internationals in Frankfort.[49]

Conflict over the Augsburg Confession (1559-1561) in the midst of growing international unrest

Theological and political conflict intensified in Calvin's Europe from 1559 to 1561. These years witnessed a confessional battle over the legitimacy of Melanchthon's *Variata*, a Huguenot assassination attempt of the French Catholic

---

[46] Calvin, *Selected Works*, 2.225. Cf. *The Register of the Company of Pastors*, 127. See Calvin, *Concerning the Eternal Predestination of God* (translated by J.K.S. Reid; London: James Clarke, 1961), 178. 'The *Consensus* had declared, "For, apart from the fact that in the sacraments nothing is appropriated except by faith, it must also be maintained that the grace of God is least of all bound to them in such a way that whoever has the sign also possesses the reality. For the signs are administered to the reprobate equally with the elect, but the truth of which they are signs belongs only to the latter"' (121).

[47] Calvin, *Selected Works*, 2.354-55.

[48] Thompson, 'Historical Background,' 10.

[49] Calvin, *Selected Works*, 6.345.

monarch and two theological Colloquies, the Naumburg Colloquy in Germany and the Colloquy of Poissy in France.

The first clash began in 1559 with Brenz's Christological teaching in relationship to the Lutheran view of the Supper.[50] But even as Brenz was solidifying Wurttemberg to the strict Lutheran view, the Palatinate began to slip even further in a Melanchthonian direction and began openly to consider the Calvinistic view of the Supper. This division between Lutheran and Reformed concerned the Lutheran princes since they were fearful of the reawakening of counter-reformational Roman Catholicism. These concerns led to the calling of the Naumburg Colloquy that was held in 1561.

Moreover, in the year preceding the Naumberg Colloquy in Germany, the first flames of the French wars of religion erupted with the Amboise conspiracy of March 1560. This was a Huguenot plot to assassinate the Catholic monarch, led by the Seigneur de La Renaudie.[51] Calvin, however, opposed the plan.[52]

Next, back in Germany, only a little over half a year after Melanchthon's death, the Lutheran princes convened the Colloquy at Naumburg in January 1561.[53] Thompson writes, 'The meaning of the Naumburg Colloquy was profound. For the first time it brought the validity of the *Variata* into open question.'[54]

These events had significance for Calvin, as a subscriber to the *Augsburg Confession* likely in its *Variata* form, particularly because the actions of Naumburg were communicated internationally.[55] These actions, colored by additional political intrigue, prompted Calvin to warn the King of Navarre, in August 1561, of the dangers of receiving the *Augsburg Confession* in France.[56] This was the first of several letters that Calvin would write to prevent the acceptance of the *Augsburg Confession* in France.

Then the following month (September, 1561) with the backdrop of the theological unrest of Germany and the political and theological instability of France, the Colloquy of Poissy was convened by the Queen Mother, Catherine de Medici. The hope was to bring stability to France by finding a workable agreement between Protestants and Catholics.[57] Calvin, however, expressed his doubts respecting the efficacy of the Colloquy on September 10, 1561, when he wrote to Theodore Beza who represented the Reformed: 'Whatever others may think, it has always been my conviction that the boasted results of the conference would come to nothing. Believe me, the Bishops will never proceed to a

---

[50] Thompson, 'Historical Background,' 20.
[51] Paul Van Dyke, *Catherine de Médici* (Charles Scribner's, 1922), 1.149ff.
[52] Van Dyke, *Catherine*, 1.149ff.
[53] See 'Naumburg' in John McCormick and James Strong (eds), *Cyclopedia of Biblical, Theological and Ecclesiastical Literature* (Harper, 1876), 6.867ff.
[54] Thompson, 'Historical Background,' 21-22.
[55] See 'Naumburg,' in *Cyclopedia*, 6.867.
[56] Calvin, *Selected Works*, 4.213.
[57] Calvin, *Selected Works*, 7.218n.1.

serious discussion.'[58] The turbulent years of 1559-1561 set the stage for Calvin's extensive correspondence to stop the entry of the *Augsburg Confession* into France.

Calvin's 1561 letters in opposition to the Augsburg Confession during the Colloquy of Poissy

Calvin composed ten letters, six in 1561 and four in 1563, to keep the *Augsburg Confession* from entering France.[59] The first six were in the context of the Colloquy of Poissy. Calvin's second set of four letters engaged a new confession that he wrote to prevent the introduction of Lutheranism into France.

Calvin's first letter was written to the King of Navarre (August, 1561). Calvin warned the King of the dangers that would emerge in France if the *Augsburg Confession* was introduced into his kingdom.[60] His five key arguments here were:

1. There already was a ratified French Confession completed in May 1559 by the General Synod of France: 'reflect how the confession of faith which the French churches have sworn to follow and maintain has been ratified'.[61]
2. The French Confession was biblical and already presented to the King: 'yet since it has been extracted from the pure word of God and presented to the king and his council, you cannot reject it, nor so huddle up the matter but that God will oppose your designs, and show you by effects that he will be listened to and believed.'
3. The inconsistency of the German Duke pushing the Augsburg since he and others had already condemned Melanchthon, its author: 'With regard to the Confession of Augsburg, how dare the Duke of Wurtemberg beg you to receive it, when we reflect that he and his like condemn the author of it, who is Melanchthon?'
4. Melanchthon's involvement in the discussion was irrelevant, since he was in ignorance: 'However, we shall leave him out of the question, since they have forced him to play a part in speaking of a thing of which he is entirely ignorant.'
5. The Lutherans were themselves divided about the confession: 'The fact is, that the most renowned persons of that party agree like dog and cat.'

---

[58] Calvin, *Selected Works*, 7.219.
[59] In chronological order, these letters were written as follows: the King of Navarre, August 1561; Theodore Beza, September 10, 1561; Admiral Coligny, September 24, 1561; Comte of Erbach, September 30, 1561; Theodore Beza, October 1, 1561; Heinrich Bullinger, November 5, 1561; the Prince of Conde, May 10, 1563; H. Bullinger, July 2, 1563; Heinrich Bullinger, September 9, 1563; the Prince of Conde, September 17, 1563.
[60] Calvin, *Selected Works*, 7.212-14.
[61] See Schaff, *Creeds*, 1.494-98.

Perhaps a reason for the King of Navarre's reticence to act on the entrance of the *Augsburg Confession* into France is found in the report of his last days. On his death bed he confessed his faith with the *Augsburg Confession*.[62]

Calvin's second letter in this period was written to Theodore Beza (September 10, 1561).[63] Calvin warned Beza in the midst of the Colloquy of Poissy of the divisive impact the *Augsburg Confession* would have on French soil. Calvin's main arguments here against the *Augsburg Confession* in France are:

1. It was a Catholic tool to create division: 'The Confession of Augsburg, as you know, is the torch of our deadliest enemy to kindle a conflagration which will set all France on fire.'
2. Melanchthon, its author, was displeased with the confession: 'The author of it repented of his work when his own faintheartedness had always been displeasing to men of energetic character.'
3. It was intended for Germany: 'In most parts, also, it is adapted to the peculiar use of Germany.'
4. It was unclear. 'I forbear to mention that it is obscure in its conciseness.'
5. It was incomplete: '[It is] mutilated by the omission of some articles of capital importance.'
6. France already had a confession: 'Besides, it would be absurd, passing by the Confession of the French, eagerly to adopt that one.'
7. It would create controversy: 'Need I mention what matter for future contention will be amassed by this manner of proceeding?'
8. It was presented as a snare not as a real matter of theological interest: 'But I am reasoning just now as if the Cardinal and his satellites sincerely embraced that confession, whereas they are only laying snares for you, that the present business being once disposed of they may throw everything in confusion.'

The third letter against the *Augsburg Confession*'s entry into France was written by Calvin (September 24, 1561), to one of the Reformed representatives at the Colloquy of Poissy, the Admiral Coligny.[64] Calvin was aware that theologians sent by the German princes to the Colloquy would seek to get the Protestants of France to commit to the *Augsburg*: 'I know . . . that they will wish to saddle them with their Confession of Augsburg.'

Calvin, here, employed five simple arguments against the introduction of the *Augsburg Confession* into France:

1. It was divisive: 'which would only be a torch to light the fire of discord'.
2. It was insufficient: '[I]t is such a meager composition.'
3. It was weak: 'so feeble'.
4. It was unclear: 'so obscure'.

---

[62] See Calvin, *Selected Works*, 7.290n.1.
[63] Calvin, *Selected Works*, 7.218-21.
[64] Calvin, *Selected Works*, 7.221-25.

ASPECTS OF REFORMING

5. It was inconclusive: 'it is impossible to stop short at its conclusions'.

The fourth letter was to the Comte of Erbach (September 30, 1561), the high chamberlain of the Palatine court.[65] Calvin warned the Comte of the danger in the plan of the German nobility to introduce the *Augsburg Confession* into France: 'How pernicious that would prove, I shall briefly explain.' He, then, proceeds to give the following ten reasons why the Comte should resist the entrance of the *Augsburg Confession* into France:

1. A French Confession already existed: 'First, a Confession has been published long ago by all the French churches, to which everyone who is admitted into the rank of a pastor gives his assent by a solemn subscription.'
2. The French Confession had been presented to leaders in state and church: 'The same Confession has been repeatedly presented to the royal council. In an assembly of all the princes and bishops, the king lately received the same from the hands of our brother Beza, and delivered it to the cardinals and bishops that the discussions of the colloquy might turn upon it. What then could be more absurd than to break off a course of proceedings so auspiciously commenced?'
3. Its discussion would cause unnecessary delay: 'Should no other damage accrue from such a proceeding except the delay, yet even that should be carefully guarded against.'
4. It would frustrate progress made and destroy hoped-for further progress: 'But if the princes now interfere with a new Confession, not only they will bring to nought all the noble transactions in which the favour of God has been so marvellously conspicuous, but by an obstacle worse than detrimental they will overturn all our hopes for the future.'
5. It will give the Catholic opponents another tool to attack the Reformed: 'For the Papists will eagerly lay hold of this subject of quarrelling; and those among them who excel in craftiness, after pretending in the first synod that they are satisfied, as soon as matters shall have taken a new turn, and they perceive the French Confession annihilated, will begin to direct their attacks elsewhere.'
6. Germans had no business legislating for the French: 'And what is to be thought of the Germans prescribing laws to us, and dictating to us, as if we were children? It cannot escape your singular perspicacity how plausible an argument this will furnish.'
7. It would confuse the hard won common faith of believers in France: 'In addition to that, it will be difficult to violate the agreement which all the pious have come to, and which they have publicly attested. Unless, then, the princes avowedly wish not only to throw into confusion their happy commencements, but to destroy entirely the fruits which the incredible labour of num-

---

[65] Calvin, *Selected Works*, 7.231-33.

bers and the blood of so many martyrs have produced, let them desist from this inauspicious conflict.'
8. It would raise great conflict: 'I say conflict, because, if they oppose their Confession to the one which has been received, dreadful disturbances will spring from it.'
9. The plan emerged from the animosity of the enemies of the Reformed Church in France: 'And that no one may doubt whence this project has proceeded, that has been already for some time the object of the machinations of all those who in France are the bitterest enemies of Christ, and who are hurried on by the most deadly animosity to effect the ruin of his kingdom.'
10. The princes should avoid the theological controversy the Lutheran theologians had already ignited in Germany with the Augsburg Confession: 'I forbear to mention that the Saxon furies, Brentz and his accomplices, have always made a bad use of the Augsburg Confession as a kind of torch to kindle a conflagration by which the whole of Germany has been set on fire. For that reason, we ought to be the more carefully on our guard lest the contagion of the evil penetrate into France.'

After these pointed arguments, Calvin confidently entrusted the matter into the hands of the Comte.[66]

Calvin's fifth letter was written to Theodore Beza (October 1, 1561), just as the Colloquy of Poissy was concluding.[67] He explained his purpose in writing to the Comte Erbach was to 'check any evil designs', to identify the 'fountainhead of the treachery' and the 'inundation' that it would unleash.

Calvin's sixth letter was sent to Bullinger (November 5, 1561). Here, Calvin mentioned his first letter written to the King of Navarre three months earlier. He, also, revealed that he had 'long ago . . . discovered' the clandestine evil plot to introduce the *Augsburg* into France. Calvin did not explain how long past this discovery had been. But one thing is clear; his earlier favorable assessment of the *Augsburg Confession* had dramatically changed for the worse.

Calvin's 1563 letters regarding his Confession written to prevent the entrance of Lutheranism into France

Eighteen months later, Calvin, again, took up the issue of the entrance of Lutheranism into France as the Wars of Religion began.[68] This started with his letter to the Prince of Conde (May 10, 1563).[69] There, Calvin explained how d'Andelot urged him to write a confession to prevent the entry of Lutheranism.

---

[66] Calvin, *Selected Works*, 7.233.
[67] Calvin, *Selected Works*, 7.233-36; cf. n.1 for historical context.
[68] On the First War of Religion (1562-1563), see Paul Henry, *Life and Times of Calvin the Great Reformer* (translated by Paul Stebbing; London: Whitaker, 1849), 396ff; Jean Paul Barbier-Mueller, *Warriors of the Word: A History of the French Wars of Religion, 1562-1598* (Geneva: Hazan, 2006), 47-68.
[69] Calvin, *Selected Works*, 7.309-13.

François d'Andelot de Coligny, a noted military leader and convert to the Protestant cause, was the brother of the Huguenot leaders, Admiral Coligny and Odet Coligny. He was tasked in November 1562 to defend the Prince of Conde's military activities before the Emperor and to address the negative reports that were being disseminated in Germany against the French Reformed. D'Andelot wrote to Calvin requesting that he compose a confession of faith to aid in that goal.[70]

The confession which d'Andelot asked for became Calvin's 'Confession of Faith, in the Name of the Reformed Churches of France, drawn up during the war to be presented to the Emperor in the diet at Frankfort, 1562'. Calvin asserted that one of the benefits of the King's signing the new confession was a wide readership of the document, even in Germany, and warned the Prince of the continuing danger of the entrance of the *Augsburg Confession* into France.[71] Calvin offered three reasons for the rejection of the *Augsburg* in France:

1. It would create entanglements: 'that they will not cease to stretch nets to entangle you in the Confession of Augsburg'.
2. It was ambiguous: 'a confession which is neither flesh nor fish'.
3. It was divisive: 'the cause of great schisms and debates among the Germans'.

A major benefit for the King's approval of the new confession was to have a ready response to those who would pressure him to accept the *Augsburg* on behalf of the Protestants of France.[72]

The second letter by Calvin in this context was to Bullinger (July 2, 1563), written hurriedly in the aftermath of great personal suffering, confiding, 'I am carefully on the watch that Lutheranism gain no ground, nor be introduced into France.'[73] He explained:

> The best means, believe me, for checking the evil would be that the confession written by me in the name of the Prince of Conde and the other nobles should be published, by which Conde would pledge his good faith and reputation, and endeavour to draw over the German princes to our party. I am waiting for his answer. The Admiral is urging him. If we could bring people to subscribe it, this proceeding would procure us some pleasant sport.[74]

There appeared a glimmer of hope, since Calvin was becoming confident that the Catholics would not accept the *Augsburg*, although he anticipated a clash with Lutheran theologians.[75]

---

[70] Calvin, *Selected Works*, 7.311n.1-2.
[71] Calvin, *Selected Works*, 7.312.
[72] Calvin, *Selected Works*, 7.312.
[73] Calvin, *Selected Works*, 7.320-23.
[74] Calvin, *Selected Works*, 7.322.
[75] Calvin, *Selected Works*, 7.322, 'Meanwhile, the condition of the churches is better than you imagine. They are permitted to make use of the confession presented to the king, as well as the catechism. In one word, things are strangely mixed up. There is

Two months later (September 9, 1563) Calvin wrote his third letter in this period, again to Bullinger.[76] He, there, made no mention of his new confession. Instead he, again, expressed his optimism that the *Augsburg* would not be welcomed in France. This was due to two reasons: the Romanists would not allow it, and Calvin's 'brethren firmly reject it'.[77] Nevertheless, this optimism was accompanied by his ongoing vigilance to prevent the *Augsburg's* entrance into France: 'We are nevertheless making the most strenuous efforts, and we shall continue to make them lest any detriment should arise from our negligence.'[78]

On September 17, 1563, Calvin, joined by Beza, wrote to the Prince of Conde. This would be his fourth and final letter on this matter.[79] They rehearsed the history of Calvin's confession and expressed their respectful impatience that he had not signed it after four months of waiting, particularly given the potentially dangerous consequences of inaction. The Prince of Conde did not answer Calvin and Beza. But neither did the *Augsburg Confession* receive an official welcome into France. Thus, Calvin secured his goal of preventing the entry of the *Augsburg Confession* into France.

Calvin's 1562 Confession and 1563 Jeremiah commentary

Calvin's 1562 confession was entitled, *Confession of Faith in the Name of the Reformed Churches of France*. The rest of the title page states: *Drawn up During the War, for presentation to The Emperor, Princes, and States of Germany, at the Diet of Frankfort; But which could not reach them, the passes being closed. Now published for the advantages which may accrue from it, and even because necessity requires it. Anno M.D. LXII.*[80] The opening statement 'To the Reader' explains the circumstances of Calvin's Confession.[81] Calvin's rebuttal of Lutheran theology is in articles 32-39.[82]

Article 32 asserts that only those with faith receive the real presence of Christ in the Supper.

Article 33 teaches that the non-believer does not receive Christ in the Supper even if he partakes of the outward signs.

Article 34 explains that the guilt of unworthy partakers is not due to having actually received the body and blood of Christ. Instead, it is because they do

---

no reason to fear, however, that the Papists will admit the Confession of Augsburg, should it be offered to them a hundred times. As my commentaries on Jeremiah will be published about the time of the next fair, I have resolved to dedicate them to the Prince Palatine. In my preface I have introduced an abstract of our whole controversy. So there is no doubt Brentz will have at me.'

[76] Calvin, *Selected Works*, 7.334-36.
[77] Calvin, *Selected Works*, 7.335.
[78] Calvin, *Selected Works*, 7.335.
[79] Calvin, *Selected Works*, 7.337-39.
[80] See Calvin, *Selected Works*, 2.137-62.
[81] Calvin, *Selected Works*, 2.138.
[82] See Calvin, *Selected Works*, 2.157-62.

not discern the presence of Christ since they reject him in unbelief. The article further explains sacramental language that sometimes identifies the sign with the thing signified.

In *Article 35* Calvin explains that the Roman Catholic doctrine of transubstantiation wrongly teaches an actual eating of the body and blood of Christ. The Roman Catholic doctrine asserts that the bread is no longer bread although it still appears to be bread. Rather, this doctrine is a failure to distinguish the sign (bread and wine) from that which it signifies (Christ's body and blood).

In *Article 36* Calvin denies Luther's view of consubstantiation. Christ is truly received by believers in the Supper but not because of Christ's descent to the earth or due to having an infinite body. Rather, this occurs by the mysterious and miraculous power of the Holy Spirit.

Article 37 further denies the Lutheran conception of the Lord's Supper by rejecting the notion of the ubiquity of the body of Christ. An infinite extension of Christ's body denies his human nature that is not lost in his union with his divine nature. This is consistent with the promise that the believer's glorified body will be like the body of the glorified Christ. This comports with the call in the Eucharist to raise one's heart on high.

Article 38 argues that this understanding of the presence of Christ does not limit the power of God, but submits to the teaching of God's word. The teachings of Scripture make clear that Christ ascended bodily into heaven from the earth. By such reliance upon the Scripture, the power of God is not lessened, but rather asserted since the union of Christ in the believer is a reality that overcomes the great distance between earth and heaven.

Article 39 declares that the Reformed understanding of the Supper has been misrepresented by injurious falsehoods. It is not true that their teaching gives no credit to Christ's words. Instead, their teaching is based on the Scriptures understood in their natural sense according to the common usage of the Holy Spirit and in accordance with the teaching of Augustine that affirms both the sign and that which it signifies in the sacrament of the Lord's Supper. Calvin's confession concludes with the plea that the German Majesty and Princes recognize this as their faith and not prejudice the truth. Thus, Calvin denied the Lutheran interpretation of the Eucharist by affirming the Reformed doctrine, stated in a respectful, yet emphatic, manner.

Calvin's final statement on the *Augsburg Confession* occurred in the preface to his commentary on Jeremiah, dedicated to Frederick III (July 23, 1563). This was composed in the context of the adoption of *The Heidelberg Catechism* six months earlier in the Palatinate. Frederick had begun his catechism project with the great skills of Ursinus and Olevianus, with a specific goal in mind. Thompson states,

> The Heidelberg Catechism was designed to put an end to the snarling partisanship of Gnesio-Lutherans versus Crypto-Calvinists and to arrive at peace and catholicity on the basis of no perishable authorities, but of God's Word alone—*das einige*

Fundament aller Tugenten und Gehorsams (the only foundation of all virtue and obedience).[83]

Calvin was aware of the struggle that was pulling the Palatinate in both Reformed and Lutheran directions. Thus, he dedicated his *Jeremiah Commentary* to Frederick III. There, Calvin states,

> I have now faithfully and plainly explained why they who boast themselves to be the followers of Luther so hastily contend with us at this day. For the same reason they pour forth their execrations on Philip Melanchthon, now dead, a man who, for his incomparable knowledge in the highest branches of literature, his deep piety, and other endowments, deserves to be remembered by all ages, and whom they have hitherto regarded as their leader: and it is strange, that in order to obtain the favour of the public, they pretend to adopt that noble Confession of Augsburg, of which he was especially the author, and ought to be deemed its true interpreter. I regard them as turbulent and unprincipled men, who possess no common courtesy and feel no shame.[84]

Calvin's respectful public remarks regarding the *Augsburg Variata* demonstrate his awareness of the tension that Frederick III was experiencing because of his leadership in bringing about the *Heidelberg Catechism* in an area under the legal authority of the *Augsburg Confession*. Calvin's deep respect for Melanchthon is, also, evident. His remarks and respect, however, in this public context were markedly milder than the tone in his private letters of 1561 and 1563. Thus, Calvin's diplomatic style gracefully cloaked his long and passionate efforts to forestall the appearance of the *Augustana* in France.

Calvin's final verdict on the *Augsburg Confession*

With the commencement of the *Heidelberg Catechism* and Calvin's publically mild statements about Melanchthon and the *Augsburg Confession*, along with his profound private resistance to it in France, this study must conclude. Of course, the story of the Lutheran and Reformed struggle over the *Heidelberg Catechism* and the *Augsburg Confession* continued for decades.[85] To summa-

---

[83] Thompson, 'Historical Background,' 25.
[84] Calvin, *Commentary on Jeremiah* (Grand Rapids: Baker, 1979), xxi.
[85] The struggle of the Lutheran and Reformed over the *Augsburg* continued from 1563 with the formal adoption of the *Heidelberg Catechism* to the publication of the Lutheran *Book of Concord* in 1580. (See Thompson, *Heidelberg Catechism*, 26.) In 1564, the *Kirchenrathsordnung* required all ministers and schoolmasters of the Palatinate to subscribe to the *Heidelberg Catechism* and were solemnly enjoined to 'apply it diligently to young and old,' avoiding all 'novelties' to the contrary (34-35). But Frederick was to pay a price for attempting to develop a new catechism under the banner of the *Augustana*. See Schaff, *Creeds*, 1.546-47. Just prior to Frederick's death (October 26, 1576), he subscribed to a single norm of doctrine beyond the Scriptures. It was the *Augsburg Confession* (Thompson, 27, 29. Cf., Bente, *Historical*

rize, then, the attempts to introduce the *Augsburg Confession* into France placed Calvin in a remarkable dilemma. He was compelled to resist the *Confession* to which he had subscribed. Believing that the introduction of the Lutheran *Augsburg* into France would divide the Reformed Church, weakening it and putting it at risk before the French Catholic royal family, he began his intense quiet campaign to prevent the admission of Lutheranism into France. As we have seen, by 1563, Calvin had written ten letters for this purpose, as well as an anti-Lutheran Confession of Faith for France.[86]

It is evident that Calvin's concerns with the *Augsburg Confession* went far beyond the small changes in Article X of the *Variata*. And, yet, Calvin had subscribed to this *Confession*, and had argued in print with Westphal, based upon that fact. Thus, we cannot escape the conclusion that Calvin had signed the *Augsburg* on the basis of a *quatenus*-subscription, rather than a *quia*-subscription. He did this even though he believed that, ideally, the latter was what ought to have been the standard for confessional subscription as was seen above in his dealings with the Athanasian Creed and his own creed to address the Italian anti-Trinitarians. Only this conclusion explains how Calvin could subscribe the *Augsburg* and, later, resist it and severely criticize it.

Thus, it is clear that Calvin would not have wanted the *Augsburg Confession* in a Reformed Confessional Collection, at least not in France after 1561.[87] Seemingly, then, the regret of President McCord didn't need to be quite so 'profound' after all. Perhaps the 'embarrassment' of Professor Cochrane was unnecessary as well. In fact, based upon this study, embarrassment and regret

---

Introductions, 247-48). With the religious peace of Westphalia in 1648 the Reformed received legal protection in German lands. Until that time a *quia*-subscription to the *Formula of Concord* forced all conscientious Calvinists to leave Lutheran lands, or to attempt to walk the confessional tight rope between the *Augustana* and the *Heidelberg* that Frederick had provided in the Palatinate.

[86] See n.59.

[87] As seen in n.4 above, Beza and other Reformed theologians included the *Augsburg* in their 1581 *Harmonia Confessionum*. Clearly Beza's opposition to the *Augsburg Confession* softened over the years. Why? Possible motives for him to reverse his earlier opposition that he held in common with Calvin include: (1) the intense opposition to the *Augsburg* had been conducted diplomatically, primarily behind closed doors with theologians and statesmen, so there was no public reason that a change in approach could not occur if circumstances dictated; (2) by 1581, the wars of religion had radically worsened the relationship of Protestants and Roman Catholics in France, closing the possibility of any Protestant creed being accepted in France; (3) it was fifteen years after Calvin's death; (4) general Reformed support for the *Augsburg* helped soften the impact on the Reformed in German lands caused by the imposed *quia* subscription to the *Formula of Concord*; (5) it gave the Reformed a potential moral advantage by open fraternal inclusiveness in the face of Lutheran intolerance; (6) as the primitive reformation confession, the Reformed saw a legitimate continuity between the *Augsburg* and their distinctive theology; (7) there was little likelihood that the *Augsburg* would attract Reformed theologians, given the extensive theological development that had occurred.

might be better felt by Reformation scholars who strive to fit Calvin into the mold of the *Augsburg Confession.*

CHAPTER 8

Calvin's school of Christ for preachers

Peter Adam

Calvin's ministry of reformation included reforming theology, the practice of the Christian life, the church, the ministry, and society. This was powerfully evident in the area of education. Leland Ryken concludes, 'One of the greatest contributions of the Reformation was in terms of education.'[1] This biblical revolution in education was profoundly influenced by the rise of Humanism. In this chapter we see Calvin's theology and practice of education as he applied it to training preachers.[2] Geneva was a 'school of Christ,' not least for preachers.[3]

Calvin's commitment to education in church and society

Preaching

Calvin's sermons were his major public mode of education for church and society. He used a new style of preaching, expository in shape, Reformed in theology, vernacular and familiar in language, and applied in presentation.[4] He

---

[1] Leland Ryken, 'Reformation and Puritan Ideals of Education' in Joel Carpenter and Kenneth Schipps (eds), *Making Higher Education Christian: the History and Mission of Evangelical Colleges in America* (Grand Rapids: Christian University Press, 1987), 38-55, 38.

[2] An earlier draft of some of this material was given as the inaugural address at the first Australasian Annual Christian Conference sponsored by Trinity College, Brisbane, and held at Emmanuel College Brisbane in June 2009. I, also, make use of some material previously given as a paper at a meeting of the Australasian Academy of Homiletics in Sydney in April 2009. Some of this was published in my chapter, '"Preaching of a lively kind"—Calvin's engaged expository preaching' in Mark D. Thompson (ed.), *Engaging with Calvin: Aspects of the Reformer's legacy for today* (Nottingham: Apollos, 2009), 13-41, and some published in two articles on 'Calvin's Preaching and Homiletic: Nine Engagements, Part 1' *Churchman* 124.3 (2010), 201-16; 'Part 2' *Churchman* 124.4 (2010), 331-42.

[3] Calvin often referred to the church as a 'school of Christ' and John Knox famously described Geneva as 'a perfect school of Christ'.

[4] On Calvin's preaching see, T.H.L. Parker, *Calvin's Preaching* (Edinburgh: T. & T. Clark, 1992); idem, *The Oracles of God: an Introduction to the Preaching of John*

preached on average five new sermons a week in the churches of Geneva.[5] Calvin was active in gospel ministry, and his preaching was a key ingredient in that ministry. It was primarily by preaching that Calvin educated the people in the message and content of the Bible, formed their theology, and shaped their lives. In the words of Ronald Wallace, '[I]t was more through his preaching than through any other aspect of his work that he exercised the extraordinary influence everyone has acknowledged him to have had.'[6]

Calvin trained ordinary people to read the Bible in his sermons.[7] This represented one of the most significant changes achieved by the reformation. Before the reformation, as Calvin wrote to Cardinal Sadoleto, 'Among the people themselves, the highest veneration paid to the Word was to revere it at a distance, as a thing inaccessible, and abstain from all investigation of it.'[8]

So the reformation had to undo the untold damage caused by the decision made by leaders of the Roman Catholic Church that the Bible was too difficult for ordinary people, and was reserved for scholars; and that instead of the Bible, the ordinary people would have statues and paintings; 'the bibles of the uneducated'.[9] This policy produced generations of people who knew Bible images, but had no idea what they meant. Calvin said of those church leaders: 'Though they may kiss the closed copies of the Scripture as a kind of worship, yet when they charge it with being obscure and ambiguous they allow it no more authority than if not a single word of it existed in writing.'[10] Christians are to know their Bibles so that they can hear God, and know, worship and serve him, and be trained and active in teaching and exhorting others. 'When, therefore, we see that there are people from all classes making progress in God's school, we acknowledge His truth which promised a pouring out of His Spirit on all flesh.'[11]

He trained lay people to assess what they heard by the Scriptures: '[T]herefore let this firm axiom stand, that no doctrine is worth believing ex-

---

Calvin (London: Lutterworth, 1947); A.G.P. van der Walt, 'Calvin on Preaching' in B.J. van der Walt (ed.), *John Calvin's Institutes: His Magnum Opus* (Potchefstroom: Potchefstroom University for Christian Higher Education, 1986); Michael Parsons, *Calvin's Preaching on the Prophet Micah: The 1550-1551 Sermons in Geneva* (Lewiston: Edwin Mellen, 2006), 147-80, and references in n.2.

[5] Parker, *Calvin's Preaching*, 62-63.
[6] Ronald S. Wallace, *Calvin, Geneva, and the Reformation: A Study of Calvin as Social Reformer, Churchman, Pastor and Theologian* (Edinburgh: Scottish Academic, 1988), 17.
[7] Here I use Randall C. Zachman, *John Calvin as Teacher, Pastor, and Theologian* (Grand Rapids: Baker Academic, 2006), 55-76.
[8] Quoted by Zachman, *Calvin*, 70.
[9] *Inst.* 1.11.5.
[10] *Comm. 1 and 2 Peter*, dedication, 225.
[11] Zachman, *Calvin*, 56-57.

cept as we perceive it to be based in the Scriptures . . . which makes it all the more clear that individuals are called to read the Scriptures.'[12]

Ordinary believers need to know their Bibles because Calvin was training the congregation as a ministry team. He wrote to Sadoleto, 'It certainly is the part of the Christian man to ascend higher than merely to seek and secure the salvation of his own soul.'[13] Christians are to serve others in ordinary matters of daily life, and, also, in bringing them the words of eternal life.[14] As Calvin preached from Deuteronomy, 'Although not all have the office of preaching the word of God, yet a private person who is a member of the church may beget spiritual children to God if he has the occasion and ability to win a poor soul and enlighten him with the faith of the gospel.'[15] He, also, warned of failing to take those opportunities: 'But when most people see that God provides an opening for them and a way to instruct the uninformed, they will remain silent, keep their mouths shut, and not say a word. . . . He will be guilty of other peoples' sin because he had the means to admonish them and did not.'[16]

Educational institutions and resources in Geneva

Calvin, also, worked to promote education in society, and to provide resources and institutions to train and educate children and young people. He created primary and secondary schools for boys and girls in Geneva.[17] These were based on schools initiated by Martin Bucer and Johann Sturm in Strasbourg.[18] These, in turn, were inspired by the Brethren of the Common Life.[19] The classes in these schools were organised according to the children's ages, and there was a graded syllabus which reflected the capacity of the children,[20] and the education was in their native French language.[21] This educational program prepared children for the senior part of the Academy. The Academy, which later became the University of Geneva, was designed to train preachers and civil servants. It provided training in Humanist skills in the liberal arts, and to these skills Calvin added a Christian understanding of God, and a theologically informed ability to read the Bible, and a Christian conviction that the purpose of

---

[12] *Comm. Acts* 17.11—quoted in Zachman, *Calvin*, 70.
[13] John Calvin, *Theological Treatises* (edited by J.K.S. Reid; London: SCM, 1954), 228.
[14] On Calvin's missiology, see Peter Wilcox, *Restoration, Reformation and the Progress of the Kingdom of Christ: Evangelisation in the Thought and Practice of John Calvin. 1555-1564* (unpublished DPhil thesis, Oxford University, 1993); Parsons, *Calvin's Preaching*, 181-225.
[15] *Serm. Deut.*25.5-12, 883 (language modernised).
[16] *Serm. Acts* 6.7-9, 337.
[17] Robert White, 'The School in Calvin's Thought and Practice,' *JCE*, 12 (1969), 5-26.
[18] Martin Greschat, *Martin Bucer, A Reformer and His Times* (Louisville: WJKP, 2004), 79-80.
[19] White, 'School,' 22.
[20] White, 'School,' 16.
[21] White, 'School,' 17.

understanding is to be able to teach the ignorant and uneducated.[22] This, too, was inspired by Strasbourg, where Calvin had lectured at the Academy set up by Martin Bucer and Johann Sturm.[23] Sturm's motto was 'learned and eloquent piety,'[24] values, also, held by Calvin. We will see below the role of the Academy in training preachers.

We, also, note Calvin's catechisms of 1536 and 1545. Both were summaries of the Christian faith. The former was designed for both adults and children, and the latter designed for children.[25] These were Calvin's provision of education for children within the church, and for all members of God's flock. Education for children is clearly reflected in the *Draft Ecclesiastical Ordinances*, which include specific mention of the education of children under the role of Doctors, and, also, clarify that all children are to attend the Sunday catechism class.[26]

Theological writing

Calvin had three styles of published writing, each with its intended purpose, genre and audience. The first was his theological writing, most notably *The Institutes*. Here he addressed the universal church and responded to its issues by tackling theological issues. The second style was exposition of the Bible texts in his commentaries, which were his lectures to students and ministers in written form. The third style was that of his sermons. These were addressed to the congregations at Geneva, by exposition and application of books of the Bible. However, from 1549 his sermons were systematically recorded by shorthand and then published. So sermons designed to be heard by the church at Geneva then became available for the wider people of God.

Calvin's personal encouragement

Calvin, also, engaged in individual education, both in personal conversations and by letter. Like the other Genevan pastors, he visited those who were ill, and those in prison. In his letters he encouraged friends in ministry, supported those facing hardship, persecution and martyrdom, and advised leaders on the best way to support the spread of gospel Christianity in Europe.[27]

---

[22] W.S. Reid, 'Calvin and the Founding of the Academy at Geneva,' *WJT* 18 (1955-56), 1-33.
[23] Greschat, *Bucer*, 146-47.
[24] Greschat, *Bucer*, 147.
[25] Calvin, *Theological Treatises*, 83-139. See, also, Robert M. Kingdon, 'Catechesis in Calvin's Geneva' in John Van Engen (ed.), *Educating People of Faith: Exploring the History of Jewish and Christian Communities* (Grand Rapids: Eerdmans 2004), 294-313; Zachman, *Calvin*, 131-46; I. John Hesselink, *Calvin's First Catechism: A Commentary* (Louisville: WJKP, 1997); T.F. Torrance, *The School of Faith* (London: James Clarke, 1959).
[26] Calvin, *Theological Treatises*, 62, 63, 69.
[27] See Calvin, *Tracts and Letters*, volumes 4-7 (edited by Henry Beveridge; Edinburgh: Banner of Truth, 2009).

ASPECTS OF REFORMING

Calvin's theology of education

We turn now to three key features of Calvin's theology of education, and then focus on his theology and practice of training preachers.[28] These three key features are three loves: love of learning, love of the truth, and love of neighbour.

We are created to love to learn

Calvin famously began *The Institutes* with his definitive statement on wisdom and knowing: 'Nearly all the wisdom we possess, that is to say, true and sound wisdom, consists in two parts: the knowledge of God and of ourselves.'[29] 'Ourselves' here is not an introspective study of the individual human, but a study of humanity, created, fallen, and restored, and the creation as the world in which humanity is set by God, and which shares the same story of creation, fall, and restoration. The ability to know and to have wisdom about God and ourselves has been implanted in us by God.

> For we see implanted in human nature some sort of desire to search out the truth to which man would not aspire at all unless he had savoured it. Human understanding then possesses some power of perception, since it is by nature captivated by love of truth.[30]

This love of truth is the deep desire to know what is true about God, about ourselves, and about the universe made by God. As we are always learning, then God is always teaching.

> [God] revealed himself and daily discloses himself in the whole workmanship of the universe.... [T]he Lord began to show himself in the visible splendour of his apparel... he shows his glory to us, whenever we and wherever we cast our gaze.
> ... [T]his skilful ordering of the universe is for us a sort of mirror in which we can contemplate God, who is otherwise invisible.[31]

And even children perceive the glory of God in the universe he has made: '[I]nfants, while they nurse at their mothers breasts, have tongues so eloquent

---

[28] For Calvin's theory and practice of education in schools see J.L. van der Walt, 'The school that Calvin established in 1559' in B.J. van der Walt (ed.), *Our Reformational tradition: a rich heritage and lasting vocation* (Potchefstroom: Potchefstroom University for Christian Higher Education, 1984), 192-201. For his general theology of education, see Ryken, 'Reformation Education'; T.M. Moore, 'Some Observations concerning the educational philosophy of John Calvin,' *WTJ* 46 (1984), 140-55. For his education in the church, see Zachman, *Calvin*, 55-71; for theological education, see Richard A. Muller, 'The Era of Protestant Orthodoxy' in D.G. Hart and R. Albert Mohler (eds), *Theological Education in the Evangelical Tradition* (Grand Rapids: Baker, 1996), 103-28.

[29] *Inst.* 1.1.1.

[30] *Inst.* 2.2.12.

[31] *Inst.* 1.5.1. See, also, Zachman, *Calvin*, ch. 11.

to preach his glory that there is no need at all of other orators.'[32] Those who have learnt to learn have clearer perceptions of reality of what God has done, and this learning is aided by the liberal arts.

> Indeed men who have either quaffed or even tasted the liberal arts penetrate with their aid more deeply into the secrets of divine wisdom. . . . [T]here is no one to whom the Lord does not abundantly show his wisdom.[33]

And this knowledge, this learning of truth, is deeply received.

> We are called to a knowledge of God: not that knowledge, which, content without empty speculation, merely flits in the brain, but that which will be sound and fruitful if we duly perceive it, and if it takes root in the heart.[34]

God's revelation in creation is effective, but that revelation is not able to lead us to saving faith in Christ.

> It is therefore in vain that so many burning lamps shone for us the workmanship of the universe to show forth the glory of its Author. Although they bathe us wholly in their radiance, yet they can of themselves in no way lead us into the right path.[35]

Though this knowledge is always available to us by the constant and gracious gift of God, and especially clearly in the Bible, we are usually blind because of our sin.

> But although the Lord represents both himself and his everlasting kingdom in the mirror of his words, with very great clarity, such is our stupidity that we grow increasingly dull towards so manifest testimonies, and they flow away without profiting us.[36]

And so, in place of knowing and loving truth, we substitute errors.

> For at the same time as we have enjoyed a slight taste of the divine from contemplation of the universe, having neglected the true God, we raise us his stead dreams and specters of our own brains, and attribute to anything else than the true sources the praise of righteousness, wisdom, goodness, and power.[37]

However although this knowing is corrupted and weakened, it is still present.

> Since reason, therefore, by which man distinguishes between good and evil, and by which he understands and judges, is a natural gift, it could not be completely

---

[32] *Inst.* 1 5 3.
[33] *Inst.* 1.5.2.
[34] *Inst.* 1.5.9.
[35] *Inst.* 1.5.14.
[36] *Inst.* 1.5.11.
[37] *Inst.* 1.5.15.

wiped out; but it was partly weakened and partly corrupted, so that its misshapen ruins appear.[38]

T.F. Torrance wrote that Calvin valued those 'natural gifts which, although they have been corrupted, still remain in man, for they are part of the groundwork of his creation'.[39]

The careful study of the universe brings blessing. As Calvin wrote, 'For astronomy is not only pleasant, but also very useful to be known: it cannot be denied that this art unfolds the admirable wisdom of God'.[40]

Indeed, he claimed that the ability to learn and invent is present among the heathen, for the Spirit's gifts are found in all humanity, both in arts and sciences, and in daily skills.

> For the invention of arts, and of other things which serve to the common use and conveniences of life, is a gift of God by no means to be despised, and a faculty worthy of commendation. . . . [T]he excellent gifts of the Spirit are diffused throughout the whole human race. Moreover the liberal arts and sciences have descended to us from the heathen. . . . [I]t is well known how far and how widely extends the usefulness of the art of the carpenter.[41]

So, gifts like justice, liberal and manual arts, jurists, philosophy, rhetoric, medicine, mathematics, and artistry come from God the Spirit. 'If we regard the Spirit of God as the sole fountain of truth, we shall neither reject the truth itself, nor despise it wherever it shall appear, unless we wish to dishonour the Spirit of God'.[42] So we should not despise these gifts, lest in doing so we despise God, the giver of the gifts. These gifts have definitive though limited value. They are

> 'Earthly things' which do not pertain to God or his Kingdom, to true justice, or to the blessedness of the future life; but which have their significance and relationship with regard to the present life and are, in a sense, confined within its bounds.[43]

Even when Calvin was commenting on Paul's words in 1 Corinthians about the futility of human wisdom in the saving plan of God, he was careful to defend the ordinary gifts of God which enrich human life.

> Paul would not be so very unreasonable as to contemn out of hand those arts, which, without any doubt, are splendid gifts of God, gifts which we call instruments for helping men carry out worthwhile activities. Therefore there is nothing irreligious about those arts, for they contain sound learning, and depend on princi-

---

[38] *Inst.* 2.2.12.
[39] T.F. Torrance, *Calvin's Doctrine of Man* (London: Lutterworth, 1949), 95.
[40] *Comm. Gen.* 1.16.
[41] *Comm. Gen.* 4.20.
[42] *Inst.* 2.2.15,16. See, also, 2.2.17.
[43] *Inst.* 2.2.1.

ples of truth; and since they are useful and suitable for the general affairs of human society, there is no doubt that they have come from the Holy Spirit.[44]

For human learning, the use of reason is worthy of honour, as it is the gift of God.

> For what is more noble than the reason of man, by which he stands out far above all animals? How greatly deserving of honour are the liberal sciences, which refine a man so as to make him truly human! Besides, what a great number of rare products they yield! Who would not use the highest praise to extol statesmanship, by which states, empires, and kingdoms are maintained?—to say nothing of other things! I maintain that the answer to this question is that Paul does not utterly condemn either the natural insight of men, or wisdom gained by practice and experience, or education of the mind through learning; but what he affirms is that all those things are useless for obtaining spiritual wisdom.[45]

Calvin, himself, benefited from his own learning, not least in his Humanist training in reading and understanding texts. Battles and Hugo note the following features of Calvin's expository style, even when used in his younger years to expound a pagan author. 'Calvin's aim is quite simple, to ensure that the reader will understand what Seneca is saying.'[46] This intention and ability requires the moral willingness to set aside one's own ideas to focus on the ideas of another, imaginative sympathy in understanding the text written by another person in a different historical context, and the ability to communicate to contemporary readers the ideas and significance of the original author. Finally, they observe Calvin's ability to paraphrase, to 'compress matter without loss of meaning,' and they commend his ability to communicate 'the whole context and underlying spirit of Seneca's words'.[47] Calvin exemplified the positive benefit of his Humanist training. We are driven by what we love, for we see implanted in human nature some sort of desire to search out the truth. It is by nature 'captivated by love of truth'.[48]

We must learn to love the truth

Whatever part of the universe and its life we are studying, we should treat it with respect. For, as Randall Zachman shows us, for Calvin, the universe is the theatre of God's glory, the living image of God and the garment of God.[49] This

---

[44] *Comm. 1 Cor.* 1.17.
[45] *Comm. 1 Cor.* 1.17.
[46] Ford Lewis Battles and André Malan Hugo, *Calvin's Commentary on Seneca's* De Clementia, *with introduction, translation and notes* (Leiden: Brill, 1969), 62.
[47] Battles and Hugo, *Calvin on Seneca*, 79.
[48] *Inst.* 2.2.12. This broad view of God's revelation is expounded in Leland Ryken, 'Calvinism and Literature' in David W. Hall and Martin Padgett (eds.), *Calvin and Culture: Exploring a Worldview* (Phillipsburg: P&R, 2012), 95-113.
[49] See Zachman, *Calvin*, 231-42.

means that we should respect the evidence we are considering, and, also, receive it with gratitude. 'Let the world become our school if we rightly desire to know God.'[50] We must, therefore, admit in God's individual works—but especially in them as a whole—that God's powers are actually represented as in a painting. Hereby, the whole of humanity is invited and attracted to recognition of him, and from this to true and complete happiness.[51]

> For the Lord, before plainly revealing to us the inheritance of immortal glory, would show himself as our Father in lesser things, that is, in his benefits that daily we receive from his hand. Since therefore this life serves us in understanding God's goodness, should we despise it as if it had no good in itself? We must, accordingly, be so disposed in mind and feeling to count it as a gift of the divine kindness that is not to be rejected.[52]

So, to love to learn is to receive God's gracious gifts.

> [A]ll the arts which contribute to the advantage of mankind, are the gifts of God, and that all that belongs to skilful invention has been imparted by him to the minds of men. . . . If we ought to form such an opinion about agriculture and mechanical arts, what shall we think of the learned and exalted sciences, such as medicine, Jurisprudence, Astronomy, Geometry, Logic, and such like? . . . Shall we not in them also behold and acknowledge his goodness, that his praise and glory may be celebrated both in the smallest and in the greatest affairs?[53]

To learn, we need the moral duty and discipline of listening with respect. This includes respect for the evidence, which Calvin exemplified in his own preaching of the Scriptures.

Calvin's normal pattern of preaching was 'expository,' accepting each book of the Bible as a text, and preaching that text by expounding it from beginning to end. For Bible texts are the complete books of the Bible, not one or more verses used as a 'text'.

Why did Calvin choose to preach books of the Bible? Calvin, as a Humanist, respected ancient texts. So, before he began his Christian ministry he expounded an ancient text, for his first published work was a commentary on Seneca's *De Clementia*, as we have seen, especially his ability to paraphrase, to pick up 'the whole context and underlying spirit of Seneca's words'.[54]

---

[50] Quoted in Zachman, *Calvin*, 242.
[51] *Inst.* 1.5.10.
[52] Quoted in Ford Lewis Battles, *The Piety of John Calvin: An Anthology Illustrative of the Spirituality of the Reformer* (Grand Rapids: Baker, 1978), 75.
[53] *Comm. Isa.* 42.19.
[54] Battles and Hugo, *Calvin*, 79.

Wimpfeling, Geiler and Surgant, Christian Humanists, were pioneers of an expository style that became common in Zürich, Strasbourg, and Geneva.[55] Calvin found examples of expository preaching in Augustine and John Chrysostom.[56] He planned a collection of Chrysostom's expository sermons,[57] to provide biblical teaching for lay people, and to show expository preaching in the early church.[58] Expository preaching was, also, sometimes found in medieval monasteries. *Homilia* was used for verse-by-verse exposition of Scripture, *sermo* for popular preaching in which exegesis was insignificant.[59] Another source could have been the late medieval innovation of teaching books of the Bible in universities.[60] Luther lectured at Wittenberg on Old and New Testament books. Among Calvin's contemporaries, Zwingli was the first to preach through books of the Bible, and began his sermons on Matthew in Zürich in 1519.[61] What had been done in Latin in monasteries and universities was now being done in the vernacular in churches.

Why did Calvin choose to preach this way? Calvin wanted to convey God's words as clearly as he could, by preaching them in their biblical shape. In this he was true to the revelation of God, and, also, to Humanist ideals. This disciplined him, and helped the congregation. He began his sermons on Psalm 119,

> I will frame myself to that manner and order which the Holy Ghost has here set down, [so] I shall enforce myself to follow as briefly as I can the plain and true meaning of the text and without continuing in long exhortations. . . . For performance thereof I determine by the grace of God to finish eight verses apart in every sermon, and to hold myself within such compass, so that the most ignorant shall easily acknowledge and confess that I mean nothing else but to make open and plain the simple and pure substance of the text.[62]

In basing his sermons on the *lectio continua* of the Bible, 'Calvin's purpose in preaching was to render transparent the text of Scripture itself.'[63] Calvin wrote of the Bible commentator,

---

[55] John H. Leith, 'Calvin's Doctrine of the Proclamation of the Word and Its Significance Today' in Timothy George (ed.), *John Calvin & the Church: A Prism of Reform* (Louisville: WJKP, 1990), 209.
[56] Parker, *Calvin's Preaching*, 79, 80.
[57] Zachman, *Calvin*, 59.
[58] There are, also, examples of expository preaching from Bernard, Anselm, Bonaventura and Aquinas—Parker, *Calvin's Preaching*, 80.
[59] Walt, 'Calvin on Preaching,' 328.
[60] David C. Steinmetz, 'John Calvin as an Interpreter of the Bible' in Donald K. McKim (ed.), *Calvin and the Bible* (Cambridge: CUP, 2006), 289.
[61] Parker, *Oracles*, 18.
[62] *Serm. Ps.* 119.5, cited in Lester De Koster, *Light for the City: Calvin's Preaching, Source of Life and Liberty* (Grand Rapids: Eerdmans 2004), 81.
[63] Leith, 'Calvin's Doctrine,' 214.

It is almost his only task to unfold the mind of the writer whom he has undertaken to expound, he misses his mark, or at least strays outside his limits, by the extent to which he leads his readers away from the original meaning of his author.[64]

To expound a text of Scripture is to respect both the human author and God the author. Torrance commented,

> he has given up the rhetorical conception of *persuasion* beloved by the humanists, one that appeals to what is attractive and desirable, and substitutes for it a mode of *persuasion* which throws the reader back upon the truth itself and its inherent validity.[65]

He wanted to avoid 'taking a text,' in the sense of taking one or two verses of Scripture out of context. In his letter to the Seigneur of Piedmont, he warned of those preachers who have only 'snatched in a passing way a few words of Holy Scripture'.[66] He wrote in his commentary on Acts 20.26: '[M]ortal man shall not be so bold as to mangle the Scripture and to pull it in pieces.'[67] 'When passages of Scripture are seized on rashly and no attention is given to context, it is not to be wondered at that errors often arise.'[68]

Calvin showed his respect for Scripture by respecting its constituent texts, the sixty-six books of the Bible. Calvin knew that in Scripture we have the intention of God (*Dei consilium*) within the intention of the human author (*mens authoris*).[69] He recognized the moral duty of the reader and preacher: 'The Golden Rule, for hermeneutic and ethics alike, is to treat others—texts, persons, God—with love and respect.'[70] Calvin respected texts, because he respected their divine and human authors. He learnt to love the truth. In this, Calvin exemplified the respectful learning which he understood to be at the heart of education, loving God's truths, and so thinking his thoughts after him.

We learn so that we may love our neighbours

We honour God when we learn the truth, and we are, also, equipped to love our neighbours: 'The works of love are such that through them we witness real righteousness. Our life shall best conform to God's will and the prescription of the law when it is in every respect most fruitful for our brethren.'[71] So, there is no room for individualism. We belong to each other as members of Christ's church.

---

[64] Comm. *Romans*, dedication, 1.
[65] T.F. Torrance, *The Hermeneutics of John Calvin* (Edinburgh: Scottish Academic, 1988), 148.
[66] Wallace, *Calvin's Geneva*, 171.
[67] Leith, 'Calvin's Doctrine,' 213.
[68] *Comm*. Isa. 14.12, cited in W.J. Bouwsma, *John Calvin: A Sixteenth Century Portrait* (New York: OUP, 1988), 118.
[69] Parsons, *Calvin's Preaching*, 17.
[70] Kevin J. Vanhoozer, *Is there a meaning in this text?* (Leicester: Apollos, 1988), 32.
[71] *Inst*. 2.8.52,54.

So if we wish to be considered in Christ, let no man be anything for himself, but let us all be whatever we are for others. This is accomplished by love; and where love does not reign, there is no edification of the Church, but mere scattering.[72]

And this love should include all humankind, not only our fellow believers.

> [W]e ought to embrace the whole human race without exception in a single feeling of love; here there is not distinction between barbarian and Greek worthy and unworthy, friend and enemy, since all should be contemplated in God, not in themselves.[73]

This love of neighbours is essential to our humanity.

> Since he has stamped his image upon us, and since we share a common nature, this ought to inspire us to provide for one another. The one who seeks to be exempt from the care of his neighbour is disfiguring himself and declaring that he no longer wishes to be a man. For whilst we are human beings, we must see our own faces reflected, as by a mirror, in the faces of the poor and despised, who can go no further and who are trembling under their burdens, even if they are people who are most alien to us, If moor or a barbarian comes to us, because he is a man, he is a mirror in which we see reflected the fact that he is our brother and our neighbour; for we cannot change the rule of nature that God has established as immutable.[74]

This includes doing our daily work to serve others. 'So therefore it becomes every man to apply his vocation in such a way that he may do all he can for his neighbours. . . . [W]e must be ready to do all good works.'[75] Some of our best good works include our daily tasks of 'digging earth . . . sewing and tailoring,'[76] for by these we honour God and benefit our neighbours. And we must do these good works with an attitude of serving others. We love our neighbours by what we do and how we do it.

> We know that the principal service that God requires of us is that we devote ourselves entirely to him; we will follow the vocation we have when we are called, without pride, ambition or envy. . . . [H]e will refrain from cheating on his neighbours, he would prefer to die rather than to wrong anyone.[77]

And such service honours God.

---

[72] *Comm. Gal.* 4.16.
[73] *Inst.* 2.8.55.
[74] *Serm. Gal.* 6.9-11, 622.
[75] *Serm. Titus* 3, 1208-1209 (modernised language).
[76] *Serm. Gal.* 5.19-23, 550.
[77] *Serm. Gal.* 5.19-23, 549.

> If the chambermaid and manservant go about their domestic tasks offering themselves in their work as a sacrifice to God, then what they do is accepted by God as a holy and pure sacrifice pleasing in his sight.[78]

All human tasks should be an expression of loving our neighbour. So our learning serves our working, and our working is a way in which we serve our neighbours. All the skills of our daily work come from God, and we must use them to serve others. So, three loves inform this theology of education: love of learning, love of the truth, and love of our neighbour. We will see how Calvin used these key features in his training of preachers, as he encouraged them to love to learn, to love the truth, and to love their congregations and audiences.

Calvin on training preachers

We now turn our attention to Calvin's theology and practice of training preachers, as an important example of his ministry of education.

Why did Calvin train preachers?

We are men and women made in God's image, restored in that image in Jesus Christ, and renewed in that image by the Holy Spirit. We must love learning, love the truth, and love our neighbour. God is our teacher, and we are members of his school, and, if we are believers in Christ then Christ, too, is our teacher.[79] God summons us and speaks to us through preachers of the Scriptures.

> God calls out that morning and evening his arms are stretched out to receive us and call us from afar. He wants nothing more than to have us under his wings, and peaceably to enjoy us. So, for our part, we must take pains to run to him to hear him, and cut off all hindrances that would hinder us from hearing the preacher.[80]

God wants his voice to be heard. 'God would even have his living voice to resound in his church . . . [so] preaching is inseparably united with Scripture.'[81] It, therefore, follows that, 'as often as the Word of God is set before us . . . God is present and calling us'.[82] So, then, preachers may say, 'When we speak, behold God, who wishes to be heard in our persons.'[83]

And, as God's voice is heard in his church in Scripture and preacher, so the church is to work to send the message of the gospel to the whole world. Calvin wanted the church in Geneva to have a global gospel vision, to take part in a strategy to convert the world to Christ in their own day, and, also, to make provision for gospel ministry in the future. For, 'God places no higher value on

---

[78] *Serm. 1 Cor.* 10.31–11.1, translated in Ronald S. Wallace, *Calvin's Doctrine of the Christian Life* (Edinburgh: Oliver and Boyd, 1959), 155.
[79] T.H.L. Parker, *Portrait of Calvin* (London: SCM, 1954), 52-54.
[80] *Serm. 2 Tim.* 4.2-5, 959.
[81] *Comm. Exod.* 13.19.
[82] *Comm. Acts* 10.33.
[83] *Serm. Job* 33.1-7, 575 (modernised language).

anything than the preaching of the gospel for he wants his kingdom to be dominant in this world, and preaching is the way to lead men to salvation.'[84] And the church in Geneva should work with God: 'To draw the world to God and to build up the Kingdom of our Lord Jesus Christ that he may rule among us.'[85] And all believers have this responsibility.

> Will we have this treasure [the gospel] remain safe and sound in our custody? First of all let every man ensure that it is locked up safe in his own heart. Yet it is not enough for us to focus just on our own salvation. For the knowledge of God must be known through the whole world, and every one must share in it, and we must take pains to bring all that wander. And we must think not only of our own time, but also of the time after our death . . . we must labour to make God known throughout the whole world.[86]

The gospel will go to the world as churches are planted, and godly ministers are provided.

> The gospel cannot be maintained without the means of which Paul speaks, that there be ministers appointed in every town, for the means to maintain the church is by preaching . . . which is the incorruptible seed by which we are born of God, it is the milk of little children, and food of the great ones. So the Church cannot but decay and perish unless it be maintained by the preaching of the word of God.[87]

Calvin employed a comprehensive strategy to raise up and train preachers for the welfare of God's people and the evangelisation of the world. Wilcox has documented Calvin's strategy and work in church planting in France and providing pastors for those churches.[88] While some preachers would work in churches that were previously Roman Catholic and were now Reformed, some would plant new churches. And two preachers from Geneva joined others from France in a mission to Brasil in 1556.

What are the implications of this? Leaders should take great care in the selection and appointment of ministers.[89] And people should think strategically and sacrificially of the need for good ministers: 'But men have so little care to serve God and his Church, that no man would have his son be a Preacher.'[90]

---

[84] *Serm. Acts* 6.1-6, 325.
[85] *Serm. 2 Tim.* 2.16-18, 808.
[86] *Serm. 2 Tim.* 2.1-3, 747, 749.
[87] *Serm. Titus* 1.5-6, 1064.
[88] Wilcox, *Restoration*, 13-81. See, also, Parsons, *Calvin's Preaching*, 181-258,
[89] *Serm. 1 Tim.* 3.1-4, 244.
[90] *Serm. 1 Tim.* 3.1-4, 240.

ASPECTS OF REFORMING

How did Calvin train preachers?

Biblical literacy in church and society
As we have seen, Calvin worked to create biblical literacy in the church and society, by preaching and teaching, and by providing a catechism for children. A church which has learnt the Scriptures, in which lay people are trained to evangelise and encourage each other, and in which the ministry of preaching is honoured, is more likely to produce preachers. He, also, established primary and secondary education in Geneva, as children who gain the ability to read, write, learn, understand, and speak are more likely to become able preachers.

Raising up and training future preachers by preaching
Calvin trained people to recognize the significance of the ministry of preaching, and he, also, trained up future preachers. This process began in the church, and was completed in the Academy. Future preachers were formed by present sermons. So, he preached of the importance of preaching, and of the need for preachers.

The congregation should be aware of the need to train preachers, and what kind of preparation was appropriate. This was important for their support of their preachers, and for those who were thinking of becoming teachers or pastors. Future preachers need more training than they can receive in sermons.[91] However, the sermons they hear in church began that training.[92] And this was to be reinforced as those who preach commend and explain the ministry of preaching, as Calvin did.

> Chose out the ablest in the world, yet they must acknowledge that they cannot speak of God with such majesty and reverence, unless God govern them and give them new speech, altering and reforming their tongues so that they may not speak after the manner of men but may show that it is the Holy Spirit who rules them.[93]

Preachers must be rigorous in orthodoxy, zealous in ministry, with a desire to honour God, and to be an example to their people.

> The first thing that is required of those whom God send to preach his word is that they continue in pure doctrine, not ending in falsehoods or going astray from true religion, but maintaining true uprightness. It is not enough for us to teach people faithfully, unless we have a zeal to edify and care for the salvation of all, and do this with a desire to honour God and show the way, and be an example to those we lead.[94]

They must be able to do public and private ministry of the Word.

---

[91] On educating preachers, see Marvin Anderson, 'John Calvin, Biblical Preacher,' *SJT* 42.2 (1989), 176-181.
[92] See Parsons, *Calvin's Preaching*, 147-180.
[93] *Serm. Deut.* 32.1-4, 1105.
[94] *Serm. 1 Tim.* 1.18-19, 103.

And then, when a man will be a preacher, it is not just a question of making a sermon, but in general and in particular it is necessary for him to know that it is to proclaim the Word of God both publicly and privately in order to edify, so that the word may be profitable.[95]

Preachers must be students of God's Word: 'No man shall ever be a good minister of God's word unless he first be a student of it.'[96] They must be able to teach and preach: 'For though a man walk uprightly and have great and excellent virtues, yet if he does not teach, he may be a good Christian, but he is no Minister.'[97] They must be willing to face hardship and suffering: 'not only diligent and indefatigable in pursing the task of teaching, but . . . ready to undergo the danger of death for the defence of the doctrine'.[98] They must be able to rebuke sin: 'When the word of God is rightly applied, then there must be conflict and war against all vices. . . . So our Lord will have his word rightly applied.'[99] They must know how to serve people: 'We cannot serve God except by serving his people.'[100] They must avoid arrogance: 'One of the greatest virtues of those who have the charge of governing the Church and preaching the Word of God, is that they guard themselves from being puffed up and have a foolish arrogance which carries them away.'[101] They must be resilient enough to face the opposition of the world and of Satan: 'they cannot preach the word of God, but Satan on the one side will do what he can to hinder them, and the world will be in an uproar'.[102] They must know what condemnation they face if they betray their trust:

> If private people who run riot against God are worthy to be condemned, then [ministers of the gospel] who do this are rightly called devils. Jesus Christ called them so in the person of Judas. So therefore those who are called to so honourable an office should take heed to themselves, because God has chosen them in his service.[103]

Preachers must use their gifts to serve others not themselves:

> Let them not seek to be esteemed for their brave babbling and lofty speech, for their subtleties, for the fine and sharp wits, for the passing bravery: all these things must be laid under foot, or else we can never serve God and his Church.[104]

They must realize the privilege and responsibility they carry:

---

[95] *Serm. 1 Tim.* 3.1-4, 239.
[96] *Serm. Deut.* 5.23-27, 258.
[97] *Serm. 1 Tim.* 4.12-13, 411.
[98] *Comm. Acts* 15.25-26.
[99] *Serm. 1 Tim.* 1.8-11, 59.
[100] *Serm. 1 Tim.* 3.6-7, 293.
[101] *Serm. 1 Tim.* 3.6-7, 289.
[102] *Serm. 1 Tim.* 1.18-19, 101.
[103] *Serm. 1 Tim.* 1.12-13, 71.
[104] *Serm. 1 Tim.* 6.20-21, 651.

ASPECTS OF REFORMING

> All they to whom God has appointed to be Ministers of his word must realize that as the keys of the kingdom are committed to them, so they must keep this treasure so that it does not perish.[105]

God's pastoral awareness is shown in providing preachers:

> We have the scripture preached to us, and by that means God allures us sweetly to him, that he could not do any more for us, except he should take us onto his lap. We feel that he takes account of our weakness, chews our food for us, and speaks to us like a nurse.[106]

God accommodates to us, so should the preacher:

> A wise teacher has the responsibility of accommodating himself to the power of comprehension of those whom he undertakes to teach . . . imparting too much would only result in loss.[107]

God accommodates to his people in Christ, in the Scriptures, and in providing preachers and teachers.[108] This, also, expressed the Humanist value of *decorum:* 'deliberate adaptation to one's audience for the sake of persuasion'.[109] Calvin exemplified this in his preaching. He preached in the vernacular French, and clearly knew the kind of responses the congregation would have to the words of Scripture in the sermon, and encouraged them to grow in faith and obedience. So, in his sermon on Ephesians 5.22-26, he articulated the instinctive responses of some in the congregation to the biblical view of our accountability to God for our marriages.

> The husband may plead, I have a dreadful and stubborn wife, or else she is proud, or has a wicked head, or else is too talkative. . . . The wife also for her part will not be without stock of excuses. For often her husband may be irritable and quarrelsome . . . some are niggardly and frequenters of taverns. . . . But when we come to God, we are bound to hang down our heads, for it will profit us nothing to be insolent towards him.[110]

Calvin preached partly in order to raise up preachers, and, also, provided a model of preaching that was expository in shape, Reformed in theology, vernacular and familiar in language, and applied in presentation. Love of learning, love of truth, and love of neighbour informed Calvin's training of preachers.

---

[105] *Serm. 1 Tim.* 6.20-21, 647.
[106] *Serm. Deut.* 4.23-26, 146.
[107] *Comm. 1 Cor.* 3.1.
[108] Peter Adam, *Speaking God's Words: A Practical Theology of Preaching* (Leicester: IVP, 1996), 137-45; and see Ford L. Battles, 'God was accommodating himself to human capacity,' *Int* 31 (1977), 19-38.
[109] Bouwsma, *Calvin*, 116.
[110] *Serm. Eph.* 5.22-26, 566.

Writings, publications and in-service training

Calvin's writings and publications, also, provided training for preachers. *The Institutes* gave a basic theological framework, the commentaries provided resources and models for those who had not had training in the liberal arts, and the published sermons provided resources for churches without ministers and models for preachers.[111]

The training that Calvin provided had a wide influence, as he trained ministers to plant churches in France, and as refugee ministers came to Geneva and were further trained in ministry. These included ministers from France, Scotland, England, Poland, Hungary, Italy, Spain, the Palatinate, and Holland. They could attend his weekday and Sunday sermons (in French), and his week day lectures (in Latin), in which he expounded the Scriptures for students at the school and for ministers who wished to attend. These lectures became his published commentaries on books of the Bible.[112]

And Calvin, also, made provision for the in-service training of preachers. The Venerable Company of Pastors met for continuing education, mutual encouragement and correction. The weekly *Congrégation* was a meeting of preachers at which a sermon was preached and discussed by those present.[113] And Calvin wrote many letters to encourage people in evangelism and ministry.

The Academy

He established the Academy, as we have seen, to train preachers and, also, to train people to serve society. This Academy provided a model for Reformed Humanist training in European universities.[114] As we have seen already, Calvin had taught at a similar Academy in Strasbourg, set up by Martin Bucer and Johann Sturm. Basic training for ministry had previously been provided by monasteries. With the closure of monasteries, universities and academies took on this role.

The Academy provided a largely Humanist education. Of the twenty-seven weekly lectures planned for the Academy at Geneva, five were in the Greek classics, three in Physics and Mathematics, five in Dialectic and Rhetoric, three in Theology, eight in Hebrew and Old Testament, and three in Ethics. This Humanist emphasis reflected both the Strasbourg model, and the training that Calvin, himself, had received at universities in France. It, also, showed Calvin's confidence in God's revelation in the world. While it was no doubt of great benefit, it might lead to confusion among students who were not theologically

---

[111] Zachman, *Calvin*, 77-102, 103-30, 59. Calvin's published sermons were especially popular in England. See Parker, *Calvin's Preaching*, 72-74.

[112] Wilcox, *Restoration*, 50-81.

[113] Jung-Sook Lee, 'Calvin's Ministry in Geneva: Theology and Practice' in Sung Wook Chung (ed.), *John Calvin and Evangelical Theology: Legacy and Prospect* (Milton Keynes: Paternoster, 2009), 211-13.

[114] Alister E. McGrath, *A Life of John Calvin: A Study in the Shaping of Western Culture* (Oxford: Blackwell, 1990), 184, 200-201.

astute, and who might learn unhelpful lessons from the Humanist sources, which might distract them from biblical faith. Calvin, himself, was less likely to import Humanist philosophy into Christianity because in his study of the Classics he had not read Christianity into those sources. As Richard Burnett comments, 'Unlike most northern European humanists, Calvin refuses to Christianize his classical sources.'[115] It could be argued that this dependence on Humanist ideals did not serve Reformed training of preachers in the long term, as it resulted in both the secularisation of those who were not theologically acute, and obsolescence of style when the Humanist focus on learning from the past was replaced by the need to be relevant to the contemporary and recently-invented present. It, also, produced situations in which training in the liberal arts was regarded as adequate training for preachers. Calvin's plan for raising up and training preachers was based on the preliminary rigorous training in the Bible, in Reformed theology and ministry, and in models of ministry provided in the church in Geneva. Without this firm foundation, training in liberal arts in the Academy would be destructive, rather than constructive.

Future preachers in the Academy, also, took part in preaching exercises, in which they would expound a passage of Scripture before some ministers and their fellow students, and get feedback on their sermons.[116] Those who were proposed for appointment as pastors were assessed by the Company of Preachers. They were examined on their life and character, their doctrine and their knowledge of the Bible, and on their communication skills including the issue of whether or not they could be heard when preaching in large buildings.[117]

So Calvin trained preachers by promoting biblical literacy and theological understanding in the church, by raising up and training preachers by his own sermons, by his writings and publications, and by setting up the Academy.

Conclusion

Calvin held a high view of humans as those who are created by God to learn, and who are called to love the truth and to love their neighbours. This led to high expectations for preachers and for congregations.

Calvin applied himself to know God by his careful and disciplined learning from the Scriptures. He benefited from his Humanist training in the liberal arts.

Calvin worked to achieve biblical knowledge and literacy in his congregations, and to train people to explain their faith in Christ to others, to encourage

---

[115] Richard Burnett, 'John Calvin on Sacred and Secular History' in David W. Hall (ed.), *Tributes to John Calvin: A Celebration of his Quincentenary* (Phillipsburg: P&R, 2010), 217-46, 223.

[116] From Statutes of the Geneva Academy (1559) cited in Alastair Duke, Gillian Lewis and Andrew Pettegee (eds), *Calvinism in Europe 1540-1610* (Manchester: Manchester University Press, 1992), 218-19.

[117] Lee, 'Calvin's Ministry,' 207-208.

each other, and to contribute to God's global gospel plan. Such congregations are more likely to produce preachers and teachers.

He recognised that the general standard of education in Genevan society needed to be improved, and so he founded schools to help achieve this. General literacy supports biblical literacy and well-trained ministers.

He provided training for preachers by founding the Academy. This training mainly comprised humanist training in the liberal arts, which provided the tools for the study of the Scriptures and the arts of thinking, reading, and communication.

Calvin, also, trained preachers by providing a model of Reformed expository preaching, by consciously addressing future preachers in the congregation in his own sermons, by publishing his sermons, by providing weekly preaching classes for students in the Academy and in-service training for preachers in the weekly *Congrégation*. He encouraged preachers to love to learn, to love the truth, and to love their congregations and audiences. He supported preachers by church-planting in France, by personal conversation, and by letter. Geneva was indeed an effective 'school of Christ' for preachers, and its influence spread across Europe and eventually around the world.

CHAPTER 9

'A new embassy': John Calvin's gospel

Martin Foord

The reformation was a theological revolution concerning the doctrine of the gospel. In contrast to Rome, the reformers (both Lutheran and Reformed) described themselves as 'evangelical'. This title drew attention to their central teaching: the gospel (*evangelium*). In Diarmaid MacCulloch's words, 'Evangelical encapsulates what was most important to this collection of activists: the good news of the Gospel'.[1] However, despite a good deal of common ground the reformers had over the gospel, there were subtle differences between the Lutheran and Reformed traditions, generally, and specific reformers, particularly. This chapter will focus on John Calvin's doctrine of the gospel and show its nuances in comparison to both the Lutheran tradition and the Western medieval tradition. It must be remembered that Calvin was not theologically regulative for the sixteenth-century Reformed tradition.[2] Dogmatic regulation was the task of the various confessions written by and for Reformed communities across Europe. Moreover, thinkers such as Huldrych Zwingli, Heinrich Bullinger, Johannes Oecolampadius, Martin Bucer, Wolfgang Musculus, John à Lasco, Peter Martyr Vermigli and Thomas Cranmer, alongside Calvin, helped found Reformed thought even if the latter was highly influential among them. But an examination of Calvin will show that characterising the reformers as having a monochrome understanding of gospel will fall foul of reductionism.[3]

---

[1] Diarmaid MacCulloch, *Reformation: Europe's House Divided, 1490-1700* (London: Allen Lane, 2003), xx.
[2] Richard Muller, 'Demoting Calvin: The Issue of Calvin and the Reformed Tradition' in A.N. Burnett (ed.), *John Calvin, Myth and Reality: Images and Impact of Geneva's Reformer* (Papers of the 2009 Calvin Studies Society Colloquium: Eugene: Cascade Books, 2011), 3-17.
[3] This reductionism is evident in works such as Scot McKnight, *The King Jesus Gospel: The Original Good News Revisited* (Grand Rapids: Zondervan, 2011); Ted Campbell, *The Gospel in Christian Traditions* (Oxford: OUP, 2009).

The medieval gospel

One cannot properly understand the reformation gospel unless it is portrayed against its medieval backdrop. The seminal figure for medieval theology, Peter Lombard, touched on the doctrine of the gospel at distinction XL in the third book of his *Sentences*.[4] Hence a significant proportion of medieval thinking about the gospel can be found in the many *Sentences* commentaries on this distinction.[5] They portray the gospel as fundamentally a 'new law' (a phrase Augustine was not fond of using). The 'new' aspect refers to salvation history. High and late medieval theology, generally, divided redemptive history into three eras.[6] First, there was the era of 'natural law' prior to Sinai, the time of the patriarchs and just beyond. Then, second, the epoch of the 'old law' began when the Torah was delivered to Israel via Moses. Finally, the age of the 'new law' commenced with the coming of Christ and will continue until his second coming. Hence, the 'new law' applied to the third era of salvation history; there was no gospel (or new law) prior to Christ. But the medieval gospel was not only 'new' it was also 'law'. This latter term referred to the new administration or arrangement that governed the new covenant people of God. It contained Christ's teaching concerning beliefs but, also, included Christ's moral commands especially found in the Sermon on the Mount (Matt. 5-7). There, Jesus contrasts the precepts of the old law ('You have heard it said . . .') with the injunctions of the new law ('but I say to you . . .').

The *Sentences'* commentators distinguished between law ('old law') and gospel ('new law') in a variety of ways. Two of them are relevant for our topic. First, the old law, understood in its 'literal' sense, issued only *earthly* promises and rewards, whereas the new law, in its literal sense, offered *eternal* promises and rewards. However, the medieval divines affirmed that eternal promises could be found in the old law when it was read in its 'spiritual' sense as shown in the New Testament use of the Old Testament. Second, the *Sentences'* commentators drew a distinction between the old law as 'letter' and the new law as 'Spirit' according to the words of 2 Corinthians 3.6, 'the letter kills but the Spirit gives life'. They, generally, believed the old law as letter 'killed' through its commands because it did not give the grace needed to do them. In this way the 'old law' could not justify. In contrast, the 'new law' as 'Spirit' (2

---

[4] Peter Lombard, III *Sententiarum* XL.i-iii, *Sententiae in IV Libris Distinctae*, 2 vols, 3rd edition (edited by Ignatius Brady; Grottoferrata: Collegii S. Bonaventurae Ad Claras Aquas, 1971-1981), 733-34.

[5] The *Sentences'* commentaries which comment upon III *Sent.* XL that I have consulted are those of Stephen Langton, Alexander of Hales, Richard Fishacre, Albert the Great, Bonaventure, Thomas Aquinas, Robert Kilwardby, Durandus of St Pourçain, Richard of Middleton, John Duns Scotus, Peter Aquila, William de la Mare, Denys the Carthusian, Gabriel Biel and Jan Hus.

[6] Hugh of St Victor structured his celebrated *On the Sacraments of the Christian Faith* according to the three eras—Hugo of St Victor, *De sacramentis christianae fidei* in J.-P. Migne (ed.), *Patrologia Latina* (Paris: 1844-1864) 176.173-618.

Cor. 3.6) was able to give life because it supplied the Holy Spirit enabling believers to follow its injunctions and so the new law could justify. This, of course, raises the question of how anyone was justified under the old law. Albert the Great answered this question by appealing to Augustine: the new law pertained backwards in time to the righteous under the old law.[7] Those justified under the old law were so because the new law applied to them.

The Lutheran gospel

Luther's gospel broke radically with the medieval notion of the new law. For Luther both law and gospel could be found *literally* in *all* of Scripture. Hence, by 1520 in his *Freedom of the Christian*, Luther could say, 'the entire Scripture of God is divided into two parts: commandments and promises', namely law and gospel.[8] The law commanded so as to be righteous before God through doing, whereas the gospel promised imputed righteousness before God through believing. Hence, law and gospel were not confined to the New Testament only but existed in the Old Testament as well. Melanchthon, in his ground-breaking 1521 *Loci communes*, contended that the gospel was first proclaimed immediately after the fall in Genesis 3.15, 'I will put enmity between you and the woman and between your seed and her seed.'[9] He says of the verse, 'This is the first promise, the first Gospel, by which Adam was raised up and understood a certain hope of his salvation, indeed, he was justified.'[10]

This construal of law and gospel entailed the characteristic Lutheran opposition between law and gospel. Unlike medieval theology, law and gospel were different in kind: the gospel was in no way a law. The law/gospel distinction was not fundamentally salvation historical but soteriological. The law terrified through its commands and drove repentant people to the gospel which consoled through its free promises. Moreover, the law/gospel distinction was, also, hermeneutical.[11] As Luther believed, the 'entire Scripture' was divided into either law or gospel in the sense that the concepts of law and gospel lay outside of salvation history and, thus, could be applied to *all* of

---

[7] 'Est tamen notandum verbum Augustini, scilicet quod justi in Veteri Testamento pertinebant ad Novum: quia justitiam in fide Novi acceperunt: et mali in Novo, timore servili, pertinent ad Vetus quoad non habere gratiam,' Albert, *Commentarii in III Sententiarum* XL.iii, Albertus Magnus, *Opera Omnia* (edited by. A. Borgnet and E. Borgnet; Paris: Louis Vivès, 1890-1899), 28.750 col.2–751 col. 1.

[8] Martin Luther, *The Freedom of a Christian* (*WA* 7:52, *LW* 31.348).

[9] Philipp Melanchthon, *Loci communes* (1521) *Quid Evangelium*, *CR* 21.140.56b.11-141.56b.12.

[10] Melanchthon, *Loci communes*, *CR* 21.141.56a.17-19.

[11] Erik Horst Herrmann, '"Why then the Law?' Salvation history and the Law in Martin Luther's Interpretation of Galatians (1513-1522)' (unpublished Ph.D. dissertation; Concordia Seminary, 2005), 236-47.

salvation history. Law and gospel 'becomes the new *sine qua non* for theological application and proclamation'.[12]

However, tensions soon arose in the Lutheran tradition over the place of repentance in the law/gospel distinction. Did repentance belong to law or gospel? Luther had spoken of repentance as law because it was a command to do something, and the believer is justified by faith alone, not works. But, as a result of his initial controversy with Johannes Agricola (1494-1566), Philipp Melanchthon began to include repentance in the gospel.[13] This understanding of the gospel appeared in his subsequent writings not least all editions from the second onwards of his influential *Loci communes*.[14] Melanchthon believed repentance was included in the gospel via Luke 24.47 where Christ spoke of 'repentance and forgiveness of sins' being preached to all nations. Other Lutheran divines, such as Erasmus Sarcerius (1501-1559) and Johann Spangenberg (1484-1550), also, included repentance in the gospel in their systems of theology.[15] But it was after Luther's death that the so-called 'Philippists' and 'Gnesio-Lutherans' properly locked horns over the place of repentance in the gospel. Jacob Andreae dates the start of the controversy to be 1559.[16] That year Matthaeus Judex, in his *Quod arguere peccata seu concionari poenitentiam*, argued that gospel in its 'proper office' excluded repentance.[17] Matthias Flacius accused the Philippist Victor Strigel of holding

---

[12] Herrmann, 'Why then the Law?' 241.

[13] 'Quia autem Evangelium continent praedicationem poenitenciae [sic], necesse est arguere et ostendere peccata,' Melanchthon, *Scholia in Epistolam Pavli ad Colossenses* (Wittenbergae, 1528), 91vo. For more on Melanchthon's controversy with Agricola see Timothy J. Wengert, *Law and Gospel: Philip Melanchthon's Debate with John Agricola of Eisleben over Poenitentia* (Grand Rapids: Baker Academic, 1997).

[14] For example, 'Definit itaque Christus Evangelium Lucae ultimo [24.47], plane ut artifex, cum iubet docere poenitentiam et remissionem peccatorum in nomine suo. Est igitur Evangelium praedicatio poenitentiae et promissio,' Melanchthon, *Loci communes* (1559) VII, *Philippi Melanchthonis Opera quae supersunt omnia* eds. Karl Gottlieb Bretschneider and Heinrich Ernst Bindseil (Wittenbergae: Apud C.A. Schwetschke et filium, 1854), 21.734.

[15] 'Evangelium est praedicatio poenitentiae et remissionis peccatorum in nomine Christi,' Erasmius Sarcerius, *Nova methodus in praecipuos scripturae divinae locos*, (Basileae: 1546), 274; 'Evangelium vero est contio de poenitentia, continens promissiones beneficii Christi,' Johann Spangenberg, *Margarita theologica Continens Praecipuos locos doctrinae Christianae* (Lipsiae: Nicolaus Wolrab, 1541), 14.

[16] Andreae, *Sechs Christlicher Predig Von den Spaltungen so sich zwischen den Theologen Augspurgischer Confession* (Tübingen: 1573), 59.

[17] Matthaeus Judex, *Quod arguere peccata, seu concionari poenitentiam, sit proprium legis, & non Evangelij, proprie sic dicti, rationes & argumenta* (Basileae: Ex officina Iacobi Parci, 1559).

to an 'Antinomian definition of the Gospel' that included repentance.[18] Johann Wigand believed the Philippists' position was a 'new Antinomianism'.[19] Yet, the Philippists, Paul Crell and Christoph Pezel, responded directly to Wigand—the latter particularly appealing to Melanchthon's reading of Luke 24.47.[20]

This controversy over repentance and the gospel appears to be a factor in the construction of Article V in the *Formula of Concord* (1577). The *Formula* resolved the dispute by noting two meanings of the word 'gospel' in Scripture. The first signifies the 'entire teaching of Christ' seen in Mark 1.15 ('repent and believe the gospel') and Acts 20.21 ('repentance toward God and faith in our Lord Jesus'). When 'gospel' is used in this sense it includes repentance. The second meaning of 'gospel' is strictly a message of grace alone embraced by faith alone and, hence, excludes the demand of repentance. It is used this way when Scripture juxtaposes law and gospel.[21] What is critical to note is that this second usage of 'gospel' is its proper (*propria*) and more important meaning. Hence, the *Formula* starkly declares,

> We therefore reject as a false and pernicious teaching when it is asserted that the Gospel is properly (*proprie*) a preaching of repentance, convicting, accusing, and damning sin, and not a preaching of God's grace alone.[22]

Therefore, the Lutheran tradition codified in the *Book of Concord* a twofold understanding of the gospel. But in its 'proper' or supreme sense, it is a message of grace alone that does not command repentance. In this way law and gospel are distinct and contrary to each other.

John Calvin's gospel

Amongst many scattered comments in Calvin's large corpus there are three key places where he especially treats the gospel as a topic. The first two are in the introductions to his harmony of the Synoptic Gospels and to John's Gospel.[23]

---

[18] Matthias Flacius, *Disputatio de originali Peccato et libero arbitrio, inter Matthiam Flacium Illyricum, & Victorinum Strigelium Vinariae* (n.p., n.c.: 1562), 341.

[19] Johann Wigand, *Collatio. De III. Argumentis Antinomicis* (Ihenae: In Officina Haeredum Christiani Rhodii, 1570) and *De Antinomia Veteri Et Nova, Collatio Et Commonefactio* (Ienae: 1571).

[20] Paulus Crellius, *Spongia de definitione evangelii, complectens propositiones centum quinquaginta, oppositas ... collationi Iohannis Wigandi* (Witebergae: Johann Schwertel, 1571); Pezel, *Apologia Verae Doctrinae De Definitione Evangelii* (Witebergae: Excudebant Clemens Schleich & Antonius Schöne, 1571).

[21] *The Formula of Concord* V.7, *Die Bekenntnisschriften der Evangelisch-Lutherischen Kirche. Herausgegeben im Gedenkjahr der Augsburgischen Konfession 1930* (Göttingen: Vandenhoeck und Ruprecht, 2010), 791.18-32.

[22] *The Formula of Concord* V neg. 1, *Die Bekenntnisschriften der Evangelisch-Lutherischen Kirche*, 792.11-16 (my translation).

[23] John Calvin, *Harmonia ex evangelistis tribus composita, Matthaeo, Marco, et Luca: adiuncto seorsum Johanne, quod pauca cum aliis communia habeat* (Genevae: Excudebant Nicolaus Barbirius et Thomas Courteau, 1563), n.p. (for Synoptics), 693-

The third is in his final 1559 edition of the *Institutes of the Christian Religion*.[24] Earlier editions had not included a separate *locus* on the gospel. Three points about Calvin's doctrine of the gospel are relevant for this discussion.

The two meanings of 'gospel'

First, Calvin believed the word 'gospel' had two meanings in Scripture, one broad and one narrow.[25] The broad sense referred to any part of Scripture that preaches the free grace of God: 'the word "Gospel" taken in a broad sense (*largè*) expresses those testimonies which God formerly gave to the fathers of his mercy and paternal favour'.[26] According to this first signification the gospel can be found in the Old Testament particularly as promises that God will be 'propitious to humans and forgives their sins'.[27] This broad meaning appears to be similar to the classic sense in which Luther defined 'gospel' (and the *Formula of Concord* codified as 'properly' meant).

In its second and narrow sense Calvin believes the word 'gospel' refers simply to the revelation of Christ: 'I take the Gospel to be the clear manifestation of the mystery of Christ.'[28] The narrowing of meaning concerns salvation history. It is not simply a message of grace *per se*, but 'the preaching of grace revealed in Christ'.[29] In this sense the gospel is *not* found in the Old Testament; it was at that time a 'mystery' *qua* unknown. According to its narrow meaning the gospel only arrives in history with Christ as a 'new form of teaching' (*nova docendi forma*).[30] Hence, Calvin can refer to the gospel as the 'New Testament' *qua* covenant. That is, the gospel is not simply the general covenant of grace but the specific new covenant established in Jesus. Calvin finds this narrow meaning taught in verses like Mark 1.14 'The beginning of the Gospel of Jesus Christ' and 2 Timothy 1.10 where Christ in his coming

---

94, (for John); *CR* 73:1-4 (for Synoptics), *CR* 75:VII-VIII (for John); *A Harmony of the Gospels Matthew, Mark, and Luke and the Epistles of James and Jude* (translated by A.W. Morrison, edited by D.W. Torrance and T.F. Torrance; Grand Rapids: Eerdmans, 1972), xi-ii; *The Gospel According to St. John: Part One 1-10* (translated by T.H.L. Parker, edited by. D.W. Torrance and T.F. Torrance; Grand Rapids: Eerdmans, 1959), 5-6.

[24] *Inst.* 2.9.

[25] Calvin, *Institutio christianae religionis, in libros quatuor* (Genevae: Oliva Roberti Stephani, 1559), 2.9.2, 145-46; *CR* 30.310-11.

[26] Calvin, *Inst.* (1559), 2.9.2, 145; *CR* 30.310.

[27] 'Quidem Evangelii nomen ad gratuitas omnes Dei promissiones extendunt, quoties se Deus propitium hominibus fore testatur, illisque peccata remittit,' Calvin, *Harmonia*, 'The Reason for John,' 693.

[28] 'Porro Evangelium accipio pro clara mysterii Christi manifestatione,' Calvin, *Inst.* 2.9.2; *CR* 30.310.

[29] *Inst.* 2.9.2, 146; *CR* 30.310.

[30] Calvin, *Harmonia ex evangelistis tribus composita, Matthaeo, Marco, et Luca* Mark 1.1-6, 80 col. 1.

'made clear life and immortality through the Gospel'.[31] Thus, he believes it is in this sense that the first four books of the New Testament are named 'Gospels' because 'they narrate that Christ appeared in the flesh, died, was raised from death, and finally was taken into heaven'.[32]

Calvin avers that the narrow definition of the 'gospel' has a 'common use' (*commune usus*) and was 'a thing sufficiently known' in the Christian tradition.[33] But, unfortunately, he nowhere gives examples of others who use it this way, presumably because he believed it was commonly known. Calvin may have had in mind Eusebius of Caesarea's *Preparation for the Gospel* which defines the gospel this way:

> But first of all, it is well to define clearly what this word 'Gospel' means to express. It is this then that brings 'good tidings' to all people of the advent of the highest and greatest blessings, which having been long since foretold have recently shone forth on all mankind.[34]

Here, the emphasis is on a new era of greater revelation. Calvin knew of Eusebius' *Preparation for the Gospel* because he explicitly refers to it in *Institutes* 1.11.4.[35] A similar definition can be found in Jacques Lefèvre d'Étaples and Johannes Oecolampadius.[36]

Indeed, Calvin's two meanings of 'gospel' are strikingly similar to Martin Bucer's analysis of 'gospel' in the introductions of his *Continuous Expositions in the Four Holy Gospels* (1527) and *Exposition of John's Gospel*.[37] Bucer contends that 'recently' (*dudum*) the idea arose that all of Scripture could be divided up into law and gospel, where the former refers to 'something required by us' and the latter to 'any promise of God's grace'.[38] This, no doubt, is a

---

[31] *Inst.* 2.9.2, 146; *CR* 30.310.
[32] Calvin, *Harmonia [...] Johanne*, 693.
[33] *Inst.* 2.9.2, 145; *CR* 30.310.
[34] Eusebius, *De Praeparatione Evangelica* 1.1, *PG* 21.24B, Eusebius, *Preparation for the Gospel*, 2 vols (translated by E.H. Gifford; Oregon: Wipf and Stock, 2002), 1.2.
[35] A.N.S. Lane, *John Calvin: Student of the Church Fathers* (Grand Rapids: Baker, 1999), 58. See, also, Irena Backus, 'Calvin's Judgment of Eusebius of Caesarea: An Analysis,' *SCJ* 22.3 (1991), 419-37.
[36] Jacques Lefèvre d'Étaples, *Commentarii Initiatorii in Quator Evangelia* (Basileae: Cratander, 1523), Matt. 4.32, 20; Johannes Oecolampadius, *Enarratio in Evangelium Matthaei* (Basileae: 1536), 1b-2a.
[37] Martin Bucer, *In sacra quatuor Evangelia, enarrationes perpetuae* (Basel: Apud Ioan. Hervagium, 1536), 1b; and *Enarratio in Evangelion Johannis*, (Argentorati, 1528), 9b-10a. For the date of the first edition of the former see Martin Greschat, *Martin Bucer: A Reformer and His Times* (translated by S.E. Buckwalter; Louisville: WJKP, 2005), 81-82.
[38] Bucer, *Enarrationes*, 1b.

reference to Luther's new understanding of the law/gospel distinction.[39] Bucer, like Calvin, believes this distinction is not wrong, but there is a second more focused meaning: 'the writings of the New Testament use the word "Gospel" for the publication of grace and redemption acquired by Christ'.[40] The emphasis of Bucer here is not so much on the greater revelation (so Calvin) but Christ's fulfilment of Old Testament promises. Bucer believes 'gospel' is used 'more for the announcement of the promises fulfilled [in Christ] than the promises' themselves.[41] Hence, Bucer may well have been an influence on Calvin.

The two relationships of law and gospel

Calvin's two definitions of 'gospel' correspond to two definitions of 'law'. As we have seen, his broad definition of the gospel (as promise) matches a broad definition of 'law':

> I acknowledge that inasmuch as the word 'Gospel' is named by Paul 'the doctrine of faith' (2 Tim. 4.10), it includes all the promises concerning free remission of sins which occur everywhere in the Law, by which God reconciles humans to himself. For there he [Paul] opposes faith to the terrors by which the conscience is distressed and vexed, if salvation is to be sought by works.[42]

Here, Calvin's understanding of the gospel, broadly taken, relates to the law as simply command, or salvation 'by works'. In this way, law and gospel are opposed to each other. This is akin to the Lutheran law/gospel distinction.

But Calvin is adamant that it is wrong *only* to understand the law and gospel in opposition: 'their error is established, who always compare the Law with the Gospel according to the merit of works and the free imputation of righteousness'.[43] He believes a second relationship between law and gospel is necessary, corresponding to the second narrower definition of 'gospel'. It entails a second definition of 'law' as the entire old covenant including its promises and ceremonies (which point forward to the gospel).[44] Calvin draws attention to Jesus' words in Luke 16.16, 'the Law and prophets were until

---

[39] An excellent account that traces Luther's move from the old salvation historical to the principial and hermeneutical distinction of law and gospel is in Herrmann, 'Why then the Law?'

[40] Martin Bucer, *In sacra quatuor Evangelia*, 1b.

[41] Bucer, *Enarrationes*, 1b.

[42] 'Fateor certe, quatenus Evangelium vocatur a Paulo [2 Tim. 4.10] doctrina fidei, eius partes censeri, quaecunque passim in Lege occurrunt promissiones de gratuita peccatorum remissione, quibus sibi Deus reconciliat homines. Fidem enim terroribus illic opponit, quibus angitur et vexatur conscientia, si ex operibus petenda sit salus,' *Inst.* 2.9.2, 145-46; *CR* 30.310.

[43] *Inst.* 2.9.4, 146, *CR* 30.312.

[44] 'It is nothing new or unusual in Scripture, that prophecies are included under the heading of Law, for all are made in reference to it, as source or end,' Calvin, *Comm. Mark* 1.1-6.

John'.⁴⁵ He notes that 'law,' there, does not refer to that which condemns but that which instructed Israel in rudimentary teaching. According to the narrower definitions, the relationship of law and gospel is that of old and new covenant. They are not opposed but in continuity:

> But in this way [the second narrower senses of law and gospel] the Gospel has not succeeded the entire Law so that it produces a different way of salvation. Rather, it confirms (*sancio*) and proves whatever scattered matters it [the law] had promised.⁴⁶

In sum, for Calvin the broad definitions of law (as command) and gospel (as promise) are opposed, whilst the narrower definitions of law (old covenant) and gospel (new covenant) are harmonious.

The second narrower definitions of law (old covenant) and gospel (new covenant), Calvin avers, particularly relate to *revelation*. They emphasise the greater disclosure of God that members of the new covenant enjoy compared to those under the old covenant. Hence, in his *Institutes*, Calvin prefaces his discussion of the two meanings of 'gospel' with a section elucidating just how immense new covenant revelation is as opposed to that of the old covenant.⁴⁷ In short, God's revelation of himself under the old covenant was 'obscure and shadowy,' whereas, he now has 'made himself visible,' as it were.⁴⁸ Hence, in the narrow sense of law and gospel, despite there being continuity (in the way of salvation) between them, there is, also, a large difference (in the amount of revelation). Thus, Calvin was keen to describe the gospel as a new 'embassy'.⁴⁹

The dominant meaning of gospel

Some have noticed that Calvin understood the word 'gospel' (and 'law') in two senses.⁵⁰ However, it has not been as carefully noted that Calvin sees one sense as dominant in Scripture and, hence, of greater importance, theologically. He contends that the second narrower sense of 'gospel' is its proper meaning in Scripture:

> Whereupon, it is correct that the word 'Gospel' properly (*propriè*) is applicable to the New Covenant. Those writers speak with insufficient accuracy, who make it

---

⁴⁵ *Inst.* 2.9.4, 146, *CR* 30.312; *Harmonia ex evangelistis tribus composita, Matthaeo* Argumentum, n.p.

⁴⁶ *Inst.* 2.9.4, 146, *CR* 30.312.

⁴⁷ *Inst.* 2.9.1.

⁴⁸ *Inst.* 2.9.1, 145; *CR* 30.309-310.

⁴⁹ *Inst.* 2.9.2.

⁵⁰ Michael Horton, 'Calvin and the Law-Gospel Hermeneutic,' *Pro Ecclesia* 6.1 (1997), 27-42; I. John Hesselink, 'Law and Gospel or Gospel and Law?—Karl Barth, Martin Luther, and John Calvin,' *RRJ* 14.1 (2005), 139-71; Andrew J. Bandstra, 'Law and Gospel in Calvin and in Paul' in D.E. Holwerda (ed.), *Exploring the Heritage of John Calvin: Essays in Honor of John Bratt* (Grand Rapids: Baker, 1976), 11-39.

> [the Gospel] common to all ages, and set the prophets no less than the apostles to be ministers of the Gospel.[51]

> What signifies the Greek word for 'Gospel' is sufficiently known. In Scripture it is taken pre-eminently (κατ' ἐξοχήν) as the joyful and happy news of the grace revealed in Christ.[52]

> But because the Spirit is accustomed to say in Scripture that the Gospel was only proclaimed when Christ came, let us retain this way of speaking.[53]

In each of these citations Calvin makes a comparison between the broad and narrow definition of the gospel, contending that the latter is Scripture's proper usage. He, thus, believes that this narrow sense should be given greater importance:

> Hence it follows that Gospel, taken in a large sense, comprehends the evidences of mercy and paternal favour which God bestowed on the Patriarchs. Still, by way of excellence, it is applied to the promulgation of the grace manifested in Christ.[54]

Therefore, whilst Calvin did hold a place for the Lutheran law/gospel distinction, it did not have the same prominence in his theology. Rather, the salvation historical emphasis took priority.

The place of repentance

Where does Calvin stand regarding repentance and the gospel? He includes it in the gospel itself:

> The sum of the Gospel is, not without good reason, made to consist in repentance and forgiveness of sins.[55]

> [T]he whole Gospel consists in two parts, remission of sins, and repentance.[56]

Calvin, here, expresses his notion of the *duplex gratia* or 'double grace' offered in the gospel. The two parts are a new position before God (justification, forgiveness of sins, reconciliation, and adoption) and a changed condition in oneself (conversion, newness of life).[57] Both forgiveness (declaration) and repentance (transformation) are free gifts received by faith alone. But Calvin is quick to affirm that faith's object is chiefly in the declarative part:

---

[51] Calvin, *Harmonia ex evangelistis tribus composita, Matthaeo, Marco, et Luca*, Argumentum n.p.
[52] Calvin, *Harmonia [...] Johanne*, 693.
[53] Calvin, *Harmonia [...] Johanne*, 693.
[54] *Inst.* 2.9.2. See *Institutes of the Christian Religion* (translated by H. Beveridge; Edinburgh: T. & T. Clark, 1863), 1:365.
[55] *Inst.* 3.3.1. See Beveridge, 1.509.
[56] Calvin, *Harmonia ex evangelistis tribus composita, Matthaeo, Marco, et Luca* Matt. 3.2, 83 col. 1.
[57] *Inst.* 3.11.1.

Nevertheless the faith which he demands we should have in the Gospel ought not to be restricted to the gift of renovation, but chiefly [*praecipué*] looks to the remission of sins.[58]

Given that forgiveness and repentance are offered in the gospel, it, thus, calls people to both faith and repentance. However, the actual faith and repentance that believers exercise are not the gospel *per se*, but its fruit. These are the works that the Holy Spirit produces in a believer, which are not meritorious.

The Reformed confessional tradition

Unlike the sixteenth century Lutheran tradition, the Reformed tradition did not have one universal set of confessional documents. Different confessions governed different reformed communities, the most important being the *Gallic Confession* (1559), *Scots Confession* (1560), *Belgic Confession* (1561), *Thirty-Nine Articles* (1563), *Heidelberg Catechism* (1563), and *Second Helvetic Confession* (1566). The one confession that explicitly articulates a doctrine of the gospel is the *Second Helvetic Confession*, which was authored by Heinrich Bullinger. It presents a gospel that is very similar to that of Calvin.

The *Second Helvetic Confession* gives two definitions of the gospel. The first is that which is akin to the Lutheran tradition in which law and gospel are 'opposed': 'The Gospel, indeed, is opposed [*oppono*] to the law: for the law works wrath, and does announce a curse; but the Gospel does preach grace and blessing.'[59] Bullinger contends that on this definition the gospel exists in the Old Testament in the form of 'evangelical promises' such as Genesis 3.15; 49.10; Deuteronomy 18.15. It was through these promises that Old Testament believers were saved. This is, basically, Calvin's broad definition of the gospel.

The second definition of the gospel in the *Second Helvetic Confession* is 'properly' (*proprié*) called 'glad and happy news' (*laetum et felix nuncium*) which did not exist in the Old Testament but was preached to the world 'first by John Baptist, then by Christ the Lord himself, and afterwards by the apostles and their successors'.[60] This 'news' concerns the fulfilment of Old Testament promises and is, particularly, narrated in the four Gospels but is, also, found scattered in the other New Testament writings. This second definition is fundamentally Calvin's narrow understanding of the gospel. Furthermore, like Calvin, Bullinger, also, explicitly includes repentance in the gospel:

---

[58] Calvin, *Harmonia ex evangelistis tribus composita, Matthaeo, Marco, et Luca* Matt. 3.2, 104 cols 1-2.

[59] Bullinger, *Confessio et expositio simplex orthodoxae fidei et dogmatum Catholicorum syncerae religionis Christianae* (Zurich: Christophorus Froschauerus, 1566), xiii, 29b; *The Creeds of Christendom* (edited by P. Schaff; Grand Rapids: Baker, 1983), 3.856.

[60] Bullinger, *The Second Helvetic Confession*, xiii; *Creeds of Christendom*, 3.857.

> The Gospel has the doctrine of repentance joined with it; for so said the Lord in the Gospel, 'In my name must repentance and remission of sins be preached among all nations.'[61]

The verse cited here to support the inclusion of repentance in the gospel is Luke 24.47, which Melanchthon particularly used to make the same point, and which appears to be in Calvin's mind when he included repentance in the gospel.

Conclusion

It can, thus, be seen that whilst there was common ground between the sixteenth century Lutheran tradition and Calvin on the doctrine of the gospel, there were, also, important differences, particularly in emphasis. Calvin and the *Formula of Concord* both propounded two definitions of the gospel. Both agreed that in one sense the gospel was to be found in the Old Testament (as promise) and was, also, opposed to the law (as bare command). But the Lutheran tradition saw this as the primary definition of the gospel, whereas for Calvin it was secondary. The latter wished to emphasise as primary his second narrow construal of the gospel as a message that was absent in the Old Testament but came to light in Christ. Moreover, Calvin's primary message of the gospel included the call to repentance, unlike the primary understanding of the gospel in the *Formula*. The difference between the *Formula* and Calvin, however, did not simply concern one theologian and the Lutheran confessional tradition. The most popular confession in the sixteenth century Reformed communities was the *Second Helvetic Confession*, which, itself, codified something like Calvin's doctrine of the gospel.

---

[61] Bullinger, *Confessio* xiv, 31b, *Creeds of Christendom*, 3.858.

3. Exegesis and theology

CHAPTER 10

The Christoscopic interpretation of John Oecolampadius on the child named in Isaiah 7-11

Jeff Fisher

The reformation era is rightly considered one of the most significant time-periods in the history of the church which shaped how evangelicals interpret Scripture. Yet despite the fact that the early sixteenth century witnessed an explosion of commentary writing, scholars have focused far less on the commentaries of reformers than on the theological writings of the time. The research that has been done on the commentaries has primarily focused on only a few well-known reformers. The purpose of this study is to look more closely at the exegesis of John Oecolampadius (1482-1531), the reformer at Basel.[1] He is one of those figures in the first generation of reform who was a very influential and greatly respected exegete, but who, for various reasons, has not received the attention of scholars and church historians in later generations.[2] Focusing on his exegesis offers us a particularly valuable perspective on the changes in exegetical practices at the time of the reformation.

Oecolampadius is a transitional figure who was ordained as a Catholic priest in 1510 and had his 'breakthrough' to the reformation understanding sometime around 1519. Through his involvement in the Humanist movement, he became

---

[1] The standard biography of Oecolampadius is Ernst Staehelin, *Das Theologische Lebenswerk Johannes Oekolampads*, QFR 21 (New York: Johnson, 1939). Primary sources are found in Ernst Staehelin, *Briefe und Akten zum Leben Oekolampads*, QFR 10, 19 (New York: Johnson, 1971). The main English biographies are Diane Poythress, *Reformer of Basel: The Life, Thought, and Influence of Johannes Oecolampadius* (Grand Rapids: Reformation Heritage Books, 2011); Gordon Rupp, *Patterns of Reformation*, 1969 (Eugene, Or: Wipf & Stock, 2009), 3-46.

[2] For examples of recent historians expressing the need for further study on Oecolampadius, see Ed Miller, 'Oecolampadius: The Unsung Hero of the Basel Reformation,' *Iliff Review* 39.3 (1982), 5; Thomas A. Fudge, 'Icarus of Basel? Oecolampadius and the Early Swiss Reformation,' *JRH* 21.3 (1997), 268; Bruce Gordon, *The Swiss Reformation* (New York: Manchester University Press, 2002), 109; Amy Nelson Burnett, 'Contributors to the Reformed Tradition' in David Whitford (ed.), *Reformation and Early Modern Europe: A Guide to Research* (Kirksville, MO: Truman State University Press, 2008), 35.

an expert in the biblical languages and the early church fathers.[3] Oecolampadius provided a large number of annotations for the first edition of Erasmus's *Novum Instrumentum* in 1515 and received his Doctorate of Divinity from the University of Basel in 1518. Near the end of 1522, Oecolampadius returned to Basel and, the following Spring, began lecturing through books of the Bible. He was quickly appointed as professor of Old Testament at the University in June 1523. His biblical lectures were unique for the time.[4] He taught in both Latin and German, and was among the few interpreters of the era who could utilize both Greek and Hebrew. His audience included up to 400 people at a time. His lectures and a few sermon series were published as 16 different commentaries, covering at least portions of 23 books of the Bible.[5] Oecolampadius was a priest, a professor, a reformer, a preacher, a pastor, and the author of numerous writings. He was not only instrumental in Basel embracing the reformation, but he, also, played a significant role in the development of biblical exegesis.

The book of Isaiah was the subject of the first series of weekly biblical lectures by Oecolampadius.[6] Even before he had completed the series, scholars of the day were writing to Oecolampadius to request his lecture notes.[7] Within weeks of completing the series in May 1524, the lectures were being prepared for its eventual publication in March 1525.[8] His was the first Protestant com-

---

[3] Oecolampadius studied Theology and the biblical languages at the universities of Heidelberg, Stuttgart, Tübingen and Basel. He had close relationships with Humanists, such as Wimpfeling, Reuchlin, Melanchthon, and Erasmus.

[4] Prior to April 1529, when Basel officially accepted the reformation, these lectures occurred weekly unless Oecolampadius had other responsibilities or Basel was in a state of upheaval. After 1529, the lectures were held daily. See Rupp, *Patterns of Reformation*, 19, 38, 42-43; Staehelin, *Das theologische Lebenswerk*, 566-67, 571.

[5] Oecolampadius's published commentaries include 1 John (1524), Isaiah (1525, 1548), Romans (1525, 1526), Malachi (1526), Haggai, Zechariah, and Malachi (1527), Daniel (1530, 1553, 1557), Job (1532, 1553, 1557, 1567), John (1533, 1535), Jeremiah, Lamentations (1533), Ezekiel (1534), Hebrews (1534), Hosea, Joel, Amos, Obadiah, Jonah, and Micah 1-2 (1535), Matthew (1536), Genesis (1536), Psalms 73-77, 137 (1544), and Colossians (1546). Ten commentaries were published for the first time after his death. Twelve went through later editions. All his previously published works on the prophets and Job were published in Geneva as one set in 1558, 1577, and 1578. During the sixteenth century, at least portions of four of his commentaries were translated or composed in German, and two were translated into French.

[6] Oecolampadius lectured on Isaiah from the Spring of 1523 until the Summer of 1524—Staehelin, *Das theologische Lebenswerk*, 189-90; Rupp, *Patterns of Reformation*, 19.

[7] Requests in 1523 came from Hedio, Capito, Brenz, Roussel, Bugenhagen, Rhegius, and Adelmann in *Briefe und Akten*, 1.216-17, 279, 284, 289-93, 319-20, 322-26, 331-32 [N°s. 149, 195, 200, 203, 221, 224, 230].

[8] See *Briefe und Akten*, 1.277, 360 (N°s. 193, 248). The commentary was published as Johannes Oecolampadius, *In Iesaiam Prophetam Hypomnematōn, Hoc Est, Commentariorum, Ioannis Oecolampadii Libri VI* (Basel: Cratander, 1525).

mentary on Isaiah, and stood as a model for how the prophet would be discussed in the early years of the reformation.[9] The lectures and subsequent commentary were well-received. Martin Luther wrote to Oecolampadius in 1523, 'Certainly we have exceedingly approved your spirit and this excellent deed. . . . May the Lord strengthen your intention in lecturing on Isaiah.'[10] Nearly a decade later, in Luther's own commentary on Isaiah (1532), he wrote, 'Oecolampadius has quite satisfactorily translated Isaiah.'[11] Zwingli, also, issued the praise, 'Oecolampadius also gave Isaiah to us . . . which truly was made clear by his comments. With respect to retaining the sense and discourse of the holy letters, no one has ever arisen from anywhere who more fairly may be called a *cornucopia*.'[12] Likewise, John Calvin recommended the Isaiah commentary by Oecolampadius to Pierre Viret in 1540. After giving his opinions about Capito, Zwingli, and Luther, Calvin wrote, 'No one, therefore, so far has engaged more diligently in this work than Oecolampadius, though he too does not always hit the mark.'[13] When Calvin published his own commentary on Isaiah (1551), Oecolampadius was one of the exegetes with whom he interacted.[14] Peter Opitz summarizes that Oecolampadius's commentary on Isaiah 'represented without a doubt a pioneering effort in "reformed" or "upper German" exposition of Scripture'.[15]

---

[9] Later Protestant commentaries on Isaiah include Zwingli (1529), Luther (1532), Münster (ca. 1540), Brenz (1550), Castellio (1551), Musculus (1557), Calvin (1559), and Bullinger (1567). See David C. Steinmetz, 'John Calvin on Isaiah 6: A Problem in the History of Exegesis,' *Interpretation* 36.2 (April 1982), 157.

[10] Luther to Oecolampadius, 20 June 1523, in *Briefe und Akten*, 1.222-23 (N° 157). See, also, Luther to Nicholas Grebel, June 1523, in *WA* 12.56. For English translations, see Martin Luther, *Luther's Correspondence and Other Contemporary Letters* (edited by Preserved Smith and Charles M. Jacobs: Philadelphia: Lutheran Publication Society, 1913), 2.187, 190 (N°s 589, 591).

[11] *WA* 31-II.2. Luther commented, 'Oecolampadius has sufficiently done good work in the grammar, although occasionally he may differ from us' (*WA* 25.88). Luther specifies disagreement in *WA* 25.152, 160.

[12] Ulrich Zwingli, *Huldreich Zwingli's Werke*, ed. Melchior Schuler and Johannes Schultness, vol. 5, Reprint (1529). (Zürich: F. Schulthess, 1828), 548. See, also, *Briefe und Akten*, 2.342 (N° 679).

[13] Calvin to Viret, 19 May 1540, in *CO* 11.36 (N° 217), my translation.

[14] See, for example, Calvin's comments in *CO* 37.262. Additionally, a letter from Bullinger to Calvin in 1553 indicates that Calvin and the Genevans were still using Oecolampadius' teachings twenty-years after his death and two years after Calvin's commentary on Isaiah had been written (*CO* 14.534).

[15] Peter Opitz, 'The Exegetical and Hermeneutical Work of John Oecolampadius, Huldrych Zwingli and John Calvin' in Magne Sæbø (ed.), *Hebrew Bible, Old Testament: The History of Its Interpretation* (Göttingen: Vandenhoeck & Ruprecht, 2008), 2.412.

Focus and methodology

In order to identify the pioneering contributions of Oecolampadius to the development of biblical interpretation, this study will use the methodology advanced by Steinmetz, Thompson, and Muller in the recent and expanding field of the history of exegesis in the sixteenth century.[16] As Timothy George notes, the reformers of the sixteenth century were in constant dialogue 'with the preceding exegetical tradition, and they used it respectfully as well as critically in their expositions of the sacred text'.[17] The focus of this study is on the exegetical dialogue of Oecolampadius on four key passages in Isaiah 7-11. In order to discern some of the ways in which his exegesis was unique and influential on later interpretive practices, the comments of Oecolampadius will be compared with important predecessors and, then, with John Calvin as a successor. Like many of his time, Oecolampadius draws on authors without acknowledging his sources, so it is not always easy to identify whose works he is using. However, we can tell from his exposition that the most relevant commentators for comparison include Chrysostom (ca. 386),[18] Jerome (ca. 410),[19] Cyril of Alexandria (ca. 428)[20] and Nicholas of Lyra (1322-1333).[21] Chrysostom, Jerome and Lyra were widely used by exegetes throughout the Middle Ages and into the reformation.[22] Additionally, Oecolampadius' particular interest in the Greek Fathers

---

[16] For a concise summary of this approach, see Richard A. Muller, 'Biblical Interpretation in the Sixteenth and Seventeenth Centuries' in Donald K. McKim (ed.), *Dictionary of Major Biblical Interpreters* (Downers Grove, IL: IVP Academic, 2007), 22-31.

[17] Timothy George, *Reading Scripture with the Reformers* (Downers Grove: IVP Academic, 2011), 123.

[18] Chrysostom's homilies on Isaiah 1-8 are in J.P. Migne (ed.), *Patrologia Graeca* (PG), vol. 56. The English translations here are from Duane A Garrett, *An Analysis of the Hermeneutics of John Chrysostom's Commentary on Isaiah 1-8 with an English Translation* (Lewiston, N.Y: Edwin Mellen, 1992).

[19] Jerome, *Commentariorum in Esaiam*, in Marcus Adriaen and Germain Morin (eds), *Corpus Christianorum, Series Latina* (CCSL), vol. 73. For an analysis of Jerome's exegesis of Isaiah, see R.G. Jenkins, 'The Biblical Text of the Commentaries of Eusebius and Jerome on Isaiah,' *Abr-Nahrain* 22 (1984), 64-78.

[20] Cyril of Alexandria, in J.P. Migne (ed.), *Patrologia Graeca* (PG), vol. 70. A sixteenth century Latin translation is available as *Divi Cyrilli Alexandriae Episcopi Commentariorum in Hesaiam Prophetam Libri Quinque* (Basel: Froben, 1563). The English translations here are from Cyril of Alexandria, *Commentary on Isaiah* (translated by Robert C. Hill; Brookline, Mass: Holy Cross Orthodox Press, 2008).

[21] Nicholas of Lyra, *Biblia: mit Postilla Litteralis von Nicolas de Lyra* (Nürnberg: Anton Koberger, 1497). For comments on Lyra's exegesis, see Philip Krey and Lesley Smith (eds), *Nicholas of Lyra: The Senses of Scripture* (Leiden; Boston: Brill, 2000); Eugene H. Merrill, 'Rashi, Nicholas De Lyra, and Christian Exegesis,' *WTJ* 38.1 (1975), 66-79.

[22] For the broader history of medieval exegesis, see Henri de Lubac, *Medieval Exegesis: The Four Senses of Scripture*, 3 vols. (Grand Rapids: Eerdmans, 1998); Beryl Smalley, *The Study of the Bible in the Middle Ages* (Notre Dame: Notre Dame University Press, 1964).

makes Chrysostom and Cyril especially relevant for comparison. At the time he was lecturing on Isaiah, Oecolampadius was, also, translating works by Chrysostom and Theophylact.[23] In addition to these Christian exegetes, Oecolampadius regularly referred to Jewish interpretations, such as those of Rashi, David Kimhi and Abraham Ibn Esra.[24]

A comparison of these exegetes on the child named in Isaiah 7-11 will demonstrate that John Oecolampadius selectively employed early Christian and medieval comments based on his own reading of the Hebrew text to continue the gradual shift from an emphasis on the fourfold sense of Scripture toward a stronger emphasis on the literal sense of the text. He particularly adapted the interpretive notion of *skopos* from the Greek Fathers as a way to understand that the genuine meaning of the text comes from both the *history* and the *mystery*, which always has Christ as its goal (*scopus*). For this reason, his approach to interpreting these texts can be called a *Christoscopic* approach.

Christoscopic approach to Isaiah

Oecolampadius presented the most important aspects of his approach to interpreting Isaiah in the dedicatory epistle, the preface and the opening of his commentary. He emphasized the importance of closely following the Hebrew text in order to discern the mind of the prophet.[25] Oecolampadius most likely used the *Biblia Rabbinica* (1517/1518) as his Hebrew text.[26] He acknowledged that the Septuagint and the Vulgate were helpful, but felt compelled to give 'a new translation, that was not lacking in Hebrew truth, which in the case of the Old Testament ought especially to be consulted and observed'.[27] He affirmed that in order to present a faithful interpretation of Isaiah, 'it was necessary to properly remember the history of the times in which he prophesied. For unless that is rightly laid before as a foundation, whatever is built on top will ruin it.'[28] He further stated:

---

[23] See *Briefe und Akten*, 1.238-45, 268-70 (N° 165, 187).

[24] See Staehelin, *Theologische Lebenswerk*, 192-93n.5; Opitz, 'Exegetical and Hermeneutical Work', 410. Oecolampadius sometimes draws Jewish interpretations from the commentaries of Jerome or Lyra.

[25] Oecolampadius, *In Iesaiam*, 4a.

[26] Before he left from Augsburg to the monastery, Oecolampadius had a copy of Felix Pratensis, *Biblia Rabbinica* (Venice: Bomberg, 1517). See Thomas Willi, 'Der Beitrag des Hebräischen zum Werden der Reformation in Basel,' *Theologische Zeitschrift* 35.3 (June 1979), 150; Staehelin, *Das theologische Lebenswerk*, 193. The *Biblia Rabbinica* included textual variants, the Targum of Johnathan, and the commentary by David Kimhi.

[27] Oecolampadius, *In Iesaiam*, 3b. Referring to his own philological skills, he rhetorically asked, '[S]ince I was able to drink from the source (*fonte*), why should I stoop to the stream?' (5b). All English translations from Oecolampadius's Isaiah commentary are mine.

[28] Oecolampadius, *In Iesaiam*, 5b.

In that way, if those [histories] are rightly treated, happily will they also be able to obtain the mysteries of allegories (*allegoriarum mysteria*), which you should not entirely despise, but also not advance unreasonably. Scripture is unworthy of either. Truly so that you may skillfully use these, understand that the prophets foretold about future things, without disregarding their own times.... Similarly, it often happens that histories, while they are true in themselves, so also obscurely prefigure mysteries, either of Christ or the Antichrist, with a certain type. So then, a diligent interpreter should disregard neither. But first to compose the history, then to remove the covers of the mysteries referred to by the apostles as well.[29]

Similar to Erasmus, Oecolampadius opposed the artificial constructions that often resulted from an uncontrolled use of the medieval fourfold sense of Scripture.[30] Oecolampadius insisted that the genuine meaning of a text could only be drawn from the historical events. Yet he did not entirely abandon the use of allegory or a spiritual sense, but looked for ways to uncover the mysteries of Christ and his kingdom to which the history pointed.[31] He appealed to Luke 4 to establish that 'in the reading of this book, Christ himself not only commended it, but also taught the way it ought to be read'.[32] He maintained that 'the sense of Scripture is disclosed to no one except those who also seek Christ and to whom Christ reveals himself'.[33] While his approach centered on Christ, Oecolampadius did not attempt to find Jesus in every detail in the way that Isidore of Seville did. Nor did he adhere to a kind of two-type exegesis that equated the literal sense with the Jewish view and a Christian sense with the traditional view like Andrew of St. Victor had done.[34] He, also, did not simply utilize a 'hermeneutic of promise and fulfillment' that located the meaning of the text strictly in the future fulfillment and tended to crowd out the historical elements.[35] Oecolampadius sought to faithfully interpret both the histories and the

---

[29] Oecolampadius, *In Iesaiam*, 5b.
[30] The four senses of Scripture in the medieval tradition were the literal, the allegorical, the tropological (moral), and the anagogical (eschatological). For an accessible explanation, see Lubac, *Medieval Exegesis*, 1.1.
[31] See Oecolampadius, *In Iesaiam*, 5a, 168b. Oecolampadius detected many ways in which Isaiah presents types of Christ, including the name *Iesaias* (4a). Sometimes Oecolampadius called the spiritual sense a *sensus mysticus* (Staehelin, *Das theologische Lebenswerk*, 192, 196). Peter Opitz, 'Exegetical and Hermeneutical Work,' 410–411, identifies that a key aspect of Oecolampadius's exegesis is that he 'interpreted salvation-historically, eschatologically, and christologically'.
[32] Oecolampadius, *In Iesaiam*, 2a.
[33] Oecolampadius, *In Iesaiam*, 2a.
[34] See Smalley, *The Study of the Bible*, 124-72; John F.A. Sawyer, 'Isaiah' in John H. Hayes (ed.), *Dictionary of Biblical Interpretation* (Nashville: Abingdon Press, 1999), 1.550-51.
[35] Muller's assertion that 'Oecolampadius recognizes no referent of the prophecy prior to the time of Christ' is oversimplified. See 'The Hermeneutic of Promise and Fulfillment in Calvin's Exegesis of the Old Testament Prophecies of the Kingdom' in

mysteries of Scripture, using a *Christoscopic* approach, modeled off the early Greek Fathers.[36] In his exposition of Isaiah, Oecolampadius affirmed that 'every Scripture looks to Christ as its goal (*scopum*)'.[37]

Exegesis of the child named in Isaiah 7-11

The exposition by Oecolampadius regarding the child named in Isaiah 7-11 reveals some aspects of how his interpretive approach worked in practice and how it was distinct from other interpreters. Oecolampadius moved through the biblical text phrase by phrase, offering philological, textual, exegetical and theological comments. His general interpretation of Isaiah 7.14-16 falls completely in line with the traditional Christian view that Isaiah predicted the birth of Jesus to a virgin, as Matthew and Luke attest.[38] Like the majority of Christian interpreters, Oecolampadius opposed the idea that the woman in this passage was either the wife of Ahaz or the wife of Isaiah. He repeated Lyra's adoption of Rashi's timeline from 2 Kings 16-18 to reject the view that Hezekiah could be the child named in 7.14.[39] Oecolampadius, also, reiterated the traditional view that this passage had to be a 'remarkable mystery (*admirabilis mysterii*) . . . greater than what anyone—either in heaven or on earth—would have asked for, and clearly transcending the order of nature. Certainly a virgin birth is that remarkable.'[40] In these respects, Oecolampadius demonstrated little difference from previous Christian exegetes.

However, in the details of his explanations, several differences distinguish Oecolampadius from his predecessors. Oecolampadius differed from the tradi-

---

David C. Steinmetz (ed.), *The Bible in the Sixteenth Century* (Durham, NC: Duke University Press, 1996), 79-81, 220-21.

[36] On the concept of *skopos* in the Greek Fathers, see Paul Blowers, 'Eastern Orthodox Biblical Interpretation' in Alan Hauser and Duane Watson (eds), *A History of Biblical Interpretation* (Grand Rapids: Eerdmans, 2009), 2.178-79, 183-85; Robert Louis Wilken, 'Cyril of Alexandria as Interpreter of the Old Testament' in Thomas Weinandy and Daniel Keating (eds), *The Theology of St. Cyril of Alexandria: A Critical Appreciation* (London: T. & T. Clark, 2003), 1-21.

[37] Oecolampadius, *In Iesaiam*, 22b.

[38] See Steven McKinnon (ed.), *Ancient Christian Commentary on Scripture: Isaiah 1-39* (Downers Grove: IVP Academic, 2004), 58.

[39] See Lyra, *Postilla Esaie*, 13a. See, also, Smalley, *The Study of the Bible in the Middle Ages*, 163; Brevard S. Childs, *The Struggle to Understand Isaiah as Christian Scripture* (Grand Rapids: Eerdmans, 2004), 174, 233. Though Rashi had used this information to conclude that the child was the son of Isaiah, both Lyra and Oecolampadius only use these calculations to prove that it could not refer to Hezekiah.

[40] Oecolampadius, *In Iesaiam*, 69a. Origen, Chrysostom, Theophylact, and Lyra all affirmed the idea stated in Jerome, *Commentariorum in Esaiam*, 102-103. Lyra, also, noted that even Rashi acknowledged that a sign ought to be something great and exceeding the faculty of a creature (Lyra, *Postilla Esaie*, 13a). Oecolampadius emphasized that the passage could not refer to an ordinary conception, because one must either 'admit that this is a pure virgin or deny that a miracle is indicated' (69b).

tional view that the verb 'conceive' in 7.14 should be translated with the future tense.[41] He argued that the Hebrew was better translated as a present tense with the prophet describing 'a future thing with prophetic eyes as if he had observed it in the present'.[42] Similarly, Oecolampadius did not find that this promise was remarkable because of the word, 'sign', but because the sentence began with 'behold'.[43] Oecolampadius, also, differed in his explanation that even though Jesus is not named Immanuel, it is rightly stated in Isaiah 7, '[b]ecause he was called Jesus, who would save people from their sins. For this is only a work of God alone . . . and he was *with us*, not only by grace as he was with the fathers, but also in bodily presence.'[44] It seems very likely that he intentionally rejected the traditional explanation that it was 'a name appropriate to the events surrounding his birth,' because, at the time, he was lecturing on Isaiah, he was, also, translating Theophylact's commentary on the Gospels, where Theophylact specifically made the assertion that 'Scripture gives this as his name, which he acquires from the event.'[45]

The most significant differences are seen in the way Oecolampadius explained that the term for the woman in 7.14 could refer to a 'young maiden' and how this 'sign' could refer to something meaningful to the people living at the time of Isaiah. Oecolampadius made no mention of the common assumption that the noun translated 'virgin' was derived from the verb meaning 'concealed,' which applied to a virgin rather than a young maiden.[46] Instead, he showed from the etymology that the term could refer to a young maiden but directly countered the Jewish argument that the use of the term in Proverbs 30.18-19 proves that the woman is not a virgin but the wife of Isaiah. Oecolampadius argued, 'If this were about the wife of Isaiah, then it would have said, "Behold your wife will bear *to you* a son" just as we read about Abraham. . . . But this is all attributed to a virgin.'[47] Similarly, in contrast to the traditional view that a sign must be new and marvelous, Oecolampadius affirmed that the promised sign in Isaiah 7.14 was *not* entirely new, but rather

---

[41] See Lyra, *Postilla Esaie*, 13a.
[42] Oecolampadius, *In Iesaiam*, 69a.
[43] Oecolampadius, *In Iesaiam*, 69a-b. See Chrysostom's view in PG 57.57; NPNF 10.31; Garrett, *Analysis of Chrysostom's Commentary on Isaiah 1-8*, 146.
[44] Oecolampadius, *In Iesaiam*, 69b, emphasis added.
[45] See Theophylact, *The Explanation of the Holy Gospel According to St. Matthew*, (House Springs, MO: Chrysostom Press, 1992), 1.21. For Chrysostom, see NPNF 10.30 and Garrett, *Analysis of Chrysostom's Commentary on Isaiah 1-8*, 150. See, also, Cyril of Alexandria in PG 70.224. Oecolampadius further opposed Theophylact's interpretation by pointing out that the command 'you shall call' is second person future.
[46] See Jerome, *Commentariorum in Esaiam*, 108; Lyra, *Postilla Esaie*, 13a. Oecolampadius, also, ignored the argument that the Jews had changed the meaning of the word. See Cyril of Alexandria in PG 70.204, *Commentary on Isaiah*, 168; Theophylact, *Explanation of Matthew*, 1.21.
[47] Oecolampadius, *In Iesaiam*, 69b.

added another specific element to the first 'sign in which all the fathers themselves were hoping for salvation' found in Genesis 3.15.[48] He located this promise with other promises made to Abraham, Isaac, Jacob, and David throughout salvation history. This is a unique aspect of Oecolampadius's *Christoscopic* approach not found in previous commentators. While Oecolampadius affirmed the traditional view that the 'ineffable mystery [of Christ's birth] is foreknown,' he provided new explanations for why this was the correct interpretation.[49]

Oecolampadius recognized the linguistic connections between 7.14-16 and 8.1-4, and supported the view that the name 'Maher-Shalal-Hash-Baz' was a second name for the Messiah. He expressly declared, 'The prophet's argument of this chapter is the same as that above. For just as there God himself promised freedom from the [kings] by calling on Immanuel not yet born, so also here he promises salvation with another name: Swift-Spoiler.'[50] This differed among some in the Christian tradition, such as Chrysostom and Aquinas, who taught that this passage referred to the son of Isaiah and not the Messiah.[51] He identified inter-textual connections to link 'plunderer' with the parable in Luke 11 where Jesus identifies himself as the 'stronger man' who overcomes the 'strong man'. Oecolampadius's argumentation most closely resembles that of Cyril, who stated that the prophet predicted that 'Christ will plunder Satan and steal his possessions'.[52] However, while Cyril and others interpreted additional elements in this passage as references to events in the early church, Oecolampadius did not find any further spiritual interpretation.[53] Instead, as he had done in chapter 7, he utilized a technique of Chrysostom to explain that the prophecy returns from the time of the future back to the time of Isaiah.[54]

---

[48] Oecolampadius, *In Iesaiam*, 69a.
[49] Oecolampadius, *In Iesaiam*, 69b.
[50] Oecolampadius, *In Iesaiam*, 72b. Oecolampadius reaffirmed that Immanuel and Swift-Spoiler are the same child in his comments on Isaiah 8.8 and 8.10 (75a).
[51] See Garrett, *Analysis of Chrysostom's Commentary on Isaiah 1-8*, 206-207. Garrett identifies this as indicative of Chrysostom's resistance to allegorizing. He notes that Chrysostom does not even mention the possibility that this could refer to a messianic interpretation.
[52] Compare Oecolampadius, *In Iesaiam*, 72b-73a, 75a with Cyril of Alexandria in PG 70.223, *Commentary on Isaiah*, 182. Oecolampadius, also, utilized an explanation similar to Cyril when he asserted, 'And this will happen to his army, that the king of the Assyrians plunders Damascus and Samaria, and in the future the spiritual Assyrian is devastated' (74a). See PG 70.225.
[53] Cyril identifies the Magi, the crucifixion, the resurrection, the apostles suffering for preaching, and other first century events in PG 70.224-225, 230; *Commentary on Isaiah*, 183-85, 189. For this approach in other exegetes, see Robert Louis Wilken, Angela Christman, and Michael Hollerich (eds), *Isaiah: Interpreted by Early Christian and Medieval Commentators* (Grand Rapids: Eerdmans, 2007), 102-104.
[54] Oecolampadius, *In Iesaiam*, 70a-b, 73b-74a. Oecolampadius taught that the phrase 'the days about to come' refers to the captivity of Jerusalem to the Babylonians. Chrysostom wrote, 'Isaiah has done here what he does continually. After the prophe-

Oecolampadius implemented his *Christoscopic* approach to show that Isaiah, 'reports with the history itself, the unusual mysteries (*cum historia haec, mysteria*). Certainly Christ is called by two names.'[55] He, specifically, rejected the view of Cyril, Lyra and others that in 8.3 the prophet had a vision of the Holy Spirit 'approaching' the virgin which 'was conveyed obliquely under the guise of intercourse'.[56] It was commonly held that it was inappropriate for God to command Isaiah to 'approach' his wife since the term normally referred to sexual intercourse. Oecolampadius discounted this view when he stated that 'nothing from the divine will is to be considered shameless—the prophet approached her in his vision'.[57] He explained that 8.3 portrayed the content of the imaginary vision written down according to 8.1 which showed that 'the prophetess is that glorious virgin Mary, who was described in the preceding chapter'.[58]

In his exposition of 9.6-7, Oecolampadius recounted the ways each title and name was true of Jesus, with specific citations from Old and New Testament passages.[59] He, explicitly, linked this passage with the others to identify that the child is Christ:

> He again established the promise with an unusual sign, that of a child born, who in chapter 7 above it says was born from a virgin and she calls Immanuel, and in chapter 8 it says he was born from a prophetess, and is called Swift-Spoiler. Now simply it says 'he is born and given to us . . . .' We attribute all those [names] to Christ, as they ought to be.[60]

---

cy he brings his message back to his historical setting' (Garrett, *Analysis of Chrysostom's Commentary on Isaiah 1-8*, 150).

[55] Oecolampadius, *In Iesaiam*, 72b-73a.

[56] Oecolampadius, also, rejected Origen's allegorical interpretation that since *ruach* is feminine, the prophetess was the Spirit. For specific views of some previous exegetes, see Jerome, *Commentariorum in Esaiam*, 115a; Lyra, *Postilla Esaie*, 15a; Cyril of Alexandria in PG 70.223; *Commentary on Isaiah*, 182. Lyra claimed to affirm Aquinas's objection to a figurative reading, but still affirmed the traditional view. Childs, *The Struggle to Understand Isaiah*, 175 calls this reading by Lyra 'both imaginative and tortuous'.

[57] Oecolampadius, *In Iesaiam*, 73b.

[58] Oecolampadius, *In Iesaiam*, 73b. Oecolampadius contended that 'there is no semblance of truth that the wife of Isaiah is called the prophetess here' (73a-b). He provided inter-textual connections on Isaiah 8.1 and examples from several Old Testament passages to demonstrate that this was a vision and not an actual event.

[59] See Oecolampadius, *In Iesaiam*, 83a-b. Oecolampadius, also, gave a brief explanation about the title 'angel of great counsel,' included in the LXX. This appears to be a summary of Jerome's explanation from Jerome, *Commentariorum in Esaiam*, 126–127. It is, also, similar to Cyril's notion that Christ was 'the messenger of the grand design' in PG 70.255.

[60] Oecolampadius, *In Iesaiam*, 82a, 82b. Oecolampadius appealed to the authority of the New Testament to immediately reject the Jewish understanding that this referred to the time of Isaiah (80a). He, also, reiterated twice more that the Swift Spoiler is Christ, the stronger man (80a, 82a).

Oecolampadius maintained that so many names were listed to confirm our hope, to be more certain about this prophecy, and so that 'we are able to learn from the names how great that boy is'.[61] He stressed that this child is not simply given to his parents, but 'indeed was born *to us* and for the salvation of all'.[62] This seems to be another unique emphasis in Oecolampadius's exposition with regard to the child named in chapters 7, 8, and 9.

Oecolampadius, also, connected the prophecy of the branch and the stump in chapter 11 with the previous chapters. He declared:

> In Christ and in no other, this prophecy resounds.... Indeed explaining the reality through a type (*per veritatem typum*), he seems to say, the boy Immanuel and Swift-Spoiler, will not only aid those trusting in him, but in the future he himself will actually be born from David, and in a while will deliver a more clear triumph over spiritual tyranny than what he now reports about Assyria.[63]

Oecolampadius specifically spoke against the allegorical interpretation of the Scholastics on the sevenfold gifts of the Spirit, as well as a 'literal' Jewish interpretation.[64] In his quest to find an interpretation between unfounded allegory and an overly literal understanding, Oecolampadius, explicitly, adopted the interpretation of Chrysostom that the 'shoot' in 11.1 symbolizes Christ as king.[65] Oecolampadius took this view further by explaining that the 'stump of Jesse' designated the tribe of David which had almost disappeared, so that the whole passage pointed to 'what kind of king the future Christ is, and then what kind of kingdom is his *in the church*'.[66]

Based on his understanding of the Hebrew text, Oecolampadius selectively embraced certain explanations from previous commentators and disregarded others. He specifically responded to Jewish interpretations and located the promises within salvation history. In each of these passages, Oecolampadius

---

[61] Oecolampadius, *In Iesaiam*, 82b. He, also, taught, 'And as above he imposed upon him the name Immanuel and Swift Spoiler, so also that now we may not distrust his promises, he includes these, by which the weakness of our faith may be helped. Indeed also he is not only called such, but actually *is* such, and always was (82a).'

[62] Oecolampadius, *In Iesaiam*, 82a. Oecolampadius applied this to his own time, 'There are many who believe that Christ was born—but not *for them*. They admit that he is Savior—but they do not dare to profess to be his (82a-82b).' See, also, *In Iesaiam*, 73b.

[63] Oecolampadius, *In Iesaiam*, 97a.

[64] Oecolampadius, *In Iesaiam*, 97a. Oecolampadius, also, criticized the exposition of the 'scholastics' on 11:9 (99b).

[65] Oecolampadius, *In Iesaiam*, 97a. He, also, incorporated Jerome's view that 'the branch bearing fruit' referred to the virgin Mary bearing a child without the seed of a man (*Commentariorum in Esaiam*, 147).

[66] Oecolampadius, *In Iesaiam*, 97a, emphasis added. Oecolampadius contended that in chapter 11, the prophet 'teaches about the church and the kingdom of Christ' (98a-b). He viewed the tamed animals as signifying the unity of the church, resulting from the savage nations which accepted the Word.

used a *Christoscopic* approach to establish the historical setting and then suggested how the mysteries about the future were present in the text and could be uncovered.

Calvin's exegesis of the child named in Isaiah 7-11

In order to see some of Oecolampadius's contribution to the exegetical tradition, it is necessary to compare his comments on Isaiah to those of John Calvin. Despite the fact that it is very difficult to identify the sources Calvin used, there is no question that Calvin was familiar with and appropriated exegetical insights from Oecolampadius.[67] James Brashler, for example, compares the interpretive approaches of Oecolampadius and Calvin to demonstrate that Oecolampadius's perspective 'is exactly the perspective of Calvin, who also stresses the historical context of the prophet Isaiah in his commentary, but at the same time he recognizes that Isaiah is also speaking of Christ at many points in his prophecy'.[68] While their overall perspectives may have been the same, Calvin only agrees with Oecolampadius on some aspects related to the child named in Isaiah 7-11.[69]

Both Calvin and Oecolampadius affirm that the passages about the child named in 7, 9 and 11 are predictions of the Messiah and not Hezekiah or the son of Isaiah.[70] However, Calvin's interpretation of the child named in chapter 8 is almost entirely the opposite of Oecolampadius. Calvin argued that the vision was of Isaiah having a child with his wife, not a vision by Isaiah of the Virgin Mary. Calvin even allowed for the fact that this could refer to an actual son of Isaiah, if there was any evidence to prove that such a child was ever born.[71] Similarly, with regard to his interpretation of 'the boy' in 7.16, Calvin acknowledged, 'Here I differ from all the commentators.'[72] He, specifically, called the view that Oecolampadius held, 'a mistake', and, later, said it 'cannot

---

[67] On Calvin's familiarity with Oecolampadius' commentary on Isaiah, see footnotes 13 and 14 above. For examples of articles that identify Calvin's use of Oecolampadius, see E.A. de Boer, *John Calvin on the Visions of Ezekiel* (Leiden; Boston: Brill, 2004); Akira Demura, 'Two Commentaries on the Epistle to the Romans: Calvin and Oecolampadius' in *Calvinus Sincerioris Religionis Vindex* (1997), 165-88; Mark W. Elliott, 'Romans 7 in the Reformation Century' in Kathy Ehrensperger and R. Ward Holder (eds), *Reformation Readings of Romans* (London: T. & T. Clark, 2008), 173-74.

[68] James Brashler, 'From Erasmus to Calvin: Exploring the Roots of Reformed Hermeneutics,' *Int* 63.2 (April 2009), 165.

[69] Calvin's comments on Isaiah 7-11 are in *CO* 36.154-250. The English translations here are from John Calvin, *Commentary on the Book of the Prophet Isaiah*, 4 volumes (translated by William Pringle: Grand Rapids: Eerdmans, 1948).

[70] *Comm. Isa.* 7.14. Calvin dismissed the idea that the child in chapter 7 refers to Isaiah's son as 'an utterly frivolous conjecture', because the title 'Immanuel' is far too illustrious to be applied to any man.

[71] *Comm. Isa.* 8.1.

[72] *Comm. Isa.* 7.16.

harmonize at all with the text'.[73] Instead, Calvin contended that the term in both 7.16 and 8.4 refers to children in general and not 'the son' in 7.14 or 8.3. Calvin, also, differed from Oecolampadius by reiterating the common view, which Oecolampadius had ignored, that the noun translated 'virgin' was derived from the verb 'to conceal', and referred to a virgin remaining hidden from the public.[74]

Perhaps the most noticeable difference is that it seems Calvin was less familiar with actual Jewish interpretations. While Oecolampadius frequently included Jewish interpretations, such as incorporating Rashi's argument to prove that the child named in Isaiah 7 was not Hezekiah, Calvin simply stated that those who think this refers to Hezekiah are ignorant of the history. Of course, this could simply be an example of Calvin seeking brevity, but his exposition of 9.6-7 reveals that he is, actually, not that familiar with the main Jewish explanation of this passage. Calvin questioned why the Jews thought it was necessary to apply *all* the names, titles, and attributes to God *here* and why 'Mighty God' was in the middle, rather than the beginning of the list.[75] Unless he was interacting with a different Jewish interpretation, it seems that Calvin did not understand that Jewish commentators asserted that all the titles belonged to God *except* 'Prince of Peace', which Hezekiah *was called* by the God with all these names. Oecolampadius had argued, 'the Hebrews so that they may falsify the sense . . . explain that God called [Hezekiah] the "Prince of Peace"'.[76] He labeled this 'plain deceit, for they explain [this verb] almost everywhere else as the impersonal, "will be called"'.[77] Calvin entirely ignored this debate over the verb tense, and, instead, simply appealed to a French idiom to explain why it was translated with a passive sense.[78]

Despite these differences, and Calvin's criticism of previous interpreters who had been 'too much at ease in handling this passage,' he actually adopted several interpretations set forth by Oecolampadius.[79] For example, Calvin echoed Oecolampadius on 7.14 when he stated, 'The word "behold" is used emphatically to denote the greatness of the event; for this is the manner in which the Spirit usually speaks of great and remarkable events in order to elevate the

---

[73] *Comm. Isa.* 7.16, 8.1. Oecolampadius had articulated that the timeframe of the two kings' collapse was before the boy named in 7.14 was even born.

[74] *Comm. Isa.* 8.4.

[75] *Comm. Isa.* 9.6.

[76] Lyra, *Postilla Esaie*, 17b. See, also, Herman Hailperin, *Rashi and the Christian Scholars* (Pittsburgh: University of Pittsburgh Press, 1963), 55. Lyra had stated, 'Rabbi Salomon and the modern Jews who follow him expound this passage as referring to Hezekiah, king of Judah, by corrupting the text.' Lyra explained how the vowel pointing of the Hebrew makes it easy to corrupt, and appealed to the LXX, a letter by Jerome, and the Chaldaic translation to support his position.

[77] Oecolampadius, *In Iesaiam*, 82b.

[78] *Comm. Isa.* 9.6.

[79] *Comm. Isa.* 7.14.

minds of men.'[80] It seems very likely that Calvin obtained this explanation from Oecolampadius since it does not appear in other exegetes. Calvin, also, embraced the explanation of Oecolampadius that Isaiah 11 refers to Jesse rather than to David to indicate that the tribe had almost disappeared from memory. This was an important component of how both exegetes described 'what will be the condition of Christ and of his kingdom'.[81] Calvin, also, picked up on Oecolampadius's emphasis that the child was given 'to us' when he wrote, 'And this giving is one of the chief articles of faith; for it would have been of little avail to us, *that* Christ was born, if he had not likewise been our own'.[82]

Probably the most significant impact of Oecolampadius's *Christoscopic* approach on Calvin is found in Calvin's response to why a promise about the future Messiah is given in the context of the deliverance of Jerusalem. Calvin answered that question with the explanation:

> [T]he prophet reminds him of the foundation of the covenant. . . . The Messiah must be born; and this was expected by all. . . . [W]e must attend to the custom of the Prophets, who, in establishing special promises, lay down this as the foundation, that God will send a Redeemer. On this general foundation God everywhere builds all the special promises which he makes to his people.[83]

In the same way that Oecolampadius had done, Calvin located the specific promise of Isaiah 7 within the context of salvation history. Though Calvin differed from Oecolampadius on some of the specific details and believed he had not always hit the mark with his exegesis, there is, certainly, significant commonality between how these two interpreters sought to interpret Isaiah.

Conclusion

Oecolampadius's explanations about the child named in Isaiah 7-11 provide several examples of how he employed a *Christoscopic* approach to interpreting Scripture. While his view was similar to Lyra's 'double literal sense' (*duplex sensus litteralis*), Oecolampadius adopted the notion of *skopos* from Eastern fathers, such as Cyril and Chrysostom, to expound both the histories and the mysteries of the text in a way that always pointed to Christ as the goal of Scripture.[84] Like his predecessors, Oecolampadius struggled with how to read Isaiah in a way that spoke to the time of the prophet, the first century, and his own

---

[80] *Comm. Isa.* 7.14. Calvin, also, echoed Oecolampadius when he disparaged those who identified the sevenfold gifts of the Spirit in Isaiah 11.2, although Calvin referred to them as 'Papists' rather than 'Scholastics' (375).

[81] *Comm. Isa.* 11.2.

[82] *Comm. Isa.* 9.6, emphasis added, though clearly implied.

[83] *Comm. Isa.* 7.14.

[84] Brevard Childs, *Struggle to Understand Isaiah*, 175, wonders if Lyra has simply incorporated the church's traditional figurative readings within his category of 'literal,' especially with texts cited in the New Testament.

time. As nearly all exegetes before him had done, Oecolampadius felt compelled to affirm that the apostolic interpretation was the genuine meaning of these texts. Previous exegetes had gone to great efforts to defend a direct correspondence between Isaiah and the New Testament. Oecolampadius sought to offer some new ways to explain how the teaching of Isaiah connected to the New Testament.

He provided background on words and phrases from the original Hebrew and later translations, identified inter-textual connections within these chapters and other books of the Bible, and located the specific promises made in Isaiah within salvation history. He sought to argue that the genuine meaning of a scripture passage was only found when the foundation of the historical events and the literal meaning was laid first and, then, the mystery was uncovered by consulting other biblical texts. This *Christoscopic* approach by Oecolampadius became influential on Calvin and later Reformed exegetes.

Evangelicals today can, likewise, embrace the aspects of this approach that encourage us to focus closely on the text in its original language and setting, remind us that there is a surplus of meaning in each text, and urge us to see Christ as the goal of all Scripture.

CHAPTER 11

Theological interpretation in the reformers: a case study of the 'Son of Man' texts in Matthew

Jason K. Lee

'So, why the interest in reformation exegesis anyway?' asks the skeptic. Is this really just a bit of pre-modern nostalgia or simply a way for historians and theologians to capture some of the more fertile publishing field of biblical studies? Or, is there a more covert reason, such as using the reformers as a way to destabilize the meaning of biblical texts and, thereby, tapping into a broader postmodern conversation about hermeneutics and the role of texts? Hopefully, instead, the renewed interest in the reformers' interpretive work is a part of a broader renewal of theological interpretation. Theological Interpretation as a contemporary movement (or scholarly sub-discipline) has drawn a variety of adherents and contributors. Some aspects of the Theological Interpretation discussion stems from a rekindled interest in the biblical authors' theological purposes and textual meanings. Efforts at theological interpretation often engage the reformers' work, recognizing the reformers as careful and faithful interpreters of the biblical texts. In this sense, contemporary and pre-modern interpreters are gathering around the common meal of the biblical text. As in any family gathering, the differing voices provide unique perspectives that can be beneficial to the individual members as they are coupled in the familial bond.

A chief characteristic found frequently in Theological Interpretation is an attempt to benefit from the church's tradition of biblical interpretation (i.e., 'pre-modern modes of interpretation') as an effort to discover meaning in biblical texts.[1] Voices from the past are being utilized as a means of creating an interpretative discussion that values the piety and liturgy of the church as a reading context. Stephen Fowl, a leading advocate for a renewal of theological interpretation, asserts, 'Thus, if we are aiming to reinvigorate a practice like theological interpretation, those eager to succeed in the present can only hope to do so in the light of the successes of the past.'[2]

---

[1] Stephen Fowl, *Theological Interpretation of Scripture* (Eugene: Cascade, 2009), 81.
[2] Fowl, *Theological Interpretation*, 55.

ASPECTS OF REFORMING

In his *Introducing Theological Interpretation of Scripture*, Daniel Treier includes this church context under the category of 'culture'. This culture 'involves not only the recognition of the various contexts in which the church has read Scripture, both rightly and poorly, across history but also the acknowledgment of our own contemporary hermeneutical locations'.[3] In engaging interpreters from the past, Treier hopes that the broadened horizons will lead to interpretations of the biblical text that reflect more theological richness. Some critics worry that the use of interpreters from the past inevitably leads to subjective interpretations. Treier acknowledges that the use of past interpreters in contemporary interpretation provides ample opportunity for the 'intrusion' of presuppositions, the supposed antithesis to interpretative objectivity. However, he resists this prejudice against presuppositions adapted from historical sources and asks, 'What if presuppositions are not a threat to objectivity but rather an aid in preserving it?'[4]

The reformers' attention to textual features in the biblical compositions is still germane to the contemporary church's interpretation and proclamation of those same biblical texts. Due to the broader influences of Humanism, the invention of the printing press and a general 'renaissance' of literature, the sixteenth century was characterized by a growing interest in texts, languages and interpretation. This interest, coupled with the religious upheaval of the reformation, caused reformation theologians to become skillful advocates of the biblical text and its theological message. To mine out the theological meaning of the biblical texts, the reformers renewed a textual interest in grammar and the 'literal sense'.

A second chief characteristic of theological interpretation of Scripture is its interaction with historical voices (and a variety of other means) to engage the interpretative question of 'what the text means'. This primary question may be one of the distinguishing factors of theological interpretation from its sometimes hostile cousin, biblical theology, which favors the interpretative question 'what the text meant'? Gerhard Hasel asserts that this 'historical reconstruction' may be one of the most problematic methodological features of biblical theology and nearly requires the collapse of the distinctions between the two questions (i.e., 'what it meant' and 'what it means').[5] So, theological interpretation may provide space for a valid use of interpretative traditions where those adhering more closely to 'biblical theology' may still resist 'theological interpretation' as a 'nonhistorical rival'.[6]

---

[3] Daniel J. Treier, *Introducing Theological Interpretation of Scripture* (Grand Rapids: Baker, 2008), 202.

[4] Treier, *Introducing Theological Interpretation*, 202.

[5] Gerhard Hasel, *New Testament Theology: Basic Issues in the Current Debate* (Grand Rapids: Eerdmans, 1978), 136-37. Hasel, also, notes that the distinction of the 'historical' interest of biblical theology from 'theological' interpretations (e.g., Stendahl) has been critiqued from within biblical theology by Childs et al.

[6] Treier, *Introducing Theological Interpretation*, 113.

The reformers did not pursue their theological endeavor of interpretation without an awareness of history as a feature in determining the meaning of an author's words. For example, though Luther and Calvin often portrayed contrasting models of biblical interpretation, they both displayed a historical interest in their theological interpretations. Gerald Bray notes that Luther's understanding of the 'literal sense' of the text has a historical sense connected, and that, even when Luther strays to an occasional use of allegory due to his theological interests, his approach is not devoid of historical awareness. In noting Luther's theological exposition of the Song of Songs, Bray asserts, 'Luther's allegory is one which the writer of the Song could have understood, and not something imposed by later church speculation.' In this approach, Luther has maintained 'the historical dimension'.[7] Bray explains that Calvin, also, sought the theological intention of a biblical author by examining 'the historical circumstances in which he wrote' and 'the grammatical form' of biblical books.[8] So, many modern theological interpreters find affinity in the reformers' pursuit of the theological meaning of a text without abandoning the historical sense of the words.

A third chief characteristic of theological interpretation is its interest in seeing the value of the whole canon for determining meaning.[9] To refer to the Scriptures as a canon indicates some level of theological commitment, especially when used in reference to a canonical reading of scripture. Theological interpreters have pointed to the canonical scriptures as 'divine address,' and, as such, have a theological end. John Webster asserts that if the canonical scriptures have the quality of divine speech 'then strategies of biblical interpretation will be judged according to their capacity to promote that end. Methods whose primary concern is (for example) the reconstruction of a text's historical or authorial origin . . . will be judged less likely to foster attention to revelation as it is presented in Scripture.'[10] So, in short, theological interpretation is furthered as it makes use of the canonical context of individual texts and recognized that the 'individual texts are to be interpreted with reference to that whole'.[11] Furthermore, as contemporary theological interpreters have drawn from the canonical approach developed by Brevard Childs and revised in some regards by Christopher Seitz, they have

---

[7] Gerald Bray, *Biblical Interpretation: Past and Present* (Downers Grove: IVP, 1996), 198.

[8] Bray, *Biblical Interpretation*, 202.

[9] For an example of how theological interpreters understand how surrounding texts 'both near and far exert canonical pressure' on interpretation, see Daniel Treier, 'A Looser "Canon"? Relating William Abraham's *Canon and Criterion in Christian Theology* to Biblical Interpretation,' *JTI* 2.1 (2008), 101-16.

[10] John Webster, 'Canon' in Kevin Vanhoozer, Craig G. Bartholomew, Daniel J. Treier and N.T. Wright (eds), *Dictionary for Theological Interpretation of the Bible* (London: SPCK, 2005), 99.

[11] Webster, 'Canon,' 100.

acknowledged that through 'the arrangement and sequencing of the material as we now have it [the canon], it is a theological statement'.[12]

Pre-critical voices, such as the reformers, are often helpful in this renewed interest in canonical context, because they often draw on the whole of the Scriptures in their interpretations. Their 'canonical reading' of the biblical texts allowed the reformers to keep in view both the unity of the testaments and the light that one part of the Bible provides for another. Kevin Vanhoozer asserts:

> Premodern interpreters had no trouble reading Scripture as a canonical whole. They were adept at understanding one part of Scripture in light of other parts, whether the parts in question were single verses or whole testaments. Such is not the case with modern interpreters who, alert to the humanity of the biblical texts—the historically and culturally conditioned nature of their composition—are more likely to highlight diversity and differences.[13]

So, as they try to revisit the canon's theological meaning, contemporary proponents of theological interpretation of biblical texts can glean from the fastidious study of the reformation exegetes with their expressed interest in the grammatical sense, theological importance and canonical context of biblical texts.

The reformers, the biblical text and the grammatical sense

Among the vast amount of religious documents in the reformation era, arguably the most influential on biblical interpretation was Erasmus' *Novum Instrumentum* (1516).[14] Erasmus' work was intended to be a revision of and improvement on the Latin Vulgate with its outdated and incorrect grammatical constructions.[15] Erasmus added two other features to justify his revisions to the approved Latin text. In parallel columns with his Latin text, Erasmus provided the Greek (Byzantine) text. Later in the work, he included his *Annotations*, which often explained why his translation revised the Latin of the Vulgate and clarified his translation's connection with the Greek text. These secondary features were to provide the textual (the Greek text) and grammatical/theological (*Annotations*) rationale behind Erasmus' Latin translation. Though Erasmus' intention may have been primarily to provide a better quality Latin

---

[12] Christopher Seitz, 'Canonical Approach' in *Dictionary for Theological Interpretation of the Bible*, 100.
[13] Vanhoozer, 'Imprisoned or Free' in Kevin J. Vanhoozer, A.K.M. Adam and Francis Watson (eds), *Reading Scripture with the Church Toward a Hermeneutic for Theological Interpretation* (Grand Rapids: Baker, 2006), 66.
[14] Erasmus' first edition (Basle, 1516) was entitled *Novum Instrumentum*. Subsequent editions in 1519, 1522, 1527 and 1535 were entitled *Novum Testamentum*.
[15] Henk Jan De Jonge, 'Novum Testamentum a Nobis Versum: The Essence of Erasmus' Edition of the New Testament,' *JTS* 35.2 (1984), 395-96. Cf. De Jonge, 'Erasmus' Method of Translation in His Version of the New Testament,' *BT* 37.1 (1986), 135-38.

text, it was his secondary features of the Greek text and his *Annotations* that would most dramatically affect the Protestant reformers, even those who rejected Erasmus' Humanist program. As H.J. De Jonge notes, 'That Erasmus was the first to make the Greek New Testament accessible to many in Western Europe by means of the printing press, remains a fact of evident importance.'[16]

Erasmus' Greek New Testament inspired an ambition for proficiency in dealing with the biblical texts, themselves, not simply the long interpretative history of these texts. His Latin-Greek text, also, drew attention to the textual features of the Bible such as its vocabulary, grammar and verbal meaning. The attention to textual features caused a more prominent focus on the literal meaning (i.e., the verbal meaning) of biblical texts instead of a prevailing interest in matters outside the biblical text, whether dogmatic or historical. Through broader accessibility of the New Testament in Greek, theological discussions often focused on the meaning of Greek words. An obvious example of the effect of this 'textual turn' initiated by Erasmus' Latin-Greek text is found in Luther's May 1518 letter to Staupitz. Luther writes,

> After this it happened that I learned—thanks to the work and talent of the most learned men who teach us Greek and Hebrew with such great devotion—that the word *poenitentia* means *metanoia* in Greek; it is derived from *meta* and *noun*, that is, from 'afterward' and 'mind'. *Poenitentia* or *metanoia*, therefore, means coming to one's right mind and a comprehension of one's own evil after one has accepted the damage and recognized the error. . . . All these definitions agree so well with Pauline theology that, at least in my opinion, almost nothing could illustrate Paul's theology better than the way they do. . . . It is evident that they [medieval theologians] were misled by the Latin term, because the expression *poenitentiam agere* suggests more an action than a change in disposition; and in no way does this do justice to the Greek *metanoein*.[17]

The reformers' interest in words and the role of grammar can be seen in their comments on the biblical text. The reformers often shed the dense style and secondary discussions found in their medieval predecessors. Though some reformation commentaries have lengthy, dogmatic discussions (e.g., Musculus, Bullinger, Piscator, Ward, Pareus, Dickson, Blackwood), a much more typical practice can be seen in Erasmus' widely read *Annotations*, which were included in the varying editions of his *Novum Instrumentum* (*Testamentum*). These notations were not restrained to points of clarity in translation issues. As Jan

---

[16] Jonge, 'Novum Testamentum,' 394. See, also, Mark Vessey, 'Erasmus' Paraphrases and the Arts of Scripture' in *Holy Scripture Speaks: The Production and Reception of Erasmus' Paraphrases on the New Testament* (Toronto: University of Toronto Press, 2002). Vessey comments, 'Erasmus seeks to resuscitate a literary and linguistic competence that could no longer be taken for granted, the loss of which had resulted, in his opinion, in the obscuring of gospel truths' (30).

[17] *LW* 48.66-68; *WA* 1.525-527. Erasmus' work on Matthew 3 (n.1) indicated that *poenitentiam agite* was not the preferred Latin rendering of *metanoia*.

Krans puts it, 'the annotations were to remain the part of Erasmus' New Testament in which he pronounced himself freely, both on text-critical and translational issues and on a vast array of other subjects. They underwent several important revisions, whereas much less attention was devoted to the printed Greek and Latin texts.'[18]

The Dutch Humanist supplemented his *Annotations* with a more expansive set of comments in his *Paraphrase* on the Gospel of Matthew (1522). This style of producing notes on the text and providing brief insights or restatements of the text became a common way of the reformers to provide commentary on the biblical texts. This style meant that the commentary relied on the structure and vocabulary of the biblical text and served as a textually-oriented reader's guide to the biblical texts, rather than a distinct work to be appreciated in its own right. Subsequent reformers, such as Zwingli, Tyndale, Luther, Oecolampadius, Melanchthon, Beza, Grotius, Diodati, Hammond, Gerhard and Cartwright, all produced annotations on the text of Matthew. In their own unique ways these notations presented insights into particular terms, phrases or other textual features of the Gospel texts.

Furthermore, when the reformers extended their comments to the other Gospels in conjunction with Matthew, they often maintained much of the qualities of the 'annotations'.[19] Bucer, Bullinger, Calvin and John Lightfoote are all leading examples of those who blended some of the characteristics of the annotations with the broader desire of producing a Gospels harmony. Strikingly, even in their attempts at a harmony of the Gospel accounts, these authors drew heavily on textual features instead of trying to resolve supposed conflicts through historical reconstruction. Understanding the author's intention in his composition, often noted in his point of view in presenting the details of a particular event, remained a main interest of the reformers even as they attempted to present a unified Gospel presentation. Moreover, the reformers' renewed interest in preaching gave a further outlet for sharing the fruits of textual study. So, the literary landscape became more densely populated with pastoral commentaries on the biblical texts, textual discussions in theological treatises and expositional sermons that drew out meaning and implications of biblical texts for their audiences.

---

[18] Jan Krans, *Beyond What is Written* (Leiden: Brill, 2006), 22.

[19] This comment, nor the previous two, does not imply that other reformers are following Erasmus slavishly or continually in content or format for their commentaries. The point is to note the paradigmatic influence of Erasmus for other reformation exegetes. See a similar comment about Bullinger following Erasmus' general approach in W.P. Stephens, 'The Interpretation of the Bible in Bullinger's Early Works,' *RRR* 11.3 (2009), 328-29.

The reformers and the biblical author's theological purpose

Two main interpretive issues face the readers who attempt to cull the reformers' thoughts for their own interpretive work: historical context and hermeneutical approach. Notably, there has been considerable development in the cultural, philosophical and theological climate since the days of the reformer. Contemporary users of reformation comments will want to garner insights in keeping with historical milieu of the original authors. The daunting task of reconstructing the proper historical context might cause great trepidation in relying on the reformers' comments for biblical insight. There is one gleaming ray of hope in this scenario. As the reformation exegetes demonstrate expressed attention to textual features of the biblical text, the verses in the text serve as an apt context for understanding the reformation authors' comments. With the biblical text being a primary focus for the reformers' comments, their own historical context effects are minimized, though not completely expunged. Some readers will sense the need to research the historical context more fully in an attempt to situate the comments within the actual historical debate or occasion. While this historical research will surely prove useful, it may be that the reformers' careful biblical comments will communicate enough textual insight that the knowledge of the reformation setting will only highlight the themes evident in the reformers' interpretations.

The reformers' hermeneutical emphases and their distinction from contemporary approaches can often be more difficult to negotiate than the historical distance from the reformation era to the current one. Some of the significant hermeneutical differences come from the reformers' commitments to canonical, theological and textual interpretations. The tendency in many contemporary approaches to scripture is to focus on a particular section (pericope or book) in isolation of its literary context in the broader Christian canon. Occasionally, modern interpreters will appeal to the larger 'Pauline corpus' or 'gospel literature' or maybe even to the Deuteronomistic history books. However, it is uncommon for modern interpreters to give extensive discussion to a verse's or narrative's role in the whole canon. Secondly, the reformers' confessional approach to biblical interpretation was disdained by scholarly exegesis in the eighteenth through twentieth century, resulting in more attention to the descriptive understanding of scripture. The close connection that the reformers affirmed between faith and valid interpretation or between scripture and doctrine was discouraged or abandoned by biblical interpreters in a later period. Much of the reformers' interest in 'what the text means' was gradually replaced by a pursuit of 'what the text meant' by their eventual successors.[20]

In their climate of increasing literary produce and revival of interest in the features of the biblical texts, many reformation authors published their thoughts

---

[20] Gerhard Maier, *Biblical Hermeneutics* (Wheaton: Crossway, 1994), 383-84.

on the life and ministry of Jesus portrayed in the canonical Gospels. These authors rarely approached the Gospel texts with the scholarly detachment of their distant successors. Furthermore, their interest in Jesus as a historical figure was not distinct from their pursuit of the theological truths he taught in word and deed. Their starting point for studying Jesus was through the textual witness of the Gospel writers within the immediate context of faithful readers of those texts. This textual approach allowed the reformers to claim apostolic authority for their theology, reforms and preaching by drawing consciously on the testimony of the apostles found in the Gospels. Particularly in the book of Matthew, the reformers heard the apostolic witness concerning Jesus' union in two natures, the necessity of repentance before entering the kingdom of God, the continuity of the Old Testament prophets and the apostolic testimony on God's purposes in Christ and the humble submission of the Son to the will of the Father. In conjunction with these prevailing themes, the reformers gave particular attention to Jesus' self-reference, 'the Son of Man,' used throughout the Gospel. Both in the reformers' commentaries and their sermons on Matthew, they considered the importance of these theological and textual features of Matthew's Gospel.

Modern exegetical concerns from the field of biblical studies deal with significantly different concerns in interpretation. A clear case in point is drawn simply from the major components of contemporary discussions of 'the Son of Man' texts in Matthew. First, a great deal of the discussion is on the use of the Aramaic phrase of 'bar nasha' in other ancient texts. The fact that this interchange focuses on Aramaic vocabulary and texts reveals that the prevailing interest of the interpreters lies in the historical occasion of Jesus' speech, rather than in the Greek text of the Gospel of Matthew.[21] Second, usually biblical scholars abbreviate any discussion of the authorial intention of the Gospel text or contrast it to Jesus' supposed consciousness in using the phrase or even in the authenticity of such a saying from Jesus.[22] While modern exegetes grapple with the identity of the Son of Man by utilizing tools that enhance the historical background of the biblical texts, the reformers spent a deal of their energies on the theological impact of the words of the texts.

The cataclysmic effect of historical critical studies on biblical interpretation causes an eclipse of the reformers' textual interests. The publication of Erasmus' Greek New Testament in 1516 inspired a renewed interest in the textual features of the Bible. The printing press allowed these Greek texts to be readily available for the reformers' use. The increased availability of the biblical texts in the original languages (first, the Greek New Testament and, then, the Hebrew Bible) stimulated the reformers to become immersed in the features of the texts themselves. For the first time, many of them began to

---

[21] E.g., Maurice Casey, 'The Jackals and the Son of Man,' *JSNT* 23 (1985), 3-22.

[22] E.g., U. Luz, 'The Son of Matthew: Heavenly Judge or Human Christ,' *JSNT* 48 (1992), 3-21.

investigate nuances of the Greek (or Hebrew) vocabulary and grammar compared to their well-known Latin texts. In the modern era, the advances of historical method enticed interpreters to a similar devoted quest. This time instead of being drawn to a deeper investigation of the textual features, the pursuit was of the actual facts of the historical events depicted in the biblical narratives. Some critical scholars used their historical tools in a way that discredited the factuality of the biblical texts, including the Gospel depictions of Jesus of Nazareth. Those biblical interpreters who were less skeptical of the reliability of the biblical texts utilized the same set of historical tools to authenticate the historicity of the biblical events. These apologetic interests lurk behind many of the discussions found in modern commentaries. Readers who are wearied by the barrage of historical data of extra-biblical details in the modern discussions will find the textual interests of the reformers to be a refreshing change. Modern interpreters interested in the grammatical, canonical and theological meaning of biblical texts will have their interpretive skills sharpened through interacting with the reformers' interpretations. In this manner, Stephen Fowl encourages that if theological interpretation 'is to flourish in the present, it will require contemporary believers to relearn the habits and practices that constituted a flourishing pattern of theological interpretation in the past'.[23]

Of course, many aspects of the reformers' interpretative approaches remain in common practice today. Modern interpreters will appreciate the reformers' interest in subtle shifts of biblical vocabulary or the Greek verbal mood. The reformers' juxtaposition of the biblical author's viewpoint and that of the characters of the narrative provides an interesting and insightful contrast. The reformers' typical practice of honing in on the theological thrust of a particular text parallels the interests of those who are teaching or preaching the biblical texts in a church context.

For the reformers, their interest in the textual features of the Scriptures meshed well with their pursuit of the theological meaning of the author. Mickey Mattox identifies this connection in Luther's expositions. Mattox writes,

> In theological terms, this meant that Luther learned to intuit the divine mysteries inscribed into the words of the biblical texts in their original languages. Theological exegesis is focused on the biblical text itself, and the divinely intended meaning of scripture is to be found through determined struggle with the words themselves, a process that requires attention to every aspect of textual and grammatical analysis.[24]

One particular interest of the reformers that resounds with many contemporary interpreters is their interest in authorial intent. The reformers' textual interest

---

[23] Fowl, *Theological Interpretation*, 55.
[24] Mickey Mattox, 'Martin Luther' in Justin S. Holcomb (ed.), *Christian Theologies of Scripture* (New York: New York University Press, 2006), 102-103.

stemmed from their perspective that authorial intention (both divine and human) was significant for textual meaning and that authorial intention could be discerned from features in the text. Particularly, in the case of Matthew, the reformers are driven by two interests in their investigations of the biblical texts. First, they had a keen interest in what Jesus said and did. Second, they were interested in the unity and diversity of the Gospel accounts. Notably, they did not see these two interests as contrasting.

Luther demonstrates these interconnected interests in a sermon on Matthew 24.15-28. He writes,

> In today's Gospel lesson our dear Lord Jesus Christ foretells the devastation of the city of Jerusalem and the Jewish homeland, as well as the end of the whole world. St. Luke (chapters 17 and 21) gives this prediction even more clearly and pointedly, item for item; St. Matthew blends both together, the end of the Jewish kingdom and the end of the world, and, as a result, is not quite as simple and clear as St. Luke. Both Matthew and Mark concentrate more on the world's end than on the devastation of the Jews, telescoping the two things together. But for better understanding we need to look at each separately, in order to see what pertains to the end of the Jewish kingdom and what pertains to the end of the world.[25]

In this selection, Luther treats the passage as a genuine address of Jesus but, also, recognizes the Gospel writers' place in retelling the story. Luther, also, recognizes differences in the intentions of the authors demonstrated in their different presentations of the material. Where modern historical critical scholars might note these differences and appeal to their respective source documents, the German reformer holds that the distinctions attest to authorial intentions. Luther claims that Matthew's presentation of Jesus' discourse reflects his theological intention in this passage (Matthew 24-25), namely, his concentration on the end of the world instead of the destruction of the Jews.

The reformers and 'canonical' interpretation

A pervasive quality of biblical interpretation among the reformers is the role of the entire canon. Whether it appears in a reformer's efforts to allow scripture to interpret scripture or in an appeal to relate Christian doctrines and practices to both Old and New Testaments, the canon provides the guidelines for these endeavors. This 'canonical' interpretation in the reformers often contrasts with modern, critical interpretation. Robert Meditz observes that the challenge for contemporary interpreters who are drawing on the reformers' insights is how 'to preserve the unity of the biblical witness in light of criticism that continuously truncates the canon and obscures its theological purpose'. So, while the reformers are comfortable drawing interconnected insights from across the biblical canon, many forms of modern, critical interpretation

---

[25] *Complete Sermons of Martin Luther*, 7.192-93.

'possess the common characteristic of dividing up the existing canon into smaller, precanonical, literary and/or theological units'.[26]

Noting the different approaches that the reformers take to certain passages is an important aspect of discerning the motives of the variety of doctrinal themes or practices among the reformers. However, these differences should not obscure their widespread commitment to the unity of the canon and the need to base doctrines on the whole of scripture as well as its parts. In a recent article, my doctoral supervisor, W.P. Stephens discusses the canonical interest of Heinrich Bullinger in biblical interpretation. Stephens comments that the use of scripture to interpret scripture is 'fundamental' to Bullinger, a commitment that can be seen in how 'Bullinger regards the New Testament as a commentary on or interpretation of the Old Testament and the Old Testament as necessary to understand the New.'[27] Bullinger's interest in the scope of the entire canon found commonality with his reforming contemporaries.

The remaining sections of this essay will use the 'Son of Man' texts in Matthew (especially chapters 24 and 25) to reflect on the reformers' interpretative produce. The reformers' comments on the grammatical sense, theological purpose and canonical context for the 'Son of Man' provide an exemplary selection of their rich, biblical work. The reformers, also, provide helpful starting points for contemporary theological interpreters.

The 'Son of Man' texts in Matthew: a case study

Having observed, earlier, Luther's comments about the place of authorial intention in understanding Matthew 24-25, our attention now turns to this pivotal Gospel text and how the reformers' interpretative interests are demonstrated in how they handle this text. Later in his sermon on Matthew 24, Luther noted the importance of recognizing the textual interplay (intertextuality) between these chapters in Matthew and some relevant texts in Daniel.[28] One specific place that the Daniel background is crucial is in the designation 'Son of Man' that is used frequently in these chapters. In the remaining sections of this essay, the work of the reformation interpreters will be mined in order to grapple with their perception of the meaning of the

---

[26] Robert Meditz, '"Too Hard for the Teeth of Time": Difficulties in Using Scripture in the Church since the Reformation,' *JTI* 2.2 (2008), 282. Throughout this review article, Meditz is interacting with Rowan Greer's *Anglican Approaches to Scripture: From the Reformation to the Present.*

[27] Stephens, 'Interpretation of the Bible,' 321.

[28] Luther comments, 'Daniel states that this will be Jerusalem's fate until the end, and St. Luke adds that the Gentiles will tread over the city until the time of the Gentiles is fulfilled. Jerusalem will not be reconstructed but must remain subject to the Gentiles until the Gentiles are converted, and so, until the world's end. That is the meaning of Christ's words here. St. Matthew has given this somewhat briefly, while the prophet Daniel and the Evangelist Luke make it very plain,' *Complete Sermons*, 7.194.

theologically rich 'Son of Man' texts in Matthew, especially in chapters 24 and 25.

A brief overview of the 'Son of Man' in the Gospel of Matthew

In an attempt to assess Matthew's compositional strategy in the author's use of the phrase 'Son of Man,' there are two chief questions to ask. First, are there any particular themes or purposes that drive the author's use of the phrase in a given passage? Second, are there contextual issues that are latent in the author's intentional employment of the phrase? These two questions will not only aid in a valid interpretation of these biblical texts, but they will, also, serve as means of drawing on the reformers' insights on these texts.

In the canonical Gospel of Matthew, the phrase 'Son of Man' is used thirty times. These thirty uses can be organized into five basic categories or themes. The most common usage (14x) refers to the future coming and reign of the Son of Man.[29] The next most common usage (8x) refers to Jesus' pending death.[30] Closely, associated with this theme are the four usages that refer to Jesus' resurrection; three of which, also, include references to his death.[31] A less frequent category (3x) is the usage of the phrase to connect Jesus with a particular divine quality.[32] The remaining three usages could be categorized as miscellaneous self-references, though there is a subtle similarity shared by them.[33]

These three self-references have an enigmatic quality of stating Jesus' identity in terms of the crowd's perception of him, while at the same time drawing attention to their assessment as a misconception. So, in almost every case 'the Son of Man' is used by Matthew as reference to Jesus in a way that there is more to him than the humble man that he is perceived to be. The multi-faceted quality of Matthew's 'Son of Man' texts was not lost on the reformers and their successors. The Puritan minister, Thomas Taylor, summarized the mysterious nature of the title and its use in the Gospels. In his comments on Matthew 16.27-28, Taylor deliberates,

---

[29] The related themes of the Son of Man's 'coming in the clouds' or 'coming in glory' or coming to reign on a 'glorious throne' can be seen in 10.23 (only mentions a 'coming'), 13.37 and 41 (this pair occurs in the Jesus' interpretation of the parable of the tares), 16.27, 16.28, 19.28, 24.27, 24.30 (two occurrences), 24.37, 24.39, 24.44, 25.31, 26.64.

[30] Jesus' looming death is predicted throughout Matthew's Gospel, with many of the explicit predictions using the 'Son of Man' phrase. Two of these occurrences relate specifically to Jesus' betrayal by Judas and are in the broader context references to his death, which is facilitated by Judas' betrayal. The references are 12.40, 17.12, 17.22-23, 20.18-19, 20.28, 26.2, 26.24 (betrayal), 26.45 (betrayal).

[31] Resurrection appears by itself in 17.9 and paired with Jesus' death in 12.40, 17.22-23, 20.18-19.

[32] Connecting Jesus with a divine quality is the theme of 9.6 (authority to forgive sins), 12.8 (Lord of the Sabbath) and 12.32 (is blasphemed).

[33] The remaining 'Son of Man' usages are 8.20, 11.19, 16.13.

> Nay, by this title our text must mean the whole Christ, God and man, the son of God, and the son of man, for though his speech expresses him as the son of man, yet the action here referred unto him (to be the just judge of all the world) proclaims him to be the Son of God; and he is indeed the son of man, but coming in the glory of his father. But why does Christ ordinarily, speaking of himself, call himself the son of man? He might have said, the Son of God shall come in the glory of his father, which might seem to have added more weight to his words.[34]

Taylor is noting that a reader might anticipate the title 'Son of God' to be used because of the association of Jesus with executing divine justice. However, Taylor continues by providing rationale for the use of 'Son of Man' as Jesus' self-referent:

> In respect of his hearers and men's judgment, who commonly esteemed him no other, and rose no higher in their judgment of him, than of a mere man, though perhaps a great and holy man. He would accommodate the weakness of his hearers; for even the disciples themselves could not yet come to acknowledge the majesty of the Son of God, in this son of man; and therefore he speaks of himself as they are able to conceive him, more intending their instruction, than his own reputation.[35]

So, with Taylor and his reforming predecessors the term 'Son of Man' reflects the Gospel writer's efforts of presenting the full christological picture. Some of the mystery surrounding the 'Son of Man' comes from the apparent contrasts of his present earthly status and his future work. Further mystery stems from a related contrast as the common perception of the 'Son of Man' by his contemporaries is compared to his true identity and role. How his contemporaries 'saw' the Son of Man is not how they will 'see' him.

The reformers and their successors understood that the phrase 'Son of Man' allows the Gospel readers to connect Jesus to his humble, earthly status at the same time pointing them to his greater role to come. The English preacher, Robert Gell, presents other biblical texts employing the 'Son of Man' both to capture the humility of Jesus' earthly position and to predict his future place. Gell explains,

> The Lord Jesus very often styles himself the Son of Man, Matt 8.20 and 9.6 and 16.20, besides many other places. And the reason is given by some that thereby he might signify his human nature, which he took upon him for man's sake, Heb 2. For what is the Son of Man, but man, as David explains one by the other, Ps 8.4. Or, when he calls himself the Son of Man, he announces, that he has a low reputation, and a contemptible estate among men. Or, he gave himself that name, by which he would be more familiarly known and called. And this is all interpreters make of this, when our Lord calls himself the Son of Man. But I

---

[34] Taylor, *Works of that Faithful Servant*, 48.
[35] Taylor, *Works of that Faithful Servant*, 48 (wording revised for clarity).

believe our Lord had greater reason than these, why he called himself the Son of Man. Nor do I doubt but he had reference unto Daniel, who was most punctual in his observation touching the Messiah, and the time of his appearing in the flesh, and his coming to judgment, he is called, Dan 7.13, The Son of Man.[36]

Furthermore, referring to similar texts in John 5.27 and Acts 17.31, Gell continues by saying that the use of the term, 'Son of Man' by Jesus is to alert his listeners to his future role as the final judge.

In Matthew's Gospel, Jesus, as the Son of Man is perceived to be a lowly person who has no personal wealth (or worth), a licentious companion of the seedy members of society but, yet, one who speaks as one of the prophets. The combination of his despicable rank among his contemporaries and his bold proclamations of his divine qualities and relationship with the heavenly Father ultimately lead to his rejection by the Jewish leaders and his death at the hand of the gentile overlords. However, Matthew's predictions of the death of the Son of Man are often paired with proclamations of his imminent resurrection, indicating that the Son of Man's death does not preclude his future role. Matthew's emphatic and, perhaps, corrective attempt to establish the identity of the Son of Man focuses on his future 'coming' in the clouds with great glory and his glorious reign that will then ensue. As Bullinger notes, the future reign of Christ begins with judgment. So, Matthew's presentation of the coming destruction of Jerusalem joins with the future coming of the Son of Man. The destruction of the world in the Son of Man's judgment is made more plausible when considering the imminent and shocking destruction of Jerusalem, the holy city. Bullinger explains, 'Forthwith by occasion of the destruction of the city, he reasons also of the destruction of the world, or of the finishing of the world, and of that glorious coming of the son of man to judgment.'[37]

Whatever humble or earthy vision Jesus' contemporaries had of the Son of Man, Matthew's Gospel presents him in a new (or renewed) heavenly portrayal that recalibrates the misconceptions of Jesus' contemporaries. Whether the Gospel of Matthew's portrayal of the Son of Man is seen to have great continuity or discontinuity with its context often depends on how that context is identified. One fundamental agreement among the reformers is that Matthew's use of the 'Son of Man' draws on the canonical context, especially the book of Daniel. So, Daniel's presentation of the Son of Man, especially in the climatic passage of 7.13-14, provides an essential background for understanding Matthew's use of the phrase.[38] Thomas Taylor writes,

---

[36] Robert Gell, *Noah's Flood Returning*, 2-3 (wording revised for clarity or style). This sermon was preached in London in 1655.
[37] Heinrich Bullinger, *Sum of the Four Evangelists*, C4.
[38] Daniel 7.13-14 reads as follows: 'I saw in the night visions, and behold, with the clouds of heaven there came one like a son of man, and he came to the Ancient of Days and was presented before him. And to him was given dominion and glory and a kingdom, that all peoples, nations, and languages should serve him; his dominion is

For the manner of Scripture in speaking of the last judgment is to use this phrase above other: Because this was appropriated to the Messiah by Daniel (7.13), to which Christ undoubtedly had reference: 'I beheld, and there came as a Son of man in the clouds of Heaven.' To show that as he showed himself in the nature of man to be judge on earth, so he would show himself in a visible manner a judge in heaven.[39]

In the Daniel text, the Son of Man comes on (ἐπὶ) the clouds and is given dominion and an everlasting kingdom with great glory and will be served by all the nations and families.[40] Matthew's frequent references to the Son of Man's coming (with glory, on the clouds, with the angels, or into his kingdom) portray imagery strikingly similar to Daniel's. For example, in Matthew 24.30, the Son of Man comes on the clouds with power and glory before all the tribes of the earth.[41]

Of particular interest to some reformers is that Matthew mentions the 'sign' of the Son of Man. Musculus states that the language of 'sign' indicates that emphasis should not be on the 'coming' of the Son of Man as much as his 'appearing'. This revelation would unveil the primary charge in the coming judgment, rejecting the Son of Man. Musculus explains that as Jesus' speaks in Matthew 24.30 he does not say that the 'Son of Man shall come in the clouds of heaven' but that 'they shall *see* the Son of Man' coming in the clouds. The text's emphasis is on the revelation that the 'coming in the clouds' is to those who have rejected him. This Son of Man is the one that they 'now despise and persecute' at that time they will 'see' him in his coming to judge with 'power and great glory'. Musculus continues by noting that Jesus was making the same point in his appearance before the high priest in Matthew 26 (v.64). There,

---

an everlasting dominion, which shall not pass away, and his kingdom one that shall not be destroyed' (ESV). One version of the Greek Old Testament reads, ¹³ἐθεώρουν ἐν ὁράματι τῆς νυκτὸς καὶ ἰδοὺ ἐπὶ τῶν νεφελῶν τοῦ οὐρανοῦ ὡς υἱὸς ἀνθρώπου ἤρχετο καὶ ὡς παλαιὸς ἡμερῶν παρῆν καὶ οἱ παρεστηκότες παρῆσαν αὐτῷ ¹⁴καὶ ἐδόθη αὐτῷ ἐξουσία καὶ πάντα τὰ ἔθνη τῆς γῆς κατὰ γένη καὶ πᾶσα δόξα αὐτῷ λατρεύουσα καὶ ἡ ἐξουσία αὐτοῦ ἐξουσία αἰώνιος ἥτις οὐ μὴ ἀρθῇ καὶ ἡ βασιλεία αὐτοῦ ἥτις οὐ μὴ φθαρῇ (LXT), sharing much verbal similarity with Matthew 24.30.

[39] Taylor, *Works of that Faithful Servant*, 48.

[40] See Michael Shepherd's insightful essay 'Daniel 7.13 and the New Testament Son of Man,' *WTJ* 68 (2006), 99-111, for more on a canonical understanding of the 'Son of Man' and the continuity between Daniel and the New Testament.

[41] Matthew 24.30 reads, 'Then will appear in heaven the sign of the Son of Man, and then all the tribes of the earth will mourn, and they will see the Son of Man coming on the clouds of heaven with power and great glory' (ESV). The NA27 reads, καὶ τότε φανήσεται τὸ σημεῖον τοῦ υἱοῦ τοῦ ἀνθρώπου ἐν οὐρανῷ, καὶ τότε κόψονται πᾶσαι αἱ φυλαὶ τῆς γῆς καὶ ὄψονται τὸν υἱὸν τοῦ ἀνθρώπου ἐρχόμενον ἐπὶ τῶν νεφελῶν τοῦ οὐρανοῦ μετὰ δυνάμεως καὶ δόξης πολλῆς

Jesus warns the high priest's court that the Jewish leaders will 'see' the Son of Man coming in 'great power'.[42]

So, for the enemies of Jesus, the coming of the Son of Man will be a revelation and a great reversal of their appraisal of him. The Son of Man's coming will reveal to his enemies the horror of their misjudgment of him. Musculus states that at the Son of Man's coming his enemies will look upon the one whom they have pierced and realize that they despised the Son of Man in his humble state and ridiculed the grace of his weakness. At that moment, they will know the sheer terror of his coming in strength and great glory because of their rejection of him in times past.[43] Musculus' discussion stems from Matthew's text, indicating that mourning will ensue at the Son of Man's coming. Musculus takes clues from the text to argue that the 'appearance' of the Son of Man is not a 'sign' for Jesus' disciples, but as a means of revealing the judgment due his enemies. Musculus notes, 'For he does not say, "And you will see me coming," but, "And they will see the Son of Man (whom they despise) coming with great power and glory".'[44] For Musculus, the appearance (or 'sign') of the Son of Man initiates the great reversal of how the nations perceive (or 'see') him.

Similarly, Martin Bucer asserts that the 'sign' of the Son of Man ushers in mourning by the nations of the earth because they now realize that they have rejected their rightful ruler. He warns that the whole world will be thrust into 'anxiety and despair' and 'they shall mourn' because the heavenly Father sends the 'sign' of the Son of Man and his glorious coming as Matthew predicts. The 'tribes of the earth' will mourn because they are left out of the heavenly city and have ignored Christ the Savior. The threat of the judgment of God overwhelms them with terror as they see the Son of Man coming with 'power and great glory'.[45] So, the Son of Man's coming will illicit great joy from the elect, but great terror for those who reject him.

---

[42] *Et videbunt filium hominis venientem in nubibus caeli cum virtute & gloria multa.]* Emphasis in eo est, quòd non simpliciter dicit: Et veniet filius hominis in nubibus caeli, &c. sed, Et videbunt filium hominis. Q.d. Quem nunc contemnunt & persequuntur, olim videbunt cum virtute & gloria magna ad iudicium venturum. Ita & infrà cap. 26. in concilio sacerdotum constitutus, dicet: Amodo videbitis filium hominis venientem in nubibus cum potestate magna. Wolfgang Musculus, *In Evangelistam Matthaeum Commentarii* (1562), 575 (emphasis added).

[43] Ita & Ioan. 19. ex Propheta citatur: Et videbunt, quem transfixerunt. Omnino nanque minatur adversariis suis adventum suum: eumque talem, per quem summo sint terrore percellendi, quemque nequeant, ut antea, imbecillitatis & ignobilitatis gratia contemnere. ad quod pertinet, quòd dicit se venturum cum virtute & gloria magna. Musculus, *In Evangelistam Matthaeum Commentarii*, 576.

[44] Non enim dicit, Et videbitis me venientem: sed, Et videbunt filium hominis (quem contemnunt) venientem cum magna virtute & gloria. Musculus, *In Evangelistam Matthaeum Commentarii*, 576.

[45] Hi igitur sentient, ita omnia misceri, & totam mundi machinam ruere, indeque, ut par est, prae summa anxietate & desperatione, planè exarescent. Atque hi plangent tum,

Bucer rejects the idea that the 'sign' of the Son of Man is some display of Jesus' humility or humanity but, rather, it is at the appearing of the Son of Man that the wicked will 'see' that the one who they have rejected as a simple 'son of man' here is the one who will reign as king in heaven and will have rule over all things.[46]

Conclusion

In their efforts to interpret these 'Son of Man' texts of Matthew 24 and 25 according to the theological intentions of Matthew's Gospel, the reformers explain that the 'Son of Man,' as a title, illustrates a theological point. From the perspective of most of his contemporaries, Jesus was just a 'son of man' or an ordinary person (cultural-historical sense of the phrase). However, Matthew asserts that they will see the 'sign' of the Son of Man and, thereby, recognize him according to the divine imagery presented in the book of Daniel (canonical-grammatical sense of the phrase). The emphasis of the reformers is that only when the nations 'see' the Son of Man coming in the clouds and great glory will they 'see' the cost of their rejection of him. This appearance (or revelation) of the Son of Man will usher in the time of final judgment. By their awareness of the multi-faceted, grammatical sense of the 'Son of Man' and aided by their appreciation of the canonical context of the phrase, the reformers presented theologically rich interpretations that still guide today's Bible readers.

---

ab parente iam in nubibus signo filii hominis, & adventum eius gloriosum ut Matthaeus habet, praedicente, sed qui tribus terrae sunt, nullum ius supernae & coelestis civitatis adepti. Christum enim salvatorem isti ignorabunt, eoque sentient intolerabile sibi iudicium Dei imminere. Quenque summa cum laetitia excipient electi, illi summo cum terrore videbunt, venientem in nubibus coeli, cum virtute & gloria multa. Martin Bucer, *In Sacra Quatuor Evangelia, Enarrationes* (1536), 465.

[46] Signum illud filii hominis, quod in coelo appariturum in Matthaeo legimus, quidam crucis imaginem fore putant sive vero ita suturum sit, sive se cus, huius enim certi nihil habemus, maiestatem virtutemque Christi, terrae coelique, ac omnium potestatem habentis, orbi indicabit, non aliter atque elata in urbibus, atque arcibus signa, eorum potestatem indicant, qui ipsarum potiuntur. Tum & impii cum videbunt, quem ut filium hominis hic contempserant, regem esse coelorum, eoque imperium habere in omnia. Bucer, *Enarrationes*, 466.

CHAPTER 12

Socinus and the Racovian Catechism on justification

J.V. Fesko

The doctrine of justification, as the article upon which the church stands or falls, is an idea that grew out of the ferment of the sixteenth-century Protestant reformation.[1] Initially, Protestant reformers, both Lutheran and Reformed, engaged the doctrine of the Catholic Church but soon after the reformation, with the closing of the Council of Trent (1565), a new theological opponent arose that caused great concern—Socinianism. The two chief founders of the Socinian movement were Laelius Socinus (1525-62) and his nephew, Faustus Socinus (1539-1604). Through their labors they brought a challenge to key tenets of catholic theology including the doctrine of the Trinity and the satisfaction of Christ. They, also, challenged chief elements of reformation soteriology by reconfiguring the doctrine of justification by faith, among other important doctrines. Though both Laelius and Faustus wrote very little theology for the masses, by comparison to other theologians of the period, their thought was eventually captured and disseminated in the Racovian Catechism—a document that spread throughout Europe and, eventually, became one of the foundational pillars of the Unitarian Church. One of the chief reasons that Protestant theologians believed that Socinianism was a great danger was because it promoted a heretical doctrine of justification.

This essay will demonstrate how Socinus' doctrine of justification diverged from accepted reformation norms and expose why seventeenth-century Reformed theologians perceived it to be a threat. But, at the same time, it will show that Socinus' heresy, identified as such by writers of the period, contains elements drawn from orthodox sources. In other words, sometimes received orthodoxy has unintended heretical consequences. Orthodoxy and heresy are often much closer to one another than some might realize. In this particular case, it was Faustus Socinus' reception of a medieval understanding of the satisfaction of Christ, an idea gleaned from one of the reformation's famous theo-

---

[1] An expanded version of this essay appears in J.V. Fesko, *Beyond Calvin: Union with Christ and Justification in Early Modern Reformed Theology (1517-1700)* (Göttingen: Vandenhoeck & Ruprecht, 2012).

logians, that created ripples throughout his theological system. These ripples affected a number of elements in his theology but, especially, had an impact upon his doctrine of justification.

The essay will proceed, first, with a brief biographical sketch so that the reader may understand something of the life of Faustus Socinus. What follows is an examination of each of the key elements of Socinus' doctrine of justification including its definition, faith, the forgiveness of sins, and the imputation of Christ's obedience. Along the way, Socinus' views, drawn from two chief works, as well as from the catechism he began to write and significantly influenced, the Racovian Catechism, will be compared with Protestant confessional norms of the period. Lastly, the essay will, briefly, explore the Reformed response to the Socinian threat. In the end, the reader will be able to see how Socinus transgressed the accepted doctrinal boundaries of his day and why Reformed theologians and those of other communions reacted so negatively to his teaching.

Brief biographical sketch

Every theologian comes from a cultural and historical context that feeds into the development of his theology. Key to Socinus' theological development is his family. He was born in Italy in 1539 to an affluent family in Tuscany in the city of Siena. His family was related not only to wealthy people but even popes, Pius II (1405-64), Pius III (1439-1503), and Paul V (1552-1621). Socinus left Italy in 1561 for Lyon, France, and quickly developed a keen interest in Theology through interaction with friends and family. One relative in particular, his uncle, Laelius Socinus, a prominent Italian anti-trinitarian, proved to be a significant influence upon Faustus.[2] Upon receiving the news of his uncle's death, Faustus went to Zürich to claim his inheritance—his uncle's writings. Faustus never received a formal theological education and never admitted to having a human teacher save one exception, his uncle's writings and notes.[3]

Laelius did not write theological treatises but, instead, carried on continued correspondence with a number of key Protestant reformers, including Heinrich Bullinger, Philip Melanchthon, John Calvin, Sebastian Castellio, and Zacharias Ursinus. In addition to these figures, Laelius studied Hebrew with Sebastian Münster and stayed with Konrad Pelikan during his travels in Basel, and he, also, developed relationships with Oswald Myconius, Simon Grynaeus, and Celio Secondo Curione. Laelius wrote to these reformers and asked them theo-

---

[2] Sbigniew Ogonowski, 'Faustus Socinus 1539-1604' in Jill Raitt (ed.), *Shapers of Religious Traditions in Germany, Switzerland, and Poland, 1560-1600* (New Haven: Yale University Press, 1981), 195.

[3] Marian Hillar, 'Laelius and Faustus Socinus, Founders of Socinianism: Their Lives and Theology, Part One,' *JRR* 10.2 (2002), 28-29.

logical questions.[4] Laelius, however, eventually wore out his welcome with some of his correspondents. In a letter to Bullinger, Calvin commented that Laelius was 'a man of insatiable curiosity' and that he was terribly irritating.[5] Bullinger was something of a father figure to Laelius, as the latter had spent much time with the former when he lived in Zürich, and, thus, he took great pains to work with him.[6] Despite his best efforts, Calvin was not convinced of Laelius' orthodoxy and wrote to Bullinger that the Italian would continue to 'vomit the poison that he had eaten'.[7] Beyond his correspondence, Laelius produced two brief works, *Concerning the Sacraments* and *Concerning the Resurrection of Bodies*, which were posthumously published in 1654 in Amsterdam. In addition to this, at the behest of Bullinger, who wanted him to respond to questions about his orthodoxy, Laelius wrote a brief confession of faith to address his critics; the confession is somewhat ambiguous but, nevertheless, satisfied Bullinger.[8]

With his uncle's writings in hand, Faustus wrote his treatise on the opening chapter of John's Gospel, which was built upon the earlier labors of his uncle.[9] He, also, made his way from Zürich back to Italy in 1563. During his time in Italy he established contacts with other like-minded theologians and pastors in Switzerland, Poland and Transylvania. Socinus, eventually, departed Italy, never to return; he first went to Basel, where he studied sotriology for three years and wrote two of his best-known works in 1578, *De Jesu Christo Servatore*, eventually published in Kraków in 1594, and *Concerning the State of the First Man Before the Fall*, which was posthumously published in 1610.[10] *De Jesu Christo Servatore* has been identified as Socinus' key theological work that embodies the core of his beliefs.[11] Socinus, later, traveled to Kolozsvàr, Tran-

---

[4] Hillar, 'Laelius and Faustus Socinus,' 24-27. The Socinus-Calvin correspondence can be found in the *Calvini Opera* (*CO*), volumes 13-17, n°s. 1191, 1212, 1231, 1323, 1341, 1361, 2219, 3100, and 3121. Four of these letters (n°s. 1191, 1212, 1231, and 1323) can be found in English translation, 'Four Letters from the Socinus-Calvin Correspondence 1549' in John A. Tedeschi (ed.), *Italian Reformation Studies in Honor of Laelius Socinus* (translated by Ralph Lazzaro Firenze: Università Di Siena, 1965), 217-30.

[5] Calvin, Letter to Bullinger, 7 Aug 1554, n° 1995, *CO* 15.208.

[6] Hillar, 'Laelius and Faustus Socinus,' 27.

[7] Calvin, Letter to Bullinger, 23 November 1554, n° 2050, *CO* 15.318; Hillar, 'Laelius and Faustus Socinus,' 27.

[8] See Laelius Socinus, *Confession of Faith (1555)* in Jaroslav Pelikan and Valerie Hotchkiss (eds), *Creeds and Confessions of Faith in the Christian Tradition* (New Haven: Yale University Press, 2003), 2.706-08.

[9] Hillar, 'Laelius and Faustus Socinus,' 29; Daniel Borvan, 'Destroying Babylon's Foundations: Continuity and Discontinuity in the Early Life and Thought of Faustus Socinus' (unpublished Masters thesis, Westminster Seminary California, 2011), 3.

[10] Fausti Socini, *Opera Omnia in Duos Tomos Distincta*, in *Bibliotheca Fratrum Polonorum quos Unitarios Vocant* (Amsterdam: 1656), vols 1-2.

[11] Hillar, 'Laelius and Faustus Socinus,' 30.

sylvania (modern-day Cluj, Romania) where he met with Giorgio Biandrata (1515-88), a well-known anti-trinitarian. During his travels Socinus made his way to Kraków and, eventually, settled in Poland where he remained until his death in 1604.[12]

Though Socinus spent the twilight of his life in Poland, he was by no means idle. In 1601 Socinus met with leading ministers in Raków to debate and discuss doctrine. Socinus presented his views in a series of theological lectures on the doctrines of Scripture, the Trinity, sin, and the sacraments. Socinus' lectures were well received and a larger group of ministers and theologians gathered the next year to continue the dialogue. The churches represented at these meetings had previously used *The Catechesis and Confession of Faith of the Polish Brethren* (1574), which was written by Georg Schomann (1530-91). Schomann originally began his theological pilgrimage as a 'stubborn Papist,' but, then, became 'a sort of Lutheran'. In 1559, Schomann met Johannes Alasco (Jan Laski) (1499-1560) when he associated himself with the Reformed churches. Schomann, eventually, embraced anti-trinitarianism.[13] It should be no surprise, then, that Schomann's catechism has been labeled 'Unitarian,' though, interestingly enough, he still incorporates Alasco's doctrine of the *munus triplex* in his Christology.[14]

Despite the widespread use of Schomann's catechism, the fruit of the Socinus lectures was a new catechism. Socinus began the work on the catechism but soon fell ill, not able to complete the work, and died in 1604. Nevertheless, Socinus' labors were not in vain as other theologians, Piotr Stoiñski (1565-1605), Hieronymus Moskorowski (1560-1625), Valentinus Smalcius (1572-1622), Johannes Crellius (1590-1633) and Johannes Vökel (ca. 1575-1618) completed the work, which was, eventually, called the *Racovian Catechism* (1605).[15] In many ways the Racovian Catechism bears the influence of Schomann's earlier work, but it, also, bears the marks of Socinus' theology.[16] Some have argued that the Racovian Catechism stands as a witness to the legacy of Socinus.[17] Others have contended that Socinus is the Thomas Aquinas of the

---

[12] Hillar, 'Laelius and Faustus Socinus,' 32-33.
[13] George (Ciachowski) Schomann, 'The Last Will and Testament Containing a Brief History of His Life as well as of sundry things done in the churches' in Stanislas Lubieniecki, *History of the Polish Reformation and Nine Related Documents* (translated and edited by George Hunston Williams; Minneapolis: Fortress, 1995), 329-30.
[14] See Georg Schomann, 'The Catechesis and Confession of Faith of the Polish Brethren (1574)' in *Creeds and Confessions*, 2.709; cf., Lubieniecki, *Polish Reformation*, 32; Johannes Alasco, 'London Confession' in James T. Dennison, Jr. (ed.), *Reformed Confessions of the 16th and 17th Centuries in English Translation* (Grand Rapids: Reformation Heritage Books, 2008), 1.563-68.
[15] Borvan, 'Destroying Babylon's Foundations,' 31.
[16] Schomann, 'Catechesis' in *Creeds and Confessions*, 2.709.
[17] Borvan, 'Destroying Babylon's Foundations,' 32; Hillar, 'Laelius and Faustus Socinus,' 36.

Unitarian church.[18] And, though the Polish anti-trinitarian movement was eventually disbanded by force under local Roman Catholic pressure by the diet of the Commonwealth of Poland in 1658, Socinus' influence spread as the Racovian Catechism was sent to King James I of England. The catechism was printed in 1651 in London; the following year Parliament ordered the document to be burned. The catechism was, also, translated into English by well-known anti-trinitarian, John Biddle (1615-62).[19] As Socinus' writings spread throughout England, John Locke (1632-1704) obtained a number of his works and became well versed in Socinian theology. The works of Socinus were, also, translated into Dutch and widely distributed in the Netherlands.[20]

Before the study proceeds, it is helpful to recognize a number of Socinus' theological views that provide the broader context for his doctrine of justification. As an anti-trinitarian, Socinus rejects the deity of the Son and the Holy Spirit.[21] He, also, rejects the common Reformed understanding of the doctrine of election.[22] Regarding his anthropology, Socinus rejects the doctrine of original sin; he believes that Adam's sin had no adverse effects upon himself or his descendants. He, therefore, did not agree with the Reformed idea of the bondage of the will—a person's will is totally free and unhindered by the noetic effects of sin.[23] Adam was created mortal and, therefore, death is not a consequence of the fall but rather the normal course of nature.[24] These different commitments help create a frame of reference for the better comprehension of Socinus' doctrine of justification.

Doctrine of justification

Standard elements of the doctrine

By the beginning of the late sixteenth century there were a number of confessional and catechetical definitions of the doctrine of justification that estab-

---

[18] Hillar, 'Laelius and Faustus Socinus,' 36.
[19] Hillar, 'Laelius and Faustus Socinus,' 36-37.
[20] Lech Szczucki, 'Socinianism' in Hans J. Hilderbrand (ed.), *The Oxford Encyclopedia of the Reformation* (Oxford: OUP, 1996), 4.84-85. For an overview of the life and influence of Socinus, see Earl Morse Wilbur, *A History of Unitarianism: Socinianism and its Antecedents* (1945; Boston: Beacon Press, 1977), 384-419.
[21] See, e.g., Alan W. Gomes, 'Faustus Socinus's A Tract Concerning God, Christ, and the Holy Spirit,' *JISCA* 1.1 (2008), 37-58.
[22] Thomas Rees (ed.), *The Racovian Catechism, with Notes and Illustrations* (London: Longman, Hurst, Rees, Orme, and Brown, 1818), 5.10, pages 336-37.
[23] Hillar, 'Laelius and Faustus Socinus,' 14; Ogonowski, 'Faustus Socinus,' 201; *Racovian Catechism*, 5.10, page 330.
[24] Faustus Socinus, *De Jesu Christo Servatore*, 3.8, page 294. All subsequent quotations are taken from Alan W. Gomes, 'Faustus Socinus' *De Jesu Christo Servatore*, Part III: Historical Introductions, Translation and Critical Notes' (unpublished dissertation: Fuller Theological Seminary, 1990); also, *Racovian Catechism*, 2.1, pages 20, 22-23.

lished a norm for both the Reformed and Lutheran wings of the reformation. Evidence of the basic agreement among the Lutherans and Reformed appears in the *Harmonia Confessionum Fidei Orthodoxarum et Reformatarum* (1581) that was compiled by Theodore Beza (1519-1605), Lambert Daneau (ca. 1535-90), Jean-François Salvart, Antoine de la Roche Chandieu (1534-91) and Simon Goulart (1543-1628).[25] This harmony was intended to be the Reformed equivalent to the Lutheran Formula Concord (1577).[26] The *Harmonia Confessionum* was approved by the pastors of Geneva, Zürich, Schaffhausen, Bern and Neustadt. Beyond the Swiss formal adoption, the *Harmonia Confessionum* was published in the name of the churches of France and Belgium.[27] The overall goal of the *Harmonia Confessionum* was to demonstrate the unity of opinion among the Reformed churches spread across Europe and the British Isles. Moreover, the intention of the work was to demonstrate Reformed agreement with Lutheran theology:

> And this was the cause why we desired to put the Confession of Augsburg, together also with those of Saxony and Württemberg, in his Harmony; that it might be the more easily known, both that we agree with them in all particular points of faith, and that there are very few matters hanging in controversy between us.[28]

Later in the seventeenth century, Reformed theologians, such as Edward Leigh (1602-71), commented that the *Harmonia Confessionum* refuted the charge that the Reformed Churches were 'variably distracted and rent in sunder with infinite differences of faith'.[29] Hence, the *Harmonia Confessionum* provides an excellent reference point for orthodox opinions on justification during the late sixteenth century, the time when Socinus and the Socinians were formulating their own views.

In the ninth chapter, 'Of Justification by Faith, and of Good Works,' the *Harmonia Confessionum* contains Lutheran and Reformed entries on the doctrine of justification from the Second Helvetic Confession (1562), the Confession of Bohemia, or Waldensian Confession (1535), the Gallican Confession (1559), the Belgic Confession (1561), the Augsburg Confession (1530), the Confession of Saxony (1551), the Confession of Würtemburg (1551) and the

---

[25] *Harmonia Confessionum Fidei* (Geneva: 1581); idem, *An Harmony of the Confessions of the Faith of the Christian and Reformed Churches, which purley profess the holy doctrine of the Gospel, in all the chief kingdoms, nations, and provinces of Europe* (Cambridge: 1586).

[26] Peter Hall (ed.), *The Harmony of Protestant Confessions of Faith* (1842; Edmonton: Still Waters Revival Books, 1992), xv-xvii; H.A. Niemeyer (ed.), *Collectionis Confessionum in Ecclesiis Reformatis Publicatarum* (Lipsiae: 1840), v, viii-ix; Jill Raitt, 'Harmony of Confessions' in *Oxford Encyclopedia of the Reformation*, 2.211-12.

[27] *Harmony*, xxix; *Harmonia Confessionum*, praefatio.

[28] *Harmony*, xxxiii; *Harmonia Confessionum*, praefatio.

[29] Edward Leigh, *Treatise of Religion and Learning and of Religious and Learned Men* (London: 1656), §13, page 169.

Tetrapolitan Confession (1530). Given that some of the confessions come from the earlier days of the reformation, there is a lack of specificity regarding elements of the doctrine of justification in some of the documents. For example, from the earliest version of the Augsburg Confession justification is simply described as the remission of sins.[30] By contrast, the Second Helvetic Confession is much more precise.

The Second Helvetic Confession was written by Heinrich Bullinger and opens the chapter on justification in the *Harmonia Confessionum*, perhaps, because it was one of the more widely accepted documents in reformation Europe. It was adopted by the Reformed churches of Switzerland (Bern, Geneva, Chur, Biel, and Mühlhausen), Scotland, Austria, Hungary (1567), Poland (1566/70), and was widely circulated in France, England and the Netherlands.[31] The Second Helvetic Confession describes justification as the remission of sins, or the non-imputation of sin, and the imputation of the righteousness of Christ. Justification is founded upon the work of Christ because he has borne the sins of the world and satisfied the justice of God. The Confession, eventually, defines justification in the following manner: 'To speak properly, then; it is God alone that justifies us, and that only for Christ, by not imputing unto us our sins, but imputing Christ's righteousness to us (Rom. 4.23-25).' The Confession is, also, clear that justification is received by faith, not by works: 'Sinful man is justified only by faith [*sola fide*] in Christ, not by the law, or by any works.'[32] The Second Helvetic Confession is not unique in its affirmation of these points, as these elements, also, appear in the Bohemian, Gallican, Belgic, Augsburg (later editions), Saxon, Würtemburg and Tetrapolitan confessions.[33] With reference to a number of these confessions, one has a suitable benchmark with which to compare the views of Socinus on justification. But, in addition to the confessions of the *Harmonia*, we will, also, use the Heidelberg Catechism (1563), given its wide dissemination, acceptance, and because the Synod of Dort (1618-19) adopted it and employed it as a canon against Remonstrant and Socinian theology.

Definition of justification
Socinus offers a definition of justification is his treatise, *Tractatus de Justificatione*, which was written sometime between 1587 and 1591. In this treatise Socinus explains that justification is a legal declaration whereby believers are

---

[30] *Harmonia Confessionum*, §9, page 187; Augsburg Confession, art. 4.
[31] *The Second Helvetic Confession (1566)*, in *Creeds and Confessions*, 2.458.
[32] *Harmony*, §9.1, page 149; *Harmonia Confessionum*, 168; Second Helvetic Confession, chapter 15.
[33] *Harmony*, § 9, pages 148-210; *Harmonia Confessionum*, 168-224; Bohemian, chapter 6; Gallian, arts 13, 20-22; Belgic, art. 22-23, Augsburg, arts. 4-5; Würtemburg, chapter. 5; Tetrapolitan, chapter. 3.

pronounced righteous by God.[34] A similar definition appears in the Racovian Catechism: 'Justification is, when God regards us as just, or so deals with us as if we were altogether just and innocent. This he does in the New Covenant in forgiving our sins and conferring upon us eternal life.'[35] This definition sounds very similar to those offered in the Lutheran and Reformed confessions of the *Harmonia Confessionum*. But, when compared to the Confession of the Polish Brethren, the predecessor of the Racovian Catechism, there is a marked difference. The Confession of the Polish Brethren states:

> What is justification? It is the forgiveness in living faith of all our past trespasses by the pure grace of God, through the agency of our Lord Jesus Christ, regardless of our works and merits; the most certain expectation of eternal life, and a true, not artificial, correction of our life by the aid of the Spirit of God, to the glory of God the Father and to the edification of our neighbors.[36]

Immediately evident is that Socinus does not incorporate the need of a reformed life, but places emphasis upon the forensic element of the legal declaration, as does the Confession of the Polish Brethren. Based upon this emphasis in his definition, some have gone as far as to say that Socinus' doctrine of justification 'deserves to be acknowledged as a legitimate variant within the Reformation' and that he 'agreed entirely with the Pauline view that we are justified by faith alone without our righteousness or good works'.[37]

The problem with such a claim is that Socinus, himself, indicated his own disagreement with standard reformation elements of justification and his disagreement was well known and praised. In his *Life of that Incomparable Man Faustus Socinus* (1636), written by Samuel Przypkowski (1592-1670), Socinus is characterized as one at odds with Reformed doctrine.[38] If Socinus' devotees recognized him as a Reformed iconoclast, then the question arises, In spite of his definition of justification, how does he depart from the Reformed norm? And by extension, How does the Racovian Catechism depart from the received Reformed orthodoxy of the late sixteenth century? The answer comes from a survey of the key elements of the doctrine of justification.[39]

---

[34] Faustus Socinus, *Tractatus Justificatione*, in *Opera Omnia*, 1.615b; John B. Godby, 'Fausto Sozzini and Justification' in F.F. Church and Timothy George (eds), *Continuity and Discontinuity in Church History* (Leiden: Brill, 1979), 254.
[35] *Racovian Catechism*, 5.11, page 346.
[36] *Catechesis and Confession of Polish Brethren*, art 2, in *Creeds and Confessions*, 2.723.
[37] Godby, 'Sozzini and Justification,' 250, 255.
[38] Samuel Przypkowski, *The Life of that Incomparable Man Faustus Socinus of Siena (1636)*, in *History of the Polish Reformation*, 386-87.
[39] For a brief survey of Socinus' doctrine of justification see, Robert S. Franks, *A History of the Doctrine of the Work of Christ in Its Ecclesiastical Development* (London: Hodder and Stoughton, 1918), 2.24-30.

ASPECTS OF REFORMING

Faith

Central to the reformation doctrine of justification is the doctrine of faith. The Scriptures are replete with references to faith. But the question is, How is faith defined? The Heidelberg Catechism, for example, defines faith as follows:

> [True faith] is not only a certain knowledge by which I accept as true all that God has revealed to us in his word, but also a wholehearted trust which the Holy Spirit creates in me through the gospel, that, not only to others, but to me also God has given the forgiveness of sins, everlasting righteousness, and salvation, out of sheer grace solely for the sake of Christ's saving work.[40]

The Catechism captures the essence of faith by emphasizing the fiduciary elements—namely, a person has knowledge and trusts in the promises of God. The Catechism emphasizes that faith alone in Christ alone is the only means by which a person is justified—the believer cannot be justified by his own works or obedience. Only the obedience and satisfaction of Christ justifies a person before the tribunal of God.[41] Socinus, on the other hand, defines faith differently. In *De Jesu Christo Servatore*, Socinus explains:

> To believe in Christ is simply to present ourselves to God as obedient to Christ's own standard and rule. Through this obedience we can expect to receive the everlasting crown of life from Christ himself. I will make this quite plain in what follows, God willing. We receive the remission of sins, which Christ provided for us through God's mercy, by penitence and a changed life.[42]

In his *Tractatus Justificatione* Socinus states that obedience is the 'substance and form' of faith.[43] He, also, states clearly, 'Faith which justifies is namely this, obedience to God.'[44] Similar statements appear throughout the Racovian Catechism. When the Catechism describes faith, it does so not only in terms of trusting in the promises of God but, also, includes obedience. Faith is

> in our Lord Jesus Christ, whereby we keep our attention fixed upon his promises, and willingly submit ourselves to obey his precepts: which faith renders our obedience more estimable and more acceptable in the sight of God; and provided it be

---

[40] Heidelberg Catechism, q. 21. All subsequent quotations from the Heidelberg Catechism are taken from *Creeds and Confessions*. The original German is cited from Philip Schaff, *The Creeds of Christendom*, 3 vols. (1931; Grand Rapids: Baker, 1990).

[41] Heidelberg Catechism, qq. 60-62.

[42] Faustus Socinus, *De Jesu Christo Servatore*, 3.2, pages 239-40. English translation cited from Gomes, 'Faustus Socinus', 30-31. See, also, Hillar, 'Laelius and Faustus Socinus,' 16; cf. Godby, 'Sozzini and Justification,' 252.

[43] Socinus, *Tractatus Justificatione*, 610: 'fides, obedientiam praeceptorum Dei, non quidem ut effectum suum, sed ut suam substantiam & formam continet atque complectitur.'

[44] Socinus, *Tractatus Justificatione*, 610: 'Fidem, hanc scilicet, qua iustificamur, Dei obedientiam esse'; Ogonowski, 'Faustus Socinus', 202.

real and sincere, supplies the deficiency of our obedience, and causes us to be justified by God.[45]

The Catechism goes on to contrast two different types of faith—a mere intellectual assent to the doctrinal truths about Christ versus a trust in Christ; but even then, this trust includes obedience. The Catechism asks, 'What is meant by trusting in God through Christ?' It then offers the following response: 'It is so to trust in God as at the same time to trust in Christ, whom he has sent, and in whose hands he has placed all things; and also both to expect the fulfillment of the promises which were given by him, and to observe the precepts which he delivered.'[46] For the Reformed faith, faith is trusting in Christ, but for Socinus it is obedience to him.

Forgiveness of sins
For the forgiveness of sins, a number of different Protestant confessions base this doctrine on the satisfaction of Christ. The Belgic Confession, for example, states:

> We believe that Jesus Christ is a high priest forever according to the order of Melchizedek—made such by an oath—and that he presented himself in our name before his Father, to appease his wrath with full satisfaction by offering himself on the tree of the cross and pouring out his precious blood for the cleansing of our sins, as the prophets had predicted.[47]

Readers should note that just because the confession invokes the term 'satisfaction' does not mean identity with the satisfaction theory of the atonement offered by St. Anselm (1033-1109).[48] In his view, Anselm advanced the dilemma that either God would accept satisfaction or punishment as an answer to humanity's fallen condition: 'Either the honor which has been taken away should be repaid, or punishment should follow. Otherwise, either God will not be just to himself, or he will be without the power to enforce either of the two options.'[49] By choosing satisfaction over punishment, Anselm eliminated the idea of substitutionary punishment. He, therefore, located Christ's satisfaction outside of the context of punishment and placed it exclusively under the rubric of merit. By his merit Christ repays the debt of honor that the sinner owes, both in

---

[45] *Racovian Catechism*, §9, page 321.
[46] *Racovian Catechism*, §9, page 322.
[47] Belgic Confession, art. 20. All subsequent quotations from the Heidelberg Catechism are taken from *Creeds and Confessions*. The French edition appears in Philip Schaff, *The Creeds of Christendom*.
[48] Louis Berkhof, *Systematic Theology* (1932-38; Grand Rapids: Eerdmans, 1996), 385.
[49] Anselm, *Why God Became Man* in Brian Davies and G.R. Evans (eds), *The Major Works* (Oxford: OUP, 1998), 1.13, page 287; idem, *Cur Deus Homo? Libri Duo* (London: David Nat, 1903), 37.

terms of what he owes God as well as recompense for the failure to give him honor. Christ restores people through his satisfaction and merit.[50]

By way of contrast, the Reformed doctrine of satisfaction differs from Anselmian version because it offers *satisfactio poenalis*, or satisfaction through punishment. It eliminates the false-dichotomy of the either-or of satisfaction or punishment and posits a both-and satisfaction *and* punishment.[51] Christ vicariously takes the place of fallen, but elect, sinners, those who are in union with Christ. Again, Belgic Confession article 21 states that Christ made satisfaction through his suffering and passion. This satisfaction is applied to the sinner through faith and union with Christ: 'But Jesus Christ is our righteousness in making available to us all his merits and all the holy works he has done for us and in our place. And faith is the instrument that keeps us in communion with him and with all his benefits. When those benefits are made ours they are more than enough to absolve us for our sins.'[52] One finds a trinitarian cast to the Reformed understanding of the satisfaction of Christ, whereby, article 20 treats the *satisfactio Christi* from the perspective of the Father, article 21 from the vantage point of Christ, and article 22 from that of the Holy Spirit.[53] The same cannot be said of Socinus' understanding of the forgiveness of sins.

Socinus engages his understanding of the Reformed view of the satisfaction of Christ from its commercial aspect—the illustration of the creditor and his debtor.[54] Socinus believed that every creditor has the right to cancel debts: 'Every creditor has the absolute right to forgive the debtor his debt—either in whole or in part—without receiving satisfaction. Surely, nobody is so ignorant, not to say mindless, to think that God cannot justly remit our debts without first receiving full satisfaction.'[55] Socinus believed that the language of Scripture that employed satisfaction terminology was not literal, but figurative. Hence, 'It is therefore quite clear that the merciful God is pleased to forgive freely our sins in the salvation provided through Christ, without any literal satisfaction.'[56]

---

[50] Anselm, *Why God Became Man*, 1.11-12, pages 282-86; Willem J. Van Asselt, 'Christ's Atonement: A Multi-Dimensional Approach,' *CTJ* 38 (2003), 60; cf. Dániel Deme, *The Christology of Anselm of Canterbury* (Aldershot: Ashgate, 2004), 91-98.

[51] Van Asselt, 'Christ's Atonement,' 61.

[52] Belgic Confession, art. 22.

[53] Van Asselt, 'Christ's Atonement,' 61.

[54] This is not to say that the Reformed view of the *satisfactio Christi* is based upon theories of commercialism and, hence, German feudal law instead of scriptural ideas. In fact, recent scholarship has discredited the caricatures of Anselm's view that God was a greedy tyrant interested only in restoring his offended dignity. Rather, Anselm employed commercial ideas, borrowed from his Germanic feudal context, as illustrations; they were not foundational to his doctrine of satisfaction (R.W. Southern, *Saint Anselm: A Portrait in a Landscape* [Cambridge: CUP, 1991], 227). For an overview of Socinus' doctrine of satisfaction, see Alan W. Gomes, '*De Jesu Christo Servatore:* Faustus Socinus on the Satisfaction of Christ,' *WTJ* 55 [1993], 209-31.

[55] Socinus, *De Jesu Christo Servatore*, 3.1, page 221.

[56] Socinus, *De Jesu Christo Servatore*, 3.2, page 240.

The Racovian Catechism contains similarly stated ideas; it decries the substitutionary satisfaction of Christ as 'false, erroneous, and exceedingly pernicious'. The Catechism states that the substitutionary satisfaction of Christ is 'repugnant to the Scriptures and right reason'. Following Socinus, the Catechism explains that God forgives men freely of their sins: 'But to a free forgiveness nothing is more opposite than such a satisfaction as they contend for, and the payment of an equivalent price. For where a creditor is satisfied, either by the debtor himself, or by another person on the debtor's behalf, it cannot with truth be said of him that he freely forgives the debt.'[57] The free forgiveness of sins is antithetical to satisfaction, according to Socinian thought. Moreover, the Racovian Catechism states that literal satisfaction would incite antinomianism, licentiousness because 'if full payment have been made to God by Christ for all our sins, even those which are future, we are absolutely freed from all liability to punishment, and therefore no further condition can by right be exacted from us to deliver us from the penalties of sin. What necessity then would there be for living religiously?'[58]

The Socinian understanding of the forgiveness of sins has at least one identifiable source of influence, namely Wolfgang Musculus (1497-1563), though the nature of influence should be qualified. The basic premise of Socinus' understanding of the remission of sins is that there is no ontological necessity in God's nature that absolutely requires satisfaction for sins. In other words, the punishment for sin is rooted in God's will and not his nature. In support of his claims, Socinus cites Musculus. In the quotation taken from his *Loci Communes*, Socinus appeals to Musculus' concept of the 'double throne' of God. Musculus states:

> Everything the Holy Scriptures say about God's grace and mercy would be in vain if God is only a just judge, and not at the same time merciful; or if he is just in such a way that he could not be merciful without threatening his justice; or if he is obligated by a legal justice which does not permit him to acquit the guilty and be merciful to whom he wills—even though rulers and magistrates can do so![59]

Socinus appeals to Musculus to substantiate the point that God may freely forgive sins; however, his appeal is selective as he demurs from Musculus' conclusions regarding justification and the remission of sins, which in his mind, 'significantly weaken the doctrine of satisfaction'.[60] So, Musculus is not a di-

---

[57] *Racovian Catechism*, 5.8, pages 304-305.
[58] *Racovian Catechism*, 5.8, page 306.
[59] Socinus, *De Jesu Christo Servatore*, 3.1, pages 224-25; cf. Wolfgang Musculus, *Loci Communes Theologiae Sacrae* (Basel: Per Sabastianum Henricpetri, 1599), *De Justificatione*, §3, pages 267-68; idem, *Common Places of Christian Religion* (London: 1563), fol. 225.
[60] Socinus, *De Jesu Christo Servatore*, 3.1, page 225.

rect source of influence but rather only a source from which Socinus culls one point but takes it in a different direction.

Imputation of Christ's righteousness

Beyond the remission of sins, another key element of the common Protestant doctrine of justification is the imputation of Christ's righteousness. Again, to quote the Belgic Confession, article twenty states: 'But Jesus Christ is our righteousness in making available to us all his merits and all the holy works.'[61] The connections between the merit (or obedience) of Christ and imputation are clear in the sampled Protestant confessions from Beza's *Harmonia Confessionum*—by faith believers receive the imputed righteousness / merit / obedience of Christ.

By contrast, Socinus rejects the concept of imputation as one commonly finds it in Protestant confessions. For Socinus the concept of substitution, one person suffering on behalf of another, is contrary to the light of reason. But Socinus, also, believes that Scripture rejects substitution. Socinus bases his rejection of substitution on Ezekiel 18.20, where the prophet states that children will not suffer for the sins of their fathers.[62] A second reason Socinus rejects substitution is his anti-trinitarian doctrine of God; he contends that the person who makes satisfaction must be utterly separate from the person who receives said satisfaction. Socinus writes:

> Common sense itself clearly teaches this, so that if you insist on saying that Christ paid all the penalties for our sins to God on our behalf, you are forced to choose between one of the following conclusions: (1) you must deny that Christ himself is eternal God and Jehovah, or (2) you must affirm the extent to which he was eternal God and Jehovah could not coincide with making that payment.[63]

Hence, Socinus attempts to pin the common Protestant assertion of substitution on the horns of a dilemma—if the one making satisfaction has to be separate from the one who receives it, then the second person of the Trinity cannot make satisfaction unless the doctrine of the Trinity is denied.

Beyond these two reasons Socinus offers additional theological explanation for his rejection of imputation that has its origins from an unlikely source, namely, from Calvin and his correspondence with Socinus' uncle, Laelius. Socinus explains that his uncle 'advised Calvin of the truth, under the pretense of inquiring into the matter' and that Calvin later incorporated his epistolary response in his *Institutes*.[64] First, Socinus appeals to the fact that Calvin rejected the idea that Christ merited reward for himself:

---

[61] Belgic Confession, art. 22. Other cited confessions in Beza's Harmony have similar statements, including the Confession of Saxony, Gallican, and Würtemburg (*Harmony of Protestant Confessions*, 9.10, page 190; xxxviii-xxxix).

[62] Socinus, *De Jesu Christo Servatore*, 3.3, page 253.

[63] Socinus, *De Jesu Christo Servatore*, 3.4, page 276.

[64] Socinus, *De Jesu Christo Servatore*, 3.6, page 285.

Calvin rules out this interpretation with sufficient clarity when he denies that Christ gained merit for himself, and censured the Scholastics who taught that he did. Calvin's censure would have been completely unwarranted if Christ could have merited reward for himself in any way at all. He felt that it was enough to show that Christ could not merit reward for himself as God for God, or as man for man. Calvin just takes it for granted that one nature could not merit reward for the other. And rightfully so.[65]

Within context, Calvin refutes the views of the 'schoolmen' (*scholastici*), though he specifically mentions Peter Lombard (ca. 1100-60) by name.[66]

The second point Socinus appeals to comes directly from the Laelius-Calvin correspondence. Though Laelius' original letter to Calvin is no longer extant, Calvin incorporated his response to Laelius in his *Institutes*: 'There are certain perversely subtle men who—even though they confess that we receive salvation through Christ—cannot bear to hear the word "merit," for they think that it obscures God's grace.'[67] From this response one can infer what the original question was: 'If the justification of men depends on the sheer mercy of God, how is it necessary that Christ's merit should at the same time intervene? How can one say both that God freely forgives and that Christ merits our forgiveness?'[68] In his response, Calvin argues that one did not have to pit Christ's merit against God's mercy; to Calvin, to do so was an absurdity. Calvin, then, invokes a common scholastic rule that, 'A thing subordinate to another is not in conflict with it.' In this case, Calvin argues that believers are 'freely justified by God's mercy alone, and at the same time that Christ's merit, subordinate to God's mercy, also intervenes on our behalf.' Calvin, also, affirms the compatibility of God's mercy and Christ's merit by arguing: 'Apart from God's good pleasure Christ could not merit anything: but did so because he had been appointed to appease God's wrath with his sacrifice, and to blot out our transgressions with his obedience.'[69]

---

[65] Socinus, *De Jesu Christo Servatore*, 3.5, page 278.

[66] Calvin, *Inst.* 2.17.6; idem, *Institutio Christianae Religionis* in *Opera Selecta* (*OS*), 3.514. Cf. Peter Lombard, *The Sentences* (translated by Giulio Silano; Toronto: Pontifical Institute of Medieval Studies, 2007-10), 3.18.1; idem, *Sententiae in IV Libris Distinctae*, 2 vols. (Grottaferrata: Collegii S. Bonavenurae Ad Claras Aquas, 1981). For Calvin's letter to Laelius see 'Responsio ad Aliquot Laelii Socini Senensis Quaestiones,' *CO*, 10.160-65.

[67] Calvin, *Inst.* 2.17.1 (*OS* 3.508).

[68] David Willis, 'The Influence of Laelius Socinus on Calvin's Doctrines of the Merits of Christ and the Assurance of Faith' in John A. Tedeschi (ed.), *Italian Reformation Studies in Honor of Laelius Socinus* (Firenze: University of Siena, 1965), 234.

[69] Calvin, *Inst.* 2.17.1 (*OS* 3.509). Elsewhere, Calvin offers the following: 'God could have redeemed us by a word or a wish, save that another way seemed to Him best for our sakes: that by not sparing His own only-begotten Son He might testify in His person how much he cares for our salvation' (*Comm. John* 15.13); idem, *Ioannis Calvini Opera Exegetica*, volume 12.2, in Helmut Feld (ed.), *Evangelium Secundum Johan-*

While Calvin maintains the necessity of the imputation of Christ's merit, he, unwittingly, left a door open for Socinus to pass through. Scholars have previously noted that Calvin's doctrine of Christ's merit and satisfaction bears the imprint of the nominalism of John Duns Scotus (ca. 1265-1308).[70] Both Calvin and Scotus affirm the idea that the worthiness of Christ's merit lies in the value assigned to it by God's decree—it has no intrinsic worth or value. God could have ordained things in such a manner as to have an angel make satisfaction and earn a sufficient amount of merit to redeem sinners.[71] Readers should keep in mind that though Calvin and Scotus overlap in their conception of the satisfaction and merit of Christ, they are interested in slightly different questions. Duns Scotus, in line with other theologians of the period such as Aquinas, was interested in the question of both what Christ merited for himself and what he merited for believers. Calvin, on the other hand, is only interested in the question of what Christ merited for others as his above-quoted rejection of Lombard demonstrates.[72]

However, the vulnerability that Calvin exposed was on the question regarding the value of Christ's merit. Based upon Calvin's idea that Christ could not merit anything apart from God's good pleasure, or his *acceptatio*, Socinus believed he was, therefore, warranted in rejecting that Christ could merit anything for another. Though, it should be noted that Calvin was not unique but merely affirmed a mainstream opinion on the matter.[73] Nevertheless, Socinus writes:

> No one can truly merit reward for another. Nor, even if it were possible for one person to gain merit for another, could the divine nature ever merit reward for anyone, since the divine nature functions as that which gives and lavishes, or if you prefer, as that which gives a suitable reward for any so-called merits. (Of course, Calvin had no doubt that the human nature could not have merited reward for the divine).[74]

Socinus goes on to contend: 'If you argue that he gained merit for us as God and in the power of the divine nature, that would be ridiculous. As we said God, or the divine nature, does not merit but bestows, paying deserved rewards

---

nem Commentarius Pars Prior (Geneva: Droz, 1997), 168; Carl Trueman, 'John Owen's *Dissertation on Divine Justice:* An Exercise in Christocentric Scholasticism,' *CTJ* 33 (1998), 90.

[70] François Wendel, *Calvin: Origins and Development of His Religious Thought* (1950; Grand Rapids: Baker, 1997), 129, 228.

[71] Joannis Duns Scoti, *Quaestiones In Librum Tertium Sententiarum* in *Opera Omnia* (Paris: 1894), 14.3.19, q. 1.7, pages 718-19; Willis, 'Influence of Laelius Socinus,' 235n.2.

[72] Willis, 'Influence of Laelius Socinus,' 235; Thomas Aquinas, *Summa Theologica* (Allen: Christian Classics, 1948), IIIa q. 1 art. 2; IIIa q. 46 arts. 1-4.

[73] Trueman, 'Christocentric Scholasticism,' 90.

[74] Socinus, *De Jesu Christo Servatore*, 3.5, page 278.

for any so-called merits.'[75] The parallel between Calvin and Socinus is thus: if God could have designed the nature of Christ's satisfaction differently, and if God only assigns value to Christ's merit because of a decision of his will rather than because it has any intrinsic value or worth, then Socinus believed he was warranted in arguing that God could simply erase the sinner's debt of sin. Socinus folds his rejection of imputation and merit into his understanding of the forgiveness of sins. Calvin, of course, would reject such a conclusion, but Socinus, nevertheless, entered through the door that Calvin left opened.

In case there is any doubt regarding this conclusion, Socinus is fairly clear as he affirms these points in his own words. Socinus is fully aware that there were theologians who 'deny that satisfaction arises from God's acceptation, basing satisfaction on Christ's very works and on the inherent power of his actual sufferings'. Socinus rejects this position as 'indefensible' because of his understanding of forgiveness and satisfaction. Instead, Socinus favorably cites Calvin on this point: 'God accepted Christ's obedience in place of satisfaction, but not because this obedience has the power to make satisfaction per se. Chief among those of this opinion appears to be John Calvin.'[76] Socinus then concludes about Calvin's view: 'Calvin—who lacked neither knowledge nor sharp judgment—recognized that Christ could not gain any merit for us or make satisfaction to divine justice for us on the strength of what he did and suffered.'[77] Socinus, therefore, believed that he had an unwitting ally in Calvin on this particular point, an alliance that Calvin, no doubt, would have rejected.

Socinus' theological argumentation does not appear in the Racovian Catechism, though the consequences of his positions certainly do surface when it explains that Christ's suffering and death was in no way a satisfaction for sin, but, merely, a moral example. When the catechism asks why Christ suffered and was crucified it replies: 'He inspires us with a certain hope of salvation, and also incites us both to enter upon the way of salvation and to persevere in it. In the next place, he is with us in every struggle of temptation, suffering, or danger, affords us assistance, and at length delivers us from eternal death.'[78] Christ, therefore, does not vicariously redeem anyone but merely demonstrates the method by which people may be saved.[79] Karl Barth, rightly, characterizes the nature and impact of Socinus' Christology upon the Racovian Catechism. The total function of Christ's prophetic office is 'to understand the historical being and work of the Mediator as merely the manifestation, declaration and exemplification of a timeless idea of reconciliation as the true *veritas coelestis*,

---

[75] Socinus, *De Jesu Christo Servatore*, 3.5, page 279.
[76] Socinus, *De Jesu Christo Servatore*, 3.6, pages 283-84.
[77] Socinus, *De Jesu Christo Servatore*, 3.6, page 285. Franks bypasses Calvin and argues that Socinus draws directly upon Duns Scotus (*Work of Christ*, 2.17).
[78] *Racovian Catechism*, 5.8, page 296.
[79] *Racovian Catechism*, 1, page 1.

and thus in short to substitute a Gospel *of* Jesus Christ for the Gospel concerning him.'[80]

The Reformed response

In one sense, there was no official response to Socinian theology that originated during the reformation (1517-65) as Socinus had not yet written or disseminated his teaching until the late sixteenth and early seventeenth century. The closest thing to Socinus' thought were the letters of his uncle, Laelius. Even then, as noted in the biographical sketch, opinions were divided over Laelius' beliefs. Laelius agitated Calvin with his persistent questions, but satisfied Bullinger with his personal confession. Other correspondents, such as Girolamo Zanchi (1516-90), had definite opinions. Zanchi acknowledged that Laelius was born of a noble family, knowledgeable of Greek and Hebrew, blameless in his comportment, but, nevertheless, 'full of diverse heresies'.[81] Socinian teaching, therefore, did not go unnoticed and as time passed, greater attention was given to this spreading doctrine.

As Socinian doctrine began to spread, the body of anti-Socinian literature grew. Hugo Grotius (1583-1645) published his *Defense of the Catholic Faith Concerning the Satisfaction of Christ Against Faustus Socinus of Siena* (1617).[82] Johannes Maccovius (1588-1644), one of the delegates to the Synod of Dort, wrote three anti-Socinian works, *The First False Adversaries, Cases of Conscience From Socinian Doctrine Arranged in a Dialogue* and *Anti-Socinus*.[83] In Reformed works like those such as Maccovius, polemical interaction with Socinian teaching became a regular feature. As one can imagine, chief topics of debate include the doctrine of the Trinity, justification and the satisfaction of Christ.[84] In fact, the number of anti-Socinian writings includes over 700 works during the period of 1595-1797. Though this number does not completely reveal the effort that went into opposing Socinian thought; professors of Theology, for example, bound student anti-Socinian dissertations together. One

---

[80] Karl Barth, *Church Dogmatics* (edited by G.W. Bromiley and T.F. Torrance; Edinburgh: T. & T. Clark, 1936-1968), IV.3/1, 15.

[81] Girolamo Zanchi, *De Tribus Elohim, Aeterno Patre, Filio, et Spiritu Sancto, Uno eodemque Iehova, libri XIII* (Neustadt Matthaei Harnisii, 1589), *praefatio*: 'plenus diversarum haereseum'.

[82] Hugo Grotius, *Denfensio Fidei Catholicae de Satisfactione Christi Adversus Fastum Socinum Senensem* (Leiden: Ioannes Patius, 1617).

[83] See Johannes Maccovius, *Johannes Maccovius Redivivus, seu Manuscripta eius Typis Exscripta* (Franeker, 1647).

[84] See, e.g., Johannes Maccovius, *Scholastic Discourse: Johannes Maccovius (1588-1644) on Theological and Philosophical Distinctions and Rules* (edited by Willem J. van Asselt, Michael D. Bell, Gert van den Brink and Rein Ferwerda; Apeldoorn: Instituut voor Reformatieonderzoek, 2009), 1.45, 2.6, 5.1, 5.6, 5.9, 5.21; pages 82, 88, 126, 128, 130, 136.

collection includes 154 dissertations and runs over 1,200 pages.[85] Another collection is over 900 pages consisting of 56 dissertations; a third combines 17 dissertations that cover 1,000 columns of text, and a fourth runs 555 pages.[86]

Perhaps one of the best examples, though, of a reaction to Socinianism comes from the pen of John Owen (1616-83). When Owen originally penned his *Death of Death in the Death of Christ* (1647), he was chiefly concerned with Arminianism. In this treatise, Owen argued against the Arminian position of what Owen called a 'universal redemption, or the general ransom'.[87] Owen engaged the Arminian argument by demonstrating that Christ's death was not absolutely necessary to redeem the elect.[88] Owen explains:

> It is true, indeed, supposing the decree, purpose, and constitution of God that so it should be that so he would manifest his glory, by the way of vindicative justice, it was impossible that it should otherwise be . . . but to assert positively, that absolutely and antecedently to his constitution he could not have done it, is to me an unwritten tradition, the Scripture affirming no such thing, neither can it be gathered from thence in any good consequence.[89]

Owen, like Calvin before him, though Owen cites Augustine (354-430) in support of his claim, grounded the necessity of Christ's satisfaction in the will of God, rather than his nature—it was based on the divine decree and the *potentia Dei ordinata*, not God's essence.[90]

By 1652 Owen had different concerns—he no longer feared Arminianism but, instead, the growing threat of Socinianism. He was concerned about the Socinian denial of the necessity of the satisfaction of Christ.[91] His concern caused him to pen *A Dissertation on Divine Justice*. Owen's subtitle is noteworthy: 'Wherein that essential property of the divine nature is demonstrated from the sacred writings, and defended against Socinians, particularly the au-

---

[85] Joannes Adamus Scherzerus, *Collegii Anti-Sociniani* (Leipzig: 1702).
[86] Josua Stegmann, *Photinianismus: hoc est, succincta refutatio errorum Photinianorum* (1623); Christiani Becmani, *Exercitationes theologicae* (Amsterdam: J. Janssonium, 1643); Ludovicus Crocius, *Antisocinismus contractus: hoc est errorum Socinianorum privatarum consequentiarum nebulis involutorum examen & brevis ostensio principiorum quibus illi XXVIII disputationibus refutantur & dogmata catholicae fidei defenduntur* (1639); Alan W. Gomes, 'Some Observations on the Theological Method of Faustus Socinus (1539-1604),' *WTJ* 70 (2008): 50n.2.
[87] John Owen, *Salus Electorum, Sanguis Jesu*; or *The Death of Death in the Death of Christ: A Treatise of the Redemption and Reconciliation that is in the Blood of Christ*, in William H. Goold (ed.), *The Works of John Owen* (1850-53; Edinburgh: Banner of Truth, 1993), 10.140-429.
[88] Trueman, 'Christocentric Scholasticism,' 89.
[89] Owen, *Death of Death*, 10.205.
[90] Trueman, 'Christocentric Scholasticism,' 89; cf. Augustine, *On the Holy Trinity*, 13.10 in Philip Schaff (ed.), *Nicene and Post-Nicene Fathers of the Christian Church*, First Series (rep.; Grand Rapids: Eerdmans, 1993), 3.174.
[91] Trueman, 'Christocentric Scholasticism,' 91.

thors of the Racovian Catechism, John Crellius, and F. Socinus himself.'[92] Owen mentions Crellius, one of several theologians who assisted in the completion of the Racovian Catechism; he, also, mentions Socinus, who being dead for nearly fifty years, was perceived by Owen to be a present threat.

In his *Dissertation*, Owen changed his position on the necessity of the satisfaction of Christ. Owen knew he was parting company with a number of significant theologians who held his former position. Owen writes that the position had the 'mighty names' of Augustine, Calvin, Musculus, William Twisse (1578-1646), moderator of the Westminster Assembly, Gerardus Vossius (1577-1649) and Samuel Rutherford (1600-61). Owen, however, now joined the ranks of other theologians who argued for the essential necessity of the satisfaction of Christ, including David Pareus (1548-1622), Johannes Piscator (1546-1625), Charles Dumoulin (1500-66), Sibrandus Lubbertus (1556-1625), André Rivet (1572-1651), John Cameron (ca. 1579-1623), Maccovius, Franciscus Junius (1545-1602) and the professors of the Academy at Saumur.[93] Some might accuse Owen of switching positions out of political expediency or out of a desire to distance himself from Socinian doctrine. However, recent analysis of his change demonstrates that Owen was driven both by theological and scriptural considerations.[94] In fact, one can rule out politics from Owen's decision because his new position is significantly closer to the position of Arminius, one for whom he reserved his greatest disdain.[95]

Conclusion

Faustus Socinus transgressed the confessional and biblical norms of his day by advocating a doctrine of justification that had people seeking to justify themselves by their own good works. Socinus' gospel was devoid of a mediator who vicariously suffered on behalf of his bride but merely pointed the way for her to follow. If she would repent of her sinful ways and place her faith in Christ, that is, obey the law of God and live an upright life, then she would be rewarded with eternal life. In the eyes of the reformers, such a gospel was in no way good news. Socinus displaced *sola fide*, *solus Christus* and *sola gratia*. In terms of Socinus' perceived impact upon the history of the church, perhaps the epitaph engraved upon his tombstone best captures it: 'Although Luther destroyed all of the house-tops of Babylon, Calvin the walls, but Socinus destroyed its founda-

---

[92] John Owen, *A Dissertation on Divine Justice* in *Works*, 10.480-624.
[93] Owen, *Dissertation* in *Works*, 10.487-88; Trueman, 'Christocentric Scholasticism,' 91n.11.
[94] Trueman, 'Christocentric Scholasticism,' 91-103.
[95] Trueman, 'Christocentric Scholasticism,' 102; cf. Jacob Arminius, *The Works of James Arminius* (edited by James Nichols; 1853; Grand Rapids: Baker, 1991), private disp. 21, 2.49-50; idem, *Disputationes, magnam partem s. theologiae complectentes, publicae & privatae, quarum index epist. dedicatoriam sequitur*, in *Opera Theologica* (Leiden: 1629), 360-62.

tions.'⁹⁶ Luther and Calvin sought to reform the doctrine of the church, but Socinus was perceived by his devotees as wanting utterly to destroy it. Adolf von Harnack (1851-1930) comments that Socinianism, as a movement, represents 'that destruction of Catholicism which could be effected on the basis of what was furnished by Scholasticism and the Renaissance while there was no essential deepening or quickening of religion. In Antitrinitarianism and Socinianism the Middle Ages and the newer period stretch hands forth to each other across the reformation.'⁹⁷ In many ways, Harnack's observations are true, though one cannot too easily dismiss the fact that Calvin was the deliveryman of the package of medieval theology that Socinus opened with glee. Nevertheless, regardless of how Socinus encountered the various ideas that he incorporated into his thought, one thing is clear: Reformed theologians for generations to come sought repeatedly to confront his teachings to preserve the truth, especially as it pertains to the doctrine of justification by faith alone in Christ alone.

---

[96] Joshua Toulmin, *Memoirs of the Life, Character, Sentiments, and Writings of Faustus Socinus* (London: J. Brown, 1777), 12; Gomes, 'Theological Method of Socinus,' 50.

[97] Adolf von Harnack, *History of Dogma* (translated by William M'Gilchrist; London: Williams and Norgate, 1899), 7.120. For a similar observation, see Franks, *Work of Christ*, 2.13.

CHAPTER 13

'Let us not . . . call God to account.'
John Calvin's reading of some difficult deaths[1]

Michael Parsons

John Thompson's fascinating study, *Writing the Wrongs*,[2] examines pre-critical commentators on some very difficult narratives that concern abuse of women in a patriarchal society. After detailed consideration of some primary texts he concludes that pre-critical commentators are 'fully capable of applying their own kinds of reading strategies to the Bible in order to deal with offensive narratives in ways that bend even the awkward silences of Scripture toward the divine norm of fairness, justice and the like'.[3] As Thompson's work indicates, even on just a cursory reading some biblical narratives are deeply disturbing and, consequently, the commentator has often felt constrained to address and to resolve the apparent dissonance. This is true, for example, of the stories that recount rape, sexual abuse and the like, as many following Phyllis Trible's seminal work, *Texts of Terror*, have shown.[4] However, it is not only commentary on the narratives of sexual abuse that portrays this characteristic. The deaths of Ananias and Sapphira in the New Testament and those of Uzzah and Uriah in the Old are, also, narratives that exemplify the problem, simply because (in the first two instances) the punishment seems to be somewhat excessive, and in the last example God appears to allow a righteous, innocent man to suffer and to die.

The interest of this essay is to examine John Calvin's response to these stories, a response which reveals the need to make some moral sense of what is happening in the narrative. A careful reading of Calvin's comments shows that he employs reading strategies in a conscious attempt to come to terms with at

---

[1] A revised version of my essay, '"Let us not be like those . . . who want to call God to account": John Calvin's reading of some difficult deaths,' *Pacifica. Australasian Theological Studies* 20.1 (2007), 1-23.
[2] John L. Thompson, *Writing the Wrongs* (Oxford: OUP, 2001).
[3] Thompson, *Writing the Wrongs*, 252.
[4] See Phyllis Trible, *Texts of Terror* (Philadelphia: Fortress, 1984). See, also, for example, Michael Parsons, 'Luther and Calvin on rape: Is the crime lost in the agenda?' *EQ* 74 (2002), 123-42.

least some of the problems in these texts, particularly problems related to the centrality of God's involvement.

Ananias and Sapphira (Acts 5.1-11)

The evangelist's account of the deaths of Ananias and Sapphira still has the ability to shock its readers and that shock is often registered as a question. Scott Spencer asks, 'How do we ever adequately make sense of the manner in which Ananias and Sapphira are taken away: suddenly struck dead by the hand of God? . . . [D]oes it warrant divine capital punishment?'[5] The shock of the incident is apparent in Calvin's commentary, and it appears as a series of questions on the severity of the punishment in relation to the crime. However, whereas Spencer's interrogative response is inclusive of himself, Calvin's is not. Even as Calvin raises the concerns of others, he himself does not share the speculative questioning of these readers—questioning he believes to be derived from a self-oriented, impious and prejudiced outlook. In commenting on verse 5[6] he says that 'some are of the opinion that the punishment was too cruel' and that they are 'displeased with the excessive severity of God,' and that others simply do not believe the narrative as it stands because it does not accord with the experience of those who today are as hypocritical but 'get off scot-free'. They argue on the grounds of an apparent discrepancy between the text and actual, lived or observed, experience. Calvin judges that the former critics contemptuously minimise Ananias' sin, evaluating it from their own and not from the divine perspective.[7]

The latter critics, however, are not as conveniently answered. Calvin is forced to argue the point in a rather complex manner. First, the reformer writes concerning the Lord's punitive intrusion during the initial stages of the nascent church, suggesting the principle that in the early church the divine punishment was as open, external and obvious as were the divine gifts. That is no longer the case, however. Things have changed. Neither the spiritual gifts nor the divine discipline are manifest in the same way today. Second, he indicates that the very visible punishment of Ananias and Sapphira reminds us that though we do not necessarily see people punished in the same way, there is divine judgement to come. The past punishment acts as a precursory warning to the contemporary church.[8]

> But as God poured out visible graces on His Church at the beginning, so that we may know with assurance that He will be present with us by the secret virtue of His Spirit, and furthermore, showed openly by external signs what we realize inwardly by the experience of faith, so He has demonstrated by the visible punish-

---

[5] F. Scott Spencer, *Acts* (Sheffield: Sheffield Academic Press, 1997), 57-58.
[6] *Comm. Acts* 5.5.
[7] *Comm. Acts* 5.8.
[8] See *Comm. Acts* 5.5; *Comm. Acts* 5.3.

ment of two persons, how horrible a judgment awaits all hypocrites, who have held Him and the Church in derision.[9]

There is clearly in Calvin's mind a parallel between the gifts of the Spirit and the punishment of sinners in the experience of the early church. The reason he suggests this is that earlier he explained the word of Peter to Ananias as proceeding from a direct revelation of the Spirit, adding that 'Luke . . . indicates that the apostles to some extent represented God (*sustinuisse Dei personam*), and acted in His stead.'[10] So, just as spiritual gifts were prominent ('visible,' 'showed openly,' 'external') in the apostolic age, so too was punishment as pronounced and public as that described in the text. 'This was an extraordinary affair'—evidently not something that one would expect to find in contemporary Europe or in the city of Geneva.[11] This line of argument has the result of pointing readers to the authoritative Word of God. Indeed, by implication, Calvin underlines this direction himself by asserting that 'the death of Ananias truly confirms the force of the Word, which Paul magnificently brings out, in saying that "it is the savour of death unto death to those who are perishing" (2 Cor 2.16)'[12]—that is, the physical, observed experience of Ananias' death is indicative, not merely of the written text, but of the powerful and poignant work of God to which that inscribed text so vividly points.

Later, Calvin defends the divine decision to punish Ananias and Sapphira on the rather obvious theological grounds that it is up to God himself to determine when and how to punish, after all he (and not us) is 'the Judge of the world'.

> [I]n the bodily punishment of these two, there has been set before us, as in a mirror, the gravity of the spiritual judgment which is still hidden. For if we think over what it means to be cast into the eternal fire, we shall not consider it the worst of evils to fall dead before the eyes of men.[13]

Here we notice that, if anything, the result of the reformer's explanation appears to be a reduction in the significance of the physical death of Ananias and Sapphira—it is not 'the worst of evils' as some no doubt contend, particularly as it contrasts with the spiritual and eternal death that judgement may usher in. Indeed its significance is seen most clearly as symbolic of 'the punishment which escapes human eyes'.[14]

---

[9] *Comm. Acts* 5.5.
[10] *Comm Acts* 5.3.
[11] *Comm Acts* 5.5.
[12] *Comm Acts* 5.5. Calvin cites Prov. 15.8; Luke 21.2; Matt. 6.3, 18.20; 1 Cor. 3.16; Isa. 11.4.
[13] *Comm Acts* 5.8.
[14] *Comm Acts* 5.5.

Calvin's Strategy

We have seen how the reformer handles the critical sceptics, but how does he, himself, handle the text—or, rather, more pointedly, how does he handle the *problem* of the text? Calvin appears to have a reading strategy that he adopts to satisfy the questions prompted by the punishment meted out against Ananias and Sapphira. We discover this in his emphases on the enormity of the couple's crime, on Satan's involvement and on the nature of God and the divine positioning in the narrative.

The enormity of the couple's crime

It is clear that if Ananias and his wife are to receive divine judgment, if they are to be condemned to on-the-spot death, then the heinousness of their crime needs to be stressed to show that in certain respects, at least, the punishment was proportionate to the crime. We discover that the reformer is at pains to demonstrate this.

On the face of it the biblical text singles out the pair's sin as deceit (5.2) and lying (5.3-4,8). However, in his initial summary, Calvin states that Ananias is condemned for only one crime, 'his wishing to deceive God and the Church with a false offering'.[15] It is significant, of course, that Calvin judges that the crime is against both God and the church, underlining the fact that the couple sin against God *in the context of* the church. He considerably expands upon this by listing no fewer than six 'evils lying behind this deceit': (1) a contempt for the living God; (2) 'sacrilegious fraudulence,' that is, a refusal to give to God what rightfully belongs to him; (3) perverse ambition and vanity, wanting to be seen in a good light before the community; (4) faithlessness; (5) ruining the church's communal strategy; (6) hypocrisy. Then, having listed the six evils, he adds, 'deliberate and audacious lying'. Later, he characteristically defines the sum total simply as 'impiety'.[16]

Calvin appears to be as certain about the eternal fate of the couple, as he is about the crimes for which they were put to death. As for the fate of Ananias, for example, that appears to be summed up in Calvin's conclusion that, "The sign of *a reprobate man* is this: he is so given over to Satan, that no room is left for the Spirit of God.'[17] Ananias was a member of the community, but he was not a true believer, not a spiritual man, not a man of faith.

It is important to note that Sapphira is treated as fully complicit with her husband and, therefore, as culpable and as deserving of the divine punishment. Though he makes nothing of the first verse that states that the wife had 'full knowledge' of her husband's duplicity, the reformer is adamant that Peter's interrogation (5.7-9) and the wife's punishment (5.10) demonstrate that she was 'no better than her husband'. Indeed, it is noticeable that Calvin emphasises this

---

[15] *Comm Acts* 5.1.
[16] *Comm Acts* 5.1; *Comm Acts* 5.8, respectively.
[17] *Comm Acts* 5.3, emphasis added. See, also, *Comm Acts* 5.5.

point. He does so by phrases that reiterate the idea, both coupling them in their sin and, also, singling Sapphira out in her own right: 'the Church saw, separately, the treacherous intention and the stubborn wickedness of each of them,' 'they were equally responsible,' 'they were on a level in wickedly lying,' 'she shows she is incurable,' 'she has no terror of God,' 'they became mutual accomplices in their crime'.[18]

So, a significant part of Calvin's strategy in dealing with the difficult situation that confronts him in this text is to emphasise the sinfulness of the recipients of divine judgement. Ananias and Sapphira demonstrate in their covert planning and actions that they are guilty before God and before the community of faith. Within this context, they deserve their fate. This is particularly highlighted by the implied contrast of Calvin's rather naïve insistence that the generous church in which these people sinned 'were more like angels than men'.[19] The contrast could hardly be drawn more sharply.

Satan's involvement
The narrative, itself, gives Calvin the cue on Satan's involvement. Peter's accusation that Satan has filled Ananias' heart, causing him to lie to the Holy Spirit, allows the reformer to speak of the devil's tactics. He comments, for example, that Satan had devised 'a trick to penetrate that holy community,' insinuating that he does so invidiously through the hypocrisy of two of its members. Calvin states this as a general rule: '[T]hat is the way Satan attacks the Church of God, when he can get nowhere with open war.'[20] Later in his exposition, commenting on Peter's explicit words ('Satan has filled your heart'), Calvin is adamant that Satan tempts everyone; it is a universal experience. However, he warns that 'when Satan takes possession of the heart he holds sway over the whole man, as if God were driven out'. This indicates that Ananias and his wife were given over to Satan, that they had 'no room left' for the Spirit of God.[21] Proof of this derives from the fact that no one would dare to be so abusive of God unless they were 'devoid of all sense and reason'. It is noticeable, though, that Calvin allows no diminishing of responsibility on Ananias' part—no necessity drove him to sin, no outside influence forced him. Despite Satan's treachery, both Ananias and Sapphira were responsible for calling the wrath of God down on their heads.[22] This adds ammunition to his argument that the crime deserved the punishment.

The nature of God and the divine positioning in the narrative
The third component that allows Calvin to handle this difficult text as he does is his view of God in the narrative. Interestingly, as Calvin expounds the pas-

---

[18] *Comm Acts* 5.8; *Comm Acts* 5.7; *Comm Acts* 5.9, respectively.
[19] *Comm Acts* 5.1.
[20] *Comm Acts* 5.1.
[21] *Comm Acts* 5.3.
[22] *Comm Acts* 5.3.

sage, it is the person of God who almost imperceptibly, but profoundly, dominates the whole episode. And, typically, it is to the Triune God that Calvin points his audience—specifically to the two important theological doctrines of providence and *coram Deo*.

Calvin realises that it might have been otherwise, but considers it to be 'the certain providence of God' that caused the church community to see 'separately, the treacherous intention and the stubborn wickedness' of both spouses.[23] In another (but related) context, John Thompson states that especially where Scripture seems obscure and offensive pre-critical commentators seek a 'rule' that will help to explain the event: '[T]hey frequently resort to providence: whatever happened in Scripture, surely God was in charge.'[24] It is in this spirit that Calvin hints at the over-arching divine providential determination of events and, as is always the case, that determination has purpose: 'it was . . . appropriate and beneficial for the edification of the Church'.[25]

The reformer, also, has a great deal to say about the fact that the events took place before God (*coram Deo*). For example, he says this following on Ananias' sin: 'At the same time it does not enter his head that he is lying and cheating *in the sight of God* (*coram Deo*), and that God will punish him for his falsehood. In effect he honours the feet of the apostles more than the eyes of God.'[26] Later, on reflection, he says that Ananias should have behaved in the community 'as if he were seeing God with his eyes'. In other words, the reformer is anxious that his audience realises that God is a present, personal and a living God in the context of the assembly. He rules the *ecclesia* through his Word, preached by the apostles—they were not acting on their own (*privati*).[27] He, also, makes the observations that it is actually Christ who 'presides in the assembly of those to whom they belong'[28] and that Ananias and Sapphira tempted the Spirit 'because they heedlessly devised their fraud as if the Spirit of God was not the Searcher (*cognitor*) of hearts'.[29]

Reflections

We can see, then, that Calvin is able to answer the difficult question that naturally surfaces on a reading of Acts 5.1-11, Why is God so severe with Ananias and Sapphira? We need to acknowledge, first of all, that Calvin sees the difficulty, but he accepts it as such largely through the eyes of others who complain. Second, we have recognised a reading strategy in Calvin's response. To allow the punishment meted out by God to be judged as deserved he does three spe-

---

[23] *Comm Acts* 5.7.
[24] Thompson, *Writing the Wrongs*, 251.
[25] *Comm Acts* 5.7.
[26] *Comm Acts* 5.2, emphasis added.
[27] *Comm Acts* 5.4.
[28] *Comm Acts* 5.8.
[29] *Comm Acts* 5.9.

cific things: he paints the couple in very bleak colours, portraying their sin as an enormous crime against both God and the church. With the help of the text he is, also, able to draw into the picture the malice of Satan, himself. Finally, he positions the Triune God in the narrative in such a way as to underline divine providence.

However, I think it would be inappropriate to say that the reformer answers the question objectively, or even comfortably. Arguably, his continual and urgent pastoral application suggests that he finds no comfort in the destruction of this couple, however sinful and culpable they are. Indeed, his heaping of fault against them points to a similar conclusion, necessitating as it does (according to Calvin) their demise and permanent removal from the pristine Christian community. Ultimately, though, they serve a broader purpose—then and now. Calvin expresses this in his comment on verse 11, 'Great fear seized the whole church and all who heard about these events.' In delineating a twofold fear the reformer suggests that, by punishing some, God calls believers back from temptation and forces unbelievers to give glory to him—'the punishment of one person was a warning for all'.[30]

On the surface, this chapter appears to recount a fairly perspicuous event, after all Ananias and Sapphira *had* clearly sinned. They were punished for what they had clearly done. But what of a text in which, though someone *is* punished, the crime is far from certain. We turn to examine how Calvin reads the passage in which Uzzah reaches out a hand to steady the ark of the covenant and is slain in the effort.

Uzzah (2 Samuel 6)

There is no doubt at all that Calvin struggles more with the narrative of Uzzah's undoing than he did with that of Ananias and his wife. His introduction to the sermon on this indicates as much: 'We have here a very strange story, that *a man attempting to honour God*, burning with a good and holy devotion, was punished like a criminal.' The reformer continues explicitly in the same vein.

> Now this certainly offends our feelings. We know that the main cause of offending God is our wicked will. . . . But . . . *when our desire is to glorify him*, and *we have no ill will in us*, even if we have erred and made a mistake, still it seems that God ought not to hold it against us. . . . It seems that this ought to be acceptable to God.[31]

Then, the inevitable question, 'Was being zealous that the ark of God should not be shamed a crime worthy of punishment?'[32] Here, the reformer clearly cannot use the reading strategy that worked in the case of Acts 5 where he was

---

[30] *Comm Acts* 5.11.
[31] Calvin, *Sermons on 2 Samuel* (translated by Douglas Kelly; Edinburgh: Banner of Truth, 1992—hereafter, *Sermons*), 244, emphasis added.
[32] *Sermons*, 244-45. See, also, *Sermons*, 249.

able to emphasise the enormity of the crime. Indeed, the way the question is framed puts a stop to that approach. In many ways Uzzah is considered to be innocent (even 'zealous'). How does the reformer tackle the problem posed by God's seemingly excessive punishment of Uzzah's hasty action?[33]

Calvin's Strategy

Calvin's approach to the problem has three elements. First, (sequentially, though not necessarily in priority) he stresses the significance of the ark. Second, he points out the enormous difference between God's wisdom and humanity's, thereby seeking to silence any complaint. This has the effect of positioning God-in-relation-to-humanity with reference to the narrative. This is where the answer is ultimately to be found. Third, he attempts to concretise the answer to the problem in human experience and fault. Here, we find that he blames Uzzah by introducing the important reformational topic of vocation (*vocatio*) and (though, rather half-heartedly) even adds the qualification that Uzzah may have been ambitious in what he did.

The significance of the ark

Given that Uzzah touched the ark and died, it is important for Calvin to show the dreadful significance of the ark. He does this in two ways. In a secondary manner, it is significant in the overall narrative. According to the reformer, chapter 6 indicates that David has turned his attention 'to restoring the integrity of the worship of God'—indeed, God has called and established him as king for that particular purpose.[34] During the previous reign the people had given up seeking God, they had no zeal or affection for him: 'Although there was an outward appearance of religion, it was coldly and grudgingly performed.'[35] Apparently, then, David wanted the ark to be 'lodged in the centre of the country' where people could worship more easily.[36] So the ark is significant because of its centrality, both to Israel's worship and to David's major task. Nevertheless, the primary significance of the ark goes well beyond that.

Calvin understandably stresses the idea that the ark is representative of divine presence.[37] Here, preaching on 2 Samuel 6, he states that 'undoubtedly the Holy Spirit wanted . . . to emphasise that this ark was a definite sign and seal of the presence of God'. Indeed, in a daring application of Psalm 27.8 ('I have ever sought your face'), the reformer likens the ark to the face of God of which David speaks.[38] This notion presents the reformer with the opportunity to pro-

---

[33] Calvin says, 'God smote him . . . because of his hastiness'—*Sermons*, 242. Calvin comments, 'Now you might consider this hastiness to be commendable zeal, but in the eyes of God it was inconsiderate zeal, and merited punishment'—*Sermons*, 249.
[34] *Sermons*, 229.
[35] *Sermons*, 230.
[36] *Sermons*, 231.
[37] He, also, speaks of it as 'a mirror in which he might be seen'—*Comm Ps.* 78.61.
[38] *Sermons*, 232.

mote the magnificence and incomprehensibility of God—an opportunity he rarely misses.

At this point Calvin is attempting to square the obvious discrepancies between what he later calls 'a box,' 'a casket of wood' and the 'greatness, majesty and power of God' whose dwelling-place it represents.[39] He adopts the familiar idea of accommodation to explain it and in so doing emphasises the enormous difference between humanity and the divine. We are 'too crude and weak,' even applying all our senses to know God he remains totally inaccessible, 'we can only crawl upon the earth, while "the heaven of heavens cannot contain him"'.

> Therefore, he must come down to us when we cannot reach up to him. And how does he come down? It is not that he changes his place as far as his essence is concerned, but he must make himself known in a familiar manner. So when he conforms himself *to our smallness*, he does it only insofar as he abases himself. Not that there is change in him, but *his coming down refers to our capacity*.[40]

The italicised words indicate clearly that Calvin has in mind that the ark is the dwelling place of God in respect to our very limited understanding—that is, it is 'a standing witness that God wanted to dwell in the midst of the people'. The reformer speaks in God's voice, 'Here am I, and when you come through these means, it is the same as if I were manifest to you and you were seeing me with the naked eye.'[41] That is what the ark means to Calvin. It represents the immediate, personal presence of the living God amongst his people.[42]

What Calvin has done in relation to the problematic situation is clear. If Uzzah is killed for touching the ark, then the significance of the ark had better be determined. The wooden box represents the very real presence of God among his people. When Israel looks at it they see his 'face'.[43] It is *that* ark that Uzzah handled.

God's unfathomable wisdom
Ultimately, according to Calvin, it is in the wisdom of God that we find the answer to the narrative's inherent problem. Calvin emphatically draws his audience's attention to the fact that the divine judgement is beyond our understanding—though, noticeably, the reformer continues to acknowledge the difficulty.

> Scripture so often warns us . . . that the judgements of God are a profound abyss. This should make us utterly astonished, so that we fear God and his judgements, and find good in all he does—*even when we are confused over it.* . . . If many of

---

[39] *Sermons*, 268, 271, 255, respectively.
[40] *Sermons*, 233. See, also, *Sermons*, 235, 236; *Inst.* 1.17.13.
[41] *Sermons*, 233.
[42] *Sermons*, 237. See, also, *Sermons*, 279, 499.
[43] *Sermons*, 232, 236, respectively.

his works still do not agree with our appetites or our reason, let us remain his captive, and realise that it is quite necessary that God should surpass all our senses.[44]

Calvin then suggests that if *we* were the judge of Uzzah he would have been absolved of any guilt because his motives were good and his zeal virtuous. Indeed, he would have been rewarded! Nevertheless, it is God's responsibility to discern between good and evil, not ours.[45] If the angels, themselves, are confused, continues Calvin, then our attitude should be one of quiet humility before the glory of God.[46]

This seems enough to settle the matter, but, interestingly, there is in Calvin's exposition a hint that the cause of Uzzah's death is still a niggling concern. Apparently, the reformer needs to find fault.

Uzzah's fault

Calvin has to move from his own perception that Uzzah was basically good[47] to the divine perception that he had offended God. It should be enough for Calvin to believe that God knows what he's about, but the reformer clearly wants to satisfy himself from a very different perspective. He needs to know that Uzzah is in some way to blame; that God justly punished him. Pastorally, this is reassuring for those who listen—they can trust God to do the right thing in relation to his people, and it is a great deal easier if we can see the problem concretely.

At this point in the reformer's argument he brings in the important reformational subject of *vocatio* in an attempt to prize open Uzzah's culpability. Calvin suggests that Uzzah went beyond the limits of the vocation to which God had called him. He defines *vocatio* as 'the duty to which God binds us' and its use 'to prove the obedience that we render him'. In vocation, God defines the limits; our task is to walk within them: 'we should not go further than is legitimate for us'. In the example of Uzzah touching the ark, says Calvin, '[W]e are instructed not to attempt to go beyond the demands of our office.'[48] It is at this juncture that Calvin begins to use words like 'presumption' and 'recklessness' and to imply Uzzah's pride and ambition, and, of course, these are displeasing to God.[49] Now Calvin feels more confident to assert God's just judgement.

> [I]f someone argues, 'Why did God exercise such excessive severity on Uzzah? Would it not have been sufficient merely to admonish him?' . . . Let us learn, therefore, to avoid such arrogance, and to adore the judgements of God—and to

---

[44] *Sermons*, 245, emphasis added.
[45] *Sermons*, 245.
[46] *Sermons*, 246.
[47] *Sermons*, 244. See, also, *Sermons*, 263.
[48] *Sermons*, 246.
[49] *Sermons*, 247.

realise that since Uzzah did not stay in his place, God had just cause to chastise him for his recklessness. . . . God was justly angry.[50]

Calvin argues further that in touching the ark Uzzah was a private person seeking to do what only consecrated people should.

In our examination of the deaths of Ananias and his wife we observed that Calvin was confident, because of their crime, that they were not people of faith, not authentic members of the Christian community, and that their fate was one of eternal judgment prefigured by their physical death. Here, in relation to Uzzah, Calvin is just as confident of Uzzah's fate—that he is a man of God, that his fate is a positive one, despite his death. God was not eternally angry with Uzzah: '[D]eath could have been profitable to Uzzah, in that being thus punished, he did not fail to obtain pardon from God,' 'it was even a mercy which God bestowed upon him when he took him out of the world'.[51] God was angry with Uzzah, but because he saw his zeal 'he punished only his body in order that his spirit might be saved'.[52] Again, the victim becomes an example to instruct, not only his own generation, but, also, future generations, including sixteenth century Geneva.

Reflections

Calvin, himself, has difficulties with the death of Uzzah. He acknowledges them and struggles to come to a conclusion. He struggles particularly with the thought that Uzzah appears to be spiritually zealous for the things of God yet that he is killed as punishment for an undisclosed wrongdoing. The reformer attempts to resolve the issue with the simple, dogmatic assertion of God's incomprehensible wisdom. However, we notice, too, that this seems somewhat less than entirely convincing (even for Calvin) and, against the text, he pursues the problematic line that Uzzah overstepped the boundaries of vocation.

It is worth pointing out what appears to be a glaring inconsistency in Calvin's argument. It has to do with his reasoning on Uzzah's situation in relation to his conclusions on David. We noticed that the reformer argues that Uzzah—though he was generally motivated by holy zeal and devotion—was guilty of overstepping the boundaries of vocation. He was smitten of the Lord because of this. However, as Calvin portrays the king, David, we see that he stands in the same difficulty but is *not* killed by God. This seems to be contradictory.

That is to say David is continually represented by Calvin as failing before God in the same area as Uzzah. Calvin suggests that David *presumed* to remove the ark, 'without being specifically commanded to do so'.[53] More relevantly, he is said to be without excuse for placing the ark of God on the new cart, 'be-

---

[50] *Sermons*, 249, 250, respectively.
[51] *Sermons*, 250. 'When God takes us from here, it is not a judgement so grievous as we think, in that we do not understand the life eternal to which he calls us.'
[52] *Sermons*, 250.
[53] *Sermons*, 231.

cause this duty was assigned to the Kohathites. .... God ordained it this way, it should have been done in obedience to him.' This speaks directly to the subject of vocation. David himself failed to recognise vocational boundaries, though he acts as he does—like Uzzah—with good intentions.[54] But according to the logic of Calvin's argument God should have smitten David.

Perhaps the answer for this inconsistency is to be found in the centrality of David to the narrative, and particularly to the soteriological significance of the king—a significance that Uzzah could not possess, of course. Indeed, Calvin sees Uzzah's example as primarily having instruction to David, and only then to others. The centrality of the king, also, plays a huge part in the final example, that of Uriah, Bathsheba's ill-fated husband.

Uriah (2 Samuel 11-12)[55]

In reading of Uriah's terrible death Calvin is clearly in a quandary. Uriah is obviously innocent of any crime. Though he does not punish Uriah (as he had Ananias and his wife and Uzzah), God is still plainly centrally involved. We might gauge the reformer's response by a paragraph in which he lists no fewer than six promises that God seems to have broken in regard to Uriah's death.

> Where were the promises by which God testified that he would never forsake his own (Ps. 37.28); that their blood would be precious to him (Ps. 72.14; Heb. 12.24); that even a hair of their head would not fall, and that they were numbered by him (Matt. 10.30); that he would guide their steps, and that he would cause them to be guided by his angels (Ps. 91.11); and that they would be fortified with a double rampart; that he would be their strength and their shield (Ps. 28.7); that he would hold them dear as the apple of his eye (Deut. 32.10; Ps. 17.8)?[56]

Calvin adds, 'and everything else that it is possible to say,' signifying a depth of concern. The inevitable question, 'Why, then, did God not help him in time of need?' follows the assertion of Uriah's innocence and precedes the poignant comment, '[I]t seems that he was frustrated *for having carefully served God.*'[57]

Calvin's Strategy

The reformer's use of Uriah defines his strategy. He presents him in stark contrast to the king. In contrast to David's shameless abuse of Uriah (both in taking his wife and in having him killed) Uriah is said to be a faithful friend to David.[58] It is Uriah, not David, who acted and spoke in a manner worthy of his vocation.[59] 'Above all,' Calvin says, 'he put God first.'[60] In this way, Calvin is

---

[54] *Sermons*, 239.
[55] Calvin speaks of Uriah as 'an innocent man'—*Sermons*, 505.
[56] *Sermons*, 507.
[57] *Sermons*, 507, emphasis added.
[58] *Sermons*, 477, 484, 507, 496.
[59] *Sermons*, 496–7. See, also, *Sermons*, 498.

able to show something of David's fall by revealing Uriah in such a contrasting and positive light.

However, there is more to Uriah in Calvin's reading of the text. He presents him as a prophet of God and this is where the doctrine of providence comes to the fore in his handling of the narrative. At the juncture where Uriah adamantly refuses to sleep with Bathsheba, Calvin makes the point that it was God who controlled his feelings. Indeed, more formally, Uriah had been prevented from sleeping with Bathsheba 'by the secret counsel of God'.[61] The reformer concludes that 'it is certain that when Uriah refused to go into his house, it was a just judgement of God on David, *to lead him to recognise his sin*'.[62] The italicised words show that Calvin (understandably) expounds the narrative with David as the central and determining character. All other characters (including Uriah) are significant only as they serve the king's situation of downfall and gracious restoration. When Uriah speaks to David, Calvin is convinced that he has been instructed by God: '[I]t is certain that God placed these words in the mouth of Uriah *in order to keep David more than convicted*.'[63]

This whole construct that Calvin pursues appears to corner him, and naturally throws up what appears to be an insurmountable question on the nature of God's love for his own people. We have already seen that Calvin realises this. He recognises that if Uriah was doing nothing less than faithfully carrying out that which the Lord had given him to do, why does he die so ignominiously?

Having asked the hard question, we find that Calvin teaches the opposite of the conclusion to which he appears to be coming. He says that far from teaching us that it is pointless to serve God, Uriah's death shows that this world is not our rest and that there is such a thing as eternal life. 'Indeed, there must be a better life than this one, for otherwise we would have to say that God was asleep in the heavens when Uriah was put to death.'[64] Again, notice the implicit reference to providence in this statement. The logic seems to be: If God is not actively involved in human affairs ('asleep in the heavens') the conclusion would be that there is nothing beyond; however, God *is* implicitly involved in Uriah's life (and, significantly, his death) and because God is loving (implied) then Uriah's death must usher in something far better than that which he leaves in this world.

This death serves as an example. In this context 'we see that this death . . . is useful to us, because it is like a mirror which represents eternal life before our eyes'.[65] The wages of the faithful are not received in this life, but in the next. The reformer cites Romans 8.28, 'And we know that in all things God works

---

[60] *Sermons*, 497.
[61] *Sermons*, 493.
[62] *Sermons*, 493, emphasis added. See, also, *Sermons*, 491, 492, 493, 496.
[63] *Sermons*, 499.
[64] *Sermons*, 508.
[65] *Sermons*, 508.

for the good of those who love him, who have been called according to his purpose,' suggesting that 'even death will be our entrance into a better life'. So, he turns a very negative problem to a positive theological conclusion in focusing on the individual eschatology involved. Enjoying God's mercy here in life ought to make us aspire to eternal rest in which we will fully know that goodness. Notice his conclusion:

> This is how we should judge the death of Uriah, and recognise that we most certainly have not been forsaken by God when he takes us to himself, for we must always go home that way. So let us not be surprised or think that God has mocked us in his promises that he wants to be our Saviour.

It is clear from this quote that Calvin has finally resolved the problem of Uriah's death. We would have to say, though, that he does this partly by ignoring the details, by normalising the death and, also, by asserting that it is in that way that God shows himself to be our Saviour (*not* our Enemy).

Reflections

It is apparent that Calvin is deeply concerned with the tragedy of Uriah. It seems to go right to the heart of a pastoral problem, perhaps *the* central pastoral question: Is God ultimately *for* his people? The reformer questions the God of the promises against the God of Uriah's death. But, finally, Calvin the pastor wants to encourage his listeners in their faith. God is to be vindicated. Pulling the rug from beneath the counter-argument, Calvin asserts that if God were *not* involved in Uriah's death there would be a greater difficulty. It is the divine involvement that assures us that Uriah was not forsaken of God (as it appears on the surface), but was mercifully taken to his eternal rest. Uriah's death was not punishment or abandonment, but rather blessing.

Conclusion

A few closing remarks might be made by way of conclusion. First, it is clear that in reading these narratives Calvin refuses to take the easy way out by ignoring the difficulties. Indeed, in each case we have discovered his acceptance of the inherent difficulty, though in the situation concerning Ananias and Sapphira he targeted the problem from the perspective of others. The reformer struggles to handle the problem in the Uzzah and Uriah narratives.

Second, we have noted that there is in the reformer's approach a casuistic analysis in which Calvin assigns blame. It appears that these narratives are dealt with more easily if culpability can be apportioned. The deaths of Ananias and Sapphira become less of a problem for Calvin by the reformer's insistence on the enormity of their crime. Uzzah's death is 'legitimised' by drawing on the reformational idea of *vocatio*, suggesting that Uzzah went beyond its boundaries. Uriah's death, of course, proves more problematic, but (naturally) the reformer still refuses to blame God.

Third, we have pointed out that Calvin's reading strategy includes introducing theological ideas. Interestingly, the reformer, himself, alludes to this in his treatment of Uzzah's death.

> Our glasses are doctrine. Through these glasses of true doctrine, we fear God and interpret his works. . . . Thus, when we have the Word of God to regulate our sense towards a proper appreciation of his works, then our judgement is right. When God exercises his judgement, we will say that it is just and equitable, and we will bow our necks beneath his yoke; we will make no complaint.[66]

The doctrine of providence is explicit in Calvin's comments on Acts 5 and Uriah's story, but it is clearly beneath the surface of his remarks on the other passage. This may appear to point to divine culpability, but the reformer's understanding is more complex than that and allows for a 'diversity of purpose' that leaves Ananias, Sapphira and Uzzah all guilty before God and without excuse.[67] At other times Calvin draws upon the ideas of *coram Deo*, *vocatio*, personal eschatology, God's wisdom and so on, in an attempt to make sense of the narratives.

Finally, it is worth noting that each death narrative forms an example for those who follow. Calvin's pastoral intention is to go beyond the text, as such, and to apply even these disturbing tales to his own people in Geneva. In that setting it is worth getting the reading strategy sufficiently watertight in order to move on to the purpose for which the passage is related, the up-building of believers in every subsequent age.

---

[66] *Sermons*, 260.
[67] See Paul Helm, *John Calvin's Ideas* (Oxford: OUP, 2004) 100. See, generally, 93-128.

CHAPTER 14

The Trinitarian shape of Calvin's theology and exegesis of Scripture

Guenter ('Gene') Haas

It has been noted by a number of scholars that Calvin's theology is 'thoroughly Trinitarian,'[1] and that his thought is structured by this doctrine.[2] Various published works have recognized that Calvin frames and expounds numerous doctrines in a Trinitarian manner, especially those constituting the divine work of salvation. Works on this theme have tended to focus on Calvin's *Institutes*,[3] with references to Trinitarian exegesis in his commentaries having a relatively minor place.

It is the intent of this chapter to contribute to Calvin scholarship by giving closer attention to the Trinitarian nature of Calvin's thought, both in his theology, but especially in his exposition of Scripture. This is done by examining the wide use that Calvin makes of the economic activity of the divine persons in expounding the doctrines of his systematic theology and in his exegesis of biblical passages that address these major doctrines. Of course, such a presentation constrained by the limitations of this publication must be selective in its references to the doctrine in the *Institutes* and to Calvin's commentaries. Yet, it is sufficient to demonstrate how extensively the doctrine of the Trinity informed his dogmatics and his exegesis of Scripture.

---

[1] I. John Hesselink states that Calvin 'was indeed theocentric, Christocentric, and pneumacentric, but all this says is that Calvin was thoroughly Trinitarian'—'Calvin's Theology' in D.K. McKim (ed.), *Cambridge Companion to John Calvin* (Cambridge: CUP, 2004), 79.

[2] Colin Gunton, *Father, Son and Holy Spirit: Essays toward a Fully Trinitarian Theology* (London: T. & T. Clark, 2003), 7; J.I. Packer, 'Calvin the Theologian' in G.S. Duffield (ed.), *John Calvin: A Collection of Distinguished Essays* (Grand Rapids: Eerdmans, 1966), 169; James B. Krohn, 'The Triune God Who Speaks: Calvin's Theological Hermeneutics,' *Koers* 66, 61.

[3] For example, see Alexandre Ganoczy, 'Observations on Calvin's Trinitarian Doctrine of Grace' in E.A. McKee and B.G. Armstrong (eds), *Probing the Reformed Tradition: Historical Essays in Honor of Edward A. Dowey, Jr.* (Louisville, Kentucky: WJKP, 1989), 96-107; Krohn, 'Triune God'; Philip W. Butin, *Revelation, Redemption, and Response: Calvin's Trinitarian Understanding of the Divine-Human Relationship* (New York: OUP, 1995).

ASPECTS OF REFORMING

This study begins by presenting Calvin's understanding of the relationship between his theology, as systematized in his *Institutes*, and his biblical commentaries. Second, we examine the key characteristics of Calvin's method of biblical exegesis. Third, I give a brief exposition of his doctrine of the Trinity, noting its key features, as found in the *Institutes*. Fourth, we survey a number of doctrines in the *Institutes*, highlighting the Trinitiarian manner whereby he explains them. Finally, this chapter examines the various passages in Calvin's commentaries in which he makes use of the Trinity to expound these passages in a manner consistent with both his exegetical method and his Trinitarian theological commitments. It is evident that his Trinitarian exegesis allows Calvin to unfold the richness of believers' relationship to God across a wide range of biblical and theological themes.

The relationship between Calvin's *Institutes* and his commentaries

In the preface to his greatly expanded second edition of the *Institutes* (1539), a preface which he included with only minor revisions in all subsequent editions of the work, Calvin clearly states his understanding of the relation between his systematic theology and his biblical commentaries.[4] Although the focus of the Christian life is the Bible, one can easily lose one's way if one does not have much practice in reading it. So, the *Institutes*, as the 'sum of Christian doctrine,' is the 'key to open a way for all children of God into a good and right understanding of Holy Scripture'. The *Institutes* does this in several ways. First, it serves to prepare and instruct people, especially candidates in sacred theology, 'for the reading of the divine Word, in order that they may be able to have easy access to it and to advance in it without stumbling'. Second, it guides the reader to know what to seek in Scripture and to what end to relate its contents.[5] Finally, the extensive theological instruction in the *Institutes* allows Calvin to have concise commentaries on the biblical texts that need not expound doctrinal matters. If people desire a deeper understanding of theological matters after reading his commentaries, they can consult the *Institutes* for this.[6]

Thus, Calvin views the relationship between the *Institutes* and his commentaries as complementary, as Thompson notes, 'by design intertwined and interdependent'.[7] The *Institutes* assumes the whole of Scripture in formulating its theology. The commentaries expound the biblical text according to the flow of the particular books. When readers use the *Institutes* as their theological guide

---

[4] John T. McNeill notes that the final paragraph of the Preface to the *Institutes* (1559) is essentially the same as the Preface to the 1539 edition. See *Inst.* 20.5n.4.

[5] *Inst.*, preface, 4. In the Preface to the French edition (1560), Calvin maintains that Scripture reveals the 'perfect doctrine' in which the 'infinite treasures' of God's wisdom are revealed (6).

[6] *Inst.*, preface, 4-5, 7.

[7] John L. Thompson, 'Calvin as a Biblical Interpreter' in McKim, *Cambridge Companion to John Calvin*, 61-62.

for the whole of Scripture, they can rightly interpret the teachings of specific biblical texts properly.[8] The commentaries assume that the reader consults the *Institutes* to gain a deeper understanding of doctrines mentioned in the biblical text.[9] So, when read together, the commentaries need not have elaborate doctrinal formulations, and the *Institutes* need not have detailed biblical exegesis.[10]

The obvious danger is that the *Institutes* might force the biblical text to fit its theological mold. To counter this, Calvin insists that Scripture is the authority over theology and the final judge of the doctrinal content of the *Institutes*. In his Preface to the 1560 French edition Calvin urges the reader 'to have recourse to Scripture in order to weigh the testimonies that I adduce from it'.[11] The clear implication is that if there is clear scriptural evidence for revision of his theology, then this must be done in accordance with the biblical teaching.

Calvin's method of biblical exegesis

Calvin published his first commentary, on Paul's epistle to the Romans, in 1540, a year after the publication of his second edition of the *Institutes*.[12] In the dedication of the commentary to Simon Grynaeus, dated 18 October, 1539, Calvin indicates his method for biblical interpretation. The biblical expositor should be guided by the virtue of 'lucid brevity' (*perspicua brevitate*). The goal should be to reveal 'the mind of the writer'. To do this one should not wander far and wide in one's explanation of the text. Rather, expositions of biblical passages should be concise (*brevitas*) and should make the meaning of the biblical authors' words easily understandable (*perspicuitas*) to the readers. Calvin claims that these exegetical guidelines stand in contrast to the commentaries by

---

[8] See David C. Steinmetz, *Calvin in Context* (New York: OUP, 1995), 19. Thomas F. Torrance, *The Hermeneutics of Calvin* (Edinburgh: Scottish Academic Press, 1988), 70, states concerning Calvin's theological and hermeneutical method: 'The fundamental purpose of theology is to serve the interpretation of Holy Scripture.'

[9] Raymond A. Blacketer, 'Commentaries and Prefaces' in Herman Selderhuis (ed.), *Calvin Handbook* (Grand Rapids: Eerdmans, 2009), 184, notes that after the completion of the final edition of the *Institutes* (1560) Calvin did have more extended discussions of new theological topics in his commentaries which he discovered in the biblical texts, notably, the Pentateuch.

[10] Richard A. Muller, *The Unaccommodated Calvin: Studies in the Foundation of a Theological Tradition* (New York: OUP, 2000), 113-14, notes that Calvin's theology generally arose from the doctrinal challenges that Calvin faced and from the catechetical needs of the church.

[11] Calvin, Preface *Inst.* (1560), 8.

[12] Calvin was obviously working on the second edition of the *Institutes* and on the commentary on Romans at the same time. The opening comments in the Preface of the former and the dedication of the latter give evidence of his thoughts on the distinction between the content of each and on their relationship to each other. John T. McNeill comments in an editorial footnote that Calvin's words to the reader (*Inst.* 1439) were written only two months prior to his words of dedication for the Romans commentary (*Inst.* 20.5n.4).

some of his contemporaries, which he describes as 'long and wordy'. They are inaccessible for 'humbler minds' because they overload readers with exegetical details or long theological discussions.[13] Calvin's goal is to keep his comments condensed and simple, illuminating the intent of the biblical author, and applying the plain or literal sense of Scripture to believers. In this context Calvin, also, appeals to the virtue of *facilitas* to promote a style of writing that is easily understood.[14] If one follows these exegetical virtues, the result is commentaries that function 'for the common good of the church'.[15]

Calvin's exegetical method flows out of his view of the relationship between the theological content of the *Institutes* and the content of the commentaries. In the preface to the French edition of the *Institutes* Calvin observes that his discussion of all the articles of the faith in that work allows him in his commentaries to have 'the greatest possible brevity,' since, if one reads the commentaries through the theology of the *Institutes*, there is no need for long theological explanations in the commentaries.[16] One simply follows the flow of the biblical author as one follows the text of the biblical book.[17] If one has any detailed theological questions, one should consult the *Institutes*. Given this relationship, Parker, rightly, insists that, for Calvin, the exposition of Scripture and dogmatic theology are complementary and equally important activities.[18] The *Institutes* provides the broad frame of reference for the exposition of individual biblical texts, since all texts must be understood within the theological teaching of the whole of Scripture. Of equal importance is the study of individual texts since they enrich and provide content for the topics of theology. Systematic theology

---

[13] *Comm. Rom.* Preface, 2-3.
[14] T.H.L. Parker, *Calvin's New Testament Commentaries* (Grand Rapids: Eerdmans, 1971), 51, notes how Calvin connects *brevitas* and *perspicuitas* to *facilitas*, thereby, relating the commentator's writing-style to the goal of making the biblical text understandable.
[15] *Comm. Rom.* Preface, 3. For discussions of Calvin's exegetical method, see Parker, *Calvin's New Testament Commentaries*, 49-68; Thompson, 'Calvin as Biblical Interpreter,' 58-73; Richard C. Gamble, '*Brevitas et Facilitas*: Toward an Understanding of Calvin's Hermeneutic,' *WTJ* 47 (1985), 1-17. Gamble notes that, for Calvin, the justification for a simple style of writing in his commentaries is found in the very style that the Spirit uses through the human authors in Scripture itself (13-15). On this point see, also, R. Ward Holder, 'Calvin as Commentator on the Pauline Epistles' in D.K. McKim (ed.), *Calvin and the Bible* (Cambridge: CUP, 2006), 243-45.
[16] Calvin, 'Subject Matter of the Present Work,' 7.
[17] Randall Zachman, *John Calvin as Teacher, Pastor, and Theologian: The Shape of His Writings and Thought* (Grand Rapids: Baker Academic, 2006), 64, states, 'When interpreting Scripture Calvin follows the order of the context of a particular book of Scripture, allowing the meaning to emerge in a natural and unforced way from the context.'
[18] T.H.L. Parker, 'Calvin as Biblical Expositor' in G.S. Duffield, *John Calvin*, 182. See, also, Elsie Anne McKee, 'Exegesis, Theology and Development in Calvin's *Institutio*: A Methodological Suggestion' in McKee and Armstrong, *Probing the Reformed Tradition*, 168.

must be biblical theology, firmly grounded in Scripture and open to correction by it. The *Institutes* arises out of the exegesis of Scripture, and is subservient to and dependent upon the divine teaching in the Bible.[19] While they have different purposes, systematic theology and biblical commentaries are necessary partners in the divine calling to the church to grow in the knowledge of God.[20]

In the light of this close relationship we can note a number of hermeneutical principles that guide Calvin in his exegesis of Scripture.[21] First, God accommodates the knowledge of himself to human capacity by using language that is adapted to our level, just as nurses 'lisp' when speaking to children.[22] This is most notable in God's revelation of himself to humans as one unified God in three persons, but it is, also, evident in the broad range of his communication with his people in the Scriptures.[23] Second, all of Scripture bears the authority of its author, the sovereign God. The Bible is the Word of God where he is known 'as the Author and Ruler over all that is made, but especially in the person of the Mediator as Redeemer'.[24] Third, biblical exegesis must take account of the two authors of Scripture, the human and the divine. The exegete must take note of the apostles' purposes in writing the particular books in regard to the needs and contexts of the intended readers. But the exposition must, also, attend to the instruction of the Spirit of God, who, while inspiring the human authors, goes beyond their specific designs to speak to the church throughout the age of the gospel.[25] An important point here for Calvin is that the message of the Spirit is not something apart from or beyond the human words.[26] Rather, it is precisely in the words of the human authors that we find the mind of the Spirit.[27] This is why the biblical exegete must be committed to dealing faithfully with the text of Scripture.[28] Fourth, there is an essential unity to the Bible, one covenant of salvation fulfilled in Christ, the Redeemer, which unites the

---

[19] Noted by Steinmetz, *Calvin in Context*, 19. Torrance, *Hermeneutics of Calvin*, 70, states concerning Calvin's theological and hermeneutical method, 'The fundamental purpose of theology is to serve the interpretation of Holy Scripture.'

[20] See David C. Steinmetz, 'John Calvin as an Interpreter of the Bible' in McKim, *Calvin and the Bible*, 291.

[21] Calvin mentions some of these in the dedication to his commentary on Romans. A concise discussion is found in Thompson, 'Calvin as Biblical Interpreter', 61-62. A more thorough study of Calvin's hermeneutics, noting a number of key principles, is found in R. Ward Holder, *John Calvin and the Grounding of Interpretation: Calvin's First Commentaries* (Leiden: Brill, 2006), ch. 2, 'Hermeneutical Principles,' 29-85.

[22] *Inst.* 1.13.1. See, also, *Comm. Gen.* 3.8; *Comm. Ps.* 78.60; *Comm. 1 Cor.* 2.7.

[23] 'God accommodates himself to our limited capacity (*ad modulum nostrum attemperat*) in every declaration which he makes of himself' (*Comm. Rom.* 1.19).

[24] *Inst.* 1.6.1.

[25] The human authors are 'organs of the Holy Spirit', communicating what God intended (*Comm. 2 Tim.* 3.16). In Scripture 'it is God who speaks with us and not mortal men' (*Comm. 2 Pet.* 1.20).

[26] *Comm. 1 Cor.* 1.19.

[27] See *Comm. Rom.* 9.14; *Comm. 1 Cor.* 2.9.

[28] See Parker, *Calvin's New Testament Commentaries*, 99.

Old and New Testaments.[29] This allows for a wide range of biblical passages from which one can draw to explain a particular theme presented in any one text.[30] Fifth, particular biblical texts must be expounded with attention given to the context. This includes the immediate context of the passage, and the context of the book as a whole. Given that God is the author of Scripture who communicates one unified message of salvation to his people, the exegete, also, needs to be aware of the context of the whole of Scripture.[31] Sixth, the exposition of Scripture must serve the good of the church as it serves the cause of the gospel.[32] This principle can, also, be understood in terms of the end of Scripture. For Calvin, the gospel, the Christian life and Scripture all find their end in Christ.[33] Christ can be known only in the Scriptures, and 'the Scriptures should be read with the aim of finding Christ in them'.[34] As Christians do this, they grow into communion with Christ, and they embody more of the life of Christ, resulting in salvation and eternal life.[35] Finally, as already noted, systematic theology, as shaped by the teaching of the whole of Scripture, is the broad frame of reference for explaining the teaching of particular biblical texts. Calvin contends that understanding this broader theological framework allows the reader to know what to seek in specific biblical texts, and how to interpret them properly. One is not distorting the text by appealing to theological themes not specifically mentioned in the text. Rather, one is expounding it by drawing upon the comprehensive doctrine revealed in Scripture.[36]

Calvin rejects the allegorical method of interpreting Scripture. Calvin argues that this approach posits deeper meanings beyond the literal sense of the words, but these are merely the speculations of the interpreters. The true meaning of Scripture is the natural and obvious meaning. Allegorical interpretations take us away from the natural or literal meaning of the words. While there may be occasional texts that invite allegorical readings, such as Galatians 4.24, such an allegorical reading is clearly indicated in Scripture, and is always consistent with the literal meaning of the text. Otherwise, one should stay away from such

---

[29] *Inst.* 2.6.4.
[30] McKee, 'Exegesis, Theology and Development,' 168, notes that this is the strength in Calvin's exegesis.
[31] See Holder, *Calvin and Grounding of Interpretation*, 80.
[32] We have previously noted Calvin's criticism of the commentaries of his contemporaries for not being accessible or useful for busy or less intelligent believers. His goal in his commentary on Romans, and presumably in all his commentaries, is 'for the common good of the church' (*Comm. Rom.* Preface, 3).
[33] Holder, *Calvin and Grounding of Interpretation*, 139-61, discusses the connection between these three.
[34] *Comm. John.* 5.39.
[35] *Inst.*, 3.2.4; *Comm. Gal.* 1.4; *Comm. 1 Cor.* 3.11.
[36] Calvin mentions these principles in his unpublished *Preface to the Homilies of Chrysostom*. Noted by Thompson, 'Calvin as Biblical Interpreter,' 63.

exegesis which is a distortion and corruption of exegesis.[37] It is the natural and plain meaning of the text that provides the mind of the Spirit.[38]

Another key point that Calvin makes about biblical interpretation is that this is not merely the result of the interpreter's learning principles and techniques of exegesis. There is no neutrality in a study of the truths revealed by God. The Spirit must strip away the false presuppositions and inventions of the mind. Calvin states, 'The Word alone will not find acceptance in men's hearts before it is sealed by the inward testimony of the Spirit.'[39] Only those who have received the Spirit of Christ have the internal testimony of the Spirit to assure them of God's goodwill toward them, enabling them to approach God as Father. The knowledge that they have of the things received by faith in Christ depends entirely upon the 'revelation of the Spirit'.[40] So, the proper interpretation of Scripture assumes the conversion of the interpreter's understanding and the assent of the interpreter's will to the promises of the gospel revealed in the Word. The Spirit, who is the author of Scripture, has the task of 'sealing our minds with that very doctrine which is commended by the gospel'.[41]

As we consider the various hermeneutical principles which guide biblical exegesis of Scripture, we note a number of preliminary implications for Trinitarian exegesis. First, an understanding of the Trinity in Scripture must involve God's accommodating his revelation to our finite human capacity. Indeed, it is precisely in his introductory comments to the doctrine of the Triune God where Calvin notes this principle of divine accommodation. Second, in bearing the authority of the divine author Scripture must be accepted as the authoritative revelation of the nature and activity of the Triune God. While the Spirit is revealed in Scripture as the divine agent of inspiration, all of the persons of the Trinity are revealed both as agents of revelation and as the content of revelation. Third, while Scripture is the product of the human authors, it is precisely through the human words that the Spirit reveals to the readers the nature of God. The interpreter must attend to these words for knowledge of God. Fourth, the essential unity of Scripture means that the whole of the Bible reveals the Triune God. While God as a Trinity of persons is not fully revealed until the New Testament, the Old Testament can be read through the fullness of the revelation of God in the New. Even so, one must not engage in fanciful speculation or the use of allegory, especially in reading the Old Testament, but one must attend to the specific content of the words of the text. Fifth, attention to the immediate context of a passage unfolds its meaning. But the context of the whole of the biblical revelation completes its meaning, especially in unfolding the activity of the Triune God. Since creation, revelation and salvation are Trin-

---

[37] *Comm. Gal.* 3.22. See, also, *Comm. Gen.* 2.8; *Comm. Is.* 33.18; *Comm. Jer.*31.24; *Inst.* 2.4.19.
[38] Parker, *Calvin's New Testament Commentaries*, 67-68.
[39] *Inst.*, 1.7.4.
[40] *Comm. 1 Cor.* 2.12.
[41] *Inst.* 1.9.1.

itarian activities, the interpreter can place the specific meaning of a text within the framework of the whole activity of God. Sixth, the principle that biblical exposition must serve the good of the church as it serves the cause of the gospel places Christ at the centre of the understanding of Scripture. For Calvin, union with Christ is the heart of the gospel, and, therefore, at the heart of the Christian life.[42] Salvation is always a Trinitarian matter. It is by the power of the Spirit that we are united to Christ so that we may have God as our Father. In other words, participation in Christ always involves participation in the community of the Trinity, which, also, involves membership in the ecclesial community.[43] Finally, it is the systematic theology of the *Institutes* that provides the broad theological framework for the interpretation of Scripture. The formulation of the doctrine of the Trinity as forged in the councils of the Church, as shaped by the whole teaching of the Bible, and as formulated in Calvin's theology provides the Trinitarian shape to the formulations of many doctrines of theology.[44] And it, also, plays a significant role of shaping the interpretation of the activities of the Triune God revealed in Scripture.

The doctrine of the Trinity in Calvin's *Institutes*

Calvin's doctrine of the Trinity in the *Institutes* 1.13 serves as the culmination of his discussion of the knowledge of God and the knowledge of self in 1.1-12. His Trinitarian theology is essentially Western and Augustinian.[45] God is one, simple, indivisible being, in whom there is a distinction between three persons or hypostases.[46] The Father, Son and Holy Spirit are equal in deity.[47] Calvin makes little reference to the traditional Old Testament texts to which medieval exegetes appealed for the Trinity.[48] Calvin appeals to the traditional New Testament Trinitarian passages, Matthew 28.19 and Ephesians 4.5. He argues that, if we are initiated into the faith of God through baptism (Eph. 4.5), the name of the one true God is indicated by the baptismal formula (Matt. 28.19). Thus,

---

[42] This has been noted by numerous Calvin scholars, such as D. Willis-Watkins, 'The *Unico Mystica* and the Assurance of Faith According to Calvin' in von Willem van 't Spijker (ed.), 77-84, *Calvin: Erbe und Auftrag* (Kampen: Kok, 1991); Dennis E. Tamburello, *Union with Christ: John Calvin and the Mysticism of St. Bernard* (Louisville, KY: WJKP, 1994).

[43] See Julie Canlis, *Calvin's Ladder: A Spiritual Theology of Ascent and Ascension* (Grand Rapids: Eerdmans, 2010), 94-98.

[44] In numerous places Calvin makes reference to his exegetical work being guided by the 'rule of faith' (*regulam fidei*) so as to be in line with the historic catholic church. For example, see *Comm. Rom.* 12.7.

[45] Robert Letham, *The Holy Trinity: In Scripture, History, Theology, and Worship* (Phillipsburg: Presbyterian and Reformed, 2004) 263.

[46] *Inst.* 1.13.1-2.

[47] *Inst.* 1.13.7, 16.

[48] The exception is Genesis 1.26, 'Let us make man in our own image'. Calvin argues that the use of the plural implies the address of the Father to the Son and the Spirit (*Inst.* 1.13.24).

God's essence must reside in the three persons designated, Father, Son and Spirit.[49] Calvin devotes most of the biblical argument in the chapter appealing to the passages where the divinity of Christ and the Holy Spirit are specifically indicated.[50] He, also, notes what these passages indicate about the relationships between the three persons.

The distinction in the persons indicates a distinction in their relations: the Son is begotten by the Father alone, and the Spirit proceeds from the Father and the Son.[51] These distinctions do not involve a hierarchy of divinity, as if the Son and Spirit receive their divine essence from the Father. Rather, each person exists as God 'of himself'. But in respect of his person—for the Son and the Spirit—each one 'exists from the Father'.[52] The distinction of persons should not undermine the unity of the persons. To emphasize this, Calvin indicates his delight in the passage of Gregory of Nazianzus, 'I cannot think on the one without quickly being encircled by the splendor of the three; nor can I discern the three without being straightway carried back to the one.'[53]

While Calvin defends the essence of God as revealed in Scripture and confessed by the teachings of the church, he rejects undue speculation about the mysteries of the Trinity. Scripture does give us some insight into the mystery of the persons of God from eternity. Nevertheless, the biblical focus is on God's activity in relation to this world and humans, that is, on the economic Trinity. Since God has revealed little about his eternal being and the intra-trinitarian relationships, we ought not to attempt to penetrate the mysteries of God beyond the revelation of Scripture.[54] Certainly, for Calvin there is a consistency between God's essential nature and the economy of his dealings with us. But it is not always clear what the revealed activity of the Trinity implies for the essential nature of God.[55] Thus, Calvin maintains the distinction between the imma-

---

[49] *Inst.* 1.13.16.
[50] *Inst.* 1.13.7-15.
[51] *Inst.* 1.13.18.
[52] *Inst.* 1.13.25. A number of authors contend that Calvin's contribution to Trinitarian theology is his clear distinction between God's essence and personhood, and his emphasis on the full deity of the Son and the Spirit over against subordinationist tendencies evident in the Nicene fathers. See B.B. Warfield, 'Calvin's Doctrine of the Trinity' in Samuel G. Craig (ed), *Calvin and Augustine* (Philadelphia: Presbyterian and Reformed, 1974), 283-84; Thomas F. Torrance, *Trinitarian Perspectives: Toward Doctrinal Agreement* (Edinburgh: T. & T. Clark, 1994), 54; Douglas F. Kelly, 'The True and Triune God: Calvin's Doctrine of the Holy Trinity; *Institutes* 1.11-13' in David W. Hall and Peter A. Lilliback (eds), *A Theological Guide to Calvin's Institutes: Essays and* Analysis (Phillipsburg: Presbyterian and Reformed, 2008), 77-78.
[53] *Inst.* 1.13.17. The quote is from Gregory's work, *On Holy Baptism*, oration xl. 41.
[54] Charles Partee, *The Theology of John Calvin* (Louisville: WJKP, 2008), 69, rightly, notes that for Calvin the doctrine of the Trinity is not designed to explain but to protect the mystery of the biblical revelation of God as Father, Son and Spirit.
[55] *Inst.* 1.13,21. Noted by Arie Baars, 'The Trinity' in Herman Selderhuis (ed.), *The Calvin Handbook* (Grand Rapids: Eerdmans, 2009), 254-55.

nent and economical Trinity, and places his own theological emphasis on the activity of the persons of God in the outworking of creation, revelation and redemption.[56]

Calvin recognizes that there is an order to the persons of God, in what we currently call the immanent Trinity: the Father is first, then from him the Son, and, finally, from both the Spirit. Consistent with this, there is, also, an order to their activity, what we currently designate as the economic Trinity: 'to the Father is attributed the beginning of activity, and the fountain and wellspring of all things; to the Son, wisdom, counsel and the ordered disposition of all things; but to the Spirit is assigned the power and efficacy of that activity'.[57] This order must be seen in the context of the unity of the three in all the works of God, for the works of the Father, Son and Spirit are connected to each other quite harmoniously.[58] So, it is in the accomplishment of these works that the cooperative activity of the persons of God is evident according to the revealed order between them.

Calvin indicates in the *Institutes* how he understands the biblical designations for God in Scripture.[59] When the name of God alone is mentioned, he understands this to designate all three persons of the Trinity. But when the name of God is mentioned in association with either the Son or the Spirit, or both, he understands the former to be referring to the Father. Concerning the term 'Lord,' Calvin notes that it sometimes is used as equivalent to the Old Testament term, 'Jehovah'. Other times 'Lord' refers to Christ, the Mediator. It is the context that directs the reader. Nevertheless, the reference to the activity of one person always implies the activity of the other two.

The Trinitarian shape of Calvin's theology

In his introductory remarks to the final edition of the *Institutes*, Calvin describes three goals for this work of theology.[60] First, he aims for brevity and simplicity of teaching as the most effective way of instructing the readers. He strives to help 'simple folk . . . in order to guide them and help them to find the sum of what God meant to teach us in his Word'.[61] Second, he strives to be comprehensive in the theology that he presents, that is, to unfold 'the sum of religion in all its parts'.[62] This is the result of his drawing upon the teaching of the whole of Scripture, faithfully handling the Word of God, so as to produce a complete doctrinal formulation of the Christian faith. Third, he aims to present

---

[56] Paul Helm, *John Calvin's Ideas* (Oxford: OUP, 2004), 46-50, argues that one must not identify the immanent and economic Trinities in Calvin's theology.
[57] *Inst.* 1.13.18.
[58] Baars, 'The Trinity,' 351.
[59] *Inst.* 1.13.20.
[60] Noted by Zachman, *Calvin as Teacher*, 86-95.
[61] Calvin 'Subject Matter of the Present Work [1560],' 6.
[62] Calvin, 'John Calvin to the Reader [1559],' 4.

the doctrines in such a way that each builds upon previous ones, and logically leads to those that follow.[63] In other words, he instructs the readers in such a way that they are persuaded of the truth of the teaching of Scripture in a systematic manner.

To accomplish these three goals Calvin makes use of the doctrine of the Trinity as a prominent paradigm to shape his theology.[64] This is obvious in his use of the Trinitarian structure of the Apostles' Creed, beginning with the second edition of 1539, as the general outline for the *Institutes*. The Trinitarian framework is clear in the titles of the four books of the 1559/1560 edition. Book One deals with 'The Knowledge of God the Creator'; Book Two deals with 'The Knowledge of God the Redeemer in Christ'; and Books Three and Four deal with the manner in which the Spirit applies the benefits of Christ to believers, and whereby the Spirit brings believers into and sustains them in the church of Christ. Through the use of this Trinitarian paradigm for his theology, Calvin sets forth the relationship between God and humans, and unfolds the implications of this for the broad range of beliefs and practices in the Christian life.[65]

Calvin begins the *Institutes* by noting the twofold knowledge of God (*duplex cognitio Dei*) available to humans: knowledge of God as Creator and knowledge of God as Redeemer 'in the face of Christ'.[66] Though God continues to reveal himself in creation, sin has corrupted humans so that they are unable rightly to know God in this revelation. God can only be known in Scripture, in and through faith and repentance in Christ,[67] confirmed by the 'inward testimony of the Spirit'.[68] Only the work of God in us opens us up to the true knowledge of God as a Trinity of persons.[69] This, in turn, opens humans up to the knowledge of all of the works of the Triune God. Thus, knowledge of the Trinitarian economy of redemption in Christ is the prerequisite for all knowledge of God.[70]

It is sin that has resulted in the need for the Trinitarian revelation and for the knowledge of God the Redeemer as the prerequisite for the knowledge of God the Creator. Prior to his fall into sin Adam was 'united and bound to his Maker' and blessed by his 'participation in God'.[71] When he broke his communion with God through his sinful rebellion, Adam broke this communion and fell from the

---

[63] Calvin 'Subject Matter of the Present Work [1560],' 8.
[64] See above, ns1-3.
[65] Noted by Butin, *Revelation*, 19.
[66] *Inst.* 1.2.1.
[67] *Inst.* 1.4.1-2.
[68] *Inst.* 1.7.4.
[69] *Inst.* 1.13.2.
[70] See Edward Dowey, *The Knowledge of God in Calvin's Theology* (New York: Columbia University Press, 1952), 46.
[71] *Inst.* 2.1.5.

uprightness of his original nature.[72] The restoration of the image in salvation involves a restoration to the state of being 'united with God'. Through the redemptive work of Christ humans are conformed to God 'by the grace and power of the Spirit'.[73]

For Calvin, both sin and salvation are framed within a Trinitarian paradigm. Sin results in the loss of communion with the Triune God. The image of God in humans, once upright, has been so deformed so that humans have lost the ability to know God or to recognize him in creation. Only Christ, 'the most perfect image of God,' can restore our image in salvation to its original integrity.[74] This activity of restoration to the Triune God through the restoration of the image of God in us is, also, a Trinitarian activity, for it is in and through Christ that 'man is made to conform to God by the grace and power of the Holy Spirit'.[75]

Calvin unfolds the various aspects of the divine work of salvation in a Trinitarian fashion. He presents the general framework of redemption as follows: 'the efficient cause of our salvation consists in God the Father's love; the material cause in God the Son's obedience; the instrumental cause in the Spirit's illumination, that is, faith; the final cause in the glory of God's great generosity'.[76] God's work of election is, also, apparent as a Trinitarian activity. Election has its source in the gracious love of God for sinners. Christ is the agent of redemption by his death on the cross. Through our union with him Christ reconciles us to God and grants us assurance of God's favour.[77] It is the Spirit who works regeneration in us through faith and confirms that we are adopted as God's children.[78] Calvin argues that the divine initiative in election does not destroy the human will, but rather renews the divine image in humans so that by God's electing grace the new nature is able to do what God calls it to do. Again, Calvin states this divine-human activity in Trinitarian terms.

> God works in his elect in two ways: inwardly, by his Spirit; outwardly, by his Word. By his Spirit illuminating their minds, and training their hearts to the practice of righteousness, he makes them new creatures, while, by his Word, he stimulates them to long and seek for this renovation. . . . Thus, our Saviour, while declaring that none can come to him but those whom the Father draws, and that the elect come after they have heard and learned of the Father [John 6.44, 45], does not lay aside the office of teacher, but carefully invites those who must be taught inwardly by the Spirit before they can make any profit.[79]

---

[72] *Inst.* 2.2.1.
[73] *Inst.* 1.15.5-6.
[74] *Inst.* 1.15.3-4.
[75] *Inst.* 1.15.5.
[76] *Inst.* 3.14.21.
[77] *Inst.* 2.16.3.
[78] *Inst.* 3.21.7; 3.24.1.
[79] *Inst.* 2.5.5.

We note the nature of the movement of redemption on the divine side and the human side. The redemptive activity of God is consistent with the order of the economic Trinity: from the Father through the mediation of the Son by the power of the Spirit. The human response to redemption is by the power of the Spirit through the mediation of the Son to reconciliation with the Father. This is the pattern followed by Calvin in his exposition of the various doctrines of redemption.

In the opening section of *Institutes* Book 3, where Calvin deals with the manner in which the grace of Christ come to believers, Calvin indicates the key role of the Spirit. The Father has poured out the benefits of salvation upon Christ. But these are useless to us as long as we are separated from Christ. So, the Spirit is the divine agent by which Christ unites us to himself so that we may enjoy all the benefits that the Father has granted to Christ for our sake.[80]

Calvin's explanation of the work of the Spirit in applying to believers the benefits of Christ begins with an exposition of faith for it is 'the principal work of the Holy Spirit'.[81] By faith believers know and receive Christ as he is revealed by the Word and offered to us by the Father. Calvin defines faith in a Trinitarian manner. It is 'a firm and certain knowledge of God's benevolence toward us, founded upon the truth of the freely given promise in Christ, both revealed to our minds and sealed upon our hearts by the Holy Spirit'.[82] Here, we note the Trinitarian order: God grants knowledge of his grace, based upon the redemptive benefits of Christ, made effective in believers by the Spirit. As the human response to God the response of faith is described by Calvin in the reverse order. The Spirit initiates and increases faith in believers so that they might firmly and steadfastly believe in Christ with the result that they are lifted up in mind and heart to the Father, and trust in his promises.[83]

Calvin, also, expounds justification in a Trinitarian manner. The righteousness which believers receive from Christ is the righteousness of his divine nature. But this does not apply to him alone, since the Father and the Spirit, also, share the same righteousness.[84] While Christ, through his sacrifice on the cross, justifies us, 'this work is the common task of the Father and the Holy Spirit'.[85]

Calvin is careful to distinguish justification from sanctification, because the former must always be seen as the gift of God's grace to his people. However, there is a necessary connection between justification and sanctification in that the latter necessarily follows from the former. As we grasp Christ by faith we receive a double grace. First, 'being reconciled to God through Christ's blamelessness, we may have in heaven instead of a Judge a gracious Father'. Second, 'sanctified by Christ's Spirit we may cultivate blamelessness and purity of

---

[80] *Inst.* 3.1.1.
[81] *Inst.* 3.1.4.
[82] *Inst.* 3.2.7.
[83] *Inst.* 3.2.24-25, 34-35.
[84] *Inst.* 3,11,8.
[85] *Inst.* 3.11.9.

life'.[86] Calvin describes the process of growth in the Christian life as an ongoing process of repentance and vivification. Here, again, he puts this in Trinitarian terms. We can only apply ourselves to repentance if we know that we belong to God, that is, that God is propitious to us in Christ. The result of our embrace of Christ by faith is that he communicates the Spirit to us so that the Spirit may reign in us in the call to holiness. So, the second aspect of the Christian life consists of the vivification of the Spirit, who creates in us the desire to live a holy life in devotion to God.[87]

Calvin presents the biblical exhortation to a virtuous life in light of the salvific activity of the Triune God. We are charged to view ourselves as bound to God not only because he is the source of our lives, but, also, because he has restored us, as adopted children, to himself as our gracious Father. We are called to imitate the example of Christ, who has united us to himself, who has cleansed us with his blood, and who has restored us to God. We are exhorted to strive to have 'God's glory shine through us' because the Spirit has dedicated us as temples to God. Calvin argues that all these activities of our triune God constitute 'the most auspicious foundations upon which to establish' our lives.[88] This Trinitarian formulation expresses the bond and unity between justification and sanctification. But even the work of sanctification is understood by Calvin as the work of all three persons of the Trinity. 'God reforms us by his Spirit into holiness and righteousness of life' through his Son 'to whom he has entrusted the whole fullness of the Holy Spirit in order that by his abundance he may supply what is lacking in his members'.[89]

If the chief work of the Spirit for Calvin is faith, then Calvin maintains that the chief exercise of faith is prayer. Just as faith is the work of the Triune God, so, also, prayer is an activity that is shaped by the activity and promises of the Trinity. Calvin states that the Spirit of adoption who seals the gospel in our hearts moves us to pray confidently to our Father and to pour out our desires to him. We have confidence in our prayers when we pray in the name of Christ, our Advocate, that God is a gracious Father who attends to our requests. Specifically, we have access in prayer to all the heavenly treasures that God offers us in Christ for we have the assurance that our heavenly Father will not withhold good gifts from his children.[90]

In Book 4 Calvin deals with the external means, namely the church and its sacraments, whereby God draws us into and sustains us in the body of Christ. Here, again, we note the various ways that Calvin unfolds the church and its ordinances in terms of the action of the Triune God. The church is central for God's redemptive activity because this is where God gathers his children for

---

[86] *Inst.* 3.11.1.
[87] *Inst.* 3.3.3-5.
[88] *Inst.* 3.6.3.
[89] *Inst.* 3.11.12.
[90] *Inst.* 3.20.1-2, 17-20.

their nourishment and guidance through the preaching of the gospel and the administration of the sacraments.[91]

Calvin defines the elect church as 'all those, who by the kindness of God the Father, through the working of the Holy Spirit, have entered into fellowship with Christ'. They are 'set apart as God's property and personal possession'. With God as their common Father and Christ as their common Head, the Spirit prompts believers in the community of love to share the benefits that God has conferred on them with one another.[92] Calvin acknowledges that not all members of the visible church who have made a verbal profession of faith are among the elect. Some are hypocrites who only have the outward forms of religion. The true members of Christ are 'those who are children of God by grace of adoption and true members of Christ by sanctification of the Holy Spirit'.[93]

For Calvin, the true worship of God by the church is the worship offered by those reconciled to God in Christ. This implies that true worshippers are those who have been regenerated by the Spirit of Christ. Calvin notes that believers are called 'a royal priesthood' in 1 Peter 2.9 because in Christ they are able to offer a sacrifice of praise to God. Worship must be offered through our Advocate. 'The Mediator interceding for us is Christ, by whom we offer ourselves and what is ours to the Father.'[94]

Calvin considers the two marks of the true church of Christ as 'the Word of God purely preached and heard, and the sacraments administered according to Christ's institution'.[95] Both offer Christ to those who receive them in faith.[96] Both confirm and strengthen our faith by presenting 'the good will of our Heavenly Father toward us'. The Spirit makes this faith effective by engraving it in our minds.[97]

For Calvin, both sacraments offer God's gracious covenant promises fulfilled in Christ to the recipients who receive them in faith. By the power of the Spirit the sacraments are the testimonies and seals of God's goodwill to us so as to nourish and confirm our faith.[98] Baptism is a sign of our engrafting into Christ, whereby we are cleansed from sin and purified by the regenerating work of the Spirit.[99] We are baptized into all three persons of the Trinity because our merciful Father has sent the Mediator to confer the benefits of salvation, and because we obtain regeneration by Christ's death and resurrection only if we are regenerated and sanctified by the Spirit. So, Calvin states concerning baptism, 'For this reason we obtain and . . . clearly discern in the Father the cause,

---

[91] *Inst.* 4.1.1.
[92] *Inst.* 4.1.3.
[93] *Inst.* 4.1.7.
[94] *Inst.* 4.18.16-17.
[95] *Inst.* 4.1.9.
[96] *Inst.* 4.14.7.
[97] *Inst.* 4.16.10.
[98] *Inst.* 4.14.7-8, 22.
[99] *Inst.* 4.15.1-3.

in the Son the matter, and in the Spirit, the effect, of our purgation and regeneration.'[100] Calvin considers the Lord's Supper our union with Christ through our partaking of the bread and wine in which the body and blood of Christ are offered to us. The elements seal and confirm God's promises of salvation to us in Christ.[101] The benefits of salvation which the Father bestowed upon Christ for the benefit of believers do not come to them through the physical eating of his flesh and blood in the bread and wine. Rather, it is by the secret power of the Spirit that the realities represented in the elements are communicated to believers. Thus, they must trust that in the efficacy of the Spirit to fulfill what is promised in the Supper. Calvin maintains that the death and resurrection of Christ are the substance of the Lord's Supper, and the effects by the Spirit on believing participants are all the benefits which Christ gives to us, especially, redemption, righteousness, sanctification and eternal life.[102]

In our survey of certain key doctrines in Calvin's theology, we have seen that the doctrine of the Trinity permeates his theology. The doctrine does not merely serve to provide an understanding of God that is faithful to Scripture and the confession of the church. This doctrine serves to inform his theology as a whole, and the articulation of the various doctrines. God has revealed himself as Father, Son and Holy Spirit. And God has acted for the redemption of his people according to the Trinitarian economy of salvation. Certainly, Calvin understood Christ to be at the heart of Scripture and at the heart of the divine work of the restoration of fallen humanity. Humans can never experience the love of God apart from the gracious work of Christ, the Redeemer. But the work of Christ is a work in communion with the Father and the Spirit. And the goal of salvation is communion with the Triune God. As a student of Scripture, Calvin had a deep understanding of this. That is why his theology is so thoroughly Trinitarian.

The Trinitarian shape of Calvin's exegesis of Scripture

We now turn our attention to Calvin's exegesis of Scripture to indicate the major role that the Trinity served to guide and frame Calvin's exegesis of Scripture. As this doctrine served as a paradigm in shaping Calvin's theology, so, also, it functioned to direct him in his exposition of numerous passages of Scripture, even when the words of the text did not refer explicitly to the three persons of the Trinity. This section can only present a representative sample of such Trinitarian exegesis. We will examine biblical passages which deal with the topics covered under the previous section on Calvin's theology. These topics are revelation, redemption, the church, baptism and the Lord's Supper.

---

[100] *Inst.* 4.15.6.
[101] *Inst.* 4.17.1-4.
[102] *Inst.* 4.17.8-11.

Revelation

As previously noted, Calvin holds to a twofold knowledge of God (*duplex cognitio Dei*) available to humans: knowledge of God as Creator and knowledge of God as Redeemer in Christ. Because of the corrupting effects of sin in all humans, they are able to know God rightly in creation. So, God must reveal himself in Scripture and confirm that this is revelation from him by means of the inward testimony of the Spirit.

Calvin's commentary on 2 Peter 1.19-21 recognizes that the Spirit is presented as the agent of revelation of the prophecy of Scripture, which Calvin understands as 'what is contained in Holy Scripture'. Scripture originates from God, revealing the fulfilment of the mysteries of his promises. This fulfilment is revealed in the truth of the gospel, in which 'Christ, the Sun of righteousness' shines forth. We can only discern 'the mysteries of God' in Scripture when we put aside our 'carnal understanding and subject ourselves to the teaching of the Holy Spirit'. The result is that the light of Christ comes to those who humble themselves before God and live 'in obedience to the guidance of the Spirit'. There are two notable features of Calvin's theological interpretation of this passage. First, although there is no explicit reference to Christ, Calvin refers to the gospel of Christ as the content of the message revealed by the Spirit through the human authors. Second, Calvin refers to the Spirit's internal work which teaches us the message of Scripture fulfilled in the gospel of Christ.

Another key passage that speaks of the origin and character of Scripture is 2 Timothy 3.16-17. Calvin understands the description of Scripture as 'inspired by God'[103] indicating that in the Bible 'God has spoken to us,' and that the prophets, 'as organs of the Holy Spirit,' stated 'only what they had been commissioned from heaven to declare'. God is the Author of Scripture, and, thus, it bears his authority. The Spirit is the divine agent who communicates divine revelation to humans via the human authors. Calvin notes that this same Spirit 'bears witness to our hearts' of these divine truths, so that 'only those who have been enlightened by the Holy Spirit have eyes to see' the true message of Scripture. Calvin describes the 'profitable' use of Scripture as the knowledge attained through faith in Christ which produces salvation and to a godly and holy life. Again, we observe that, although the passage only makes reference to Scripture as 'inspired by God,' Calvin exegetes the passage in a Trinitarian fashion, with reference to the internal testimony of the Spirit.[104]

This Trinitarian pattern of exegesis is repeated in Calvin's commentaries on other passages that refer to Scripture as divine revelation, but where the emphasis is on Christ. In Calvin's remarks on Ephesians 2.20 where Christ is presented as the 'chief cornerstone' of the church which was 'built on the foundation

---

[103] The Greek word here is Θεόπνευστος. The NIV Bible translates this as 'God breathed.'

[104] There is a reference to salvation through faith in Christ in 2 Timothy 3.15 to which Calvin refers in his comments on 3.17.

of the apostles and prophets,' Calvin notes that it is the Spirit's speaking to us through the mouths of the prophets and apostles that results in the Word of God. Because Christ is the end of the law, and 'the sum of the Gospel,' the faith of the church must be built on the pure doctrine of Christ. If believers want to grow in their knowledge of the Scriptures, 'everything must be directed to Him'. This is why he is the only foundation of the church (on Eph. 2.20).

Commenting on 1 Peter 1.10-11 where the emphasis is on the 'Spirit of Christ' speaking through the prophets in their predictions of the sufferings and glories of the Messiah, Calvin recognizes that the passage teaches that Christ ruled over the prophets' message. Yet, while the prophecies were dictated by Christ, Calvin explains that Christ directed the Spirit from heaven to the prophets so that they proclaimed 'the testimony of the Spirit'. Moreover, we must recognize that the gospel ultimately comes from God (on 1 Pet. 1.10-11). No matter which person of the Trinity is emphasized in Scripture, Calvin's exegetical comments retain the Trinitarian harmony in the process of revelation.

In his comments on the various places where the Gospels record Jesus' words on the knowledge of the Father and the Son, Calvin inevitably makes reference to the Spirit. Consider the following examples. When Jesus says, 'No one knows the Son except the Father, and no one knows the Father except the Son and those to whom the Son chooses to reveal him' (Matt. 11.27), this implies 'guidance of the Spirit'. While the Father makes the Son known and the Son reveals the Father, Calvin notes that it is 'by the Spirit' that our minds are open to that which otherwise would be hidden from us (on Matt. 11.27). Calvin repeats this pattern of including the Spirit in his comments on passages where reference is only made to the Father and the Son concerning Jesus' knowledge, revelation and reconciliation to God (on John 1.14, 6.44-46, 14.10).[105]

Calvin's commentaries reflect his theological understanding that revelation is always a Trinitarian matter. Divine revelation is always the work of the Father, Son and Holy Spirit. Calvin, also, includes references to the internal work of the Spirit. There is no knowledge of the Father through the incarnate Son, as revealed in Scripture, 'till the Spirit of God seal our minds and hearts' (on John 15.27). This Trinitarian economy of self-revelation shapes Calvin's exegesis of passages on this doctrine.

Redemption

Calvin expounds the Trinitarian nature of salvation as rooted in election. Calvin's commentary on the passage on election in Ephesians 1.3-14 in which there is reference to the three persons of the Trinity is an extended discussion of the role each divine person has in the grace of election, whereby God calls and justifies those whom he chooses. Calvin unfolds the 'good pleasure of the will of God' as the efficient cause of salvation in his comments on verses 5-6.[106]

---

[105] *Comm. John* 1.14; *Comm. John* 6.44-46; *Comm. John* 14.10.
[106] *Comm. Eph.* 1.5-6.

Christ is presented as the material cause of salvation, who by his death has reconciled us to God and has appeased the Father toward us in verses 7-12.[107] Calvin concludes this section by presenting the work of the Spirit in sealing the truth of the gospel of salvation in believers' hearts. The Spirit seals our faith in Christ by enlightening the intellect in the gospel and confirming its promises to us: 'For as God promises in His Word that He will be to us a Father, so by the Holy Spirit, He gives us the testimony of His adoption.'[108]

We have previously noted that Calvin considers salvation as consisting in the restoration of the image of God in humans by conformity to the image of Christ. Calvin unfolds this renewal in his comments on passages where all members of the Trinity are mentioned, such as 2 Corinthians 3.17-18. He states that 'the purpose of the Gospel is the restoration in us of the image of God'. This is accomplished by the work of the Spirit whom Christ sends to us. 'Christ is the Spirit because he animates us with the life-giving power of the Spirit.'[109] Calvin makes similar remarks in his commentary on Romans 8.9. The children of God are those who have been renewed into the holiness of Christ, by the Spirit who is equally the Spirit of the Father and the Son. Because Christ is our Mediator, Calvin notes that in this text the apostle wisely moves from the Father to Christ to the indwelling of the Spirit.[110]

Calvin describes this renewal of election in Trinitarian terms even when all three persons are not mentioned. Romans 8.29-30 refers to those whom God predestined 'to be conformed to the image of his Son' resulting in justification and glorification. God adopts people to be conformed to the image of Christ so that they may become heirs of his kingdom. Even though there is no explicit reference to the Spirit in this passage, Calvin makes reference to the work of the Spirit as both inwardly drawing people to Christ and effecting their sanctification in conformity to the image of Christ.[111] Calvin's exegesis is similarly Trinitarian in other passages that are not explicitly so. For example, on John 17.21, where Jesus prays that believers may be one by being united to the Son and the Father, Calvin indicates the role of the Spirit in this. '[W]e are one with Christ . . . because by the power of His Spirit He communicates to us His life and all the blessings He has received from the Father.'[112] Other passages where Calvin's comments refer to the renewing work of the Spirit even though reference is only made to the Father and the Son are John 1.9, John 3.16, Romans 6.9, and 2 Corinthians 4.6.[113]

Calvin's exegesis of Scripture often indicates the Trinitarian nature of the application of redemption to believers whether or not the passage is overtly

---

[107] *Comm. Eph.* 1.7.
[108] *Comm. Eph.* 1.13.
[109] *Comm. 2 Cor.* 3.17-18.
[110] *Comm. Rom.* 8.9.
[111] *Comm. Rom.* 8.29-30.
[112] *Comm. John* 17.21.
[113] *Comm. John* 1.9; *Comm. John* 3.16; *Comm. Rom.* 6.9; *Comm. 2 Cor.* 4.6.

Trinitarian. In John 14.16-17, where all three persons are indicated, Calvin unfolds election as the source of faith. The grace which God bestows on the elect is the grace of the Spirit. Christ, 'our Mediator and Intercessor,' receives the grace of the Spirit from the Father, and bestows the Spirit on believers so that believers receive 'heavenly illumination' through the experience of faith.[114] Commenting on Jesus' words to the Father in John 17.6, 'I have revealed you to those whom you gave me out of the world,' Calvin, again, highlights the Trinitarian nature of election that produces faith. Christ's work is efficacious only for the elect 'by the inward teaching of the Spirit'. '[T]hat faith that flows from the eternal predestination of God' is granted to those who belong to Christ because the Father gave them to him.[115] This theme of election as the Trinitarian source of faith is found in numerous other exegetical comments by Calvin, such as John 17.8, 1 Corinthians 2.5, and 2 Corinthians 3.18.[116]

Calvin presents the nature of faith in his exposition of John 3.16. Faith is receiving Christ 'as he is given to us by the Father'. Specifically, it embraces the reconciliation to God accomplished by the death of Christ and our deliverance from eternal destruction. So, the essence of faith is 'placing Christ before one's eyes and beholding in Him the heart of God poured out in love'. Christ 'regenerates us by His Spirit' so that we receive by faith the divine gifts of pardon and righteousness.[117] We find similar Trinitarian accounts on the nature of faith as embracing the loving promises of God in Christ, and as the result of the renewing and sealing work of the Spirit, in Calvin's comments on John 1.13, 2 Corinthians 1.21-22 and Hebrews 6.4-5.[118]

Calvin, also, describes various facets of salvation in a Trinitarian fashion. This is evident in Calvin's accounts of adoption, justification and sanctification. Concerning Galatians 4.6 Calvin observes that adoption by God is the cause, and that the testimony by the Spirit is the result. It is only by the 'incitement of the Spirit of Christ' that we dare to call God our Father. 'We are the sons of God because we are endowed with the same Spirit as His only Son.'[119] Commenting on Romans 3.21-22 Calvin describes justification as the righteousness of God which we receive from God along with the remission of our sins, all through faith. The efficient cause of justification is the mercy of God; the substance of justification is Christ, and the instrument of justification is faith. Faith is the result of the renewing work of the Spirit, as is evident in the example of Abraham.[120] Similar Trinitarian accounts of justification are found in Calvin's

---

[114] *Comm. John* 14.16-17.
[115] *Comm. John* 17.6.
[116] *Comm. John* 17.8; *Comm. 1 Cor.* 2.5; *Comm. 2 Cor.* 3.18.
[117] *Comm. John* 3.16.
[118] *Comm. John* 1.13; *Comm. 2 Cor.* 1.21-22; *Comm. Heb.* 6.4-5.
[119] *Comm. Gal.* 4.6. A similar Trinitarian account of adoption is found in *Comm. Rom.* 13.14.
[120] *Comm. Rom.* 3.21-22.

comments on Ephesians 2.8-10 and Galatians 2.20.[121] Calvin explains sanctification, as evident in John 17.19, as Trinitarian. 'It is because He consecrated Himself to the Father that His holiness might come to us. . . . God's Spirit cleanses us by the holiness of Christ and makes us partakers of it.' But Christ has, also, presented us to the Father in his own person so that 'we may be renewed to true holiness by His Spirit'.[122] A similar Trinitarian account of sanctification is found in Romans 13.14.[123]

The confidence and assurance that believers have in prayer is presented in a Trinitarian fashion in Calvin's comments on Romans 8.15-17. We dare to call on God in prayer because the Spirit testifies to us that we are children of God. The assurance of our adoption by the Spirit gives us the confidence to address God as Father knowing that he has a 'fatherly love' for us. The basis for this is participation in the inheritance of Christ which he accomplished on the cross. Because we receive this by the grace of God, we pray, not with doubt, but with 'a loud voice to heaven without fear'.[124] Calvin makes a similar point in his exegesis of Galatians 4.6. The testimony of the Spirit to our adoption as children of God convinces us of 'God's Fatherly attitude towards us,' and incites us to dare call God our Father with the 'full confidence' that he hears our prayers.[125]

Although many of these passages on the various aspects of redemption do not refer to the Holy Spirit, Calvin's Trinitarian exposition makes reference to him. This reflects his conviction that the Spirit and Christ belong together, and that to receive one is to receive another. '[T]he Spirit will be found nowhere but in Christ, . . . Nor can Christ be separated from His Spirit.'[126] Calvin, also, recognizes that in Scripture 'the Spirit is sometimes referred to as the Spirit of God the Father and sometimes as the Spirit of Christ without distinction'. There are two reasons for this. First, the Spirit's fullness is poured out on Christ as our Mediator and Head so that each believer might receive a portion from him. Second, 'the same Spirit is common to the Father and the Son, who have one essence'. Thus, they have a common purpose in the economy of salvation.[127]

The church, baptism and the Lord's Supper

Calvin gives a Trinitarian exposition of the nature and unity of the church. He understands Ephesians 1.4-6 to teach that there is one unified church reflecting the unity of Father, Son and Holy Spirit as one God. The church consists of the members of Christ, who are united under the rule of Christ. 'By the Spirit of sanctification, God pours himself forth through all the members of the Church,

---

[121] *Comm. Eph.* 2.8-10; *Comm. Gal.* 2.20.

[122] *Comm. John* 17.19.

[123] *Comm. Rom.* 13.14.

[124] *Comm. Rom.* 8.15-17.

[125] *Comm. Gal.* 4.6.

[126] *Comm. Eph.* 3.17.

[127] *Comm. Rom.* 8.9.

embraces all in His government, and dwells in all.'[128] Expounding John 17.21, Calvin avers that the unity that the church experiences under the rule of Christ is the unity of the Son with the Father the power of which is diffused through the whole body of believers. For 'we are one with Christ . . . because by the power of His Spirit He communicates to us His life and all the blessings He has received from the Father'.[129] The only way that we can know the union between us and Christ, and between Christ and the Father, is when Christ 'pours His life into us by the secret efficacy of the Spirit. And this is the experience of faith.'[130]

The 'living stones' which 1 Peter 3.5 designates as the members of the church are, according to Calvin, those in whom God dwells by his Spirit. They have been united to Christ by faith and have experienced the grace of God in Christ. They alone are able to worship God in a manner that is pleasing to him. He accepts them, not because our worship merits favour with God, but only because of the merit of Christ. '[W]e offer sacrifices through Christ, that they may be acceptable to God.' This is why faith is necessary for the proper worship of God.[131] Calvin expounds Hebrews 12.28 to present the Trinitarian nature of acceptable worship to God as follows: '[W]hen we embrace the Gospel we are given the Spirit of Christ to worship God with reverence and holiness.'[132]

In the description of circumcision as a sign and seal in Romans 4.11, Calvin finds the indication that sacraments are 'testimonies by which God seals His grace on our hearts'. Though not specifically mentioned, this implies the grace of God in Christ. Sacraments are instruments of God's grace 'by the secret grace of His Spirit' who makes them effective in the elect.[133] This is evident in both sacraments. Commenting on the Trinitarian formulation in Matthew 28.16, Calvin describes baptism as a sign and seal of the grace of God's adoption whereby he engrafts us into Christ so as to be part of his flock. Calvin considers it appropriate to mention all three persons in baptism due to the economy of salvation. Because of the free mercy of the Father, he 'reconciles us to Himself through the only-begotten Son'. This is accomplished through the sacrificial death of Christ. This is realized by the Spirit through whom Christ 'cleanses and regenerates us all, and, finally, makes us partakers of all his benefits'.[134] Calvin gives similar Trinitarian explanations in his remarks on Acts 2.38 and 1 Corinthians 1.13. The efficacy of baptism derives from Christ. But 'Christ can-

---

[128] *Comm. Eph.* 4.5-6.
[129] *Comm. John* 17.21.
[130] *Comm. John* 14.20.
[131] *Comm. 1 Pet.* 2.3-5.
[132] *Comm. Heb.* 12.28.
[133] *Comm. Rom.* 4.11.
[134] *Comm. Matt.* 28.19.

not be grasped by faith without the Father by whom He was given to us and the Spirit by whom He renews and sanctifies us'.[135]

In Calvin's extensive exposition of the Lord's Supper in 1 Corinthians 11.23-29 he makes use of the Trinitarian economy. This sacrament is beneficial for those in whom Christ dwells and who are united to him through faith. In our partaking of the bread and wine we are made one with him so that 'He imparts Himself to us . . . by the secret power of the Holy Spirit'. The benefit to the recipients is 'a share in redemption, and the application to us of the benefit of His sacrifice'. The cup of the new covenant in Christ's blood signifies Christ's blood poured out to reconcile believers to God. Calvin comments that 'now we drink it spiritually in order to have a share in that reconciliation'.[136] So, those who partake of the elements worthily, that is, in faith, are assured of the promises of God in Christ, and God's faithfulness to them.[137]

This survey has examined Calvin's exegesis of a number of passages that deal with the same doctrines that we noted previously in his theology. Just as Calvin often gives a Trinitarian shape to his doctrines, so, also, we note the same Trinitarian pattern at work in his exposition of these themes in Scripture. This follows the divine economy of God's dealings with the world and humanity. Revelation and salvation follow the Trinitarian design of God's engagement with men and women: from the Father, through the mediation of the Son, by the power of the Spirit. Human fellowship with the Father occurs in and through Christ, but it is by the power of the Spirit who unites us to Christ that we are reconciled to God. This pattern from God and to God shapes Calvin's exegesis of Scripture. Even when only one or two of the persons of the Trinity are explicitly mentioned, Calvin frequently completes the Trinitarian economy, since the activity of all three make explicit what is implicit in the various aspects of divine salvation. Thus, similar to his theological formulations in the *Institutes*, Calvin's exegesis provides a rich and thorough understanding of the nature of salvation and the benefits that flow to believers from the redemptive activity of the Triune God.

Conclusion

Several observations can be made in the light of the survey of Calvin's Trinitarian formulations of doctrine and his Trinitarian exposition of Scripture. First, as Calvin states in the preface to the *Institutes*, the systematic theology found therein, and specifically the theology of God as a Trinity of persons, shapes Calvin's reading and interpretation of the teachings of Scripture. While Scripture and Calvin's exegetical work remain primary, the theology of the *Institutes* draws upon the teaching of Scripture as a whole to provide a framework for reading individual passages correctly. This prevents a misreading or distortion

---

[135] *Comm. Acts* 2.38. See, also, *Comm. 1 Cor.* 1.13.
[136] *Comm. 1 Cor.* 11.25.
[137] *Comm. 1 Cor.* 11.27.

of individual texts when interpreted in isolation for the teaching of the whole of Scripture. The Trinitarian economy of salvation serves as the overarching context for understanding specific biblical texts that deal with specific facets of God's redemptive work and the means of grace. The parts must always be read and applied in the context of the whole.

Second, Calvin's Trinitarian exegesis of Scripture does not necessarily contradict his stated goal of 'lucid brevity' in his commentaries. On the surface, his references to the activity of the persons of the Trinity when they are not explicitly mentioned in passages may appear to be going beyond the words of the author. But, as noted in the section on Calvin's exegesis, one of Calvin's hermeneutical principles is that one is dealing not simply with a human author but, also, with the divine author. That which the divine author reveals in one section of Scripture must take into account the whole teaching of Scripture by that same divine author. With reference to the Trinity, Calvin states that any thoughts on one person of the Trinity should immediately involve a consideration of all three. This, also, applies to their activities, since the three persons cooperate in the works of creation, revelation and salvation. Thus, when a text refers to the activity of only one or two members of the Trinity, it is consistent with the united activity of the three to make explicit the activity of the Father, Son and Spirit. In filling out the meaning of the text Calvin can still be considered as conforming to his exegetical goals.

Third, Calvin's Trinitarian exegesis of Scripture allows him to indicate the interrelationships between a wide variety of seemingly diverse texts.[138] Unfolding various texts according to the Trinitarian economy of salvation allows Calvin to draw connections between revelation, sin, election, restoration of the image of God, justification, sanctification, prayer, the church, worship, and the sacraments. This theological framework of the activity of the Trinity embodied in the exegesis of various texts builds an understanding of the Bible that is comprehensive and coherent.

Finally, both Calvin's Trinitarian formulation of many doctrines of theology and his Trinitarian exegesis in Scripture reinforce the consistency between his theology and his exegesis of Scripture. If the articulation of the economy of salvation is faithful to the teachings of Scripture, then the exposition of Scripture according to the work of the Father, Son and Holy Spirit serves to shed light on the meaning of various passages of Scripture. Each serves to reinforce the truthfulness of the other. Of course, there is a danger here that this may become a 'closed circle,' which forces biblical texts into a preconceived theological mould. But this danger exists for any biblical exegete, since no one can avoid assumptions, theological or otherwise, in interpreting biblical texts. The key point is that theological assumptions and paradigms used in the exposition of biblical texts are confirmed insofar as they accurately unfold the meaning of

---

[138] McKee, 'Exegesis,' 168, makes this point about Calvin's theological exegesis of Scripture.

the texts. The evidence presented in this chapter suggests that Calvin's Trinitarian exegesis of Scripture serves to reinforce the truthfulness of the Trinitarian formulation of his theology.

In conclusion, this chapter has given abundant evidence of the prominent role of the doctrine of the Trinity in Calvin's theology and exegesis of Scripture. Calvin considered it of central importance to understand the Christian faith in terms of the Triune God who has spoken and acted for the salvation of his people. This means that our knowledge of God via Scripture and theology necessarily has a Trinitarian structure. Moreover, salvation has to do with more than merely knowledge about the Triune God. It consists of our knowing and being reconciled to God as Father, Son and Holy Spirit. If this is the central message of Scripture, then it should be central to our theology. For Calvin, both the theologian and the biblical exegete must do their work, not as detached observers, but as those who have experienced the promises of God in Christ. As such, their calling is to engage in theology and biblical exegesis to lead the readers to an encounter with the Triune God. That is why for Calvin, the Trinity is central to his theology and biblical exposition. For in both endeavours one is unfolding and proclaiming for the readers the salvific activity of the Triune God.

CHAPTER 15

Reformed worldviews and the exegesis of the Apocalypse

Rodney L. Petersen

Seismic social changes swept through the sixteenth century. These have been channeled in our time by the residue of churches, political assumptions, cultural institutions, and the patterns of understanding left behind. While spirited renewal movements have continued to emerge since the sixteenth century, the West has lived in the light of patterns set down then.[1] No where is this more true than with historical consciousness. The book of Revelation, the Christian Apocalypse, has often been the lens through which history has been read. Its imagery of trumpets, seals and bowls of wrath have fired the imagination of temporal progression toward end-time judgment even as its depiction of final prophets and the lion who is a lamb offer intimations of consolation.

Visions of renewal, restoration, or reform have been a part of that historical vision, shaped by the Apocalypse. In the sixteenth century much of this visionary and imaginative work swirled around questions of final prophets (e.g., Rev. 11) portending an end to history or, at least, marking visions of what true social and religious reform might mean as it coalesced around the work of various reformers.[2] While we usually mark the beginning of the reformation with Martin Luther, significant historical thinking for purposes of social renewal as derivative of the Apocalypse and its vision of end-time prophets can find a point of departure in Zürich and with the civic religious reformer Heinrich Bullinger.[3] The pattern for defining prophecy in Zürich became a model for the Reformed in the Swiss German and Rhineland centers of Reformation and beyond.[4]

---

[1] Diarmaid MacCulloch, *The Reformation* (New York: Viking, 2003), 674-83.
[2] This essay is a reworking of material found in my study, *Preaching in the Last Days: The Theme of Two Witnesses in the Sixteenth and Seventeenth Century* (New York: OUP, 1993).
[3] See Peter Opitz, *Heinrich Bullinger als Theologe* (Zürich: Theologischer Verlag Ag, 2004).
[4] Philippe Denis, 'La Prophétie dans les églises de la Réforme au XVle siècle,' RHE, 72 (1977), 289-316. Cf. G.R. Potter, *Zwingli* (Cambridge: CUP, 1976), 211-24.

The company of prophets

Commenting on Revelation 11, Heinrich Bullinger notes that in the previous thirty years a company of prophets (*communis prophetia*) like Mirandola, Reuchlin, Erasmus, Luther, Zwingli, Oecolampadius, Melanchthon and 'innumerable others' have arisen to take up the prophetic mantle. Many have stepped forward to prophesy with the new vernacular Bible in hand, thus raising a question about the definition of prophecy, of prophetic legitimacy and of the nature of renewal or reform.[5]

Turning first to the city of Zürich, it was in this early Reformed setting that Luther was first referred to as an 'Elijah,' and by Zwingli, raising the question of whether this implied moral reform or an end-time witness to some greater renewal. What motivated Zwingli? Was it the same series of events that may have caused Thomas Müntzer to begin his reputed apocalyptic timetable? The dating is the same, around 1519. In any case, several years later when Zwingli wrote his treatise on the nature of the ministry, *The Shepherd* (*Der Hirt*), there were no references to special prophets or adventual witnesses heralding the end of history. His was an Erasmian and moral reform rather than that set in a particular apocalyptic framework.[6]

Zwingli's answer to the larger question of prophecy is seen, in part, in the institution of the *Prophezei*, which in its very structuring heralded the *viva vox evangelii*, the living word of the gospel, rather than the sacramental altar—to say nothing of end-time scenarios.[7] This institution, symbolic of the Reformed turn from prayer and ritual to prayer and prophecy, functioned without specific

---

[5] Gottfried Locher, 'How the Image of Zwingli Has Changed in Recent Research,' *Zwingli's Thought: New Perspective* (Leiden: Brill, 1981), 61. Bibliographies on the ecclesiology of the reformers can be found in Emile G. Leonard, *A History of Protestantism*. volume 1, *The Reformation* (edited by H.H. Rowley, translated by J.M.H. Reid; London: Nelson, 1965).

[6] On the nature of civic humanism and the reworking of apocalyptic and ideological patterns of thought so as to stress a new human responsibility, see Eugenio Garin, *Italian Humanism: Philosophy and Civic Life in the Renaissance* (New York: Harper and Row, 1965); Hans Baron. *The Crisis of the Italian Renaissance: Civic Humanism and Republican Liberty in an Age of Classicism and Tyranny* (Princeton: Princeton University Press, 1966).

[7] Begun in June 1525, 'prophesyng' took the form of public lectures in the Grossmünster, replacing the former canonical hours of Prime, Terce, and Sext. After canons, the students listened to a sermon in Latin. Then, as further citizens from the city gathered, a sermon was delivered in German. See Locher, 'In Spirit and in Truth,' *Zwingli's Thought*, 27-30; cf. J. Figi, *Die innere Reorganisation des Grossmünstersstiftes in Zürich von 1519 bis 1531* (Affoltern am Albis, 1951), 73-93; Oskar Farner, *Huldrych Zwingli* (Zürich: Zwingli Verlag, 1954), 3.554-63. Note the role of 1 Cor. 14.34. On the deep cultural implications of such civic orientation, or lack thereof, in northern German society, see Lionel Rothkrug, 'Religious Practices and Collective Perceptions: Hidden Homologies in the Renaissance and Reformation,' *Historical Reflections* 7.1 (Spring 1980).

apocalyptic concerns.[8] It focused upon the proclamation of the gospel as God's Word was heard through the exposition and application of Scripture.[9] The concerns of the Christian disciple were to be shaped by the leading themes of Scripture, increasingly the rediscovery of the covenant in relation to the current state of society, more than by the suppositions of an apocalyptic timetable.[10] Parallels were drawn between the contemporary reform of public affairs and the work of the Old Testament prophets who urged national renewal.[11] In his comments on Revelation 10:11, Bullinger, one with Zwingli in the institution of the *Prophezei*, finds a legitimate commission for Reformed ministers (citing I Cor. 11 and 14) by recourse to models of prophetic calling in the Old and New Testaments, not through an apostolic order in history.[12]

The place and function of prophecy

The question of the place of prophecy, of who was appropriately endowed, continued to be a lively issue through the sixteenth century.[13] If looked at through the lens of the Apocalypse some of the key points of tension that arose over the place of prophecy in the Christian community can be discerned. Several commentaries on the Apocalypse in the sixteenth century provide indications for how prophesy was being conceived. We might begin with the work of Francis Lambert of Avignon.

Francis Lambert of Avignon

The Apocalypse commentary by Francis Lambert of Avignon was used to express support for a wide vision of prophecy as being the work of all of God's people. Lambert's commentary on the Apocalypse was the earliest 'Protestant'

---

[8] Rudolf Pfister traces the roots to Bullinger, together with the monks at the Kappel cloister in 1523, and to Zwingli since 1525 at the cathedral in Zürich ('Prophezei,' in RGG V [Tübingen: Mohr, Paul Siebeck, 1961], col. 638); cf. Emil Egli, 'Prophesying' in *The New Schaff-Herzog Encyclopedia of Religious Knowledge* (New York: Funk and Wagnalls, 1911), 9.278; F. Schmidt-Clausing, 'Das Prophetzeigebet: Ein Blick uber Zwinglis liturgische Werkstatt,' *Zwingliana* 12 (1964), 10-34.

[9] The Zürich translation of the Bible resulted from the Prophezei, to be revised in every generation. See 'Die Prophezei' in *Die Züricher Bibel 1531* (Zürich: Theologischer Verlag, 1983), 1383-87.

[10] Locher, 'Huldrych Zwingli's Concept of History' in *Zwingli's Thought*, 102-3. Zwingli speculates on Antichrist's nature (*De vera et falsa religione commentarius* [1525] in CR, 90.894), but not on the witnesses.

[11] Siegfried Rother, *Die religiösen und geistigen Grundlagen der Politik Huldrych Zwingli* (Erlangen: Palm & Enke, 1956), 63-72; cf., Bernd Moeller, *Imperial Cities and the Reformation*, 103-10.

[12] Heinrich Bullinger, *In Apocalypsim conciones centum* (Basel: Oporinus, 1557), 135.

[13] Robert Kolb, *Reformers Define the Church, 1530-1580* (St. Louis: Concordia, 1991); cf., Gert Haendler, *Amt und Gemeinde bei Luther in Kontext der Kirchengeschichte* (Stuttgart: Calwer Verlag, 1929).

commentary on the book of Revelation.[14] Lambert, formerly a Franciscan, travelled to Zürich in 1522, where he sat under Zwingli's tutelage. Moving then to Wittenberg, Lambert found support from Luther. During Lambert's subsequent sojourn in Strassburg, he heard the Strassburg prophets.[15] From there he came finally to Hesse, in 1526, where he was called by Philip, Landgrave of Hesse, to reorganize the Church.[16]

An ardent biblicist and learned philologist, it is tempting to see in Lambert's authorship of commentaries on the prophets of the Old Testament his intent and his concern for prophetic models discerned in Israel's past. When he comments on the Apocalypse at least three things can be noted. First, the focus of the book of Revelation is upon the present life of the Christian. God's prophets convey his consolation and judgment to the contemporary church. Scripture is the rod for doing this. It is held by God's prophets, known by the spiritual qualities and prophetic gifts delineated in Revelation 11.[17] The description of prophetic witnesses found there offers Lambert the opportunity to draw upon prophetic models from the Old Testament.[18] This contributes to the Apocalypse's purpose, the strengthening of the church between the Incarnation and Consummation.[19]

Second, the authority of the Apocalypse is the revelation of Jesus Christ. He is its central story. Everything in Revelation has to do with him, even mystically.[20] The church is Christ's body. The book of Revelation shows us how he rules his church (the Holy Jerusalem)[21] through Spirit, Word, and ministry. Servants of Christ are servants of his Word, the measuring rod (Rev. 11.1).

Third, the *'antichristus mysticus'*[22] is embodied in the papacy and Turk. It is with this identification that time and development enter Lambert's commen-

---

[14] Francis Lambert (d'Avignon), *Exegeseos in sanctum divi Joannis Apocalypsim Libri VII* (Marburg, 1528; Basel, 1539).

[15] Williams hypothesizes that Lambert may have been influenced in laicizing prophecy by the Strasburg prophets, Wolfgang Schultheiss and John Campanus, the latter having written on the topic before 1531. See Williams, *Radical Reformation*, sec. 11.4.

[16] Gerhard Muller, *Franz Lambert von Avignon und die Reformation in Hessen* (Marburg: N.C. Elwert, 1958), 53-69. The Zürich Prophezei was to influence similar institutions, e.g., in the Palatinate, East Friesland, the Netherlands, and, via John à Lasco, England.

[17] Müller cites the first of several 'Paradoxa' put forward by Lambert as official points for debate by the Homberg Synod (Oct. 21-23, 1526). The first item: 'Titulus primus. Omnia reformanda, que deformata. et per quid' (*Paradoxa,* fol. 2v).

[18] Further in the *Paradoxa* (fol. 6r) Lambert writes, 'Fursten und Obrigkeiten sollen mit starker Hand wie Josia ausführen, was jene lehren' (cited by Müller, *Franz Lambert*, 40-41). Contemporary parallels with the rediscovery of the law under Israel's King Josiah, and the reform which followed, will become favorite Protestant themes.

[19] Bullinger, *In Apocalypsim,* fols. 189r-19Iv.

[20] Bullinger, *In Apocalypsim,* fol. 1v; cf. his summary at sig. A7v.

[21] Bullinger, *In Apocalypsim,* sig. A3r; cf. Muller, *Franz Lambert,* 66. Note the trace of Tyconian exegesis in this connection of body and rule.

[22] Wilhelm Bousset, *Die Offenbarung Iohannis* (Gottingen: Vandenhoeck und Ruprecht, 1906), 86.

tary. There is a muted sense of development in his discussion of the seals.[23] In line with the recapitulative method, the seven trumpets parallel the seals, constituting an allegorical description of the true proclamation of the mysteries of God as the seals are opened.[24] When Lambert reaches the fourth seal, he discusses the growth of Turkish power. Both pope and Turk are preludes to a deeper spirit of Antichrist growing in the world. The effect of this is that more weight is given to the key imagery of Revelation 11 than seems implied in the general and spiritual interpretation given the text. Adumbrated under the sixth seal is a picture of the last time, the revival of the gospel and the growth of persecution, illustrated in chapters 11 and 13 of Revelation.[25]

Sebastian Meyer

A second early commentary on the Apocalypse, that by Sebastian Meyer, should be mentioned for the light it sheds on the way in which tribulation is to be handled through the lens of the Apocalypse.[26] Meyer, another former Franciscan, became a minister in the city of Bern. Together with Bertold Haller (1492-1528) he took a lead in the reformation of that city after the disputation of 1528.[27] Casper Megander would further this work of reform by the institution of the *Prophezei* following the example of Zürich. Meyer's commentary adds a clear historical element to the work of the prophets of Revelation 11 in what is otherwise a spiritual and allegorical handling of the text.

Meyer's outline of the Apocalypse is thoroughly Christocentric in its structure. The person and work of Christ defines and shapes the imagery of the text, an illustration of the extent to which Meyer applies Tyconius's rules in an effort to make sense of the book's visions. By doing this, Meyer appears to be telling us that the place of prophecy is in that church that represents Christ. As this is a community in travail, it is one that bears the wounds of Christ, or fills out the sufferings of Christ in its generation.[28] Each portion shows forth some new dimension of Christ and the trials through which his body, the church, goes in time: his presence in the seven churches (Rev. 2-3), his exaltation and the victory of God's people (Rev. 4-7), the constancy of his gospel and his people (Rev. 8-11), the afflictions of his body (Rev. 12-14), new persecutions (Rev. 15-16),

---

[23] Lambert, *Exegeseos*, fols. 117v-149v.
[24] Lambert, *Exegeseos*, fol. 150r.
[25] Lambert, *Exegeseos*, fol. 1125r. and 130.
[26] Sebastian Meyer, *In apocalypsim Johannis Apostoli* (Zürich: Froschouer, 1539); I refer to the edition of 1554 (Zürich: Froschouer). See Bousset, *Offenbarung*, 86-87.
[27] On the bitter anti-papalism and acerbic form of Meyer's efforts at reform, see Steven Ozment, *The Reformation in the Cities* (New Haven: Yale University Press, 1975), 56-61. Ozment cites Oskar Vasella, *Reform und Reformation in der Schweiz. Zur Würdigung der Anfänge der Glaubenskrise* (Münster in Westfalen, 1958), 28-34, 36, 62.
[28] See I Pet. 2.21; 3.12-18—ideas which betray Meyer's Franciscan background.

judgment and damnation (Rev. 17-18), and the marriage of Christ and the church (Rev. 20-22).[29]

There is some sense of temporal development in the visions of the seals, but Meyer appears to be most interested in the way the first five seals illustrate the events of the life of Christ and find a parallel in the church's experience through history.[30] The trumpet visions present an occasion for a discussion of the theme of judgment throughout Scripture. There is little sense of temporal development here until one comes to the fifth trumpet. Muhammad and the papacy ascend out of the bottomless pit (Rev. 9.2) at this point.[31] However, one does not yet find the same desire to correlate vision and event as will be evident in later Protestant writers. When Meyer comes to the two witnesses of Revelation 11, he goes beyond Lambert in his identification of them with the emerging Protestant reform. The witnesses are the few preachers of the gospel throughout history, especially now in the great cities of Germany. Furthermore, he draws in a history of martyrdom under the vision of the slaying of the witnesses by the beast (Rev. 11.7). The list points to Hus, Jerome of Prague, Savonarola, the Fraticelli, the poor men of Lyons, and Bohemian Waldensians.[32]

If this is not the first, it is at least one of the earliest, delineations of a 'history' of proto-Protestantism under the imagery of the Apocalypse. It is a line of development which Bullinger stimulates and to which the early Lutheran apologist and historian Mathias Flacius Illyricus (1520-1575) will contribute as well as the later English playwright and apocalypticist John Foxe (1516/17-1587). Meyer's history of martyrdom comes in a commentary with little explicit interest in correlating prophecy and event. The locus of Revelation 11 is one of the few such places. This has the effect of drawing a parallel between Christ's suffering with that of his body, the church, and the adventual witnesses.[33] Meyer's tropological, or moral, interests pull in a literal reading of our text where he seeks to understand reforming efforts of his time. The adventual witnesses are Christ's body. Under their figure the true church is imaged much as it had been earlier for Tyconius, but now it is identified explicitly as those in opposition to the Roman Antichrist.

---

[29] Meyer, *In apocalypsim Johannis*, sig. A5v.
[30] Meyer, *In apocalypsim Johannis*, fols. 21r-23v. The sixth seal is said to be either the calling of the gentiles or various cataclysms in the church's history.
[31] Meyer, *In apocalypsim Johannis*, fol. 33r. Meyer does add the unloosing of Satan in A.D. 1000 (fol. 80v).
[32] Meyer, *In apocalypsim Johannis*, fol. 42r.
[33] Meyer, *In apocalypsim Johannis*, sig. A5v-A6r; in particular Tyconius's first rule: 'De Dominio et corpore eius.' It might be surmised that Meyer is drawing upon a text like Col. 1.24 in which Paul counsels the Christian to accept suffering in order to complete the sufferings of Christ 'for the sake of the body, that is the Church'.

ASPECTS OF REFORMING

The Academy of Geneva

The place of prophecy as it was defined in the growing pan-Protestant movement, despite its differences as Lutheran or Reformed after 1529, was with the church as the body of Christ and was located in the nascent theological academies.[34] In Strasburg and Geneva, which saw no commentaries on the Apocalypse written by prominent Reformed theologians, particular events promoted a 'regularization' of prophecy at a time when the Lutheran Church visitations were now underway. Strasburg, noted as a center of radical prophetic activity, and of possible significance for the laicization of the *Prophezei*, was the place where Melchior Hoffman, having accepted his role as the Elijah under of Revelation 11, met his end.[35] Reform in Strasburg, as instituted by Martin Bucer and the city officials, sought to regulate any similar or further outbursts of prophetic inspiration.[36] As Spiritualist unrest increased, the City Council placed interdicts upon unauthorized groups gathering to read Scripture outside of the control of Synod and Council.[37] In reaction to this radical prophetism, an official and apocalyptically-restrained definition of prophecy was formulated by Bucer and Wolfgang Capito.[38]

Prophecy was carefully defined and its place located in the Academy of Geneva.[39] Teaching became the form for prophecy at the Academy. It is, also, what was done at weekly meetings of pastors and laity for prayer and the dis-

---

[34] Menna Prestwich, 'Introduction' in *International Calvinism, 1541-1715* (Oxford: Clarendon, 1985), 4.

[35] Hofmann's convert Cornelius Polderman was Enoch to Hofmann's Elijah as reported by Obbe Philips, *Bekenntniss*, BRN, 7.126 (Williams's translation in SAW, 206-25).

[36] Denis develops parallels with the Zurich Prophezei ('Prophétie,' 292-94). See E.W. Kohls, *Die Schule bei Martin Bucer in ihrem Verhältnis zu Kirche und Obrigikeit* (Heidelberg: Quelle & Meyer, 1963), 48, 57-58, 65-66. On reform in Strassburg, see Miriam Chrisman, *Strasbourg and the Reform* (New Haven: Yale University Press, 1967), 81, 98-114.

[37] Chrisman, *Strasbourg and Reform*, 177-201; cf. Manfred Krebs and Hans Georg Rott (eds.), *Quellen zur Geschichte der Taufer, Elsass I und II* (Guttersloh: Gerd Mohn, 1959, 1960), 355, 358-59, for examples. Another example is Wolfgang Schultheyss, who warned the city officials not to neglect prophecy. See his *Ermanung zum geistlichen Urteyl* (1531).

[38] Ozment, *Reformation in the Cities*, 146-48. On Bucer's theology, see August Lang, *Der Evangelienkommentar Martin Butlers und die Grundzüge seiner Theologie* (Leipzig: 1900), 150ff.

[39] Calvin, *Comm. Heb.* 11.5, 161-62. Compare Calvin's commentary on Genesis 5.22-24. Heinrich Quistorp, *Die letzten Dinge im Zeugnis Calvins* (Guttersloh: Bertelsmann, 1941), 116. In addition to an Erasmian doubt, Calvin's aversion to the Apocalypse was occasioned by what he felt was its misuse by the radicals of the reformation. See Otto Weber, 'Calvins Lebre von der Kirche' in *Die Treue Gottes in der Geschichte der Kirche* (Neukirchen: Neukirchen Verlag des Erziehungsvereigns, 1968), 2.103.

cussion of Scripture.⁴⁰ Prophecy as charismatic foretelling was rare and generally limited to the apostolic age. The church during the time of Calvin had Christ; its prophets were tellers of this highest gift. Special prophets and latter-day prophecies were not needed. Peter Martyr, a Florentine reformer at Zürich, Basel, and then Strasburg, cited as evidence the growing numbers of books and numerous teachers of the time.⁴¹

The first edition of Calvin's *Institutes* (1536), following the debacle of Münster (1535-1536), was written both to explain the evangelical faith and to defend the Reform movement from charges of social sedition and ideas characteristic of religious radicalism.⁴² In the Strasburg congregation of French Protestant refugees where Calvin was briefly pastor, some were reportedly Melchiorite sympathizers.⁴³ Calvin was openly critical of their leaders, whom he identified as Thomas Müntzer, Melchior Hoffman and Nicholas Storch.⁴⁴ It is possible that Calvin had in mind not only 'adventual witnesses' like these when he spoke of 'curious men [who] harass themselves,' but, also, Michael Servetus (1511-1553), who prophesied of an imminent third Elijah, drawing upon Revelation 11, in his *Christianismi Restitutio*.⁴⁵ Willem Balke adds that this work may have been a 'countermeasure' to Calvin's *Institutes*.⁴⁶

Without denying God's direction in final temporal events, Calvin's references to last things laid primary stress upon God's judgments in time. However, as his reading of the prophetic texts demanded a technical interpretation, Calvin developed a methodology in his exegesis that related biblical promises to patterns of fulfillment. Promises in the Old Testament found their fulfillment in the New Testament and in the establishment of Christ's kingdom. That king-

---

⁴⁰ Denis notes that for the sake of purity and agreement in doctrine, Calvin organized regular 'Conferences de l'Ecriture' as part of his *Ecclesiastical Ordinances*. Through such meetings, it was hoped that all of the prophets of the city would speak with one voice in order to expose error and seek agreement around the proper interpretation of Scripture ('Prophétie,' 299).

⁴¹ Peter Martyr noted that there is no need for special prophets since books and teachers are now so numerous (*Loci communes* [Zürich: Froschouer, 1580], 1.19). See Elizabeth L. Eisenstein, *The Printing Press as an Agent of Change: Communication and Cultural Transformations in Early-Modern Europe* (Cambridge: CUP, 1979).

⁴² I am following Willem Balke, *Calvin and the Anabaptist Radicals* (translated by William J. Heynen; Grand Rapids: Eerdmans, 1981; Amsterdam, 1973), 39-71.

⁴³ Deppermann, *Hoffman*, 331-32.

⁴⁴ CO 9.96. Calvin refers to these three self-proclaimed prophets as 'Thomas Monetarius,' 'Melchior Pellionius,' and 'Nicholas Pelagius'—phrases written in defense of the Reformed position against Joachim Westphal's charges that the Reformed were one with the radicals; cf. Balke, *Calvin and the Anabaptist Radicals*, 297.

⁴⁵ Michael Servetus, *Christianismi Restitutio* (Vienna, 1553; repro Frankfurt: Minerva, 1966). After identifying Rome with Sodom on the basis of Revelation 11 and 17 (447), Servetus writes of the spiritual mystery of the law, of Christ and of a third Elijah who will appear before the final resurrection to deal with the need for the restitution of all things (Mal. 4, Matt. 17, Rev. 11).

⁴⁶ Balke, *Calvin and the Anabaptist Radicals*, 200.

dom began with Christ's first Advent. It continues, though under siege, since that Advent in a tension between promise and fulfillment as that kingdom is increasingly manifest. Richard Müller, using the term 'kerygmatic analogy,' illustrates the way in which Calvin developed the idea of an extended meaning of the text, permitting its literal reading while, nevertheless, finding, often through the medium of preaching, a contemporary application or meaning of the text. In this way the logic, or dynamism, of the text, though located in history, might carry us into a future meaning.[47]

By applying the logic of this exegetical method with what many have seen as an optimism about the prospects for human betterment or analogy with the growth of Christ's kingdom, Calvin has been seen to contribute to the idea of progress in human history, a kind of historical meliorism wherever the gospel is heard and appropriated.[48] This exegetical integrity gave an inner logic to the idea of the kingdom of God in Martin Bucer's theology, an idea that impressed Calvin during his sojourn in Strasburg.[49] Calvin's meliorism would contribute to an enduring, if less apocalyptic, interest in the nature of Christ's kingdom among the Reformed. A proleptic sharing in Christ's resurrection and session in glory might be seen to work its way backwards to present times insofar as one believed that the present times stood in the shadow of the end of history.

Circles of Reformed theological thought that took their cue from Calvin excluded special prophets and prophecy, locating such in Christ the last 'prophet' whose ministers herald his name. This tended to mean that the tension between whether the gift of the charisma for prophecy was given to the whole congregation of believers (1 Cor. 14.26-32) or alone to those duly trained and approved (1 Tim. 2.2) was one of demonstrable Christ-centered piety rather than Spirit ecstasy. Christ's heralds were those set against Antichrist. As Revelation 11 was read in this context a number of implications became clear that would ensure its longevity and contribute to a new form of chiliasm that looked not to a new age following the second Advent of Christ but rather to an age of increasing spiritual, and often derivatively, material improvement prior to Christ's return for his bride, the church, which has made itself ready for his return (Rev. 19.7).

---

[47] Richard A. Muller, 'The Hermeneutic of Promise and Fulfillment in Calvin's Exegesis of the Old Testament Prophecies of the Kingdom' in *The Bible in the Sixteenth Century* (Durham: Duke University Press, 1990), 68-82, especially, 71-76.

[48] Quistorp. *Die letzten Dinge*, 113.

[49] Thomas F. Torrance, *Kingdom and Church. A Study in the Theology of the Reformation* (Edinburgh: Oliver and Boyd, 1956). Although Barnes is accurate, to my mind, on the extent to which apocalyptic ideas were generated and developed by Luther-oriented reformers, it seems clear to me that following the work of Bucer, Bullinger and Calvin, among others, that a more integral development of eschatological ideas occurred among the Reformed (cf. Robert Barnes, *Prophecy and Gnosis* [Stanford: Stanford University Press, 1988], 3-6 *et passim*) and would be borne out in the different millennial configurations of biblical scholars.

A visionary mission: three different agendas

Through the course of the sixteenth century the great company of prophets divide over different visions of the future drawn from the texts. The commentaries on the Apocalypse authored by Francis Junius, James Brocard and David Pareus illustrate three paradigmatic tendencies. These will be identified in the nineteenth century as post-millennial, pre-millennial and a-millennial visions of historical progress, each with its own ideal for social and religious reform.

Francis Junius: rebuilding the temple

The notes to the Apocalypse found in the Geneva Bible of 1560[50] drew from Francis Junius,[51] spreading his Reformed understanding of prophesy across national boundaries in this area as in so many other points of doctrine. The gloss on the text of Revelation 11 (1560 edition) identifies the two witnesses as Joshua and Zerubbabel, an interpretation congruent with the muted optimism of Reformed eschatology. It was these two who were charged with the reconstruction of the temple in the days of old Israel's return to Jerusalem following the Babylonian captivity.[52]

That same Bible refers in its notes to Queen Elizabeth as 'our Zerubbabel for the erecting of this moste excellent temple'.[53] The gloss (Zech. 4.3-14) describes the task. As Joshua and Zerubbabel faced the job of reconstructing the temple after exile, so in the sixteenth century faithful preachers worked to restore the church. They are opposed by the 'beast that cometh out of the bottomless pit'. In the gloss the beast is 'the Pope which hathe his power out of hel'.[54] The names of Elijah and Enoch, seen so frequently in association with Revelation 11, are now replaced by Joshua and Zerubbabel, reflecting the task which lay before the Protestant reformers.

This personally self-confident but acerbic, anti-papal line of interpretation can be traced through the glosses of successive editions of the Geneva Bible.[55] Francis Junius (1545-1602), born in Bourges (France), educated at Lyons, and called as a pastor (1565) to the Walloon congregation of Antwerp, fled the city

---

[50] *Geneva Bible: A Facsimile of the 1560 Edition*, with an introduction by Lloyd E. Berry (Milwaukee: University of Wisconsin Press, 1969), 118, for commentary on Revelation 11.3.

[51] Lewis Lupton, *A History of the Geneva Bible* (London: Olive Tree Press, 1975), 7.153-77. After 1594, Junius's commentary was increasingly used to supply the notes to the Apocalypse. See Berry, 'Introduction to the Facsimile Edition,' *Geneva Bible*, 15. Richard Bauckham, *Tudor Apocalypse* (Oxford: Sutton Courtenay Press, 1978), 49, argues that early notes may have come from Bullinger.

[52] *Geneva Bible*, 118.

[53] Francis Junius, *Apocalypsis. A Briefe and Learned Commentaire upon the Revelation of Saint John the Apostle and Evangelist, applied unto the historie of the Catholike and Christian Church* (London, 1592), fol. iir.

[54] Junius, *Apocalypsis*, fol. 1l8r.

[55] See Lupton, *History of Geneva Bible*, 7.153-77.

(1567) in the face of Roman Catholic and Anabaptist opposition. After accompanying Prince William of Orange he was eventually called to Heidelberg (1573) where he assisted Immanuel Tremellius in the translation of a Protestant Latin Bible. The edition of 1599, bearing Junius's notes, was widely read, both on the Continent among the Reformed and in English Puritan circles. With respect to the text, Junius notes that there are two histories to the church. We might describe them as the church under the cross (Rev. 11.1-13) and the church victorious (Rev. 11.14–19). The first finds its fuller explanation in Revelation 1-16, the second in Revelation 20, the textual locus for the millennium.

On the one hand, Junius's commentary follows the historicist tendencies of Nicholas of Lyra. This is clear in Revelation 1-16 (cf. Rev. 11.1-13), the history of the church under the cross. However, the trials of this church are told under a polyvalent symbolism as one finds it in chapter 12 of Revelation. The vision of chapter 12 adumbrates the inception, growth, and conflict of the church in the first century (cf. Rev. 11.2) and later history. That later history is continued in chapter 13 (cf. Rev. 11.7).[56] Junius fills out his view of the church's past through his description of the seals and trumpets. The fifth (Rev. 9.1) and sixth (Rev. 9.13) trumpets of the Apocalypse both occurred during the period of papal hegemony in society. The fifth trumpet marks the end of the binding of Satan, occurring during the reign of Gregory VII (1075).[57] Following the end of this first millennial period the world was vexed by the dragon for 150 years until the reign of Gregory IX (1227-1241). Conflict continued with the 1260-year ministry of the witnesses ending under Boniface VIII, who literally slew them. The prophetic 1260 days of the witnesses' activity (Rev. 11.3) are added to the approximate length of Christ's life, yielding the year when Boniface was made bishop of Rome (A.D. 1294).[58]

Prophecy was revived after Boniface but was opposed again by the dragon and the beasts and would be so until Christ's descent, pictured in Revelation 14.[59] This period will be followed by judgment (Rev. 15-16) and victory (Rev. 17-19). While the slaying of the witnesses was literally fulfilled when certain Christians were hanged in Rome in the thirteenth century, Junius's comments on our text still offer a history of Protestantism and a present agenda for the church. God's true prophets in the sixteenth century are those who work like Joshua and Zerubbabel to reestablish the true worship of God. The history of this restoration from Boniface VIII until the Consummation is adumbrated by Revelation 11.14-19, a seeming millennial age.[60] The meanings woven into the text by Junius helped to create a powerful anti-papal thrust and a sense of millennial mission for Protestantism that the movement will bear well through the

---

[56] Junius, *Apocalypsis*, fols. fols. 115v-116r and 116r-117r.
[57] Junius, *Apocalypsis*, fol. 114r; cf. fol. 120r.
[58] Junius, *Apocalypsis*, fol. 114v.
[59] Junius, *Apocalypsis*, fol. 11v.
[60] Junius, *Apocalypsis*, fol. 115v.

nineteenth century. The spiritual Temple of God was in process of reconstruction. The Geneva Bible and popular pamphlets heightened the impact of Junius's interpretation.

James Brocard: a millenarian vision

The commentary on the book of Revelation by James Brocard presents a different reformed paradigm for the future.[61] Brocard's work illustrates a blending of Reformed and Joachite elements; as such, the ways in which an earlier radical reading of the Apocalypse helped to shape a growing Reformed understanding of the visions set forth in that book.[62] Running through the commentary is an apocalyptic or chiliastic hope for restoration in history predicated upon an opening Age of the Holy Spirit subsequent to the Protestant reformation. It outlines a far-reaching vision for Protestant historical and institutional development, which, Jürgen Moltmann argues, influenced the thought of Johannes Coccenius (1603-1669) whose own work helped to alter scholastic Reformed theology by introducing into it the history of salvation and a millenarianism predicated upon the doctrine of successive covenants.[63]

Brocard's work illustrates Reformed theology intermixed to a great degree with Joachite spirituality and historical momentum. Two points stand out in this commentary. First, the Reformed doctrine of predestination is melded with argumentation drawn from Joachite prophetic speculation, thus creating a kind of historical determinism and illustrating a transformationist and progressive historical development toward the kingdom of God. As such, the commentary is a fine example of what Heinrich Quistorp argued was the bias in Calvin's theolo-

---

[61] The commentary on the Apocalypse to which I have had access is an English edition entitled *The Revelation of S. Ihon reveled* (London, 1582; orig. Latin, 1580); cf. Bousset, 95. Brocard belonged first to the French Reformed and, later, Dutch Reformed Church. The name James Brocard is found on the title page of the English translation of his commentary on the Apocalypse (Latin orig., 1580). His works include *De Prophelia Libri Duo* (Lyon, 1581), *The Revelation of S. [hon reveled . . . Englished by J. Sanford* (London, 1582), *Mystica el Propetica Libri Levitici Interpretatio* (Lyon, 1580), *Mystica et prophetica libri Geneseos interpretatio* (Bremen, 1585).

[62] See Jürgen Moltmann, 'Jacob Brocard als Vorläufer der Reich Gottes theologie und der symbolisch-propetischen Schriftausleguing des Johann Coccenius,' ZKG 71 (1960), 110-29. In drawing out Brocard's significance, Moltmann illustrates how Brocard came to know one of the chief reformers of Bremen, Christoph Pezel. Through Pezel, Tholuck argued, Brocard's ideas influenced the development of the 'Kingdom of God' theology of Coccenius (111-12).

[63] Moltmann in 'Jacob Brocard' draws out the connection, arguing for Brocard's influence upon the anti-papal and recapitulative lines of analysis in Coccenius's exhaustive systematic 'septenary' illustrating the totality of his kingdom theology. See Gottlob Schrenk's summary of Coccenius's Apocalypse commentary: *Gottesreich und Bund im älteren Protestantismus, vornehmlich be; Johannes Coccenius* (Gütersioh: C. Bartlesmann, 1923), 335-47.

gy toward the triumph of God in time.[64] This is illustrated both in the preface to Brocard's commentary on the Apocalypse and throughout the body of the text.[65] Additionally, this primacy granted to divine initiative is developed by Brocard so as to see a certain parallelism, both in the initial creative activity of God and in the final denouement of history.[66]

Having referred briefly to the Reformed provenance of the commentary, it is the more prophetic dimensions that are of interest to us. It is, also, such speculation that kept Brocard on the move as he faced scholastic Reformed hostility until eventually he found a home in Bremen and protection under Christoph Pezel. Born in 1563 in Venice, Brocard travelled to France but was condemned by the Calvinist National Synod for his prophetic interpretation of Scripture. Expelled from the Netherlands for similar reasons, Brocard found refuge with the Reformed at Bremen. Here he published several works, including a commentary on Genesis, one on the Song of Solomon, and another on the book of Revelation. His life and publication history were clearly bounded by the age of Philip II of Spain (1527-1598) and the Dutch Wars of Independence (1568-1648). This political history adds an additional element of interest to Brocard's work on the book of Revelation. The commentary becomes an early place for analyzing the transition of thought in the late sixteenth and early seventeenth centuries from a transcendent apocalyptic expectation to a more political hope expressive of the new national religious orders reshaping the social and religious map of Europe.[67]

In his exposition on the Apocalypse, Brocard notes three states of history, of which the third, belonging to the Holy Spirit, will be a Sabbath of 'opened prophecy'.[68] There are seven ages of the world. The sixth age is that of new prophets and the seventh that of the second Advent. There are seven divisions in Brocard's Age of the Son. The seventh began with Luther's preaching of the gospel. There are then seven seasons of the Age of the Holy Spirit, the first from the preaching of Luther to the ascent of the Swiss Reformed movement, the second and third in such places as England and Denmark, the fourth having come with the 'French troubles'. A fifth season runs from those troubles through the 'slaughter of the Gospellers', and a sixth would last until 'the conflicte of hostes, when in thicke cloudes of the sky Chryst shalbe present to turne his Judgement agaynst ye Papistes'.[69] The source of his vision, Brocard writes in numerous places in his Apocalypse commentary, is the work of 'Abbot Joachimus'.[70] Reeves argues that 'Joachim is the key prophet of the sixth age and

---

[64] Quistorp, *Die letzten Dinge*, 116.
[65] Brocard, *Revelation*, fol. 10v.
[66] Brocard, *Revelation*, fol. 12v.
[67] Koppel Pinson, *Pietism as a Factor in the Rise of German Nationalism* (New York: Columbia University Press, 1934), 58-59, 78, 180-206.
[68] Brocard, *Revelation*, fol. 5r. See Reeves, *Influence of Prophecy*, 488n.11; 494-99.
[69] Brocard, *Revelation*, fol. 5v.
[70] Brocard, *Revelation*, fol. 17v.

the chief medieval influence upon Brocard's thought.'[71] In arguing such, Reeves draws out Brocard's use of Ezekiel's wheel, the apocalyptic trumpets, and sacrifice of Elijah on Mt. Carmel, each of these sets of symbols characteristic of the work of Joachim.[72] Such patterns can, also, be discerned in Brocard's commentary on the book of Genesis.[73]

Contemporary religious and attendant social reform movements play a role in shaping Brocard's thinking about contemporary history. God's Son comes in the Spirit, preaching renewal.[74] Such thinking is applied to Brocard's own day. Texts from chapters 9-11 of Revelation are used to picture that renewal, comparable to a birthing process, seen in the contemporary persecution of Protestants in France. This renewal is said to begin with the Word, which is given as a measuring rod to all ages now entering the last.[75] For forty-two months, that is, since the days of Pope Sylvester I (314-335), gentiles have trodden down the holy city. Throughout this period, paralleled by the 1260 years of the witnesses' preaching in Revelation 11, the gospel was heard. All who have continued in the gospel are the two apocalyptic prophets,[76] but the vision is uniquely applicable to Brocard's own day.[77]

Accordingly, Christ will bring the church out of the desert (the sixth age) by the year 1573, a date based on adding the 1260 day-years to A.D. 313, when the church became perverted under Sylvester.[78] This occurs together with the emergence of a spiritually empowered ministry. Discussing the two olive trees and candlesticks before God, Brocard writes that these two are the Holy Spirit and Christ. Because true ministers are bearers of these members of the Trinity, they can be referred to by these figures. Thus, Brocard emphasizes a mystical component to our two witnesses. They are 'ministers of the Gospel and of the

---

[71] Reeves, *Influence of Prophecy*, 495.

[72] Reeves, *Influence of Prophecy*, 495-99.

[73] Within the threefold economy of the Trinity there are eight ages of history as found in Scripture: (1) that of Abraham, (2) the Law, (3) the prophets, (4) the Evangel, (5) the Apostolic Church, (6) the woman (Church) hidden in the wilderness, (7) that of new prophets, and (8) eternity (Brocard, *Praef. in Gen.*, fols. 20v, 153v; as cited in Moltmann, 'Jacob Brocard,' 120). Moltmann, 'Jacob Brocard,' 110-29.

[74] Brocard, *Revelation*, fol. IIIr. This Spiritualist exegesis is not only reminiscent of Joachim, but, also, of Joachim's later disciple, Peter John Olivi, who, also, held to a second coming in the spirit, in Francis of Assisi.

[75] Brocard, *Revelation*, fol. 109r. Although peace appeared to come for Protestants in 1570, further measuring was to occur as Christ cleansed his church (fols. 109v-110r).

[76] Brocard, *Revelation*, fols. 109v-110r.

[77] Brocard, *Revelation*, fol. 110r-v.

[78] This merits comparison with the perspective of John Foxe. See Patrick Collinson, *The Birthpangs of Protestant England: Religious and Cultural Change in the Sixteenth and Seventeenth Centuries* (New York: Macmillan, 1988).

word of Prophecy'.[79] Their power comes from the doctrine and spirit that they bear.[80]

For forty years, to the beginning of persecution in France, the gospel has been faithfully preached by these witnesses. This preaching is 'the work of Chrysts second coming'.[81] Now the prophecies of old begin to be fulfilled. Christ himself reminds us of his words in Matthew 24.[82] The apocalyptic battle begins as the beast arises from the pit 'to play the Devill'. These events came to pass in France in 1572.[83] Now we stand on the verge of Christ's kingdom.[84]

The tensions evident in the late sixteenth century between theologies of hope dependent upon either an Augustinian/Thomist or Joachite theological perspective are tensions that will now divide Protestantism and Protestant renewal movements into the contemporary period. Both commentaries by Junius and Brocard, as widely different as they are—the first standing within one millennial age and looking to another, and the second more pessimistically located in the present and looking to God's intervention with a millennial age—will now mark the Reformed movement. The commentaries of Junius and Brocard, caught between the worlds of Reformed and radical exegeses, offer promising avenues of analysis for understanding in the way from the dogmatic theologians of the sixteenth century to the apocalyptic theologians of the seventeenth century—and in their own way the onset of modernity.[85]

The chiliastic tendencies among the Reformed, visible already in Francis Lambert, were heightened by Brocard but given fresh respectability particularly with the work of Johann Heinrich Alsted (1588-1638) as well as others.[86] That

---

[79] Brocard, *Revelation*, fol. 110v
[80] Brocard, *Revelation*, fol. 111r.
[81] Such argumentation is reminiscent of that of Peter John Olivi (c. 1248-1298), a disciple of Joachite thought. Olivi had argued in the thirteenth century that a 'second coming of Christ had occurred in the person and preaching of Francis of Assisi'.
[82] Brocard, *Revelation*, 'That is as I thinke, after that the Gospel shalbe preached [?] 40. yeres & more. & upon the beginning of the French troubles the worke of Chrysts second coming shalbe declared to haue bene present: when those thinges shall begin to come to passe, whych the Prophetes have reported, and Chryst himselfe hath put us in minde of the 24. cap. Math.'
[83] Brocard is referring to the St. Bartholomew's Day massacre, August 23-24, 1572.
[84] Brocard, *Revelation*, fol. 113r.
[85] Moltmann, 'Jacob Brocard,' 111-12.
[86] Johann Heinrich Alsted, *Diatribe de Mille annis Apocalyptics* (orig., 1627). I have used the edition Francofurti: Conradi Eifridi, 1630. This treatise, a commentary on Revelation 20, is said by the author to connect all of the preceding and subsequent chapters of the Apocalypse. The history of the church is seen in four periods: (1) John the Baptist to the Jerusalem Council (A.D. 50); (2) A.D. 51 to the millennium; (3) the millennial church; and (4) from the end of the millennium to universal judgment (16-25). Our witnesses are found from Boniface III to the years of the Protestant reformation (18, 26-65). Alsted's work stands in need of focused attention.

of Junius would be further developed with enduring significance in the Anglo-American world by Thomas Brightman (1562-1607).

David Pareus: a perpetual reformation

We complete our survey of these commentaries and what they have to say about prophesying, by turning next to David Pareus (1548-1622). His commentary retains[87] an anti-chiliastic, anti-papal line of interpretation.[88] Its purpose is to give a vision of perpetual reformation to the church with special reference to the Protestant reformation.[89] In addition to following Bullinger at many places, Pareus develops a complex recapitulative approach to the imagery of the text.[90]

Pareus writes of the series of seals and trumpets as illustrating similar eras in the history of the church. The bowls of wrath are reserved for the end of history. A large portion of the commentary is devoted to the work of the adventual witnesses of Revelation 11. They illustrate Pareus's recapitulative methodology as their work is correlated with the last four great acts of God in history: (1) the calamities of the church brought on by tyrants and heretics (especially by Apollyon [the Devil] and Muhammad) and seen in the six trumpets (Rev. 8,9); (2) the comfort promised the afflicted (Rev. 10); (3) the amplification of the previous calamities, that is, the conflict of the church with the Western (!) Antichrist and its cleansing (Rev. 11:1-15); and (4) the sound of the last trumpet, the call to judgment and the great reward.[91]

Its story is divided into two visions, a general command to measure the temple, that is, to reform the church (Rev. 11:1-2), and a specific description of the reformation through the work of the witnesses (Rev. 11:3-14). All is concluded with the sound of the last trumpet (Rev. 11:15). Four aspects of the work of reformation are detailed in the text as Pareus sees it: (1) a description of the witnesses (Rev. 11:3-6), (2) their war with the beast (Rev. 11:7-10), (3) the way in which God's prophets are avenged (Rev. 11:11-13), and (4) the victorious conclusion with judgment and divine vindication (Rev. 11:14-15).

Pareus fills in this outline of reform by drawing upon the history of the interpretation of the passage. He rejects Nicholas of Lyra's application of it to the

---

[87] David Pareus, *Commentarius in apocalypsim* (Frankfurt, 1618). The edition I used was the *Commentary Upon the Divine Revelation . . . Evangelist John* (Amsterdam, 1644). The substance of this work was delivered as a series of lectures at the Reformed Academy in Heidelberg (1608), and published ten years later.

[88] Bousset, *Offenbarung*, 96.

[89] Pareus, *Divine Revelation*, 242. See Günther Brinkmann, *Die Irenik des David Pareus: Frieden und Einheit ihrer Relevanz zur Warheitfrage* (Hildesheim: Gerstenberg, 1972). We might speculate that this understanding of reformation served to strengthen Pareus in his endeavor toward toleration and conciliation among Protestants.

[90] Bousset, *Offenbarung*, 96.

[91] Pareus, *Divine Revelation*, 209-10.

sixth century as frivolous. John is called to measure the church (Rev. 11:1-2).[92] This signifies its reformation through the Word of God (the measuring rod) in the days when it has been destroyed by the Western Antichrist. He argues pointedly against Francis Ribeira and Catholic theories of the church's indefectibility.

Pareus now proceeds to argue that as the old temple needed restoration, so does the new. Various analogies are drawn between Israel's religious practices and those of the church.[93] When he comes to the forty-two months of gentile destruction (Rev. 11:2), Pareus applies this period to the time of Antichrist's persecution. Analyzing a variety of opinions,[94] he concludes (agreeing essentially with Bullinger), that the forty-two months represent a definite figure for an indefinite period.

Having sketched the prophecy of a future reformation in general, Pareus turns to the specific program for reform, its instruments, development, success, and history. He notes Theodore Beza's point that this vision is God's promise: When it appears that prophecy is extinct and that Antichrist is victorious, God will restore prophecy so 'that the city of God may be rebuilt'.[95] Augustine's (*sic*, Tyconius) interpretation that the witnesses are the Old and New Testaments, as well as the opinion of Bede and Brightman, is rejected. The text appears to call for personalities, Pareus writes. Some, he adds, find here two powerful teachers 'with the power and spirit of Elias' in the last days. This, however, is uncertain. Pareus concludes, 'I will follow the opinion of Bullinger. and some others of our best interpreters who understand the two witnesses indefinitely, to be diverse reformers of religion in Antichrist's times.'

The time of the preaching of the witnesses is said to be 1260 days (Rev. 11:3). This period of time is the same as the forty-two months (Rev. 11:2).[96] Considering a variety of opinions, Pareus follows again an indefinite line; it is enough that God knows the period precisely. If, he adds, one asks why should some other number not be proposed, it is because there is some sense to this figure. It may be applied to the period running from Boniface III forward. At any rate, it refers to a period of oppression mixed with success as the power of

---

[92] Pareus, *Divine Revelation*, 212-13. Following Rupert of Deutz, Pareus identifies the little book given John to eat (Rev. 10.2,8-10) with the measuring rod (Rev. 11.1), the Word of God.

[93] Pareus, *Divine Revelation*, 213-16.

[94] Pareus, *Divine Revelation*, 216-20. Pareus rejects four different interpretations of our text. He generally agrees with Bullinger that the 42 months (1260 years) ran from A.D. 666 to the Last Judgment (historicist). The four rejected positions are: (1) Bellarmine (a specific period of 42 months in the future—futurist; (2) Junius and the Magdeburg centurators (1260 years from Christ's passion to Boniface VIII—historicist; (3) Foxe (two periods of persecution in the early and then last days of the Church—futurist; and (4) Alcasar (a period of time in the first century—preterist.

[95] Pareus, *Divine Revelation*, 221.

[96] Pareus, *Divine Revelation*, 225.

Antichrist increases. During all this time Christ's true prophets appear contemptible in their sackcloth garb, but they are dignified by the oil of the Spirit and the light of God's Word, 'by which they shall drive away Antichristian darknesse, and kindle againe the lost light of the Gospell in the Church'.[97]

Conclusion

Bullinger's sermons on the Apocalypse, which began our search on the Reformed use of our text, contributed to the increasingly historicist and anti-papal line of interpretation. The rules for reading a text found in Tyconius, as well as Joachite prophecies of Antichrist, were central to this development. Furthermore, the search for a moral understanding of history, together with a desire to make sense of the vicissitudes of the gospel through time, fostered a growing literalization of the vision inspired by our text.[98] While further tendencies may be discovered in the authors we have discussed, such as those leading to a closer historical and critical analysis of the text,[99] this development will come to fruition only after Protestantism has been significantly marked in its consciousness by the vision of God's two adventual witnesses. Following the works of Junius, Brocard, and Pareus we have seen that vision layout these different paradigms for historical understanding. Junius's vision caught us up in an increasing second millennial age following the identification of the witnesses. Brocard placed that age beyond the tribulation of the present and Advent of Christ. Pareus's understanding was more recognizably Augustinian, but tinctured by a historicism that would work to keep further speculation alive.

Each one of these three paradigms for history was developed in relation to strong civic interests and a desire to shape civil society in different ways. This makes for striking comparison with Luther and visions for the end of history, which appeared within Lutheranism to be less related to immediate interests in social meliorism. The issue of community in relation to the kingdom of God will come to the fore with increasing force following the work on our text by John Foxe. John Foxe added an integral and politically significant national piety to the growing historicization of our text that will bear upon the interests of Anglo, and then Anglo-American, understanding of community and communal values.

---

[97] Pareus, *Divine Revelation*, 228.
[98] This historicist exegesis stimulated Jesuit preterist (Alcasar) and futurist (Ribeira, Bellarmine) responses, offering a different literalization.
[99] R.H. Charles, *Studies in the Apocalypse* (Edinburgh: T. & T. Clark, 1913), 33; cf. Bousset, *Offenbarung*, 97-99, 102-6.

BIBLIOGRAPHY

PRIMARY WORKS

Alsted, Johann Heinrich, *Diatribe de Mille annis Apocalyptics* (orig., 1627; Francofurti: Conradi Eifridi, 1630).

Andreae, Jacob, *Sechs Christlicher Predig Von den Spaltungen so sich zwischen den Theologen Augspurgischer Confession* (Tübingen: 1573).

Anselm, *Cur Deus Homo? Libri Duo* (London: David Nat, 1903).

—. *Why God Became Man*. In Brian Davies and G.R. Evans (eds), *The Major Works* (Oxford: Oxford University Press, 1998).

Arminius, Jacob. *Disputationes, magnam partem s. theologiae complectentes, publicae & privatae, quarum index epist. dedicatoriam sequitur*. In *Opera Theologica* (Leiden: 1629).

—. *The Works of James Arminius*, 3 volumes (edited by James Nichols; 1853; Grand Rapids: Baker, 1991).

Aquinas, Thomas. *Summa Theologica*, 5 volumes (Allen: Christian Classics, 1948).

Augustine, *Commentaries on the Psalms*. In *Ancient Christian Writers: The Work of the Fathers in translation*, 30 volumes (translated by Scholastica Hebgin and Felecitas Corrigan; New York: Newman, 1969).

—. *On the Holy Trinity*. In Philip Schaff (ed.), *Nicene and Post-Nicene Fathers of the Christian Church*, First Series, 13 volumes (reprinted; Grand Rapids: Eerdmans, 1993).

Becmani, Christiani, *Exercitationes theologicae* (Amsterdam: J. Janssonium, 1643).

Beza, Theodore, et al., *An Harmony of the Confessions of the Faith of the Christian and Reformed Churches, which purley profess the holy doctrine of the Gospel, in all the chief kingdoms, nations, and provinces of Europe* (Cambridge: 1586).

—. *Harmonia Confessionum Fidei* (Geneva: 1581).

Bibliander, Theodore, *Ad omnium ordinum reip* (Basel: Oporinus, 1545).

Book of Concord, The (translated and edited by Theodore G. Tappert; Philadelphia: Fortress, 1978).

Brocard, James, *De Prophelia, Libri Duo* (Lyon, 1581).

—. *The Revelation of S. [hon reveled . .. Englished by J. Sanford* (London, 1582).

—. *Mystica el Propetica Libri Levitici Interpretatio* (Lyon, 1580).

—. *Mystica et prophetica libri Geneseos interpretatio . . .* (Bremen, 1585).

Bucer, Martin, *De Regno Christi libri duo* (orig., 1550; edited by Francois Wendel; Paris: Presses Universitaires de France, 1955).

—. *Enarratio in Evangelion Johannis* (Argentorati, 1528).

—. *In sacra quatuor Evangelia, enarrationes perpetuae, secundum recognitae, in quibus praeterea habes syncerioris theologiae locos communes supra centum, ad scripturarum fidem simpliciter, & nullius cum insectatione tractatos, adiectis etiam aliquot locorum retractationibus* (Basel: Apud Ioan, Hervagium, 1536).

Bullinger, Heinrich, *Confessio et expositio simplex orthodoxae fidei et dogmatum Catholicorum syncerae religionis Christianae* (Zurich: Christophorus Froschauerus, 1566).

—. *In Apocalypsim conciones centum* (Basel: Oporinus, 1557).

—. *In Sacrosanctum Iesu Christi Domini Nostri Evangelium Secundum Matthaeum Commentariorum Libri XII* [*Commentary on Matthew*] (Zurich: Apud Froschoverum, 1542).

—. 'The Second Helvetic Confession.' In P. Schaff (ed.), *The Creeds of Christendom* (Grand Rapids: Baker, 1983), 3.831-909.

—. *The Summe of the Foure Evangelists* (translated by J. Tomkys; London: For W. Ponsonby, 1582).

Calvin, John, *A Harmony of the Gospels Matthew, Mark, and Luke*, CNTC, volumes 1-3 (translated by A.W. Morrison; edited by D.W. Torrance and T.F. Torrance; Grand Rapids: Eerdmans, 1972).

—. *Commentaries on the Book of Genesis* (Grand Rapids: Baker, 1981).

—. *Commentaries on the First Twenty Chapters of the Book of the Prophet Ezekiel*, COTC, volume 1 (translated by Thomas Myers; Grand Rapids: Eerdmans, 1963).

—. *Commentaries on the Four Last Books of Moses Arranged in the Form of a Harmony*, CTS, volume 1 (translated by Charles William Bingham; Grand Rapids: Eerdmans, 1952).

—. *Commentaries on the Four Last Books of Moses Arranged in the Form of a Harmony*, CTS, volume 4 (translated by Charles William Bingham; Grand Rapids: Eerdmans, 1963).

—. *Commentaries on the Twelve Minor Prophets*, CTS, volume 1, *Hosea*, CTS, volume 5, *Malachi* (translated by John Owen; Grand Rapids: Eerdmans, 1963).

—. *Commentarij in Epistolam Pauli ad Romanos*, Strassburg: Vuendelinum (Rihelium, 1540).

—. *Commentary on Isaiah 33-66* (Grand Rapids, Baker, 1981).

—. *Commentary on Jeremiah* (Grand Rapids: Baker, 1979).

—. *Commentary on the Book of Isaiah*, CTS, volumes 1-4 (translated by William Pringle; Grand Rapids: Eerdmans, 1963).

—. *Commentary on the Book of Psalms*, CTS, volumes 1-4 (translated by James Anderson; Grand Rapids: Eerdmans, 1963).

—. *Commentary on the Epistles of James and Jude*, CNTC volume 3 (translated by A.W. Morrison; edited by D.W. Torrance and T.F. Torrance: Grand Rapids: Eerdmans, 1972).

—. *Concerning the Eternal Predestination of God by which He has chosen some men to salvation and left others to their own destruction and Concerning the Providence of God by which He governs all human affairs:*

The Agreement of the Pastors of the Church of Geneva (translated by J.K.S. Reid; London: James Clarke, 1961).
—. 'Four Letters from the Socinus-Calvin Correspondence 1549.' In John A. Tedeschi (ed.), *Italian Reformation Studies in Honor of Laelius Socinus* (translated by Ralph Lazzaro; Firenze, Università Di Siena, 1965), 217-30.
—. *Harmonia ex evangelistis tribus composita, Matthaeo, Marco, et Luca: adiuncto seorsum Johanne, quod pauca cum aliis communia habeat* (Genevae: Excudebant Nicolaus Barbirius et Thomas Courteau, 1563).
—. *Harmony of Exodus, Leviticus, Numbers and Deuteronomy* (Grand Rapids: Baker, 1981).
—. *Hebrews and 1 and 2 Peter* (Grand Rapids: Eerdmans, 1963).
—. *Institutio christianae religionis, in libros quatuor* (Genevae: Oliva Roberti Stephani, 1559).
—. *Institutio Christianae Religionis.* In Petrus Barth and Guilelmus Niesel (eds), *Opera Selecta*, 5 volumes (Munich: 1926-52).
—. *Ioannis Calvini Opera Exegetica*, vol. 12.2, In Helmut Feld (ed.), *Evangelium Secundum Johannem Commentarius Pars Prior* (Geneva: Droz, 1997).
—. *Ioannis Calvini Opera quae Supersunt Omnia*, 59 volumes (edited by Johann Wilhelm Baum, August Eduard Cunitz, and Eduard Reuss; Brunsvigae: C.A. Schwetschke et Filium, 1863-1900).
—. *Selected Works* (Grand Rapids: Baker, 1983).
—. *Sermons on Deuteronomy* (Edinburgh: Banner of Truth, 1987).
—. *Sermons on Galatians* (Edinburgh: Banner of Truth, 1997).
—. *Sermons on Job* (Edinburgh: Banner of Truth, 1993).
—. *Sermons on the Acts of the Apostles*, chapters 1-7 (Edinburgh: Banner of Truth, 2008).
—. *Sermons on the Epistle to the Ephesians* (Edinburgh: Banner of Truth, 1973).
—. *Sermons on Timothy and Titus* (Edinburgh: Banner of Truth, 1983).
—. *Sermons on 2 Samuel* (translated by Douglas Kelly; Edinburgh: Banner of Truth, 1992).
—. *The Acts of the Apostles*, volume 1 (CNTC, volume 6, Grand Rapids: Eerdmans, 1979).
—. *The Epistle of Paul the Apostle to the Hebrews and the First and Second Epistles of St. Peter* (edited by D.W. Torrance and T.F. Torrance; Grand Rapids: Eerdmans, 1963).
—. *The Epistles of Paul to the Galatians, Ephesians, Philippians, and Colossians* (Edinburgh: Oliver and Boyd, 1965).
—. *The Epistles of Paul to the Romans and Thessalonians*, volume 8 (CNTC, Grand Rapids: Eerdmans, 1973).
—. *The First Epistle of Paul to the Corinthians* (CNTC, Grand Rapids: Eerdmans, 1963).

BIBLIOGRAPHY

—. *The Gospel According to St. John 11-21* (edited by T.F. Torrance and David Torrance; Grand Rapids: Eerdmans, 1996).

—. *The Institutes of the Christian Religion*, 2 volumes (translated by Henry Beveridge; Edinburgh: T. & T. Clark, 1863).

—. *The Institutes of the Christian Religion* (The Library of Christian Classics, volumes 20-21; edited by John T. McNeill; London: SCM, 1960).

—. *Theological Treatises* (translated by J.K.S. Reid; London: SCM, 1954).

—. *Tracts and Letters*, volumes 4-7 (edited and translated by Henry Beveridge; Edinburgh: Banner of Truth, 2009).

Chrysostom, John, *Homilies on the Gospel of St. Matthew*. In Philip Schaff (ed.), *A Select Library of Nicene and Post-Nicene Fathers of the Christian Church*, volume 10 (Grand Rapids: Eerdmans, 1978).

Clement of Alexandria, 'The Instructor.' In Alexander Roberts and James Donaldson (eds), *The Ante-Nicene Fathers: Translation of the Writings of the Fathers down to AD 325* (Grand Rapids: Eerdmans, 1956), 1.6.

Crell, Paul, *Spongia de definitione evangelii, complectens propositiones centum quinquaginta, oppositas ... collationi Iohannis Wigandi* (Witebergae: Johann Schwertel, 1571).

Crocius, Ludovicus, *Antisocinismus contractus: hoc est errorum Socinianorum privatarum consequentiarum nebulis involutorum examen & brevis ostensio principiorum quibus illi XXVIII disputationibus refutantur & dogmata catholicae fidei defenduntur* (1639).

Cyril of Alexandria, *Commentary on Isaiah* (translated by Robert C. Hill; Brookline, MA: Holy Cross Orthodox Press, 2008).

—. *Divi Cyrilli Alexandriae Episcopi Commentariorum in Hesaiam Prophetam Libri Quinque* (Basel: Froben, 1563).

D'Étaples, Jacques Lefèvre, *Commentarii Initiatorii in Quator Evangelia* (Basileae: Cratander, 1523).

Die Bekenntnisschriften der evangelisch-lutherischen Kirche (Gottingen, 4th ed. 1959).

Erasmus, Desirderius. *Novum Instrumentum* (Basle: 1516).

—. *The Essential Erasmus* (edited by John P. Dolan; New York: New American Library of World Literature, 1964).

—. *The First Tome or Volume of the Paraphrase of Erasmus upon the New Testament* (London: E. Whitchurche, 1548).

Eusebius, *Preparation for the Gospel*, 2 volumes (translated by Edwin Hamilton Gifford; Oregon: Wipf and Stock, 2002).

Flacius, Matthias and Victor Strigel, *Disputatio de originali Peccato et libero arbitrio, inter Matthiam Flacium Illyricum, & Victorinum Strigelium Vinariae* (n.p., n.c.: 1562).

Gell, Robert. *Noah's Flood Returning: Or, A Sermon Preached August the 7th, 1655* (London: J.L. to be sold by Giles Calvert, 1655).

Geneva Bible: A Facsimile of the 1560 Edition (with an introduction by Lloyd E. Berry; Milwaukee: University of Wisconsin Press, 1969).

Gerhard, Johann. *Annotationes Posthumae in Evangelium D. Matthaei* (Jena: Georgi Sengenwaldi, 1663).

Grotius, Hugo, *Denfensio Fidei Catholicae de Satisfactione Christi Adversus Fastum Socinum Senensem* (Leiden: Ioannes Patius, 1617).

Jerome, *Commentariorum in Esaiam*. In Marcus Adriaen and Germain Morin (eds), *Corpus Christianorum Series Latina*, volume 73 (Turnholti: Brepols, 1963).

Judex, Matthaeus, *Quod arguere peccata, seu concionari poenitentiam, sit proprium legis, & non Evangelij, proprie sic dicti, rationes & argumenta* (Basileae: Ex officina Iacobi Parci, 1559).

Junius, Francis, *Apocalypsis Joannis* (Heidelberg. 1591).

—. *Apocalypsis. A Briefe and Learned Commentaire upon the Revelation of Saint John the Apostle and Evangelist, applied unto the historie of the Catholike and Christian Church* (London, 1592).

Krebs, Manfred and Hans Georg Rott (eds), *Quellen zur Geschichte der Taufer, Elsass I und II* (Guttersloh: Gerd Mohn, 1959, 1960).

Lambert, Francis (d' Avignon), *Exegeseos in sanctum divi Joannis Apocalypsim Libri VII* (Marburg, 1528; Basel, 1539).

Leigh, Edward, *Treatise of Religion and Learning and of Religious and Learned Men* (London: 1656).

Lombard, Peter, *Sententiae in IV Libris Distinctae* (edited by Ignatius Brady; 3rd edition, 2 volumes; Grottoferrata: Collegii S. Bonaventurae Ad Claras Aquas, 1971-1981).

—. *The Sentences* (translated by Giulio Silano; Toronto: Pontifical Institute of Medieval Studies, 2007-10).

Luther, Martin, *Annotationes in Aliquot Capita Matthei* (1538). In *Opera Omnia Domini Martini Lutheri* (Wittenberg: Per Iohannem Lufft, 1554).

—. Ausgewählte Werke, ed. By H.H. Borcherdt/ Georg Merz, 6 volumes, third edition (München: Chr. Kaiser Verlag, 1951).

—. *D. Martin Luthers Werke: Kritische Gesamtausgabe* (Weimar: Hermann Böhlaus Nachfolger, 1883- 87).

—. *Large Confession* in *Die Bekenntnisschriften der evangelisch-lutherischen Kirche, herausgegeben im Gedenkjahr der Augsburgischen Konfession 1930* (Göttingen: Vandenhoeck & Ruprecht, 1959).

—. *Letters of Spiritual Counsel* (translated by Theodore Tappert; Vancouver: Regent College Publishing, 2003).

—. *Luther's Correspondence and Other Contemporary Letters* (edited by Preserved Smith and Charles M. Jacobs; Philadelphia: Lutheran Publication Society, 1913).

—. *Luther's Works*, 56 volumes (edited by Jaroslav Pelikan and Helmut Lehmann; St Louis: Concordia, 1955-1986).

—. *On The Ineffable Name and On Christ's Lineage* (1543) in Gerhard Falk, *The Jew in Christian Theology: Martin Luther's Anti-Jewish Vom Schem*

Hamphoras, Previously Unpublished in English, and Other Milestones in Church Doctrine Concerning Judaism (North Carolina: 1992).

—. *Table Talk*, 'Of The Jews: DCCCXIV', http://biblestudy.churches.net/CCEL/L/LUTHER/ TABLE_TA/TABLE_45.HTM.

The Complete Sermons of Martin Luther: Sermons on Gospel Texts, volumes 5-7 (edited by Eugene F.A. Klug; Grand Rapids: Baker, 2000).

—. *The Precious and Sacred Writings of Martin Luther*, volumes 10-14 (edited by John Nicholas Lenker; Minneapolis: Lutherans in All Lands, 1904-07).

—. *The Sermons of Martin Luther* (Grand Rapids: 1996), 1.62—available online at http://www.orlutheran.com/html/mlselk21.html.

—. *Thirty Foure Special and Chosen Sermons of Dr. Martin Luther* (London: Thomas Paine for Francis Tyton, 1649).

—. *Vorlesung über den Römerbrief 1515/ 1516*, Lateinisch-deutsche Ausgabe, 2 volumes (Darmstadt: Wissenschaftliche Buchgesellschaft, 1960).

Lyra, Nicholas de, *Biblia: Mit Postilla Litteralis von Nicolaus de Lyra* (Nürnberg: Anton Koberger, 1497).

Maccovius, Johannes, *Johannes Maccovius Redivivus, seu Manuscripta eius Typis Exscripta* (Franeker, 1647).

—. *Scholastic Discourse: Johannes Maccovius (1588-1644) on Theological and Philosophical Distinctions and Rules* (edited by Willem J. van Asselt, Michael D. Bell, Gert van den Bring, and Rein Ferwerda; Apeldoorn: Instituut voor Reformatieonderzoek, 2009).

Magnus, Albertus, *Opera Omnia*, 38 volumes (edited by Auguste Borgnet and Emil Borgnet; Paris: Louis Vivès, 1890-1899).

Mayer, John. *A Commentarie upon the New Testament*, volume 1 (London: Thomas Cotes for John Bellamie, 1631).

Melanchthon, Philipp *Annotationes et Conciones in Evangelium Matthaei*. In *Philippi Melanthonis Opera Quae Supersunt Omnia*, volume 14 (edited by Carolus Gottlieb Bretschneider; Halis Saxonum: C.A. Schwetschke et Filium, 1847. Reprinted as *Corpus Reformatorum: Melanchthonis Opera*, volume 14 (New York: Johnson Reprint Corporation, 1963).

—. *Philippi Melanchthonis Opera quae supersunt omnia*, Corpus Reformatorum, 29 volumes (edited by Karl Gottlieb Bretschneider and Heinrich Ernst Bindseil; Wittenbergae: Apud C.A. Schwetschke et filium, 1834-1860).

—. *Scholia in Epistolam Pavli ad Colossenses* (Wittenbergae: 1528).

Meyer, Sebastian, *In apocalypsim Johannis Apostoli* (orig., Zürich: Froschouer, 1539; Zürich: Froschouer, 1554).

Musculus, Wolfgang, *Common Places of Christian Religion* (London: 1563).

—. *Loci Communes Theologiae Sacrae* (Basel: Per Sabastianum Henricpetri, 1599).

—. *In Evangelistam Matthaeum Commentarii* (1548) (reprinted Edition; Basel: Ex officina Hervagiana, 1562).

Oecolampadius, Johannes, *Enarratio in Evangelium Matthaei* (Basileae: 1536).
—. *In Iesaiam Prophetam Hypomnematōn, hoc est, Commentariorum, Ioannis Oecolampadii Libri VI* (Basel: Cratander, 1525).
Owen, John. *The Works of John Owen*, 24 volumes (edited by William H. Goold; 1850-53; Edinburgh: Banner of Truth, 1993).
Pareus, David, *Commentarius in apocalypsim* (Frankfurt, 1618)
—. *Commentary Upon the Divine Revelation . . . Evangelist John* (Amsterdam, 1644).
Pezel, Christoph, *Apologia Verae Doctrinae De Definitione Evangelii* (Witebergae: Excudebant Clemens Schleich & Antonius Schöne, 1571).
Plass, Ewald (ed.), *What Luther Says* (St. Louis: Concordia, 1959).
Register of the Company of Pastors of Geneva in the Time of Calvin, The (edited and translated by Philip E. Hughes; Grand Rapids: Eerdmans, 1966).
Sarcerius, Erasmus, *Nova methodus in praecipuos scripturae divinae locos* (Basileae: 1546).
Servetus, Michael, *Christianismi Restitutio* (Vienna, 1553; repro Frankfurt: Minerva, 1966).
Socinus, Faustus, *Opera Omnia in Duos Tomos Distincta*, in *Bibliotheca Fratrum Polonorum quos Unitarios Vocant*, volumes 1-2 (Amsterdam: 1656).
Scherzerus, Joannes Adamus, *Collegii Anti-Sociniani* (Leipzig: 1702).
Scotus, John Duns, *Quaestiones In Librum Tertium Sententiarum*. In *Opera Omnia*, volume 14 (Paris: 1894).
Spangenberg, Johann, *Margarita theologica Continens Praecipuos locos doctrinae Christianae* (Lipsiae: Nicolaus Wolrab, 1541).
Staehelin, Ernst, *Briefe und Akten zum Leben Oekolampads* (reprint. QFR 10, 19; New York: Johnson, 1971).
Stegmann, Josua, *Photinianismus: hoc est, succincta refutatio errorum Photinianorum* (1623).
Tappert, Theodore G. (ed.), *The Book of Concord: The Confessions of the Evangelical Lutheran Church* (Philadelphia: Fortress, 1959).
Taylor, Thomas. *The Works of that Faithful Servant of Christ* (London: T.R. and E.M. for John Barlet the elder and John Barlet the younger, 1653).
Theophylact, *The Explanation of the Holy Gospel According to St. Matthew*. In *Theophylact's Explanation of the New Testament*, volume 1 (House Springs, MO: Chrysostom Press, 1992).
Vatican Council II: The Conciliar Documents (edited by Austin Flannery, O.P.; Northport: Costello, 1979).
Wigand, Johann, *Collatio. De III. Argumentis Antinomicis* (Ihenae: In Officina Haeredum Christiani Rhodii, 1570).
—. *De Antinomia Veteri Et Nova, Collatio Et Commonefactio* (Ienae: 1571).
Zanchi, Girolamo, *De Tribus Elohim, Aeterno Patre, Filio, et Spiritu Sancto, Uno eodemque Iehova, libri XIII* (Neustadt Matthaei Harnisii, 1589).

BIBLIOGRAPHY

Zwingli, Huldrych, *Annotationes Huldrici Zwinglii in Evangelium Matthaei*. In *Huldreich Zwingli's Werke*, Erste vollstandige Ausgabe durch Melchior Schuler und Joh. Schulthess, volume 6.1 (Zurich: Turici ex Officina Schulthessian, 1836).

—. *Commentary on True and False Religion* (edited by Samuel Macauley Jackson and Clarence Nevin Heller; Durham, NC: Labyrinth Press, 1981).

—. *De vera et falsa religione commentarius (1525)* in *Corpus Reformatorum*, 90.

—. *Huldreich Zwingli's Werke*, volume 5 (edited by Melchior Schuler and Johannes Schultness; reprint [1529] Zürich: F. Schulthess, 1828).

SECONDARY WORKS

Abrahams, Israel, *Jewish Life in the Middle Ages* (London: MacMillan, 1896; reprint BiblioBazaar 2011).

Achtemeier, Elizabeth, 'Exchanging God for "no gods": A Discussion of Female Language for God.' In A. Kimel Jr. (ed.), *Speaking the Christian God* (Grand Rapids: Eerdmans, 1992), 1-16.

Acklin-Zimmermann, Beatrice, *Die Gesetzesinterpretation in den Römerbriefkommentaren von Peter Abaelard und Martin Luther. Eine Untersuchung auf dem Hintergrund der Antijudaismusdiskussion* (Frankfurt a.M. 2004).

Adam, Peter, 'Calvin's Preaching and Homiletic: Nine Engagements, Part 1,' *Churchman* 124.3 (Autumn 2010), 201-216; 'Part 2' *Churchman* 124:4 (Winter 2010), 331-342.

—. '"Preaching of a lively kind"—Calvin's engaged expository preaching.' In Mark D. Thompson (ed.), *Engaging with Calvin: Aspects of the Reformer's legacy for today* (Nottingham: Apollos, 2009), 13-41.

—. *Speaking God's Words: A Practical Theology of Preaching* (Leicester: InterVarsity Press, 1996).

Aland, Kurt (ed.), Lutherlexikon (4th edition; Göttingen: Vandenhoeck & Ruprecht, 1983).

Althaus, Paul, *The Theology of Martin Luther* (translated by Robert C. Schultz; Philadelphia: Fortress, 1970).

Anderson, Marvin, 'John Calvin, Biblical Preacher,' *Scottish Journal of Theology*, 42.2 (1989), 176-181.

Asendorf, Ulrich, *Die Theologie Martin Luthers nach seinen Predigten* (Göttingen: Vandenhoeck & Ruprecht, 1988).

Baars, Arie, 'The Trinity.' In Herman Selderhuis (ed.), *The Calvin Handbook* (Grand Rapids: Eerdmans, 2009), 245-257.

Backus, I., 'Calvin's Judgment of Eusebius of Caesarea: An Analysis,' *Sixteenth Century Journal* 22.3 (1991), 419-437.

Bainton, Roland, *Here I Stand* (New York: Abingdon-Cokesbury, 1950).

Balke, Willem, *Calvin and the Anabaptist Radicals* (translated by William J. Heynen; Grand Rapids: Eerdmans, 1981; Amsterdam, 1973).

Bandstra, A.J., 'Law and Gospel in Calvin and in Paul.' In D.E. Holwerda (ed.), *Exploring the Heritage of John Calvin: Essays in Honor of John Bratt* (Grand Rapids: Baker, 1976), 11-39.

Barbier-Meuller, Jean Paul, *Warriors of the Word: A History of the French Wars of Religion, 1562-1598* (Geneva: Hazan, 2006).

Barnes, Robert, *Prophecy and Gnosis* (Stanford: Stanford University Press, 1988).

Barnhouse, Ruth Tiffany and Urban T. Holms, III (eds), *Male and Female: Christian Approaches to Sexuality* (New York: Seabury, 1976).

Baron, Hans, *The Crisis of the Italian Renaissance: Civic Humanism and Republican Liberty in an Age of Classicism and Tyranny* (Princeton: Princeton University Press, 1966).

Barth, Hans-Martin, Der Teufel und Jesus Christus in der Theologie Martin Luthers, FKDG 19 (Göttingen: Vandenhoeck & Ruprecht, 1967).

Barth, Karl, *Church Dogmatics*, 14 volumes (edited by G.W. Bromiley and T.F. Torrance; Edinburgh: T. & T. Clark, 1936-68).

Battles, Ford Lewis, 'God Was Accommodating Himself to Human Capacity.' In *Readings in Calvin's Theology* (Grand Rapids: Baker, 1984). [Also, found in *Interpretation* 31 (1977), 19-38.]

—. *The Piety of John Calvin: An Anthology Illustrative of the Spirituality of the Reformer* (Grand Rapids: Baker, 1978).

—. and André Malan Hugo, *Calvin's Commentary on Seneca's De Clementia, with introduction, translation and notes* (Leiden: Brill, 1969).

Bauckham, Richard, *Tudor Apocalypse* (Oxford: Sutton Courtenay, 1978).

Bayer, Oswald, *Martin Luthers Theologie. Eine Vergegenwärtigung* (2nd edition; Tübingen: 2004).

Beeke, Joel R. and Sinclair B. Ferguson (eds), *Reformed Confessions Harmonized* (Grand Rapids: Baker, 1999).

Bellardi, W., *Wolfgang Schultheyss. Wege und Wandlungen eines Strassburger Spiritualisten und Zeitgenossen Martin Bucers* (Frankfurt: Erwin von Steinbach-Stiftung, 1976).

Bente, F., *Historical Introductions to the Book of Concord* (St. Louis: Concordia, 1965).

Berger, Heinrich, *Calvins Geschichtsauffassung* (Zürich: Zwingli Verlag, 1955).

Berkhof, Louis, *Systematic Theology* (1932-38; Grand Rapids: Eerdmans, 1996).

Bienert, Walther, *Martin Luther und die Juden, Ev. Verlagswerk* (Frankfurt: Ev. Verlagswerk, 1982).

Billings, J. Todd, *The Word of God for the People of God: An Entryway to the Theological Interpretation of Scripture* (Grand Rapids: Eerdmans, 2010).

Blacketer, Raymond A., 'Commentaries and Prefaces.' In Herman Selderhuis (ed.), *The Calvin Handbook* (Grand Rapids: Eerdmans, 2009), 181-192.

Bloesch, Donald G., *Is the Bible Sexist?* (Westchester, IL: Crossway, 1982).

BIBLIOGRAPHY

Blowers, Paul, 'Eastern Orthodox Biblical Interpretation.' In Alan Hauser and Duane Watson (eds), *A History of Biblical Interpretation*, volume 2 (Grand Rapids: Eerdmans, 2009).

Boockmann, H., Kirche und Frömmigkeit vor der Reformation. In G. Bott (ed.), *Martin Luther und die Reformation in Deutschland. Ausstellung zum 500. Geburtstag Martin Luthers. Veranstaltet vom Germanischen Nationalmuseum Nürnberg in Zusammenarbeit mit dem Verein für Reformationsgeschichte* (Frankfurt a.M.: Insel-Verlag, 1983), 41-72.

Bornkamm, Heinrich, *Luthers geistige Welt* (2nd edition; Gütersloh: Bertelsmann, 1953).

—. *Luther's World of Thought* (St. Louis: Concordia, 1958).

Borvan, Daniel, 'Destroying Babylon's Foundations: Continuity and Discontinuity in the Early Life and Thought of Faustus Socinus' (Masters Thesis, Westminster Seminary California, 2011).

Bosseder, Johannes, *Luthers Stellung zu den Juden im Spiegel seiner Interpreten. Interpretation und Rezeption von Luthers Schriften und Äußerungen zum Judentum im 19. und 20* (München: Hueber, 1972).

Bousset, Wilhelm, *Die Offenbarung Iohannis* (Gottingen: Vandenhoeck und Ruprecht, 1906).

Bouwsma, William J., 'Calvin and the Renaissance Crisis of Knowing,' *Calvin Theological Journal* 17 (1982), 190-211.

—. *John Calvin: A Sixteenth Century Portrait* (Oxford: Oxford University Press, 1988).

—. 'Renaissance and Reformation: An Essay in the Affinities and Connection.' In Heiko A. Oberman (ed.), *Luther and the Dawn of the Modern Era* (Leiden: Brill, 1975), 127-149.

Brashler, James, 'From Erasmus to Calvin: Exploring the Roots of Reformed Hermeneutics,' *Interpretation* 63.2 (April 2009), 154-166.

Bray, Gerald. *Biblical Interpretation: Past and Present* (Downers Grove: IVP, 1996).

Brecht, Martin, *Martin Luther*, volume 2 (Philadelphia: Fortress, 1990).

Brecht, Martin, *Martin Luther*, Bd. 1: *Sein Weg zur Reformation, 1483-1521* (Stuttgart: Calwer, 1983).

—. Bd. 2: *Ordnung und Abgrenzung der Reformation, 1521-1532* (Stuttgart: Calwer, 1986).

—. Bd. 3: *Die Erhaltung der Kirche, 1532-1546* (Stuttgart: Calwer, 1987).

Brinkmann, Günther, *Die Irenik des David Pareus: Frieden und Einheit ihrer Relevanz zur Warheitfrage* (Hildesheim: Gerstenberg, 1972).

Browning, D.S., *Practical Theology* (San Francisco: Harper & Row, 1983).

Burnett, Amy Nelson, 'Contributors to the Reformed Tradition.' In David Whitford (ed.), *Reformation and Early Modern Europe: A Guide to Research* (Kirksville, MO: Truman State University Press, 2008), 25-56.

Burnett, Richard, 'John Calvin on Sacred and Secular History.' In David W. Hall (ed.), *Tributes to John Calvin: A Celebration of his Quincentenary* (The Calvin 500 Series, Phillipsburg: Presbyterian and Reformed, 2010), 217-246.

Butin, Philip W., *Revelation, Redemption, and Response: Calvin's Trinitarian Understanding of the Divine-Human Relationship* (New York: Oxford University Press, 1995).

Canlis, Julie, *Calvin's Ladder: A Spiritual Theology of Ascent and Ascension* (Grand Rapids: Eerdmans, 2010).

Casey, Maurice. 'The Jackals and the Son of Man,' *Journal for the Study of the New Testament* 23 (1985), 3-22.

Chadwick, Owen, *The Reformation* (Harmondsworth: Penguin, Reprint 1973).

Charles, R.H., *Studies in the Apocalypse* (Edinburgh: T. & T. Clark, 1913).

Childs, Brevard S., *The Struggle to Understand Isaiah as Christian Scripture* (Grand Rapids: Eerdmans, 2004).

Chrisman, Miriam, *Strasbourg and the Reform* (New Haven: Yale University Press, 1967).

Christensen, Carl C., *Art and the Reformation in Germany* (Athens, OH: Ohio University Press, 1979).

Clayton, Joseph, *Luther and his Work* (Milwaukee: Bruce Publishing, 1937).

Cochrane, Arthur C., 'Reading the *Augustana* from the Reformed Tradition.' In *Currents in Theology and Mission* (St. Louis: Faculty of Concordia Seminary in Exile, 1980).

Collinson, Patrick, *The Birthpangs of Protestant England: Religious and Cultural Change in the Sixteenth and Seventeenth Centuries* (New York: Macmillan, 1988).

Cooke, Bernard, 'Non-Patriarchal Salvation,' *Horizons* 10 (1983), 22-31.

Coolman, B.T., *The Theology of Hugh of St. Victor: An Interpretation* (New York: Cambridge University Press, 2010).

Dau, W.H.T., *Luther Examined and Re-examined: A Review of Catholic Criticism and a Plea for Revaluation* (St. Louis: Concordia, 1917).

Davis, Ellen F. and Richard B. Hays (eds), *The Art of Reading Scripture* (Grand Rapids: Eerdmans, 2003).

de Boer, E.A., *John Calvin on the Visions of Ezekiel* (Leiden: Brill, 2004).

de Greef, Wulfert, *The Writings of John Calvin. An Introductory Guide* (translated by Lyle Bierma; Louisville: Westminster John Knox, 2008).

de Jonge, Henk Jan. 'Erasmus' Method of Translation in His Version of the New Testament,' *The Bible Translator* 37.1 (Jan 1986), 135-138.

—. 'Novum Testamentum a Nobis Versum: The Essence of Erasmus' Edition of the New Testament,' *Journal of Theological Studies* 35.2 (Oct 1984), 394-413.

de Koster, Lester, *Light for the City: Calvin's Preaching, Source of Life and Liberty* (Grand Rapids: Eerdmans 2004).

Delius, Hans-Ulrich, *Martin Luther, Studienausgabe*, 6 volumes (Berlin/Leipzig: Ev. Verlagsanstalt, 1979-1999).

BIBLIOGRAPHY

Deme, Dániel, *The Christology of Anselm of Canterbury* (Aldershot: Ashgate, 2004).

Demura, Akira, 'Two Commentaries on the Epistle to the Romans: Calvin and Oecolampadius.' In Wilhelm H. Neuser, and Brian G. Armstrong (eds), *Calvinus Sincerioris Religionis Vindex* (Kirksville, MO: Sixteenth Century Journal Publishers, 1997), 165-188.

Denis, Philippe, 'La Prophetie dans les eglises de la Reforme au XVIe siecle,' *RHE* 72 (1977), 289-316.

Dennison, Jr., James T., *Reformed Confessions of the 16th and 17th Centuries in English Translation*, 3 volumes (edited by James T. Dennison, Jr.; Grand Rapids: Reformation Heritage Books, 2008-).

Dingel, Irena, '"Dass wir Gott in keiner Weise verbilden": Die Bilderfrage zwischen Calvinismus und Luthertum.' In Andreas Wagner, Volker Hörner, Günter Geisthardt (eds), *Gott im Wort—Gott im Bild: Bilderlosigkeit als Bedingung des Monotheismus?* (n.p.: Neukirchener Verlag, 2005), 97-111.

Doberstein, John W., 'Introduction' to *Luther's Works*, volume 51: *Sermons* I, xiv-xv.

Douglass, Jane Dempsey, 'Calvin's Use of Metaphorical Language for God: God as Enemy and God as Mother,' *The Princeton Seminary Bulletin* 8 (1987), 19-32.

Dowey, Edward, *The Knowledge of God in Calvin's Theology* (New York: Columbia University Press, 1952).

Duke, Alastair, Gillian Lewis and Andrew Pettegee (eds), *Calvinism in Europe 1540-1610* (Manchester: Manchester University Press, 1992).

Eastwood, Cyril, *The Priesthood of All Believers: An Examination of the Doctrine from the Reformation to the Present Day* (Minneapolis: Augsburg, 1962).

Ebeling, Gerhard, *Evangelische Evangelienauslegung: Eine Untersuchung zu Luthers Hermeneutik* (Darmstadt: Wissenschaftliche Buchgesellschaft, 1962).

—. *Luther: An Introduction to His Thought* (London: William Collins, 1970).

Edwards, Mark U., Jr., *Luther's Last Battles* (Ithaca: 1983; reprint, Fortress, 2005).

Egli, Emil, 'Prophesying.' In *The New Schaff-Herzog Encyclopedia of Religious Knowledge*, volume 9 (New York: Funk and Wagnalls, 1911).

Eire, Carlos, 'Iconoclasm.' In Hans J. Hillerbrand (ed.), *Oxford Encyclopedia of the Reformation* (New York: Oxford University Press, 1996), 2:302-306.

—. *War Against the Idols: The Reformation of Worship from Erasmus to Calvin* (Cambridge: Cambridge University Press, 1986).

Elliott, Mark W., 'Romans 7 in the Reformation Century.' In Kathy Ehrensperger and R. Ward Holder (eds), *Reformation Readings of Romans* (London: T. & T. Clark, 2008), 173-174.

Estes, J.M., 'The Role of the Godly Magistrate in the Church: Melanchthon as Luther's interpreter and collaborator,' *Church History* 67.3 (September, 1998), 463–483.

Falk, Gerhard, *The Jew in Christian Theology: Martin Luther's Anti-Jewish Vom Schem Hamphoras, Previously Unpublished in English, and Other Milestones in Church Doctrine Concerning Judaism* (Jefferson, NC: McFarland, 1992).

Farley, E., 'Theology and practice outside the clerical paradigm.' In Don. S. Browning (ed.), *Practical Theology* (San Francisco: Harper & Row, 1983).

Farner, Oskar, *Huldrych Zwingli*, volume 3 (Zurich: Zwingli Verlag, 1954).

Faustel, Heinrich, *D. Martin Luther. Sein Leben und Werk* (Holzgerlingen: Hänssler, 2008).

Fesko, J.V., *Beyond Calvin: Union with Christ and Justification in Early Modern Reformed Theology (1517-1700)* (Göttingen: Vandenhoeck & Ruprecht, 2012).

—. 'Socinus and the Racovian Catechism on Justification' (paper given at the 2011 Evangelical Theological Society's Annual Meeting in San Francisco).

Figi, J., *Die innere Reorganisation des Grossmünstersstiftes in Zürich von 1519 bis 1531* (Affoltern am Albis, 1951).

Fowl, Stephen. *Theological Interpretation of Scripture* (Eugene, Or: Cascade, 2009).

—. with L. Gregory Jones, *Reading in Communion: Scripture and Ethics in Christian Life* (Grand Rapids: Eerdmans, 1991).

Franks, Robert S., *A History of the Doctrine of the Work of Christ in Its Ecclesiastical Development*, 2 volumes (London: Hodder and Stoughton, 1918).

Freitag, Albert, 'Veit Dietrichs Anteil an der Lutherüberlieferung.' In Karl Drescher (ed.), *Lutherstudien zur 4. Jahrhundertfeier der Reformation veröffentlicht von den Mitarbeitern der Weimarer Lutherausgabe* (Weimar: Hermann Böhlaus Nachfolger, 1917), 170-202.

Frymire, John M., *The Primacy of the Postils: Catholics, Protestants, and the Dissemination of Ideas in Early Modern Germany* (Leiden: Brill, 2010).

Fudge, Thomas A., 'Icarus of Basel? Oecolampadius and the Early Swiss Reformation,' *Journal of Religious History* 21.3 (October 1997), 268-284.

Gamble, Richard C., '*Brevitas et Facilitas*: Toward an Understanding of Calvin's Hermeneutic,' *Westminster Theological Journal* 47 (1985), 1-17.

Ganoczy, Alexandre, 'Observations on Calvin's Trinitarian Doctrine of Grace.' In Elsie Anne McKee and Brian G. Armstrong (eds), *Probing the Reformed Tradition: Historical Essays in Honor of Edward A. Dowey, Jr.* (Louisville, KY: Westminster/ John Knox Press, 1989), 96-107.

Garin, Eugenio, *Italian Humanism: Philosophy and Civic Life in the Renaissance* (New York: Harper and Row, 1965).

BIBLIOGRAPHY

Garrett, Duane A., *An Analysis of the Hermeneutics of John Chrysostom's Commentary on Isaiah 1-8 with an English Translation* (Lewiston, N.Y.: Edwin Mellen, 1992).

George, Timothy, *Reading Scripture with the Reformers* (Downers Grove, IL: IVP Academic, 2011).

German Evangelical Kirchentag's Proceedings of Annual Meeting (Berlin: Evangelical Alliance, 1853) in *Evangelical Christendom*, volumes 7-8.

Gerrish, Brian A., 'Priesthood and Ministry in the Theology of Luther,' *Church History* 34 (1965), 404–422.

—. *The Old Protestantism and the New* (Chicago: University of Chicago Press, 1982).

Godby, John B., 'Fausto Sozzini and Justification.' In F.F. Church and Timothy George (eds), *Continuity and Discontinuity in Church History* (Leiden: Brill, 1979), 250-264.

Gomes, Alan W., '*De Jesu Christo Servatore:* Faustus Socinus on the Satisfaction of Christ,' *Westminster Theological Journal* 55 (1993), 209-231.

—. 'Faustus Socinus's *A Tract Concerning God, Christ, and the Holy Spirit*,' *Journal of the International Society of Christian Apologetics* 1.1 (2008), 37-58.

—. 'Faustus Socinus' *De Jesu Christo Servatore*, Part III: Historical Introductions, Translation and Critical Notes' (unpublished dissertation: Fuller Theological Seminary, 1990).

—. 'Some Observations on the Theological Method of Faustus Socinus (1539-1604),' *Westminster Theological Journal* 70 (2008), 49-71.

Gordon, Bruce, *The Swiss Reformation* (New York: Manchester University Press, 2002).

Gounelle, André, 'Le sacerdoce universel,' *Études Théologiques et Religieuses* 63 (1988), 429–434.

Graham, William A., *Beyond the Written Word: Oral Aspects of Scripture in the History of Religion* (Cambridge: Cambridge University Press, 1987).

Grayzel, Solomon, *A History of the Jews From the Babylonian Exile to the Present* (New York: Mentor, 1968).

Greschat, Martin, *Martin Bucer, A Reformer and His Times* (Louisville: Westminster John Knox, 2004).

Grimm, H.J., *The Reformation Era: 1500–1650* (New York: Macmillan, 1973).

Grisar, Hartmann, *Luther* (translated by E.M. Lamond, edited by L. Cappdelta; London: Trubner, 1915).

Gritsch, Eric, *Martin—God's Court Jester: Luther in Retrospect* (Philadelphia: Fortress, 1983).

—. *Martin Luther's Anti-Semitism. Against His Better Judgment* (Grand Rapids: Eerdmans, 2012).

—. 'The Unrefined Reformer,' *Christian History* 39 12.3. ChristianHistory.net: http://www.christianitytoday.com/ch/1993/issue39/3935.html.

—. 'Was Luther Anti-Semitic?' *Church History* 39. 12.3 ChristianHistory.net: http://www.christianitytoday.com/ch/1993/issue39/3938.html.
Guder, Darrell L., *The Continuing Conversion of the Church* (Grand Rapids: Eerdmans, 2000).
Gunton, Colin E., *Father, Son and Holy Spirit: Essays toward a Fully Trinitarian Theology* (London: T. & T. Clark, 2003).
—. *Theology Through Preaching: The Gospel and the Christian Life* (London: T. & T. Clark, 2001).
—. *The Theologian as Preacher: Further Sermons from Colin Gunton* (London: T. & T. Clark, 2004).
Hailperin, Herman, *Rashi and the Christian Scholars* (Pittsburgh: University of Pittsburgh Press, 1963).
Hall, Peter (ed.), *The Harmony of Protestant Confessions of Faith* (1842; Edmonton: Still Waters Revival Books, 1992).
Hasel, Gerhard, *New Testament Theology: Basic Issues in the Current Debate* (Grand Rapids: Eerdmans, 1978).
Hauerwas, Stanley, *Unleashing the Scripture: Freeing the Bible from Captivity to America* (Nashville: Abingdon, 1993).
Heimmel, Jennifer P., *'God is our mother': Julian of Norwich and the medieval image of Christian feminine divinity* (Salzburg, Austria: Institut fur Anglistik und Amerikanistik, Universitat Salzburg, 1982).
Heintze, Gerhard, *Luthers Predigt von Gesetz und Evangelium* (München: Chr. Kaiser Verlag, 1958).
Heitink, G., *Practical Theology: history, theory, action domains: manual for practical theology* (Grand Rapids: Eerdmans, 1999).
Helm, Paul, *John Calvin's Ideas* (Oxford: Oxford University Press, 2004).
Hendel, Kurt, 'The Material as a Vehicle of the Divine,' *Currents in Theology and Mission* 28 (2001), 326-34.
Hendrix, Scott H., *Luther and the Papacy: Stages in a Reformation Conflict* (Philadelphia: Fortress, 1981).
Henry, Paul, *Life and Times of Calvin the Great Reformer* (translated by Paul Stebbing; London: Whitaker, 1849).
Herrmann, E.H., '"Why then the Law?" Salvation history and the Law in Martin Luther's Interpretation of Galatians (1513-1522)' (doctoral dissertation; Concordia Seminary, 2005).
Hesselink, I. John, *Calvin's First Catechism: A Commentary* (Louisville: Westminster John Knox, 1997).
—. 'Calvin's Theology.' In Donald K. McKim (ed.), *The Cambridge Companion to John Calvin* (Cambridge: Cambridge University Press, 2004), 74-92.
—. 'Law and Gospel or Gospel and Law?—Karl Barth, Martin Luther, and John Calvin,' *Reformation and Revival Journal* 14.1 (2005), 139-171.
Heyns, L.M. and H.J.C. Pieterse, *A Primer in Practical Theology* (Pretoria, SA: Gnosis, 1990).

BIBLIOGRAPHY

Hillar, Marian, 'Laelius and Faustus Socinus, Founders of Socinianism: Their Lives and Theology, Part One,' *A Journal from the Radical Reformation* 10.2 (2002), 18-38.

Hillerbrand, Hans. J., (ed.), *The Oxford Encyclopedia of the Reformation*, 4 volumes (Oxford: Oxford University Press, 1996).

Hirsch, Emanuel, introductory comments in *Luthers Werke in Auswahl*, volume 7: *Predigten* (Berlin: Walter de Gruyter, 1962).

Holder, R. Ward, 'Calvin as Commentator on the Pauline Epistles.' In Donald K. McKim (ed.), *Calvin and the Bible* (Cambridge: Cambridge University Press, 2006), 224-255.

—. *John Calvin and the Grounding of Interpretation: Calvin's First Commentaries* (Leiden: Brill, 2006).

Holmio, Armas K.E., *Luther-Friend or Foe* (Chicago: National Lutheran Council, 1949).

Holwerda, David E., 'Eschatology and History: A Look at Calvin's Eschatological Vision.' In D.E. Holwerda (ed.), *Exploring the Heritage of John Calvin: Essays in Honor of John Bratt* (Grand Rapids: Baker, 1976).

Horton, M.S., 'Calvin and the Law-Gospel Hermeneutic,' *Pro Ecclesia* 6.1 (1997), 27-42.

Hughes, R.A., *Lament, Death and Destiny* (New York: Peter Lang, 2004).

Jenkins, R.G., 'The Biblical Text of the Commentaries of Eusebius and Jerome on Isaiah,' *Abr-Nahrain* 22 (1984), 64-78.

Jung-Sook Lee, 'Calvin's Ministry in Geneva: Theology and Practice.' In Sung Wook Chung (ed.), *John Calvin and Evangelical Theology: Legacy and Prospect* (Milton Keynes: Paternoster, 2009), 199-218.

Karant-Nunn, Susan, *The Reformation of Feeling. Shaping the Religious Emotions in Early Modern Germany* (Oxford: Oxford University Press, 2010).

Kaufmann, Thomas, *Luthers 'Judenschriften'* Ein Beitrag zu ihrer historischen Kontextualisierung (Tübingen: Mohr Siebeck, 2011).

Kelly, Douglas F., 'The True and Triune God: Calvin's Doctrine of the Holy Trinity; *Institutes* 1.11-13.' In David W. Hall and Peter A. Lillback (eds), *A Theological Guide to Calvin's Institutes: Essays and Analysis* (Phillipsburg, NJ: Presbyterian & Reformed, 2008), 65-89.

Kingdon, Robert M., 'Catechesis in Calvin's Geneva.' In John Van Engen (ed.), *Educating People of Faith: Exploring the History of Jewish and Christian Communities* (Grand Rapids: Eerdmans 2004), 294-313.

Klappert, Bertold, 'Erwählung und Rechtfertigung.' In Heinz Kremers (ed.), *Die Juden und Martin Luther—Martin Luther und die Juden: Geschichte, Wirkungsgeschichte, Herausforderung* (Neukirchen-Vluyn: Neukirchner Verlag, 1987), 368-410.

Klaus, Bernhard, *Veit Dietrich: Leben und Werk* (Nürnberg: Verein für bayerische Kirchengeschichte, 1958).

Klotsche, E.H., *Christian Symbolics or Exposition of the Distinctive Characteristics of the Catholic, Lutheran and Reformed Churches as well as the Modern Denominations and Sects Represented in this Country* (Burlington: Lutheran Literary Board, 1929).

Klug, Eugene F.A. (ed.), *Sermons of Martin Luther: The House Postils* (Grand Rapids: Baker, 1996).

Köhler, Walter, 'Das Täufertum in Calvins *Institutio* von 1536,' *Mennonitische Geschichtsblätter*, 2 (1936).

Kohls, E.W., *Die Schule bei Martin Bucer in ihrem Verhältnis zu Kirche und Obrigikeit* (Heidelberg: Quelle & Meyer, 1963).

Kolb, Robert, *Luther and the Stories of God: Biblical Narratives as a Foundation for Christian Living* (Grand Rapids: Baker Academic, 2012).

—. *Martin Luther as Prophet, Teacher, and Hero: Images of the Reformer, 1520-1620* (Grand Rapids: Baker, 1999).

—. *Martin Luther. Confessor of the Faith* (Oxford: Oxford University Press, 2009).

—. *Reformers Define the Church, 1530-1580* (St. Louis: Concordia, 1991).

—. and T.J. Wengert, *The Book of Concord: The Confessions of the Evangelical Lutheran Church* (Minneapolis: Fortress, 2000).

Krans, Jan, *Beyond What is Written* (Leiden: Brill, 2006).

Krey, Philip and Lesley Smith (eds), *Nicholas of Lyra: The Senses of Scripture* (Leiden: Brill, 2000).

Krohn, James B., 'The Triune God Who Speaks: Calvin's Theological Hermeneutics,' *Koers* 66.1 & 2, 53-70.

Lane, A.N.S., *John Calvin: Student of the Church Fathers* (Grand Rapids: Baker, 1999).

Lang, August, *Der Evangelienkommentar Martin Butlers und die Grundzüge seiner Theologie* (Leipzig: 1900).

Leith, John H., 'Calvin's Doctrine of the Proclamation of the Word and Its Significance Today.' In Timothy George (ed.), *John Calvin & the Church: A Prism of Reform* (Louisville: Westminster John Knox, 1990), 206-229.

Leroux, Neil, *Luther as Comforter. Writings on Death* (Leiden: Brill, 2007).

—. *Luther's Rhetoric: Strategies and Style from the Invocavit Sermons* (St. Louis: Concordia Academic, 2002).

Letham, Robert, *The Holy Trinity: In Scripture, History, Theology, and Worship* (Phillipsburg, NJ: Presbyterian and Reformed, 2004).

Lidgett, J. Scott, *The Fatherhood of God in Christian Truth and Life* (London: Epworth, 1903).

Lillback, Peter A., 'Confessional Subscription Among 16th Century Reformers.' In David Hall (ed.), *The Practice of Confessional Subscription* (University Press of America, 1995).

Lindberg, Carter, 'Tainted Greatness: Luther's Attitudes Toward Judaism and their Historical Reception' in Nancy A Harrowitz (ed.), *Tainted Greatness:*

Antisemitism and Cultural Heroes (Philadelphia: Temple University Press, 1994), 15-35.

Locher, Gottfried, 'Huldrych Zwingli's Concept of History;' 'How the Image of Zwingli Has Changed in Recent Research;' and 'In Spirit and in Truth.' In *Zwingli's Thought: New Perspective* (Leiden: Brill, 1981).

Lohse, B., *Martin Luther: An introduction to his Life and Work* (Philadelphia: Fortress, 1986).

—. *Martin Luther's Theology: Its Historical and Systematic Development* (edited and translated by Roy A. Harrisville; Minneapolis: Fortress, 1999).

Loy, Matthias et al, *Sermons on the Gospels for the Sundays and Principal Festivals of the Church Year by Dr. Martin Luther* (Rock Island, IL: Augustana Book Concern, 1871).

Lubac, Henri de, *Medieval Exegesis: The Four Senses of Scripture* (Grand Rapids: Eerdmans, 1998).

Lubieniecki, Stanislas, *History of the Polish Reformation and Nine Related Documents* (edited and translated by George Hunston Williams; Minneapolis: Fortress, 1995).

Lupton, Lewis, *A History of the Geneva Bible*, volume 7 (London: Olive Tree, 1975).

Luz, U. 'The Son of Matthew: Heavenly Judge or Human Christ?' *Journal for the Study of the New Testament* 48 (1992), 3-21.

MacCulloch, Diarmaid, *Reformation: Europe's House Divided, 1490-1700* (London / New York: Allen Lane, 2003).

—. *The Reformation: A History* (Viking Adult, 2004).

MacKenzie, 'The Evangelical Character of Martin Luther's Faith.' In Kenneth J. Stewart and Michael Haykin (eds), *The Advent of Evangelicalism: Exploring Historical Continuities* (Nashville: B&H Academic, 2008), 171-98.

Mackinnon, James, *Luther and the Reformation*, volume 4 (New York, 1962).

Maier, Gerhard, *Biblical Hermeneutics* (Wheaton: Crossway, 1994).

Mattox, Mickey. 'Martin Luther.' In Justin S. Holcomb (ed.), *Christian Theologies of Scripture* (New York: New York University Press, 2006), 94-113.

McGrath, Alister E., *A Life of John Calvin: A Study in the Shaping of Western Culture* (Oxford: Blackwell, 1990).

McKee, Elsie Anne, 'Exegesis, Theology and Development in Calvin's *Institutio*: A Methodological Suggestion.' In Elsie Anne McKee and Brian G. Armstrong (eds), *Probing the Reformed Tradition: Historical Studies in Honor of Edward A. Dowey* (Louisville, KY: Westminster John Knox, 1989), 154-72.

McKim, Donald K. (ed.), *Dictionary of Major Biblical Interpreters* (2nd ed. Downers Grove, IL: IVP Academic, 2007).

Mackinnon, James, *Luther and the Reformation*, volume 4 'Vindication of the Movement (1530-1546)' (New York: Russell & Russell, 1962).

McKinnon, Steven A. (ed.), *Ancient Christian Commentary on Scripture: Isaiah 1-39* (Downers Grove, IL: InterVarsity Academic, 2004).

McLaughlin, Eleanor L. 'Male and Female in Christian Tradition: Was there a Reformation in the sixteenth century?' In Ruth Tiffany Barnhouse and Urban T. Holmes, III (eds), *Male and Female: Christian Approaches to Sexuality* (New York: Seabury, 1976).

Meditz, Robert. '"Too Hard for the Teeth of Time": Difficulties in Using Scripture in the Church since the Reformation,' *Journal of Theological Interpretation* 2.2 (2008), 275-283.

Merrill, Eugene H., 'Rashi, Nicholas De Lyra, and Christian Exegesis,' *Westminster Theological Journal* 38.1 (1975), 66-79.

Meuser, Fred W., 'Luther as Preacher of the Word of God.' In Donald K. McKim (ed.), *The Cambridge Companion to Martin Luther* (Cambridge: Cambridge University Press, 2003), 136-148.

—. *Luther the Preacher* (Minneapolis: Augsburg, 1983).

Miller, Ed L., 'Oecolampadius: The Unsung Hero of the Basel Reformation,' *Iliff Review* 39.3 (Fall 1982), 5-25.

Moeller, Bernd, H.C. Erik Midelfort and Mark Edwards, *Imperial Cities and the Reformation: Three Essays* (Labyrinth, 1982).

Mollenkott, Virginia, *The Divine Feminine: the Biblical Image of God as Female* (New York: Crossroad, 1983).

Moltmann, Jürgen, 'Jacob Brocard als Vorlaüfer der Reich Gottes theologie und der symbolisch-propetischen Schriftausleguing des Johann Cocceius,' *ZKG*, 71 (1960).

Montgomery, John W., *In Defense of Martin Luther* (Milwaukee: NPH, 1970).

Moore, T.M., 'Some Observations concerning the educational philosophy of John Calvin,' *Westminster Theological Journal* 46 (1984), 140-155.

Muhlhan, B., *Being Shaped by Freedom* (Eugene Oregon: Pickwick, 2012).

Müller, C.: 'Luthers Haltung zu den Juden.' In Wolfgang Kraus (ed.), *Auf dem Weg zu einem Neuanfang. Dokumentation zur Erklärung der Evangelisch-Lutherischen Kirche in Bayern zum Thema Christen und Juden* (München: Chr. Kaiser Verlag, 1999), 135-149.

Muller, Gerhard, *Franz Lambert von Avignon und die Reformation in Hessen* (Marburg: N.C. Elwert, 1958).

Muller, Richard A., 'Biblical Interpretation in the Sixteenth and Seventeenth Centuries.' In Donald McKim (ed.), *Dictionary of Major Biblical Interpreters* (2nd ed. Downers Grove, IL: IVP Academic, 2007), 22-31.

—. 'Demoting Calvin: The Issue of Calvin and the Reformed Tradition.' In A.N. Burnett (ed.), *John Calvin, Myth and Reality: Images and Impact of Geneva's Reformer* (Papers of the 2009 Calvin Studies Society Colloquium, Eugene: Cascade Books, 2011), 3-17.

—. 'The Era of Protestant Orthodoxy.' In D.G. Hart and R. Albert Mohler (eds), *Theological Education in the Evangelical Tradition* (Grand Rapids: Baker, 1996), 103-128.

BIBLIOGRAPHY

—. 'The Hermeneutic of Promise and Fulfillment in Calvin's Exegesis of the Old Testament Prophecies of the Kingdom'. In David C. Steinmetz (ed.), *The Bible in the Sixteenth Century* (Durham, NC: Duke University Press, 1996), 68-82.

—. *The Unaccommodated Calvin: Studies in the Foundation of a Theological Tradition* (New York: Oxford University Press, 2000).

'Naumburg.' In John McClintock and James Strong (eds), *Cyclopedia of Biblical, Theological and Ecclesiastical Literature* (New York: Harper, 1876), 6.867.

Ngien, Dennis, *Luther as a Spiritual Adviser* (Milton Keynes: Paternoster, 2007).

Niemeyer, H.A. (ed.), *Collectionis Confessionum in Ecclesiis Reformatis Publicatarum* (Lipsiae: 1840).

Nijenhuis, Willem, *Calvinus Oecumenicus: Calvijn en de eenheid der kerk in het licht van zijn briefwisseling* (La Haye, 1958).

Oberman, Heiko A., *Luther: Man Between God and the Devil* (New York: 1989).

—. *Luther: Mensch zwischen Gott und Teufel* (Berlin: Siedler Verlag, 1991).

—. *The Impact of the Reformation* (Grand Rapids: Eerdmans, 1994).

—. *The Roots of Anti-Semitism* (Philadelphia: Fortress, 1984).

Ong, Walter J., *Orality and Literacy: The Technologizing of the Word* (New York: Routledge, 2005).

Opitz, Peter, *Heinrich Bullinger als Theologue* (Zürich: Theologischer Verlag Ag, 2004).

—. 'The Exegetical and Hermeneutical Work of John Oecolampadius, Huldrych Zwingli and John Calvin.' In Magne Sæbø (ed.) *Hebrew Bible, Old Testament: The History of Its Interpretation* (Göttingen: Vandenhoeck & Ruprecht, 2008), 2.407-413.

Osmer, R.R., *Practical Theology: An Introduction* (Grand Rapids: Eerdmans, 2008).

Ozment, Steven, *The Reformation in the Cities* (New Haven: Yale University Press, 1975).

—. *The Serpent and the Lamb: Cranach, Luther, and the Making of the Reformation* (New Haven: Yale University Press, 2011).

Packer, J.I. 'Calvin the Theologian.' In G.S. Duffield (ed.), *John Calvin: A Collection of Distinguished Essays* (Grand Rapids: Eerdmans, 1966), 149-175.

Parker, T.H.L. 'Calvin as Biblical Expositor.' In G.S. Duffield (ed.), *John Calvin: A Collection of Distinguished Essays* (Grand Rapids: Eerdmans, 1966), 176-186.

—. *Calvin's New Testament Commentaries* (Grand Rapids: Eerdmans, 1971).

—. *Calvin's Preaching* (Edinburgh: T. & T. Clark, 1992).

—. *Portrait of Calvin* (London: SCM, 1954).

—. *The Oracles of God* (London: Lutterworth, 1947).

Parsons, Michael. *Calvin's Preaching on the Prophet Micah: The 1550-1551 Sermons in Geneva* (Lewiston: Edward Mellen, 2006).

—. '"Let us not be like those . . . who want to call God to account": John Calvin's reading of some difficult deaths,' *Pacifica. Australasian Theological Studies* 20 (2007), 1-23.

—. *Luther and Calvin on Grief and Lament. Biblical Text and Life-Experience* (Lewiston: Edwin Mellen, forthcoming).

—. *Luther and Calvin on Old Testament Narratives. Reformation Thought and Narrative Text* (Lewiston, NY: Edwin Mellen, 2004).

—. 'Luther and Calvin on rape: Is the crime lost in the agenda?' *Evangelical Quarterly* 74 (2002), 123-142.

—. *Martin Luther's Interpretation of the Royal Psalms: the Spiritual Kingdom in a Pastoral Context* (New York: Edwin Mellen, 2009).

—. *Reformation Marriage* (Eugene: Wipf & Stock, 2011).

Partee, Charles, *The Theology of John Calvin* (Louisville, KY: Westminster John Knox, 2008).

Pattinson, S. and J. Woodward, 'An Introduction to Pastoral and Practical Theology.' In J. Woodward and S. Pattinson (eds), *The Blackwell Reader in Pastoral and Practical Theology* (New Jersey: Blackwell, 2000), 1-16.

Payton, Jr., James R., 'The Background and Significance of the Adopting Act of 1729.' In *Pressing Toward the Mark* (Philadelphia: The Committee for the Historian of the Orthodox Presbyterian Church, 1986).

Pelikan, Jaroslav and Valerie Hotchkiss (eds), *Creeds and Confessions of Faith in the Christian Tradition* (New Haven: Yale University Press, 2003).

Petersen, Rodney L., *Preaching in the Last Days: The Theme of Two Witnesses in the Sixteenth and Seventeenth Century* (New York: Oxford University Press, 1993).

Pfister, Rudolph, 'Prophezei.' In *RGG* V (Tübingen: J.C.B. Mohr, Paul Siebeck, 1961), col. 638.

Pieterse, H., *Contextual Theology for Ministry* (Perth, WA: Snowgoose Media, 2011).

Pinson, Koppel, *Pietism as a Factor in the Rise of German Nationalism* (New York: Columbia University Press, 1934).

Po-chia Hsia, R., 'Jews as Magicians in Reformation Germany.' In Sander L. Gilman and Steven T. Katz (eds), *Anti-Semitism in Times of Crisis* (New York: New York University Press, 1991).

Potter, G.R., *Zwingli* (Cambridge: Cambridge University Press, 1976).

Poythress, Diane, *Reformer of Basel: The Life, Thought, and Influence of Johannes Oecolampadius* (Grand Rapids: Reformation Heritage, 2011).

Prestwich, Menna, 'Introduction.' In *International Calvinism, 1541-1715* (Oxford: Clarendon, 1985).

Quistorp, Heinrich, *Die letzten Dinge im Zeugnis Calvins* (Gtittersloh: Bertelsmann, 1941).

Rees, Thomas (ed.), *The Racovian Catechism, With Notes and Illustrations* (London: Longman, Hurst, Rees, Orme, and Brown, 1818).

Reeves, Marjorie, *The Influence of Prophecy in the Later Middle Ages* (Oxford: Clarendon, 1969).

Reid, W.S., 'Calvin and the Founding of the Academy at Geneva,' *Westminster Journal of Theology* 18 (1955-56), 1-33.

Reinis, A., *Reforming the Art of Dying* (Aldershot: Ashgate, 2007).

Richard, James William, *books.google.comhttp://books.google.com/books/about/Philip_Melanchthon_the_Protestant_precep.html?id=3fYEAAAAYAAJ&utm_source=gb-gplus-sharePhilip Melanchthon, the Protestant preceptor of Germany, 1497-1560.*

—. *Philip Melanchthon, the Protestant Preceptor of Germany, 1497-1560* (New York: Putnam, 1898).

Robbert, George S., 'Martin Luther's Later Years,' *Church History* 39. 12.3 ChristianHistory.net:http://www.christianitytoday.com/ch/1992/issue34/3451.html.

Rother, Siegfried, *Die religiösen und geistigen Grundlagen der Politik Huldrych Zwingli* (Erlangen: Palm & Enke, 1956).

Rupp, Gordon, *Martin Luther and the Jews* (London: Council of Christians and Jews, 1972).

—. *Patterns of Reformation* (reprint 1969; Eugene, OR: Wipf & Stock, 2009).

Ryken, Leland, 'Calvinism and Literature.' In David W. Hall and Martin Padgett (eds), *Calvin and Culture: Exploring a Worldview* (Phillipsburg: Presbyterian and Reformed, 2012), 95-113.

—. 'Reformation and Puritan Ideals of Education.' In Joel Carpenter and Kenneth Schipps (eds), *Making Higher Education Christian: the History and Mission of Evangelical Colleges in America* (Grand Rapids: Christian University Press, 1987), 38-55.

Sawyer, John F.A., 'Isaiah.' In John H. Hayes (ed.), *Dictionary of Biblical Interpretation*, volume 1 (Nashville: Abingdon Press, 1999).

Sbigniew Ogonowski, 'Faustus Socinus 1539-1604.' In Jill Raitt (ed.), *Shapers of Religious Traditions in Germany, Switzerland, and Poland, 1560-1600* (New Haven: Yale University Press, 1981), 195-210.

Schaff, Philip, *The Creeds of Christendom*, 3 volumes (1931; Grand Rapids: Baker, 1990).

Schmidt-Clausing, F., 'Das Prophetzeigebet: Ein Blick uber Zwinglis liturgische Werkstatt,' *Zwingliana* 12 (1964), 10-34.

Schrenk, Gottlob, *Gottesreich und Bund im älteren Protestantismus, vornehmlich be; Johannes Cocceius* (Gütersioh: C. Bartlesmann, 1923).

Schwarz, Berthold, 'Martin Luther and the Jewish People with Implications for Jewish Missions.' In David Parker (ed.), *Jesus, Salvation and the Jewish People* (Milton Keynes: Paternoster, 2011), 85-117.

Scott, David, 'Speaking to Form: Trinitarian-Performative Scripture Reading,' *Anglican Theological Review* 77 (1995), 137–159.

Seitz, Christopher, 'Canonical Approach.' In Kevin Vanhoozer, Craig G. Bartholomew, Daniel J. Treier and N.T. Wright (eds), *Dictionary for Theological Interpretation of the Bible* (London: SPCK, 2005), 100-102.

Shakespeare, William, *Romeo and Juliet, Norton's Anthology* (Chicago: Hampton, 2004), 55-104.

Shepherd, Michael. 'Daniel 7:13 and the New Testament Son of Man,' *Westminster Theological Journal* 68 (2006), 99-111.

Smalley, Beryl, *The Study of the Bible in the Middle Ages* (Notre Dame: Notre Dame University Press, 1964).

Smith, D.A., 'The Preaching Community' (unpublished dissertation, 2007).

Southern, R.W., *Saint Anselm: A Portrait in a Landscape* (Cambridge: Cambridge University Press, 1991).

Spencer, F. Scott, *Acts* (Sheffield: Sheffield Academic, 1997).

Spitz, Lewis W., *The Protestant Reformation (1517-1559)* (New York: Harper & Row, 1985).

Staehelin, Ernst, *Das theologische Lebenswerk Johannes Oekolampads* (QFR 21; New York: Johnson, 1939).

Stauffer, Richard, *The Quest for Church Unity: From John Calvin to Isaac d'Huuisseau* (Allison Park, PA: Pickwick, 1986).

Steinmetz, David C., *Calvin in Conflict* (New York: Oxford University Press, 1995).

—. 'John Calvin as an Interpreter of the Bible.' In Donald K. McKim (ed.), *Calvin and the Bible* (Cambridge: Cambridge University Press, 2006), 282-291.

—. 'John Calvin on Isaiah 6: A Problem in the History of Exegesis,' *Interpretation* 36.2 (April 1982), 156-170.

Stephens, W.P. 'The Interpretation of the Bible in Bullinger's Early Works,' *Reformation and Renaissance Review* 11.3 (Dec 2009), 311-333.

Stetina, Karin Spiecker, 'Abba Father: Calvin's Biblical Image of the Fatherhood of God.' In Michael Parsons (ed.), *Since we are Justified by Faith. Justification in the Protestant Theologies of the Reformation* (Milton Keynes: Paternoster, 2012), 72-85.

Stolt, Birgit, *Martin Luthers Rhetorik des Herzens* (Tübingen: Mohr Siebeck, 2000).

Strand, Kenneth A., 'Current Issues and Trends in Luther Studies,' *AUSS* 22.1 (1984).

'Subscription.' In John McClintock and James Strong (eds), *Cyclopedia of Theological Literature* (New York: Harper, 1881), 10.3-4.

Swan, James, Martin, *Luther's Attitude Toward The Jews*, 2005 http://tquid.sharpens.org/luther_Jews.htm.

Tamburello, Dennis E., *Union with Christ: John Calvin and the Mysticism of St. Bernard* (Louisville, KY: Westminster John Knox, 1994).

Thompson, Bard, 'Historical Background of the Catechism.' In *Essays on the Heidelberg Catechism* (Philadelphia: United Church, 1963).

BIBLIOGRAPHY

Thompson, John L., 'Calvin as a Biblical Interpreter.' In Donald K. McKim (ed.), *The Cambridge Companion to John Calvin* (Cambridge: Cambridge University Press, 2004), 58-73.
—. *Writing the Wrongs* (Oxford: Oxford University Press, 2001).
Tonkin, John, 'Word and Image: Luther and the Arts,' *Colloquium* 17(1985), 45-54.
Torrance, Thomas F., *Calvin's Doctrine of Man* (London: Lutterworth, 1949).
—. *Kingdom and Church. A Study in the Theology of the Reformation* (Edinburgh: Oliver and Boyd, 1956).
—. *The Hermeneutics of Calvin* (Edinburgh: Scottish Academic Press, 1988).
—. *The School of Faith* (London: James Clarke, 1959).
—. *Trinitarian Perspectives: Toward Doctrinal Agreement* (Edinburgh: T. & T. Clark, 1994).
Toulmin, Joshua, *Memoirs of the Life, Character, Sentiments, and Writings of Faustus Socinus* (London: J. Brown, 1777).
Treier, Daniel J. 'A Looser "Canon"? Relating William Abraham's *Canon and Criterion in Christian Theology* to Biblical Interpretation,' *Journal of Theological Interpretation* 2.1 (2008), 101-116.
—. *Introducing Theological Interpretation of Scripture* (Grand Rapids: Baker, 2008).
Trigg, Jonathan D., *Baptism in the Theology of Martin Luther* (Leiden: Brill, 1994).
Trueman, Carl, 'John Owen's *Dissertation on Divine Justice:* An Exercise in Christocentric Scholasticism,' *Calvin Theological Journal* 33 (1998), 87-103.
Trible, Phyllis, *Texts of Terror* (Philadelphia: Fortress, 1984).
Van Asselt, Willem J., 'Christ's Atonement: A Multi-Dimensional Approach,' *Calvin Theological Journal* 38 (2003), 52-67.
Van der Walt, A.G.P., 'Calvin on Preaching.' In B.J. van der Walt (ed.), *John Calvin's Institutes: His Magnum Opus* (Potchefstroom: Potchefstroom University for Christian Higher Education, 1986), 326-341.
Van der Walt, J.L., 'The school that Calvin established in 1559.' In B.J. van der Walt (ed.), *Our Reformational tradition: a rich heritage and lasting vocation* (Potchefstroom: Potchefstroom University for Christian Higher Education, 1984), 192-201.
Van Dyke, Paul, *Catherine de Médici* (London: Charles Scribner's, 1922).
Vanhoozer, Kevin J., 'Imprisoned or Free.' In K.J. Vanhoozer, A.K.M. Adam and F. Watson (ed), *Reading Scripture with the Church* (Grand Rapids: Baker, 2006), 51-93.
—. *Is there a meaning in this text?* (Leicester: Apollos, 1988).
—. *The Drama of Doctrine: A Canonical-Linguistic Approach to Christian Theology* (Louisville: Westminster John Knox, 2005).
Van Oudtshoorn, D.A., 'Video as effektiewe Bedieningsmiddel in die Plaaslike Gemeente' (unpublished dissertation: University of South Africa, 1988).

Vasella, Oskar, *Reform und Reformation in der Schweiz. Zur Würdigung der Anfänge der Glaubenskrise* (Münster in Westfalen, 1958).

Mark Vessey, 'The Tongue and the Book: Erasmus' *Paraphrases on the New Testament* and the Arts of Scripture.' In H.M. Pabel and M. Vessey (eds), *Holy Scripture Speaks* (Toronto: University of Toronto Press, 2002), 29-58.

Von Harnack, Adolf, *History of Dogma*, 7 volumes (translated by William M'Gilchrist; London: Williams and Norgate, 1899).

Wallace, Ronald S., *Calvin, Geneva, and the Reformation* (Edinburgh: Scottish Academic Press, 1988).

—. *Calvin's Doctrine of the Christian Life* (Edinburgh: Oliver and Boyd, 1959).

Wallmann, Johannes, *Kirche und Israel im Mittelalter und in der Reformationszeit, KI* 34 (Kassel: Ev. Presseverband, 1989), 69-90.

Warfield, B.B. 'Calvin's Doctrine of the Trinity.' In S.G. Craig (ed.), *Calvin and Augustine* (Philadelphia: Presbyterian & Reformed, 1974), 189-284.

Webb, Stephen H., *The Divine Voice: Christian Proclamation and the Theology of Sound* (Grand Rapids: Brazos, 2004).

Webster, John, 'Canon.' In Kevin Vanhoozer, Craig G. Bartholomew, Daniel J. Treier and N.T. Wright (eds), *Dictionary for Theological Interpretation of the Bible* (London: SPCK, 2005).

Weimer, Christopher, 'Luther and Cranach on Justification in Word and Image,' *Luther Quarterly* 18 (2004), 387-405.

Wendel, François, *Calvin: Origins and Development of His Religious Thought* (1950; Grand Rapids: Baker, 1997).

Wengert, T.J., *Law and Gospel: Philip Melanchthon's Debate with John Agricola of Eisleben over Poenitentia* (Grand Rapids: Baker, 1997).

—. *The Pastoral Luther: Essays on Martin Luther's Practical Theology* (Grand Rapids: Eerdmans, 2009).

Wessel-Roth, Ruth, *Thomas Erastus: Ein Beitrag zur Geschichte der reformierten Kirche und zur von der Staatssouveranität* (Lahr/Baden, 1954).

White, Robert, 'The School in Calvin's Thought and Practice,' *Journal of Christian Education*, 12 (1969), 5-26.

Wilbur, Earl Morse, *A History of Unitarianism: Socinianism and its Antecedents* (1945; Boston: Beacon Press, 1977).

Wilken, Robert Louis, 'Cyril of Alexandria as Interpreter of the Old Testament.' In Thomas Gerard Weinandy and Daniel A. Keating (eds), *The Theology of St. Cyril of Alexandria: A Critical Appreciation* (London: T. & T. Clark, 2003), 1-21.

—. with Angela Russell Christman and Michael J. Hollerich (eds), *Isaiah: Interpreted by Early Christian and Medieval Commentators* (Grand Rapids: Eerdmans, 2007).

Wilcox, Peter, *Restoration, Reformation and the Progress of the Kingdom of Christ* (unpublished doctoral thesis, University of Oxford, 1993).

BIBLIOGRAPHY

Willi, Thomas, 'Der Beitrag des Hebräischen zum Werden der Reformation in Basel,' *Theologische Zeitschrift* 35.3 (June 1979), 139-154.

Williams, George H., *The Radical Reformation* (Kirksville, Mo.: Sixteenth Century Journal Publishers, 1992).

Willis, David E., 'Rhetoric and Responsibility in Calvin's Theology.' In Alexander J. McKelway (ed.), *The Context of Contemporary Theology* (Atlanta: John Knox, 1974), 43-64.

—. 'The Influence of Laelius Socinus on Calvin's Doctrines of the Merits of Christ and the Assurance of Faith.' In John A. Tedeschi (ed.), *Italian Reformation Studies in Honor of Laelius Socinus* (Firenze: University of Siena, 1965), 233-241.

Willis-Watkins, D., 'The *Unico Mystica* and the Assurance of Faith According to Calvin.' In von Willem van 't Spijker (ed.), *Calvin: Erbe und Auftrag* (Kampen: Kok, 1991), 77-84.

Wingren, Gustaf, *The Christian's Calling: Luther on Vocation* (Edinburgh: Oliver and Boyd, 1957).

Winkler, Eberhart, 'Luther als Seelsorger und Prediger.' In Helmar Junghans (ed.), *Leben und Werk Martin Luthers von 1526 bis 1546* (Göttingen: Vandenhoeck und Ruprecht, 1983), 1.225-39, 2.792-97.

Wyatt, Peter, *Jesus Christ and Creation* (Allison Park, Penn: Pickwick, 1996).

Zachman, Randall, *John Calvin as Teacher, Pastor, and Theologian: The Shape of His Writings and Thought* (Grand Rapids: Baker, 2006).

WEBSITES

Augsburg Confession http://www.elca.org/Who-We-Are/Our-Three-Expressions/Churchwide-Organization/Office-of-the-Presiding-Bishop/Ecumenical-and-Inter-Religious-Relations/Full-Communion-Partners.aspx.

Calvin's Catechism http://camosun.ca/learn/programs/history/johnston/120_topic3.pdf.

Hochkirchliche Vereinigung Augsburgischen Bekenntnisses (*High Church Union of the Augsburg Confession*) is at http://en.wikipedia.org/wiki/Hochkirchliche_Vereinigung_Augsburgischen_Bekenntnisses

The Protestant Church in the Netherlands (PCN) http://www.google.com/#sclient=psy-ab&hl=en&source=hp&q=The+Protestant+Church+in+the+Netherlands.

Author Index

Achtemeier, E., 91n.44
Acklin-Zimmermann, B., 31n.2
Adam, P., xii, 118-137, 134n.108
Althaus, P., 5, 10, 46n.52, 48n.56
Anderson, M., 132n.91
Anizor, U., xi, 1-15
Asendorf, U., 17n.3

Baars, A., 225n.55
Backus, I., 144n.35
Bainton, R., 39n.19, 43n.35, 49
Balke, W., 249
Bandstra, A.J., 146n.50
Barbier-Mueller, J.P., 111n.68
Barnes, R., 250n.49
Baron, H., 243n.6
Barth, K., 197-198
Battles, F.L., 84, 85n.12, 125, 134n.108
Bauckham, R., 251n.51
Beeke, J.R., 18n.5
Bente, F., 96n.1
Berkhof, L., 191n.48
Berry, L.E., 251n.50
Billings, J.T., 14, 14n.57
Blacketer, R.A., 219n.9
Bloesch, D., 94n.56
Blowers, P., 156n.36
Boockmann, H., 40n.22
Borvan, D., 184n.9
Bousset, W., 245n.22
Bouwsma, W., 85n.14, 86n.20, 128n.68
Brasher, J., 161
Bray, G., 167
Brecht, M., 20n.18
Browning, D.S., 55, 66n.52, 67n.53
Buchwald, G., 22n.27, 31n.75
Burnett, R., 136

Butin, P.W., 217n.3

Campbell, E., 138n.3
Canlis, J., 224n.43
Casey, M., 172n.21
Chadwick, O., 50n.66
Charles, R.H., 259n.99
Childs, B.S., 156n.38, 167
Chrisman, M., 248n.36
Christensen, C.C., 20n.16
Cochrane, A.C., 97, 98n.9
Collinson, P., 255n.78
Cooke, B., 95n.57

Davis, E.F., 13, 13n.53
de Boer, E.A., 161n.67
de Greef, W., 104n.41
de Jonge, H.J., 168n.15, 169
de Koster, L., 127n.62
de Lubac, H., 153n.22
Deme, D., 192n.50
Dempsey Douglass, J., 89n.37, 93n.52
Demura, A., 161n.67
Denis, P., 242n.4, 249n.40
Dingel, I., 16n.1, 98
Doberstein, J.W., 21n.23
Dowey, E., 227n.70
Duke, A., 136n.116

Eastwood, C., 11n.47
Ebeling, G., 18n.12, 21n.23
Edwards, M.H., 37n.11, 42, 46n.51
Egli, E., 244n.8
Eire, C., 16n.1
Eisenstein, E.L., 249n.41
Elliott, M.W., 161n.67
Estes, J.M., 59n.30

Falk, G., 45n.47
Farley, E., 55

INDEXES

Farner, O., 243n.7
Ferguson, S.B., 18n.5
Fesko, J.V., xii, xiii, 97n.4, 182-201, 182n.1
Figi, J., 243n.7
Fisher, J., xiii, 150-164
Flannery, A., 96n.3
Foord, M., xii, 138-149
Fowl, S., 11, 165, 173
Franks, R.S., 189n.39
Freitag, A., 22, 22n.24
Frymire, J.M., 21n.23, 22
Fudge, T.A., 150n.2

Gamble, R.C., 220n.15
Ganoczy, A., 217n.3
Garin, E., 243n.6
Garrett, D.A., 153n.18, 158
Gerrish, B.A., 8n.31
George, T., 153
Graf, A., 54
Graham, W.A., 12n.52
Grayzel, S., 38n.13
Greschat, M., 120n.18
Grimm, H.J., 59n.29
Grisar, H., 43n.36, 48n.58
Gritsch, E., 36n.7, 39, 47n.53
Gomes, A.W., 186n.21, 186n.24, 192n.54, 201n.96
Gordon, B., 150n.2
Gounelle, A., 14n.56
Guder, D.L., 14n.58
Gunton, C.E., 13n.53, 217n.2

Haas, G., xiii, 217-241
Haendler, G., 244n.13
Hailperin, H., 162n.76
Hall, D.W., xi-xiv, 99n.13
Harnack, A. von, 201
Hasel, G., 166
Hauerwas, S., 11n.50
Hays, R.B., 13, 13n.53
Heimmel, J., 87n.26
Heintze, G., 17n.3

Heitink, G., 56n.18
Helm, P., 216n.67, 226n.56
Hendel, K., 19n.15
Hendrix, S.H., 28n.58
Henry, P., 11n.68
Herrmann, E.H., 140n.111
Hesselink, I.J., 121n.25, 146n.50, 217n.1
Heyns, L.M., 52, 56, 57, 64-65
Hillar, M., 183n.3
Hirsch, E., 22n.27
Holder, R.W., 220n.15, 221n.21, 222n.33
Horton, M., 146n.50
Hughes, R.A., 82n.60
Hugo, A.M., 125

Jenkins, R.G., 153n.19
Jones, L.G., 11

Karant-Nunn, S., 78n.42, 81n.56
Kelly, D.F., 225n.52
Kingdon, R.M., 121n.25
Klaus, B., 22n.24
Klappert, B., 36n.10
Klotsche, E.H., 98n.10
Klug, E.F.A., 23n.31
Kohls, E.W., 248n.35
Kolb, R., 2, 2n.1, 2n.2, 2n.8, 3, 17n.3, 24n.40, 244n.13
Krans, J., 169-170
Krey, P., 153n.21
Krohn, J.B., 217n.2

Lane, A.N.S., 144n.35
Lang, A., 248n.38
Lee, J.K., xiii, 165-181
Lee, J.-S., 135n.113
Leith, J.H., 127n.55
Leonard, E.G., 243n.5
Leroux, N.R., 18n.10, 68, 73n.24
Letham, R., 224n.45

Lillback, P.A., xii, 96-117, 99n.13
Lindberg, C., 36n.8, 36n.10
Locher, G., 243n.5
Lohse, B., 5, 26n.48, 63n.46
Lupton, L., 251n.51
Luz, U., 172n.22

MacCulloch, D., 138, 242n.2
MacKenzie, C., xi, 16-32, 25n.42
Maier, G., 171n.20
Mattox, M., 173
McGrath, A.E., 135n.114
McKee, E.A., 220n.18, 222n.30, 240n.138
McKinnon, S., 156n.38
McKnight, S., 138n.3
McLaughlin, E.L., 93n.56
McNeill, J.T., 218n.4, 219n.12
Meditz, R., 174
Merrill, E.H., 153n.21
Meuser, F.W., 17n.3
Miller, E., 150n.2
Moeller, B., 244n.11
Mollenkott, V., 88n.28
Moltmann, J., 253
Moore, T.M., 122n.28
Muhlhan, B.J., xi, 52-67, 61n.39
Muller, G., 245n.16
Muller, R.A., 122n.28, 138n.2, 153, 219n.10, 250

Nelson, A., 150n.2
Ngien, D., 69n.8
Nijenhuis, W., 98n.10

Oberman, H., 35, 36, 36n.10, 40, 46, 47, 47n.54, 48
Ogonowski, S., 183n.2
Ong, W.J., 12n.51
Opitz, P., 152, 154n.24, 155n.31, 242n.3
Ozment, S., 20n.16, 246n.27

Packer, J.I., 217n.2
Parker, T.H.L., 118n.4, 130n.79, 135n.111, 220
Parsons, M., xii, xiii, 52, 68-82, 71n.12, 119n.4, 131n.88, 132n.91, 202-216, 202n.4
Partee, C., 225n.54
Pattinson, S., 55
Payton, J.R., 98n.12
Petersen, R.L., xiii, 242-259, 242n.2
Pfister, R., 244n.8
Philips, O., 248n.35
Pieterse, H.J.C., 52, 53n.7, 54, 56, 64-65
Pinson, K., 254n.67
Plass, E., 34n.3, 46n.51
Potter, G.R., 242n.4
Poythress, D., 150n.1
Prestwich, M., 248n.34

Quistorp, H., 248n.39, 253

Rees, T., 186n.22
Reeves, M., 254
Reid, W.S., 121n.22
Reinis, A., 70n.10
Richard, J.W., 101
Robbert, G.S., 35n.4
Rother, S., 244n.11
Rothkrug, L., 243n.7
Rupp, G., 37, 37n.12, 40n.26, 45, 150n.1
Ryken, L., 118, 122n.28, 125n.48

Sawyer, J.F.A., 155n.34
Schaff, P., 96n.2, 96n.3, 101
Schmidt-Clausing, F., 244n.8
Schrenk, G., 253n.63
Schwarz, B., xi, 33-51
Scott, D., 15n.60
Shakespeare, W., 83
Shepherd, M., 179n.40

INDEXES

Smalley, B., 153n.22, 156n.39
Smith, D.A., 55n.16
Smith, L., 153n.21
Smith, P., 58n.26
Smith, R.R., 56, 59
Spencer, S., 203
Spitz, L.W., 35n.4, 50n.66
Staehclin, E., 150n.1
Stauffer, R., 98, 98n.10, 100
Steinmetz, D., 127n.60, 152n.9, 153, 219n.8, 221n.19, 221n.20
Stephens, W.P., 170n.19, 175
Stetina, K.S., xii, 83-95, 83n.3
Strand, K.A., 33n.1
Szczucki. L., 186n.20

Tamburello, D.E., 224n.42
Tappert, T.G., 16n.2, 68n.4, 73
Thompson, B., 100n.19, 107
Thompson, J.L., 202, 207, 218, 221n.21, 222n.36
Tonkin, J., 20n.16
Torrance, T.F., 121n.25, 124, 128, 219n.8, 221n.19, 225n.52, 250n.49
Toulmin, J., 201n.96
Treier, D.J., 11n.49, 166
Trible, P., 202
Trigg, J.D., 4n.11, 6n.24
Trueman. C., 195n.69

Van Asselt, W.J., 192n.50
van der Walt, A.G.P., 119n.4
van der Walt, J.L., 122n.28
Van Dyke, P., 107n.51

Vanhoozer, K.J., 13n.55, 14, 168
van Oudtshoorn, D.A., 53n.7
Vessey, M., 169n.16

Wallace, R.S., 119n.6, 130n.78
Warfield, B.B., 225n.52
Webb, S.H., 13n.54
Weber, O., 248n.39
Webster, J., 167
Weimer, C., 20n.16
Wendel, F., 196n.70
Wengert, T.J., 2n.1, 52, 58n.26, 66n.51
White, R., 120n.17
Wilbur, E.M., 186n.20
Wilcox, P., 120n.14, 135n.112
Wilken, R.L., 156n.36
Willi, T., 154n.26
Williams, G.H., 245n.15
Willis, D., 195n.68
Willis, E.D., 86n.20
Willis-Watkins, D., 224n.42
Wingren, G., 19n.12
Winkler, E., 17n.3
Woodward, J., 55

Zachman, R.C., 119n.7, 122n.28, 125, 135n.111, 220n.17

Scripture index

Genesis
1 2; **1.26** 224n.48; **3.1-18** 87;
3.15 140, 148, 158; **22** 80; **49** 31;
49.10 148

Exodus
3.14 84; **19.5-6** 14; **20** 19; **20.4**
19; **20.5** 19; **32** 17; **37.7** 19

Numbers
21.9 19

Deuteronomy
18.15 148; **32.10** 213

2 Samuel
6 208-213; **11-12** 213-215

2 Kings
16-18 156; **18.4** 19

Job
1.21 69; **2.10** 74; **33.6** 87

Psalms
8.4 177; **17.8** 213; **23** 87; **24** 87;
27.8 209; **28.7** 213; **37.28** 213;
57 89; **61** 89; **61.3** 89, 89n.38;
72.14 213; **91** 89; **91.11** 213; **102**
89; **102.6** 89, 89n.38; **119** 127

Proverbs
15.8 204n.12; **30.18-19** 157

Isaiah
7 157, 158, 159, 160, 161,
161n.70, 163; **7-11** 156-164; **7.14**
156, 157, 162, 162n.73; **7.14-16**
156, 158; **7.16** 161, 162; **8** 159,
160; **8.1** 159, 159n.58; **8.1-4** 158;
8.3 159, 162; **8.4** 162; **9** 160,
161; **9.6-7** 159, 162; **11** 160,
160n.66, 161, 163; **11.1** 160; **11.2**
163n.8; **11.4** 204n.12; **22.17** 103;
31.5 92; **40.18** 86; **42.13-14** 90;
45.5-12 87; **46.3** 90; **49.15** 87,
92; **66** 92n.69; **66.12-13** 92

Jeremiah
8.18 87; **17.5-8** 87; **23.6** 40; **31.9**
91

Ezekiel
18.20 194

Daniel
3 17; **7.13** 178, 179; **7.13-14** 178,
178n.38

Zechariah
4.3-14 251

Malachi
1.6 91; **4** 249n.45

Matthew
1.21 34; **3** 169n.17; **5-7** 139; **5.1-12** 25; **5.20** 26; **5.20-26** 26; **5.39**
62; **6.3** 204n.12; **7.15** 10; **8.20**
176n.33, 177; **9.6** 176n.32, 177;
10.23 176n.29; **10.30** 213; **11.19**
176n.33; **11.27** 234; **12.8**
176n.32; **12.32** 176n.32; **12.40**
176n.30, 176n.31; **13.37** 176n.29;
13.41 176n.29; **16.6** 10; **16.13**
176n.33; **16.19** 3, 9n.36; **16.20**
177; **16.27** 176n.29; **16.27-28**
176; **16.28** 176n.29; **17** 249n.45;
17.9 176n.31; **17.12** 176n.30;
17.22-23 176n.30, 176n.31; **18.15-20** 9; **18.20** 204n.12; **19.28**
176n.29; **20.18-19** 176n.30,
176n.31; **20.28** 176n.30; **21.1-9**
25; **22.30** 93n.50; **23** 89; **23.16**

49; **23.33** 49; **23.37** 83; **24** 175, 176, 181, 256; **24-25** 174, 175; **24.4-5** 10; **24.15-28** 174; **24.27** 176n.29; **24.30** 179, 179n.41, 176n.29; **24.37** 176n.29; **24.39** 176n.29; **24.41** 176n.29; **25** 176, 181; **25.31** 176n.29; **26.2** 176n.30; **26.24** 176n.30; **26.45** 176n.30; **26.64** 179, 176n.29; **28.16** 238; **28.19** 6, 224

Mark
1.14 143; **1.15** 142; **10.35-45** 87; **16.16** 6

Luke
2.13-14 27; **2.25-32** 27n.52, 31; **3.7** 49; **4** 155; **6.36-42** 26; **8.4-15** 28n.57; **11** 158; **16.16** 145; **17** 174; **21** 44n.41, 174; **21.2** 204n.12; **22.19** 8; **24.47** 141, 142, 149

John
1.9 235; **1.13** 236; **1.14** 234; **1.19-28** 28, 29; **3.16** 235; **3.16-21** 25; **5.27** 178; **6.1-15** 28n.57; **6.44** 228; **6.44-46** 234; **6.45** 228; **7.20** 49; **8.12** 94-95; **8.44-45** 49; **10.5** 10; **10.27** 10; **14.6** 34; **14.10** 234; **14.12-14** 70; **14.16-17** 236; **14.26** 10; **15.27** 234; **17.6** 236; **17.8** 236; **17.19** 237; **17.21** 235, 238; **20.28** 50

Acts
2.38 238; **4.12** 34; **5** 216; **5.1-11** 203-208, 207; **5.2** 205; **5.3-4.8** 205; **5.5** 203; **5.7-9** 205; **5.10** 205; **5.11** 208; **13.10** 49; **17** 19; **17.31** 178; **20.21** 142; **20.26** 128

Romans
3.21-22 236; **4.11** 238; **4.23-25** 188; **6.9** 235; **8.9** 235; **8.15-17** 237; **8.28** 214; **8.29-30** 235; **12.1** 9; **12.14** 38; **13** 63, 64; **13.1-7** 63; **13.6** 64; **13.14** 237; **13.27** 64

1 Corinthians
1.13 238; **2.5** 236; **3.16** 204n.12; **4.12-13** 38; **11** 244; **11.23** 8; **11.23-29** 239; **11.24** 8; **11.24-26** 4; **14** 244; **14.26-32** 250

2 Corinthians
1.21-22 236; **2.15** 10; **2.16** 204; **3.6** 139, 140; **3.17-18** 235; **3.18** 236; **4.6** 235; **4.13** 10

Galatians
1.8 49; **2.20** 237; **3.28** 36; **4.6** 236, 237; **4.24** 222

Ephesians
1.3-14 234; **1.4-6** 237; **1.5-6** 234; **1.6** 87; **1.7-12** 235; **2.8-10** 237; **2.20** 233, 234; **4.5** 224; **5.22-26** 134

Philippians
3.2 49; **3.7-8** 30; **4.7** 80

Colossians
1.24 247n.33; **2.4** 49; **2.5** 49

1 Thessalonians
5.21 10

1 Timothy
2.2 250; **2.5** 34

2 Timothy
1.10 145; **3.15** 233n.104; **3.16-17** 233; **4.10** 145

Titus
1.10 49

Hebrews
2 177; **6.4-5** 236; **12.24** 213; **12.28** 238

James
1.18 90, 91n.43

1 Peter
1.10-11 234; **2.5** 9; **2.9** 7, 15, 231; **2.21** 246n.28; **3.5** 238; **3.12-18** 246n.28

2 Peter
1.19-21 233

1 John
2.27 10

Revelation
1-6 252; **1-16** 252; **2-3** 246; **4-7** 246; **8** 257; **8.11** 246; **9** 257; **9.2** 247; **9.13** 252; **9-11** 255; **10** 257; **10.11** 244; **11** 242, 243, 245, 246, 247, 248, 249n.45; **11.1** 245; **11.1-2** 257, 258; **11.1-13** 252; **11.1-15** 257; **11.2** 252, 258; **11.3** 252, 258; **11.3-6** 257; **11.3-14** 257; **11.7** 247, 252; **11.7-10** 257; **11.11-13** 257; **11.14-15** 257; **11.14-19** 252; **11.15** 257; **12** 252; **12-14** 246; **13** 246, 252; **15-16** 246, 252; **17** 249n.45; **17-18** 247; **17-19** 252; **19.7** 250; **20** 252; **20-22** 247

INDEXES

General Index

Academy, the Genevan, 120-121, 132, 135-136, 137, 248-250
accommodation, 84, 86, 89, 90, 92, 95, 134, 177, 210, 221, 221n.23
Adam, 12, 27, 84, 140, 186, 227
Agricola, Johannes, 141
a'Lasco, John, 138
alter Christus, 82
Ambiose conspiracy, 107
Anabaptists, 2n.2
Anselm, 191-192, 192n.54
Antichrist, the, 28n.58, 47, 58, 155, 247, 250, 257, 258, 259
apostles, 5, 5n.18
Apostles' Creed, the, 227
Aquinas, Thomas, 158, 185, 196
Augsburg Confession, xii, 96-117, 188
Augustine, 2n.2, 47n.54, 87, 89, 114, 127, 139, 140, 199, 200, 258

baptism, 2, 3-4, 6, 6n.22, 8, 15, 237-239
Berndt, Ambrose, 70-72, 75
Beza, Theodore, xii, 97n.4, 107, 109, 110, 113, 116n.87, 187, 258
Biddle, John, 186
blasphemy, 27, 27n.52, 35, 37, 39, 45, 46
Brenz, Johannes, 107, 111, 112n.75
Brocard, James, 253-257, 259
Bucer, Martin, 101, 102, 103, 120, 121, 135, 138, 144-145, 170, 180-181, 248, 250, 250n.49
Bullinger, Heinrich, 103, 104, 138, 148, 169, 170, 175, 178, 183, 184, 188, 198, 242, 243, 244, 247, 250n.49, 257, 258, 258n.94, 259

Calvin, John, ix, xi, xii, xiii, 18, 83-95, 96-117, 118-137, 138, 142-149, 152, 161-163, 164, 167, 170, 183, 184, 194-201, 202-216, 217-141, 248n.39, 249, 249n.40, 250, 250n.49, 253
Capito, Wolfgang, 248
Caroli, Peter, 99
Castellio, Sebastian, 183
children, 120-121, 131, 132, 194, 221, 230
Christian freedom, 18, 41, 53, 59, 60-64
Christology, 16
Chrysostom, John, 127, 153, 154, 158, 158n.51, 160, 163
church, 93, 129, 160, 203, 205, 208, 222, 224, 230, 231, 234, 237-239, 240, 245, 246, 247, 250, 252, 252, 255, 257
Clement of Alexandria, 87
Colloquy of Poissy, the, 107, 108, 109, 111
community, 10, 11, 14, 14n.58, 54, 57, 59, 205, 206, 207, 224, 246, 259
confession, 12
conscience, 4n.15, 20
consubstantiation, 114
coram Deo, 207, 216
Cordatus, Conrad, 72-73, 75, 81
Cyril of Alexandria, 153, 154, 158, 158n.52, 158n.53, 159, 159n.59, 163

death, 6, 25, 26, 31
Decalogue, the, 18, 19

293

devil, the (Satan), 6, 20, 27, 48, 48n.58, 58, 78, 133, 158, 205, 206, 208, 247n.31, 252
Diet of Augsburg, 22, 40n.26
Dietrich, Veit, 21-24, 30n.70, 31, 73
discipline, 12
doctrine, 24, 216, 218, 234, 256

Eck, Johann, 49, 49n.64
education, xii, 118-137
Erasmus, Desiderius 17, 17n.4, 151, 151n.3, 155, 168-169, 170, 172, 243
eschatology 46, 215, 216, 250n.49
eternal life, 25
Eucharist, the, 16, 102-104, 114
Eusebius of Caesaria, 144
Eve, 27
exorcism, 16n.1

faith, ix, 3, 3n.6, 4, 4n.11, 4n.14, 4n.15, 12, 20, 24, 25, 26, 31, 32, 34, 43, 44, 53, 61, 62, 62n.42, 69, 70, 71, 72, 73, 80-81, 106n.46, 113, 123, 134, 142, 148, 160n.61, 188, 190-191, 192, 200, 201, 215, 227, 228, 229, 230, 231, 233n.104, 235, 236, 238, 239
Farel, 101, 102
first commandment, the, 16
forgiveness, 2, 3, 3n.6, 4, 5, 6, 9, 12, 25, 26, 32, 61, 147, 148, 176n.32, 189, 190, 191-194, 195
Foxe, John, 247, 259

Gell, Robert, 177
God, 68, 81, 122, 188
   Creator, 2, 87
   Father, 77, 81, 87, 88, 90, 91, 92, 92n.47, 93n.54, 95, 126, 178, 192, 224n.48, 224-226, 228, 229, 230, 235, 238
   glory of, 122-123, 126, 189, 211, 230
   grace of, ix, 2, 4, 14n.58, 25, 27, 34, 57, 72, 74, 75, 76, 77, 81, 106n.46, 123, 127, 144, 147, 157, 195, 228, 229, 236, 237, 238
   holy, 14, 50
   immutable, 86
   Judge, 15, 193, 204, 229
   judgement of, 42, 205, 206, 211, 245, 247, 249, 252, 257
   kindness of, 76-77, 86
   love of, 26, 70, 77, 78, 92, 228
   majesty of, 89
   mercy of, 2, 12, 26, 27, 57, 87, 143, 190, 192, 195, 212, 215, 231, 236
   presence of, 77, 210
   promises of, 3, 6, 12, 213, 215, 229, 233, 235, 236, 239, 241, 249, 258
   Saviour, 15, 87, 215
   speaking, 2
   transcendence of, 85
   triune, 15
   will of, 2, 63, 69, 72, 74, 82, 199
   wisdom of, 210-211, 212, 216
   wrath (anger) of, 37, 38, 44, 44n.41, 74, 86, 206, 257
gospel, ix, xii, 2, 3, 3n.5, 5, 8, 9, 9n.37, 10, 11n.47, 12, 14, 14n.58, 17, 25, 26, 27, 30n.68, 31, 34, 35n.5, 38, 41, 42, 46, 47, 50, 53, 55, 56, 57, 61, 66, 120, 131, 138-149, 190, 198, 222, 223, 224, 230, 233, 234, 235, 238, 243, 246, 247, 250, 255, 256
grief, xii, 68-82

INDEXES

Grotius, Hugo, 198

Hausmann, Nicholas, 57
Heinze, Wolf, 76
hermeneutical principles, 221-234, 240
Hoffman, Melchior, 148, 149
Holy Spirit, the, ix, 2-3, 2n.2, 4n.15, 9, 10, 14, 31, 34, 63, 84, 85, 114, 119, 124, 125, 127, 130, 132, 140, 147, 148, 159, 160, 163n.80, 186, 189, 190, 192, 203, 204, 205, 206, 207, 209, 220n.15, 221, 221n.25, 223, 224, 224n.48, 226, 227, 228, 229, 230, 231, 233, 235, 236, 237, 238, 239, 245, 253, 254, 259
house postils, 16-32
humility, 30
hypocrisy, 26

idolatry, xii, 16-32, 91
idols, 17, 17-21, 28-29
Illyricus, Flacius, 247
images, 16n.1, 17, 18, 19, 20, 27, 30, 119
Invocavit Sermons, 18
Israel, 12

Jerome, 153
Jesus Christ, ix, xi, 2, 3, 3n.5, 4, 5, 8, 12, 14, 14n.58, 17, 20, 25, 26, 29, 32, 34, 36, 39, 44, 48, 51, 62n.42, 68, 73, 77-78, 82, 123, 129, 130, 134, 139, 143, 155, 159, 160, 163, 164, 172, 177, 182, 188, 190, 191, 200, 201, 222, 226, 227, 228, 232, 233, 236, 237, 238, 239, 241, 245, 246, 247, 252, 255
death, 2, 53, 77-78, 93n.54, 113, 114, 176, 176n.30, 178, 197, 199, 235

grace of, 25
Judge, 177, 178, 179, 180
Mediator, 78, 237
presence of, 5, 114
Redeemer, 221, 232
return of, 176n.29, 178, 179
righteousness of, 194-198, 229
Saviour, 25, 30, 32, 50, 53, 157, 160n.62, 180, 228
Son, 224-226, 229
'Son of Man,' 172-181
Suffering of, 4, 192, 197, 200, 234
type, 78, 246, 259
Jews, the, 33-51
Joachim of Anhalt, 77
Junius, Francis, 251-253, 256, 259
justification by faith, xii, 25, 26, 28n.58, 32, 48n.56, 50, 51, 62, 65, 147, 182, 186-198, 201, 229, 235, 236, 240

Karlstadt, Andreas, 6, 16, 18, 18n.8, 19, 20
kingdom of heaven (of Christ), 25, 124, 131, 155, 160, 160n.66, 163, 172, 235, 249, 250, 253, 256, 259
King of Navarre, the, 107
knowledge, ix, 122-123, 224, 227, 233, 234
Knox, John, 118n.3
Knudsen, John, 79

Lambert, Francis, 244-246
Latomus, 48
Law/gospel distinction, 60-61, 140-142, 145
law, the, 26n.48, 31, 41, 60, 61, 188
Lefévre, Jacques, 144
Leigh, Edward, 187

295

Lightfoote, John, 170
Locke, John, 186
Lombard, Peter, 139, 195, 196
Lord's Prayer, the, 8-9
Lord's Supper, the, 3-5, 6, 98, 100, 103, 113, 114
Luther, Elizabeth, 73, 82
Luther, John, 78
Luther, Katherine, 73, 78n.42
Luther, Magdalene, 78-79, 78n.42, 82
Luther, Martin, ix, xi, xii, 16-32, 33-51, 52-67, 68-82, 100, 101, 102, 103, 104, 127, 140, 152, 167, 169, 173, 174, 200, 242, 243, 245, 254, 259

Maccovius, Johannes, 198
Marburg Colloquy, the, 22
Margaritha, Antonius, 40n.26, 41n.27
Mary, 30-31, 30n.68, 30n.70, 41n.27, 43, 44, 46, 159, 161
Melanchthon, Philip, xii, 56, 57, 59, 60, 63-64, 78, 96, 98, 100, 103, 104, 105, 107, 108, 109, 115, 140, 141, 142, 149, 151n.3, 183, 243
metaphors for God, 86-87
  Beloved, 87
  Comforter, 87
  King, 87
  Mother, 87, 91-92, 92n.47
  mother bird, 89
  nurse, 90
  Physician, 87
  Shepherd, 87
  Teacher, 87, 130
  woman in labour, 90
  womb, 90-92, 93n.50
Metzler, Catherine, 79, 81
Meyer, Sebastian, 246-247
ministry, 1
mission, 14

monasticism, 26, 30
Müntzer, Thomas, 243, 249
Musculus, Wolfgang, 138, 169, 179, 180, 193-195, 200
New Testament, the, ix, 5, 34, 139, 140, 143, 164, 175, 222, 223, 258
Nicholas of Lyra, 41n.27, 153, 156, 159, 159n.56, 162n.76, 163n.84, 237

Oecolampadius, Johannes xiii, 101n.23, 138, 144, 150-164
Old Testament, the, ix, 5, 17, 40, 41n.27, 139, 140, 154, 175, 222, 223, 245, 258
Osiander, Andrew, 79, 80
Owen, John, 199-200

Pareus, David, 257-259
Paul of Burgos, 41n.27
Pauli, Benedict, 73-75
Peasants' War, the, 57, 59, 60, 63
penance, 3, 3n.6
persecution, 32, 38, 43n.36, 103, 121, 246, 258n.94
Pfefferkorn, Johann, 37
Poach, Andreas, 22
power of the keys, the, 9, 9n.36
prayer, 70, 93, 230, 235, 237, 240, 243
preachers, xii, 130-136, 247, 251
preaching, ix, xii, 2, 3, 7, 12, 14, 15, 19, 21n.23, 22, 26, 47, 118-120, 126, 127, 130, 131, 133, 207, 231, 256, 258
priesthood of believers, 1-15
priestly functions, 6-7
prophecy, 243-258
providence, 50, 81-82, 207, 214, 216

Queen Mary of Hungary, 76

INDEXES

Racovian Catechism, 182-201
redemption, 234-237
Reineck, John, 72
repentance, 141, 142, 147-148, 172, 227, 230
resurrection, 34, 77, 82, 176, 176n.31, 178, 250
Reuchlin, 37, 151n.3, 243
revelation, 84-86, 123, 135, 146, 180, 181, 221, 223, 225n.54, 227, 229, 233-234, 236, 240, 245
Rorer, Georg, 22

sacraments, 3n.6, 4n.11, 13, 185, 237-239, 240
sacrifice, 9
Sadoleto, Jacob, 119, 120
saints, 17, 29, 32
salvation, 6
scatology, 48
Schomann, Georg, 185
Scotus, John Duns, 52, 196
second commandment, 18
Servetus, Michael, 249
sin, 21, 25, 26, 31, 32, 34, 78, 120, 123, 133, 157, 185, 186, 188, 189, 194, 203, 205, 227, 233, 240
Socinus, Faustus, xii, xiii, 182, 183-186
Socinus, Laelius, 182, 183, 184
sola fide, 50, 188, 200
sola gratia, 50, 200
solus Christus, 33, 34, 35, 200
sola scriptura, 50, 88, 96
Spalatin, George, 57, 60
spiritual kingdom, the, 58
Storch, Nicholas, 249
Sturm, Johann, 120, 121, 135

Taylor, Thomas, 176-177, 178-179

theological interpretation of Scripture, 1-15, 165-168
things indifferent, 18
transubstantiation, 114
Trinity, the, xiii, 44, 87, 99, 182, 185, 194, 198, 218, 223, 224-226, 227, 229, 231, 234, 240, 255

union with Christ, 192, 232, 235, 238, 239
University of Wittenberg, the, 18
Ursinus, Zacharias, 183

Vermigli, Peter Martyr, 138, 249, 249n.41
Viret, Pierre, 152
Visitation (1527), the, xi, 57-67
vocation, 211-212, 213, 215
von Staremberg, Bartholomew, 68-70, 75
von Taubenheim, John, 80

Wernsdorfer, Vincent, 69
Westphal, 103, 106, 116
Word of God, the, (Scriptures, the) ix, xii, 1-6, 25, 29n.64, 31, 34, 43, 44n.41, 45, 49, 53, 60, 68, 69, 72, 73, 84-85, 85n.19, 98, 108, 114, 130, 133, 160n.66, 185, 204, 207, 216, 218, 221, 226, 231, 234, 244, 245, 255, 258, 259
works righteousness, 21, 29
worship, 14, 14n.58, 17, 19, 24, 28, 84n.9, 93, 119, 209, 231, 238, 240, 252

Zanchi, Girolamo, 198
Zink, John, 75
Zoch, Lawrence, 77
Zwickau, 72

Zwingli, Huldrych, 5, 17, 22, 101n.23, 102, 103, 127, 138, 152, 170, 243, 244n.8, 245

www.ingramcontent.com/pod-product-compliance
Lightning Source LLC
Chambersburg PA
CBHW061429300426
44114CB00014B/1601